The Cambridge Companion to K-Pop

How did Korea come to create a vibrant pop culture scene that would enthrall not only young Asian fans but also global audiences from diverse racial and generational backgrounds? From idol training to fan engagement, from studio recording to mastering choreographic sequences, what are the steps that go into the actual production and promotion of K-pop? And how can we account for K-pop's global presence within the rapidly changing media environment and consumerist culture in the new millennium? As an informed guide for finding answers to these questions, *The Cambridge Companion to K-Pop* probes the complexities of K-pop as both a music industry and a transnational cultural scene. It investigates the meteoric ascent of K-pop against the backdrop of increasing global connectivity wherein a distinctive model of production and consumption is closely associated with creativity and futurity.

SUK-YOUNG KIM is Professor of Theater and Performance Studies at the University of California, Los Angeles. She is the author of *Illusive Utopia*, *DMZ Crossing*, and *K-Pop Live* and frequently comments on Korean cultural politics for BBC, CNN, and National Public Radio.

Cambridge Companions to Music

Topics

Composers

The Cambridge Companion to Richard Strauss
Edited by Charles Youmans

The Cambridge Companion to Michael Tippett
Edited by Kenneth Gloag and Nicholas Jones

The Cambridge Companion to Vaughan Williams
Edited by Alain Frogley and Aiden J. Thomson

The Cambridge Companion to Verdi
Edited by Scott L. Balthazar

Instruments

The Cambridge Companion to Brass Instruments
Edited by Trevor Herbert and John Wallace

The Cambridge Companion to the Cello
Edited by Robin Stowell

The Cambridge Companion to the Clarinet
Edited by Colin Lawson

The Cambridge Companion to the Guitar
Edited by Victor Coelho

The Cambridge Companion to the Harpsichord
Edited by Mark Kroll

The Cambridge Companion to the Organ
Edited by Nicholas Thistlethwaite and Geoffrey Webber

The Cambridge Companion to the Piano
Edited by David Rowland

The Cambridge Companion to the Recorder
Edited by John Mansfield Thomson

The Cambridge Companion to the Saxophone
Edited by Richard Ingham

The Cambridge Companion to Singing
Edited by John Potter

The Cambridge Companion to the Violin
Edited by Robin Stowell

The Cambridge Companion to

K-POP

....

EDITED BY

Suk-Young Kim
University of California, Los Angeles

CAMBRIDGE
UNIVERSITY PRESS

CAMBRIDGE
UNIVERSITY PRESS

Shaftesbury Road, Cambridge CB2 8EA, United Kingdom

One Liberty Plaza, 20th Floor, New York, NY 10006, USA

477 Williamstown Road, Port Melbourne, VIC 3207, Australia

314–321, 3rd Floor, Plot 3, Splendor Forum, Jasola District Centre, New Delhi – 110025, India

103 Penang Road, #05–06/07, Visioncrest Commercial, Singapore 238467

Cambridge University Press is part of Cambridge University Press & Assessment, a department of the University of Cambridge.

We share the University's mission to contribute to society through the pursuit of education, learning and research at the highest international levels of excellence.

www.cambridge.org
Information on this title: www.cambridge.org/9781108837057

DOI: 10.1017/9781108938075

© Cambridge University Press & Assessment 2023

First published 2023

A catalogue record for this publication is available from the British Library.

Library of Congress Cataloging-in-Publication Data
Names: Kim, Suk-Young, 1970– editor.
Title: The Cambridge companion to K-pop / edited by Suk-Young Kim.
Description: [1.] | Cambridge, United Kingdom ; New York, NY : Cambridge University Press, 2022. | Series: Cambridge companions to music | Includes bibliographical references and index.
Identifiers: LCCN 2022046605 (print) | LCCN 2022046606 (ebook) | ISBN 9781108837057 (hardback) | ISBN 9781108940030 (paperback) | ISBN 9781108938075 (epub)
Subjects: LCSH: Popular music–Korea (South)–History and criticism. | Sound recording industry–Korea (South)–History. | Popular music–Korea (South)–Production and direction. | Music and transnationalism.
Classification: LCC ML3502.K6 C35 2022 (print) | LCC ML3502.K6 (ebook) | DDC 781.63095195–dc23/eng/20220927
LC record available at https://lccn.loc.gov/2022046605
LC ebook record available at https://lccn.loc.gov/2022046606

ISBN 978-1-108-83705-7 Hardback
ISBN 978-1-108-94003-0 Paperback

Contents

Figures

Tables

Contributors

Thomas Baudinette is Senior Lecturer in Japanese and International Studies at Macquarie University.

Michelle Cho is Assistant Professor of East Asian Studies at the University of Toronto.

Stephanie Choi is Adjunct Assistant Professor in East Asian Studies at New York University.

Candace Epps-Robertson is Assistant Professor in English at the University of North Carolina at Chapel Hill.

Hye Won Kim is Assistant Professor in English and Asian Studies at Kennesaw State University.

Kyung Hyun Kim is Professor in East Asian Studies and Visual Studies at the University of California, Irvine.

Suk-Young Kim is Professor of Theater and Performance Studies at the University of California, Los Angeles.

Youngdae Kim is a freelance ethnomusicologist and music critic.

Jung-Min Mina Lee is Instructor in Asian and Middle Eastern Studies at Duke University.

So-Rim Lee is Korea Foundation Assistant Professor at the University of Pennsylvania.

Roald Maliangkay is Professor in Korean Studies at Australian National University.

Chuyun Oh is Associate Professor in Dance at San Diego State University.

Youjeong Oh is Associate Professor of Asian Studies at the University of Texas at Austin.

CedarBough T. Saeji is Assistant Professor in Korean and East Asian Studies at Pusan National University.

Hyunjoon Shin is Professor in Cultural Studies and Social Theories at Sungkonghoe University.

Acknowledgments

Anyone working on popular culture knows well that time is at once their best friend and worst enemy. In the fast-changing world of pop culture, every day offers scholars a windfall of new materials to swim in, but with each minute's passing they also become inevitably outdated. No matter how hard one tries, one can never have a full and comprehensive perspective on something evolving so quickly. My collaborators whose work is highlighted in this volume saved me from being outdated or, at least, helped slow down the pace. Thanks to their fresh perspectives and keen insights, they inspired me to examine this dynamic field with a renewed appreciation and a much deeper understanding.

Qianxiong Yang was a smart and reliable editorial assistant, who stepped in to provide much needed help. Thanks to Stephanie Sakson, whose editorial work improved the book, and to Abi Sears, who patiently guided me through each step of the production process. Kate Brett first presented the idea of making this book, for which I am grateful. A Korea Foundation Small Grant supported the production of the index and funded a series of online lectures, allowing me to feel a sense of community during the difficult days of the Covid-19 pandemic. Particular thanks go to Chungmin Lee, who supported this endeavor in many way, both big and small.

Researching K-pop requires one to repeatedly renew their perspective. It is like chasing a storm that leaves you strides behind. Day after day, minute after minute, new songs are released and fresh faces step into limelight. But my media-savvy students are always ahead of me, and writing this book is my belated gesture to acknowledge their contribution to the field of K-pop. This book is dedicated to my students, past, present, and future.

Notes to Readers

- For transliteration of Korean words, the volume will consistently use the official Korean language Romanization system released by South Korea's Ministry of Culture and Tourism in 2000, also referred to as Revised Romanization of Korean. Exceptions are made for proper names well known in the English-speaking world by alternate Romanizations (e.g. Lee Soo-man rather than Yi Su-man); for authors who published their names in alternate Romanizations (e.g. Suk-Young Kim rather than Suk-yeong Gim); for performers who deliberately use alternate Romanizations for their names (e.g. Lee Hi rather than Yi Ha-i).
- Although East Asian convention dictates that surnames precede given names (e.g. Lee So-Rim), in this volume, East Asian names appear with the given name first followed by surnames (e.g. So-Rim Lee). Exceptions are made for stage names and artistic names, which have been widely used in the music and entertainment industry (e.g. Bang Si-hyuk rather than Si-hyuk Bang).
- K-pop band names like BLACKPINK or Agust D are left in their own Anglicized spellings since they deliberately use idiosyncratic spellings for professional purposes and are known as such in both Korean and international media.
- All translations not otherwise credited are contributor's own.
- When quoting others' work, author's use the transliteration system originally chosen by other authors.

Introduction

Korea's Moment in the Limelight

SUK-YOUNG KIM

Vibrant colors, swaggering idols, and enthralled arena. Constellations of fans who exude transformative energy that buoys the brilliance of the moment. Jovial melodies on heart-racing tracks. Hooks that rush straight to your memory. A shining light has been illuminating the K-pop stage since the dawn of the millennium. What started out as a local craze has now become a truly global phenomenon. The interest in various K-pop bands and their prolific performances has only intensified over the years. What magnetic forces are at work to elate the worldwide fan community and heighten the splendor of the constantly evolving scene called K-pop?

The versatility of K-pop has always made it difficult to box the genre into one or a few categorical definitions. For those hoping to grasp this ever-morphing cultural scene, any single classification of it will be too constricting. For some Koreans, K-pop became an epicenter for rallying ethnocentric pride, touting the growing influence of Korean culture worldwide. For other Koreans, it is a symptomatic ailment of the media-saturated youth of today. For the Asian diasporic community, it carries the refreshing banner of Asian cool. For some critics in the West, K-pop idols have reconfirmed their long-standing prejudice against Asians as mechanical, machinelike disciplinarians devoid of humanity. For the dedicated fandom, K-pop has enabled an unprecedented degree of community building, whereas for the business community, it has presented a prime case of branding and marketing in the age of the metaverse.

The many faces of K-pop have invited scholarly scrutiny, often directed toward unpacking the manifold meanings of the "K" in K-pop. Elsewhere, I introduced the new phrase "keyboard/keypad" pop as a way to emphasize the centrality of digital consumerism in the K-pop world, as most of this music consumption takes place via digital platforms; "Kleenex pop" to emphasize the quick turnover of top songs and trends; and "ketchup pop" to indicate their manufactured taste and flavor. And never to be forgotten, Korea looms large behind "K," sustaining the conversation on how K-pop can buoy a nation's soft power beyond everyone's wildest dreams.[1] Who would have imagined that it would take a glitzy pop music scene to transform one nation's public image from a war-torn country into a trendy hub of popular culture in less than half a century?

While many discussions have taken place around the range of meanings of "K," the "pop" side of K-pop has been given less critical treatment.[2] To be fair, "pop" holds an equal share with "K" in gauging the genre's supple soundscape. Dominating the sonic spread of K-pop are American pop (most notably teen pop, bubblegum pop) heavily infused with all sorts of global music trends of the twentieth century (hip hop, R&B, gospel, jazz, rock, swing). K-pop also harnesses a broader range of "pop," including Eurodance music and J-pop trends, among the increasing streak of traditional Korean musical themes.

But the most crucial ingredient in "pop" is ironically what is missing in rock music. For its rapacious adaptability, the "pop" in K-pop connotes passing trends at best, standing as a marker of triviality, which is often projected as the diametric opposite of "rock authenticity." The lack of awareness of K-pop's rising influence or, even worse, open prejudice against music from Asia often prompts critics of K-pop to label it as factory-manufactured music.

The rock/pop contrast is nothing new and existed long before K-pop entered the global music scene as a major force. Richard Middleton pointed to how the field of musicology has repeatedly confronted the tenuous relationship between rock authenticity and the suspicious validity of "pop" music:

> Within popular music culture, the discourse of authenticity is familiar. Typically, it is taken to mark out the genuine from the counterfeit, the honest from the false, the original from the copy, roots from surface – oppositions which in turn often map on to further distinctions: feeling as against pretense, acoustic as against electric, subculture as against mainstream, people as against industry, and so on.[3]

The oppositions listed here characterize the dichotomization of rock versus pop. This bifurcation denotes the idea that pop music cannot stand the test of time. It sits on a pressurized time clock that will shortly announce that it is high time for this passing trend to pop. To this effect, John Lie likewise indicated that the term "'popular' almost always signifies the less prestigious in a series of binary distinctions; elite, high, or refined against mass, low, or vulgar."[4]

But underneath such condescending discourse on "pop" lie much more complex dimensions. "Pop" accentuates the spectacularly **performative** aspect of today's pop music, in which K-pop finds no rivals: **personality** of idols; **picturesqueness** of dance, makeup, fashion, and music videos; but most importantly, a highly dedicated **populace** – fans – generating and sustaining the heat. These various facades again hark back to the rooted condescension toward frivolous music that is enjoying temporary success, but they also explain the unique strength of pop music in the age of rapid digital transformation, where viral media exercise unprecedented power – so much so that they have the clout to topple the aforementioned music hierarchy.

The rapid leap forward into digital consumption truly has transformed the face of the global music industry. From sound mixing to music promotion, the way music interfaces with fans and critics alike has changed foundationally. Especially with the rise of music and video streaming platforms such as Spotify and YouTube, the amorphous concept of popularity has turned into easily quantifiable streaming and viewing counts. One could dismiss this transformation as a frivolous popularity contest, but like it or not, it is here, asking us to map the contours of the pop music industry in a fundamentally different way. K-pop's rise to global prominence merged precisely with this digital transformation; even more, K-pop was pioneering the process as the vanguard to showcase how digital platforms should catch up with the chimerically diversifying modes of expression. Digital platforms in the current ecosystem of the music industry are no longer just an arena to showcase popular music but a major stimulant expediting changes in the ways music is produced and consumed.

But to place our fingers only on the pulse of today is to miss out on the extensive genealogy of K-pop. To be sure, K-pop has many decades of history under its belt, and the genre's resilience is due in large part to its evolving survival strategy cultivated and refined through generations. The history of K-pop can be traced alongside Korea's national history at the turn of the millennium that influenced the nation's cultural industry and the broader development of the global popular music industry, with important considerations of the way music has been produced and consumed, locally and globally. To begin, how did Korea with a small-scale music industry come to create a vibrant pop culture scene that would enthrall not only generations of young Asian consumers but also global audiences from diverse racial and generational backgrounds? Who are the main players in the K-pop ecosystem? From idol training to fan engagement, from studio recording to mastering choreographic sequences, what are the steps that go into the actual production and promotion of K-pop? And how can we account for K-pop's global presence within the rapidly changing media environment and consumerist culture in the new millennium?

This book serves as an informed guide for finding answers to these questions by casting a double look at the synchronic and diachronic development of the K-pop industry. It probes into multiple facets of K-pop as both a music industry and a transnational cultural scene while situating this performance genre in the historical context from late colonial Korea (1930–40) to today's hyperdigitized world. It investigates the meteoric ascent of K-pop against the backdrop of increasing global connectivity, wherein a distinctive model of production and consumption is closely associated with creativity and futurity. Tracing these inquiries can be done meaningfully only when we closely consider the "technology paradigm,"[5] which had a profound impact on the way music is produced and consumed. For example, the way we encounter K-pop has shifted not just along with the transition from vinyl records to CDs to mp3s but also along the trajectory of televisions to computers to cell phones. The technology paradigm extends the playing field of today's K-pop from social media to the AI-driven metaverse, at times shifting the focus from music and performance to the limits of the tech industry itself.

While technological shifts have had a formative influence on the range of sound and visual production, what makes K-pop a truly unique cultural scene is its sticky human relationships – timeless networks that preceded the rise of technological wonders. A colossal energy builds among a dedicated fan community around their shared love for individual idols, bands, and social causes, but what also matters is the affective exchange between individual idols, between music artists from various generations, and among the adjacent labor force (production staff, volunteer translators in online fan communities). At the same time, the sweat-and tear-stained training process of each idol implies much human labor and sacrifice, often rendered invisible under blinding limelight.

For the most part, the analysis in this volume concerns idol-centered pop music that has emerged since the 1990s, primarily featuring young performers for multimedia entertainment catering to the younger generation of fans and consumers. While the majority of the chapters work around this specific definition of K-pop, much broader forces in the Korean music world have nourished, contextualized, and influenced the idol music industry. Rock and jazz musicians, balladeers, and folk singers of the 1970s and '80s make occasional appearances to help us envision the ins and outs of the idol music and entertainment of today.

Following these multiple threads of investigation, this book interweaves the historical, technological, and affective registers of K-pop by mapping first its genealogy and production models, then the ways K-pop travels in multiple directions across global networks woven by transmedia platforms and multiracial fan communities. It is organized first to impart an overarching understanding of K-pop as both an industry and a network of cultural practices, then to move on to the backstage reality of the industry, ending with how K-pop is globally circulated. Individual chapters in each part collaborate to produce a cohesive vison of the industry, artistry, and human entanglements.

Part I, "Genealogies," provides a broad contextualization of K-pop, from its roots in 1930s–1940s Korean popular music under Japanese colonial rule to South Korea's burgeoning record industry of the 1980s and '90s. This broad scope is balanced by the close-up exposition of K-pop's musical traits to showcase an array of industry structures, which sheds light on its unique soundscape, role division, and transnational network of talents. Roald Maliangkay's "Sticking It to the Man: Early Neoliberalism in Korean Pop Music" illustrates the deployment of the talent system in Korean music industry during the late colonial era. This chapter discusses case studies that predate the K-pop idol system by half a century, foreshadowing how talents are discovered and promoted in an increasingly commercializing music world. The chapter analogizes how the record companies of the 1930s–1940s worked as the precedents of today's entertainment conglomerates. Hyunjoon Shin's "Itaewon Class, Gangnam Style, and Yeouido Star: The Industrial Revolution of Korean Pop in the 1990s" brings the genealogy of K-pop closer to the immediate past – to the nascent moment of the present-day K-pop industry. By focusing on the transforming structures of entertainment companies and talents who moved around various networks in the music and dance scene, Shin provides a comprehensive view of how the Korean music industry evolved before the millennium – in conjunction with the changing sociopolitical environment – and created the conditions for the present-day K-pop to emerge on the global stage.

Part II, "Sounding Out K-Pop," delves into the technicalities of the K-pop soundscape. The two complementary chapters give us a tour of the ins and outs of sound production and analysis. Jung-Min Mina Lee's "Finding the K in K-Pop Musically: A Stylistic History" presents a structuralist analysis of how sound, rhythm, and cadence constructed K-pop's unique sonic registers. The chapter reveals the stylistic versatility of K-pop seen through a valuable insight of a musicologist who closely listens and reads iconic K-pop songs from various eras. Hye Won Kim's "Recording the Soundscape of K-Pop" treats us to a rare backstage view on how the recording process is crucial for paving a rich aural palette for diverse acoustic expressions of the K-pop world. Rich in its empirical evidence, the chapter illustrates the evolution of the soundscape of K-pop as the recording technology has evolved, the working relationship between a songwriter and performer, and the distinctive concepts of the temporal and spatial nature of sound.

Part III, "Dancing to K-Pop," takes a similar structure as Part II, first offering a dance practitioner's structuralist reading of various typologies of

K-pop choreography, which is followed by how they are practiced by various cover dance groups. The two chapters posit gender expression as a critical focus of analysis, which leads to contradicting effects of K-pop movements – sometimes liberating but at other times reaffirming the constricting gender norms. Chuyun Oh's "K-Pop Dance Music Video Choreography" walks readers through various techniques of K-pop movement and video production, highlighting the diversity of bodily movements that go into the making of K-pop visual effects. The choreographic typologies as presented by Oh mostly observe binary gender expressions, leading her to identify various shades of femininity and masculinity in motion. CedarBough Saeiji's "Embodying K-Pop Hits through Cover Dance Practices" unpacks the fan-driven cover dance practices that create affective communities whereby Korea becomes a global cultural hub that can bypass the dominance of American popular culture. This ethnographic chapter provides an insight into how the line between passive viewing and active practicing of K-pop dance is easily blurred, showing that the major fuel of K-pop fandom is creative movements that emerge out of communal choreographic practices.

Part IV, "The Making of Idols," highlights the Korean idol production system and its transnational adaptation. The two chapters in this part excavate the emotive aspect of the K-pop world, including idols' intimate labor and kinetic storytelling that are maximally commodified for profitability. They also ask foundational questions about who gets to do K-pop by presenting a case of idol production by nonethnic Koreans outside Korea. Stephanie Choi's "K-Pop Idols: Media Commodities, Affective Laborers, and Cultural Capitalists" sheds light on the realities of the idols' and trainees' working conditions. By carefully engaging with the human toll the process has on young aspiring entertainers, Choi exposes what is often left out in the blinding success stories of top performers. Giving fairhanded treatment to both the K-pop industry and the Western pop music world in her critique of entertainers' lack of agency, Choi ultimately projects the K-pop world as a "critical site in which diverse social relations are created, subverted, and negotiated." So-Rim Lee's "From K-Pop to Z-Pop: The Pan-Asian Production, Consumption, and Circulation of Idols" warns about techno/ethnocentric nationalism and minor-scale imperialism against less developed nations within ASEAN (the Association of Southeast Asian Nations), which often have been the first landing points of global K-pop bands. Now that some ASEAN nationals are forming their version of pop, the chapter investigates how "the South Korean corporatized monopoly of K-pop" may sustain itself in the age of deeper multinational entanglements of talent, capital, and fan communities.

Part V, "The Band That Surprised the World," fully confronts the discursive routes of K-pop's global circulation, with a particular focus on the group BTS as the K-pop phenomenon of the new millennium. Kyung Hyun Kim's "BTS, Transmedia, and Hip Hop" presents a polemical appraisal of how hip hop and rap music have been embraced as a major tenet of K-pop. By examining BTS's early career, Kim provides a critical assessment of how the group's phenomenal success in large part owes to their engagement with hip hop and rap music.

Kim argues that the sense of "home" and "locality," so central to the US hip hop tradition, lacks an authentic counterpart in the works of BTS. Instead, BTS and its fans found an alternative home and belonging in cyberspace, especially with the launching of Bangtan Universe. Suk-Young Kim and Youngdae Kim's "The BTS Phenomenon" presents an alternate view on authenticity by exploring how BTS's self-written lyrics, not shying away from the dialects of their hometowns, exude locality. The chapter suggests that the notion of authenticity itself might be a fraught convention articulated by a Western hegemony that constantly marginalizes newcomers to the established music scene. The chapter shows that BTS's global aspirations present a compelling alternative to the US-driven pop music industry by analyzing the band's viral storytelling technique, the significance of BTS's winning major music awards, and the band's presence on social media platforms. Candace Epps-Robertson's "Transcultural Fandom: BTS and ARMY" provides a smooth segue into Part VI with a brief panoramic view of K-pop fandom conventions. Presenting the BTS fan community of ARMY as a case in point, the chapter highlights their activities, which go beyond supporting BTS: social and political activism and mutual support of ARMY members' career needs. Epps-Robertson's chapter shows why K-pop is much more than music and media products for consumption; it is also a rallying point for millennials and those of Generation Z who value participatory culture.

Part VI, "Circuits of K-Pop Flow," traces the discursive routes of K-pop's circulation and consumption, with particular focus on new media's role, fans' translation of K-pop content, fan fiction, and K-pop tourism akin to pilgrimage. Michelle Cho's "K-Pop and the Participatory Condition: Vicarity, Serial Affect, and 'Real-Life Contents'" is a theoretical reflection on the transforming modes of media consumption as they redefine the shape of liveness in today's media ecosystem. By positing K-pop as one of the most conspicuous global media movements today, the chapter illustrates how K-pop had been forecasting the significance of contagion and virality all along before they became the key to success. Thomas Baudinette's "Idol Shipping Culture: Exploring Queer Sexuality among Fans of K-Pop" presents multiple ways idols as floating symbols of desire can unexpectedly galvanize queer reception and re-creation of the original K-pop content. By closing in on the parallels between the Japanese and the Korean shipping culture (a particular kind of fan culture where fans project an imagined relationship between two idols), Baudinette's work confirms the well-known thesis that culture is identified with the place of its circulation rather than with the place of its origin. Youjeong Oh's "Following the Footsteps of BTS: The Global Rise of K-Pop Tourism" illuminates how K-pop aficionados often transform ordinary places into extraordinary sites to visit. The chapter illustrates how the narratives emerging from K-pop storytelling – whether from promotional images for albums, from music videos, or from idols' Instagram photos – are able to authenticate any location, effectively elevating it into the holy land of K-pop pilgrimage.

With the mainstream success of Korean popular culture in recent years (think *Parasite*, *Squid Game*, BTS, and BLACKPINK), many still wonder how it all happened. Why Korea? Why now? Circling back to the beginning of this introduction will provide some insight: a high saturation of talented entertainers and fierce competition among them, a highly supportive but also critical fan base who constantly raise the bar for performers, the resilient hybridity of music styles, and Korea's rapid embrace of digital transformation, which enabled Korean content to reach a worldwide audience. These are just a few highlights, and the full answers will be found in the pages of this book.

Notes

1 Suk-Young Kim, *K-Pop Live: Fans, Idols, and Multimedia Performance* (Stanford, CA: Stanford University Press, 2018).
2 I thank Ian Condry for having first suggested this idea.
3 Richard Middleton, *Voicing the Popular: On the Subject of Popular Music* (London: Routledge, 2006), 200.
4 John Lie, *K-Pop: Popular Music, Cultural Amnesia, and Economic Innovation in South Korea* (Oakland: University of California Press, 2015), 14.
5 Jeffrey Funk, *Technology Change and the Rise of New Industries* (Stanford, CA: Stanford Business Books, 2013), 5.

PART I

Genealogies

1 Sticking It to the Man

Early Neoliberalism in Korean Pop Music

ROALD MALIANGKAY

Open Competition

In cultural studies, as well as in many other disciplines, the use of the term "neoliberalism" has become increasingly prevalent. Outside the field of economics, to which it was once tied more closely, it has become a blanket term for capitalist measures that include deregulation, reductions in public expenditures, and an emphasis on individual entrepreneurship, competition, and free trade. Terry Flew notes that when interpreted as an approach to economic policy, it may be endorsed by left-leaning policy makers due to its inherent goal to reduce the cost of bureaucracy, but it is more frequently associated with ruthless approaches to capitalist gain.[1] Nick Couldry argues that neoliberal strategies pose a danger when they promote a worldview that regards markets as the ideal sociopolitical form of organization and allows its principles to drown out alternative criteria. While neoliberalism may, for example, appear to foreground the voices of individuals, including those of fan communities, he warns that "the notion of freedom underlying neoliberalism is abstracted from any understanding of the social processes that underpin 'voice' in its full sense as an embodied process of effective speech."[2] In the workplace, the corporate identity does indeed risk obfuscating truly individual, personal experience and value, and while one might posit that the self-branding so common in popular culture is a triumph of individual expression, Couldry contends that it merely represents the "opportunity to compete as a commodity."[3] Since neoliberal values have become internalized and very much part of our culture, championing a more introspective and less performative account of the non-market-driven needs and emotions of individuals may prove quite challenging.

The business of Korean popular music is driven by neoliberalism in a range of different ways. According to Inkyu Kang, it is responsible for the hypercommodification and hyperrationalization of K-pop, as evidenced by the creation of "talents" through years of training, the wide range of spin-off products, and the frequent use of lip-synching. And it explains, he argues, the deindividualization of group members and their replaceability within idol formations.[4] But neoliberalism can be identified in another equally important aspect of K-pop, namely the semantics of K-pop performances. In conformist and (from a Korean point of view) politically correct fashion,[5] many idol formations passionately endorse the voices of their fans through messages of individuality, girl power, and self-love. The phenomenon of Seo Taiji and Boys demonstrated,[6] however, that emphasis on personal empowerment and symbols of nonconformity can be used to promote major brands, including idol formations, luring fans into portraying themselves as critical consumers who happen to have developed a "bias." There is one other realm where the connection between neoliberalism and today's K-pop industry is predominant. It is where competition and public scrutiny allow individuals a chance to break out as rising stars through the reality talent show.

Over the past decade, reality talent shows have experienced a dramatic surge in popularity on South Korean TV networks. Examples include Mnet's *Superstar K* (2009–2016), *The Voice of Korea* (2012–2013), *I Can See Your Voice* (*Neo-ui moksori-ga boyeo*, since 2017), and *Produce 101* (2016–2019); tvN's *Korea's Got Talent* (2011–2012); SBS's *Survival Audition K-Pop Star* (2011–2017); KBS's *Top Band* (2011–2015) and *Singing Battle* (*Norae ssaum*, 2016–2017); and MBC's *Star Audition: The Great Birth* (*Seuta odisyeon widaehan tansaeng*, 2010–2013) and *I Am a Singer* (*Na-neun gasuda*, 2011–2015). Even Marvel's comic book character Luna Snow, the K-pop idol turned superhero, was introduced in 2019 as a member of 4L1T, "winners of the idol origins contest."[7] Reality talent shows revolve around a small panel of noted individuals judging music performances by amateurs over the course of competitive elimination rounds. As they play into the general public's distrust of the music industry's manipulative power and gatekeeping, viewers are asked to cast their vote, either live or online. Meanwhile, the amateur status of contestants and the name of a show like *The Voice of Korea* fuel the sentiment that audiences are playing a role in curating true talent.

Hyeonu Han argues that the talent shows are more competitions than auditions. He believes an audition is a way of seeing how well you fit a particular role, while a competition focuses on how well a predetermined song is played: "The main concern is who sings the designated song better and who goes up to the higher pitch."[8] But although the element of competition is undeniable and will also play out among the fans, the shows equally encourage the audience to assess whether a candidate is "fit" to win. As important as their voices, backstories serve as evidence of contestants' authenticity. Critics note that viewers are made to judge a limited range of renditions of well-established styles of music based on vague criteria.[9] Indeed, for the television shows to be successful, and for the successful contestants to earn the lucrative rewards that will allow them to commit themselves fully to their artistic ambitions, the undefined criteria for performance cannot completely shun stylistic conventions or be perceived as superimposed; the contestants must emulate existing conventions to win the maximum number of votes. The business of popular entertainment favors those with the greatest commercial promise, and despite the outcome arguably being predetermined, by seemingly defying the cultural hegemony the notion of raw talent promotes sales. As Jeremy Gilbert notes, the idea of the "innate talent" of individuals serves to "justify the obviously self-perpetuating nature of inegalitarian institutions and social relations."[10] Adorno's idea of pseudo-individualism therefore applies to both the business model and the supposed talent of the contestants.[11] The considerable commercial importance of the shows – some have generated viewer ratings as high as 20 percent – can cast doubts upon the validity of the polls. After all, judges and producers may have a vested interest in selecting contestants who, for better or worse, appeal to a large percentage of the population. When in spite of the format's popularity and reliance on viewer voting, Mnet's producers feared that the 2019 installment of their *Produce* series would produce an unfavorable outcome, they rigged the voting process.[12]

John Fiske defines fandom as a minority's act of appropriating "certain performers, narratives or genres" from mainstream pop. "It is," he finds, "typically associated with the cultural tastes of subordinated formations of the people, particularly with those disempowered by any combination of gender, age, class and race."[13] The definition is helpful because it identifies the crucial factor of empowerment, which may take different forms and could be taken to comprise cultural, social, and economic involvement or recognition. Although K-pop and talent shows have come under increasing scrutiny by fans, the criticism does not immediately pose a challenge to the business model per se. Critics may genuinely oppose aspects of the industry's hegemony and have a significant effect on sales but may ultimately be driven by a desire to find unity in a common purpose, promote their fandom and ability to scrutinize, or compete with fans of other idols. Since fandom presents an avenue for young people to distinguish themselves, even strong criticism of talent shows may be geared less toward generating systemic change than toward generating likes. Pop culture fandom is aspirational; it yields greater agency to the subordinated, even though the majority of critically engaged fans may not seek control over particular media to reverse their subordination, however loud their voices.

Selling Records

In the first few decades of the twentieth century, record companies' primary source of revenue was the sale of physical copies. The wonders of new media technologies and the foreign scenes and sounds they produced certainly drew in affluent consumers, but as soon as prices began to drop and the size of the middle class began to grow, the business became a dominant feature of daily life. In Korea, too, talent shows, radio broadcasts, and countless advertisements promoting the latest records could be found everywhere. While the elements of cost, sound quality, and uniqueness remained considerable selling points for some time, the growing phenomenon of celebrity stardom eventually turned fandom into a fourth major factor driving sales. Enjoying the accolades of connoisseurship and cosmopolitanism that their involvement awarded, many young urbanites kept up to date on the activities of their idols and emulated their style. They bought magazines and frequented record shops and popular music venues to follow the latest developments and share experiences and opinions.

Having steadily grown an interest in Korean talent among Korean and Japanese middle-class consumers, in the late 1920s the companies began to increasingly bring out modern, faster arrangements of traditional songs called "new folk songs" (*sin minyo*) and *yuhaengga* (*yuhaeng*, popular; *ga*, song). Because they followed Japan's pentatonic *yonanuki* scale, they could become popular with both Koreans and Japanese domestically, opening up the possibility of a Japanese-language release. Even so, in 1928, F. H. Goldsmith, a recording engineer for Victor Japan, said that across northeast Asia people were primarily interested in their own music, with native pop genres generally holding little commercial promise overseas.[14] Jazz was the last of the three primary pop song styles to emerge and thrive. Unlike the other two styles, which could be described as melancholic, jazz songs were mostly upbeat. Because many of them corresponded with passionate dance sequences admired on the silver screen, they felt decidedly more modern and, on account of their more playful character, may have symbolized conformity to the political status quo. Indeed, Yongwoo Lee finds that in Korea's context, young people turned jazz music into a commodity that tied them to America's utopic contemporaneity.[15] Rather than merely emulating aspects of Western culture, however, Koreans sought to own it. To a Westerner, Korean jazz may have seemed flattering, but to Koreans it was defiantly progressive; its very existence denied foreign patency and allowed it to be embedded with Korean sensibilities. Despite having no control over any particular medium or genre, Koreans were able to create "glocalized" forms of entertainment that highlighted their own potential and expressed uniquely Korean sentiments. But while Korean successes overseas were important for their self-image, Korean jazz did not sell abroad and was not even popular with Korea's own elite, who preferred Western classical music.[16]

By the early 1930s, the primary companies competing for a slice of the Korean music market were Columbia and Victor, closely followed in terms of market share by Chieron, Polydor, Okeh, and Taepyeong (Taihei in Japanese). I estimate their total annual income to have hovered around 35 million won around the mid-1930s, equivalent to approximately US$350 million today. In a discussion with noted pop singers and record company representatives in January 1936, *Samcheolli* (Our land) magazine editor Donghwan Kim claimed that sales of traditional Korean music ("Joseon soripan") accounted for a third of the total volume of 1.5 million records sold,[17] which suggests that until the early 1940s, when the production of records collapsed, the Korean market was dominated by "new folk songs" and *yuhaengga*, jazz songs, and Western classical music. Korean pop music accounted for more than half of record sales, and some pop songs, whether foreign or Korean, sold thousands of copies almost overnight. But like today, due to the high cost of production, record companies rarely took chances; although nudity had long proven to sell live acts regardless of artistic talent, gramophone recordings had to ideally be sold before they ended up on the shelves.

Music fandom grew considerably in the 1930s, but few contemporary publications discussed the phenomenon in detail. The first use of the English term "fan" (*paen*) in regard to admirers of pop culture in Korea may be in the Japanese-language paper *Pusan nippo* from June 1925, which reported that fans in Busan, presumably all Japanese, were excited about the arrival of actress Makino Teruko.[18] Another, from December 1926, referred to Korean followers of Hollywood star Rudolph Valentino.[19] The term "fan" retained its association with things foreign for some time and was still placed between quotation marks in an editorial on popular music a decade later.[20] While it was used to refer to sports fans, too, when it was applied to popular music, not a realm dominated by men, it appears to have carried negative connotations. The many complaints by Koreans about the ill effects of modern urban culture in the early 1930s show that some believed pop music was having a druglike effect on Korean youth, with gramophone technology often receiving partial blame. In an editorial from January 1930, for example, an impression of an evening at Café Baron in Seoul reads: "When the sound of jazz belches from a gramophone player, waitresses twitch their shoulders and wriggle their bums. These unsightly mechanical rhythms are springing up everywhere."[21] In a piece on the effect of pop music on children published four years later, a critic wrote: "When I walk down an alley, I often hear a phonograph playing. The lyrics are usually quite meaningless and messy."[22] And in 1935, folklorist Seokha Song lamented that records with "empty pop songs" (*pyetoehan yuhaengga*) were now playing virtually everywhere around the country.[23] It is ironic that criticism of the medium took decades to come to the fore, and that when it finally did, due of course in part to the emergence of print media – in the 1920s and 1930s important platforms for the discussion of popular culture included the magazines *Samcheolli*, *Byeolgeongon* (Another world), and *Jogwang* (Dawn) – Koreans were playing a greater role in the record industry than ever before. Not only were they increasingly involved in the production of records both behind the scenes and in front of the microphone, but even the voice of Korean fans had become difficult to ignore: Many wrote letters to their idols, followed them around after performances, sent gifts like cosmetics or chocolate, and they sometimes demanded that the radio play their favorite music.[24] Indeed, in January 1940, pop singer Song Geumnyeong acknowledged that "today's fans of popular songs (*yuhaengga*) have certainly become more knowledgeable and better at their hobby."[25] What is more, despite growing criticism of the involvement of *gisaeng* (young hostesses or courtesans) in popular culture, which extended even to their use of fashion accessories,[26] record companies and the radio provided talented ones with better career opportunities than they had ever had.

Recognizing Talent

Newspapers and the radio played a significant role in the promotion of the new repertoires, while fandom and conformity did their part to urge consumers to keep up to date. To be at the forefront of new developments in popular culture, or at the very least aware of them, has always been a major driver of fandom. In May 1933, when portraits of individual artists were regularly featured in ads and on records and lyric sheets, the music label Chieron debuted an anonymous singer simply called Ms. Chieron. It challenged fans to show themselves to be true connoisseurs by identifying the hidden identity of the vocalist. Columbia Records followed suit in September 1934 with a Ms. Korea, whose face on lyric sheets was made unrecognizable by a black banner across her eyes. A Ms. Regal and Mr. Columbia debuted in 1934 and 1935, respectively.[27] An ad in the *Maeil sinbo* (Daily report) again a year later also played into the pressure to be in the know. Using small profile pictures of two women, a record shop challenged readers to work out the identity of the popular singers based on a few small hints.[28] In these and other ways record companies promoted their products widely and aggressively; shoppers, movie audiences, and journal subscribers were all subjected to countless advertisements and promotions. While shop owners did their part distributing flyers and lyric sheets for a new record or gramophone player, record companies and the radio advertised live radio shows and public events where audiences could witness the latest or future stars performing live.

Unlike *gisaeng*, who could rely on their management to provide introductions, talented singers with no ties to the music industry could make a name for themselves by winning a prize in a contest. The idea may not have been adopted from abroad, but if it was, it certainly shows that Korea's entertainment industry followed developments elsewhere. The 1935 Hollywood production *Every Night at Eight*, about a singing trio trying to break through using an amateur radio hour, was the first to piggyback on the popularity of the amateur hour concept in the United States.[29] In the United Kingdom; in Japan, where *Every Night at Eight* opened in April 1936; and in China, too, talent shows were becoming a regular feature on the radio.[30] In Hong Kong in January 1932, the chairman of the Broadcasting Committee issued an invitation to local talent for a singing contest.[31] And in Shanghai in November 1935, an amateur contest was organized with the help of several local radio stations under the auspices of the RCA-Victor record company. Running over the course of a week and decided by the listeners based on "popular vote," it sought to support talented contestants and in the process "point to all the stars who began at the bottom."[32]

In Korea, from October 1933, for approximately six months, Columbia Records staged a pop music singing contest in ten cities across the country with a record contract on the line, as well as the possibility of an acting gig with the Japanese film studio Shōchiku Kinema. Hye Eun Choi writes that in the 1930s record companies regularly held contests like these "as a means to recruit new artists as well as raise their revenues."[33] Indeed, the events promoted the companies' brand names and their association with talent, and sometimes sales of a particular hit song or recital. Sponsoring Columbia Records's contest was the *Joseon ilbo* (Korea daily), which sought to increase sales through regular updates on the proceedings and presented the contestants to readers with a photo in its first major announcement.[34] The events were held in the evening, and each week time allowed for only three contestants to sing one designated song and one of their own choosing.[35] Yujeong Jang notes that, because popular music still lacked the reputation of Western classical music, only noted specialists of the latter genre were asked to serve as judges. On this occasion they were Prof. Mary Young of Ewha College, Prof. Jemyeong Hyeon of Yeonheui College, and pianist and soprano Seongdeok Yun.[36] At the finals, held on February 17, 1934, emerging stars Jeong Ilgyeong and Go Boksu came in first and second place, respectively (see Figure 1.1).

The success of the scheme prompted other record companies to follow suit. After similar contests had been held by Okeh in 1935–1936 and

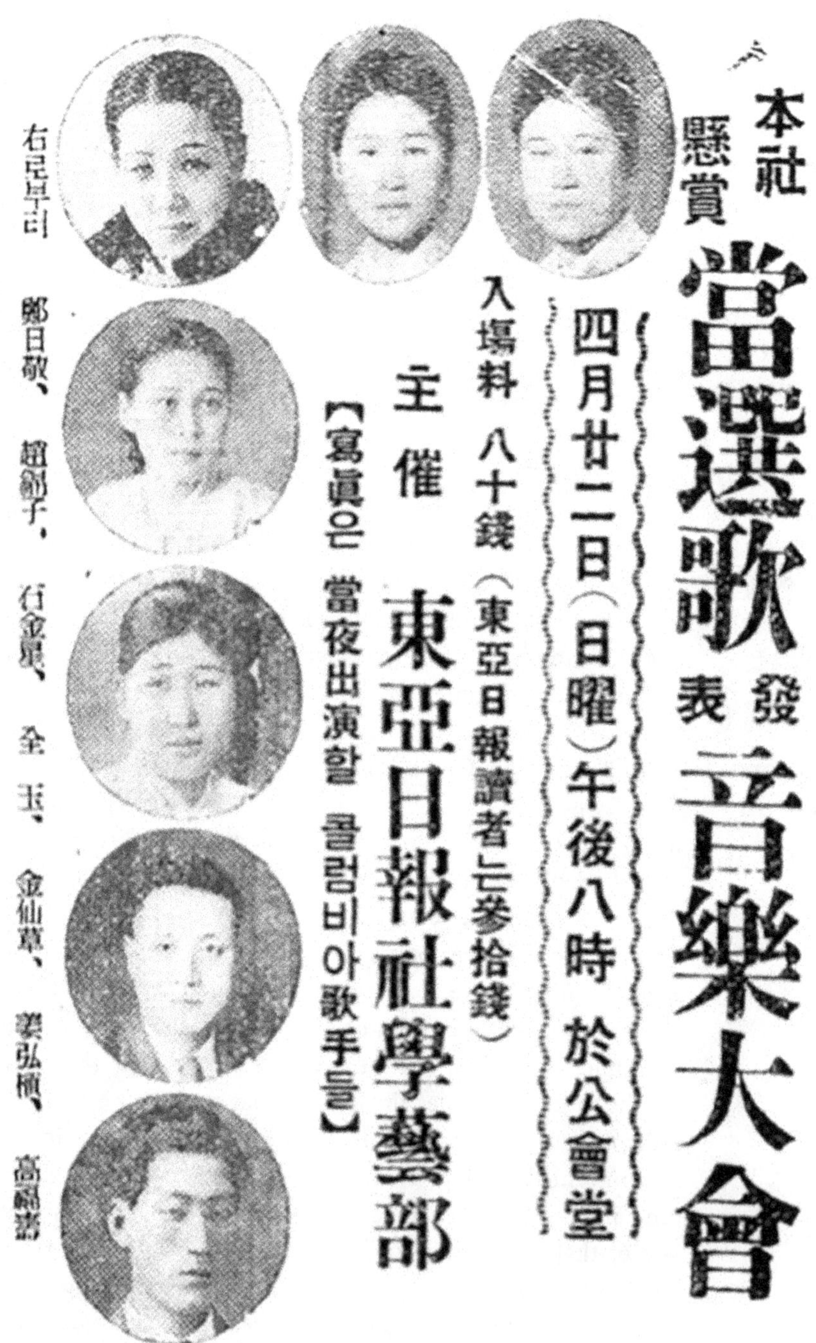

Figure 1.1 Advertisement for a concert by Columbia singers includes photos of Jeong Ilgyeong, in the top right corner, and Go Boksu, at the bottom (*Donga ilbo*, April 19, 1934, 6).

Victor in early 1939,[37] on July 29, 1939, Taepyeong Records announced another nationwide contest, again in collaboration with the *Joseon ilbo*.[38] This time, however, judges were chosen from among notable figures from the popular music scene, namely composer Jeon Gihyeon and lyricist

Cheon Ato. Finalists had to sing Chae Gyuyeop's hit song "Bukkuk ocheon kiro" (The northern country's 5,000 kilometers, Taihei8600), which the company had released in January that year, and one song of their own choosing.[39] A few months later, it was Polydor Japan's turn to organize a nationwide "New Singer Contest" (Sinin gasu seonbal daehoe), with support from the *Donga ilbo* (East Asia daily). The contest also played out over six months, but the repertoire was fully predetermined and comprised songs released by Polydor in the year prior: three particular songs for male contestants and three for female ones. Judging was once more done by well-established insiders of the popular music scene: actor and lyricist Pyeong Wang, Polydor's local head of A&R, and composers Mun Howol and Jeon Gihyeon.[40] In 1942, Taepyeong Records announced what would be the last national pop music singing contest to be held before the end of colonial rule.[41]

Noted vocalists who were "discovered" through talent shows include Ilgyeong Jeong, Boksu Go, Sejeong Jang, Geumja Jo, Bangnam Jin, Nana Baek, and Yeongchun Kim.[42] Hye Eun Choi finds that successful singers like Boksu Go would generally enjoy a greater reputation than their female counterparts.[43] Although the neoliberal nature of the contest, the idea that anyone could be a star, was intriguing, the negative perception of *gisaeng* persisted, and not because the young women's music training gave them an unfair advantage. Despite the prevalence of *gisaeng* in everyday life and the high salaries of some former *gisaeng*-turned–pop stars, the association of *gisaeng* with popular music long tainted the latter. The negative association may have led to the term *yeoryu myeongchang* being introduced. Used to refer to acclaimed *gisaeng* performers of traditional music, the first part of the term (*yeoryu*), Choi argues, indicates that the women were educated and "socially successful."[44] But although the *gisaeng* past of female stars was thus rarely celebrated, despite the rigorous training they had undergone, women's working-class backgrounds could work in their favor as long as they did not call their virtue into question. That the talent of contestant Jang Sejeong was discovered while she was "working as a salesgirl at Hwasin Department Store in Pyongyang," for example, may have boosted her appeal, especially since department store saleswomen were known to be selected on the basis of their looks.[45]

Similar to the popular *Korea's Got Talent*–like TV shows of today, the contests entailed the public auditioning of contestants performing a limited range of music in popular styles in front of a panel of people working for the record company and a collaborating entertainment agency.[46] The range of well-established pop songs was much more limited at the time, so in order to promote their own productions and have them regarded as the standard, contestants were required to cover the record companies' own hit songs. From a marketing point of view, little could go wrong, but the commercial importance of the talent shows still cast doubts upon the selection criteria applied. Despite its own involvement in the formula from the start, on April 25, 1940, the *Joseon ilbo* published an editorial that criticized the commercialism of talent shows, arguing that it was wrong of record companies to ask contestants to buy two records and pay a participation fee.[47] Since it did not mention which company it had in mind, the critique is likely to have been aimed at Taepyeong Records and Polydor, which had both charged an application fee of 3 won the previous year. Amounting to the cost of a record, it was a relatively high fee that may have been partly intended as a form of preselection due to the high number of applications.[48] A month later, the paper published another critique of the shows, this time focused on the absence of proper criteria and bias toward pretty female contestants and those with *aegyo* (winsomeness).[49] Criticism of the alleged bias was likely fueled by the looks of female contestants frequently coming up in public discourse, as well as by the faces of both male and female entertainers having been customarily printed on flyers, newspaper advertisements, and posters since the mid-1920s. Since the emphasis on the looks of female entertainers was not limited to the shows or the record industry, a critique like this could not have much effect. A newspaper report on Taepyeong Records's second contest in early 1942 lists the songs – all Taihei hits – on which the contestants would be judged, but again omits any discussion of criteria.[50]

Critics of the talent shows and the social hierarchies they upheld could not overturn their own role as consumers, let alone their status as colonized subjects. They were reminded of this on May 22, 1933, when the government promulgated the Gramophone Record Regulations (Chugeumgi rekodeu chwiche gyuchik), which banned many albums for being disturbing or immoral.[51] But the shared recognition of raw talent, that subjective social standard that had been cultivated over years, may have felt no less magical than finding the perfect partner.[52] Although the format invited the opinions of privileged citizens too, the audiences' efforts to serve cultural justice by giving recognition to amateur music talents brought the colonized together over matters of taste.[53] The shows were premised, after all, on individuals' mastery in *their* popular culture. Especially when living under colonial rule, finding commonalities in defiance of the political hegemony, the formula's cultivation of shared norms, would have been gratifying. Apart from the element of public scrutiny, the talent shows' native embedding of authenticity was crucial. Annette Hill posits that "The more emphasis is placed on spectacle and style, the more audiences look for authenticity in people's behavior, emotions and the settings for representations of reality."[54] Although the record industry had not yet been hit by major controversies or scandals, the decades-long seeming absence of the general public's immediate participation led some to question the notion of "popular" (*yuhaeng*) entertainment regardless of the involvement of Koreans in the creative production process.[55]

Despite Koreans having no control over any particular medium or genre and the judging catering to a Korean audience, the talent shows were a platform for uniquely Korean sentiments and highlighted the potential of the subordinated. That finalists would have a chance of success with Japanese and Japanese colonial subjects overseas was important for Koreans' self-image. But although an article in the *Maeil sinbo* from June 1925 boasted that "Korean [traditional] vocal music will reverberate in foreign ears,"[56] the reality was that outside Korea, few people were interested in Korean renditions of Western music. Only a handful of Korean stars enjoyed success in Japan, where in 1940, Korean music made up less than 2–3 percent of all records produced.[57] Records released under a Japanese pseudonym were either Japanese translations of Korean songs or songs specifically written for the Japanese market. While a few Korean virtuosos were able to briefly escape their colonial subjectivity in Japan by working under a pseudonym, Western audiences would not look beyond their ethnicity. Korea's foremost celebrity, dancer Choe Seung-hui, for example, found that foreign audiences did not care much for Asians performing Western dance, in original or adapted forms. In spite of her wide range of styles, they preferred an "oriental" musical accompaniment to one involving Western instruments, which forced her to find Korean Americans to accompany her on Korean traditional instruments during her tour in the United States.[58]

Conclusion

As the above examples demonstrate, fandom in colonial Korea comprised a very complex range of emotions and aspirations that deserves much more careful attention than is paid here. Apart from infatuation with a celebrity or the social distinction that music could provide, from early on pop music fandom was driven by the beauty of the melodies and lyrics and the music's association with a modern, Western view on life. Fandom was liberating, as it appealed to modern sensibilities around class, gender, and community. By lending them a voice and highlighting their economic and cultural capital, it gave fans a sense of empowerment. Although foreign companies seldom acknowledged either the talent of a Korean pop star or the importance of their Korean fans, they allowed fans to imagine a connection to peers outside their social circle and provided opportunities to collect experiences and items that quickly grew in prestige. The careers of some female singers were launched by the neoliberal "stick it to the man" formula that proved popular with many Koreans, but misogyny prevailed. Some Koreans were concerned about the degrading effect of *gisaeng*'s prominence on the sanctity of Korean pop entertainment, but not equally concerned about traditional forms of entertainment. This may be in part because the latter did not invite comparison with Japanese or Western entertainment and in part because of the notion that women trained as courtesans ought not to represent modern Korea. It is ironic, because eroticism helped promote Korean popular culture among both Koreans and Japanese, and it frequently relied on association with the *gisaeng* institution.

Although opportunities to become a professional entertainer with one of the largely Japanese-owned businesses were relatively small in number, already in the 1920s aspiring artists managed to cultivate their unique performing skills and to land contracts by way of private auditions, public talent shows, and radio gigs. The small- to medium-sized events groomed talents to serve both Korean and foreign audiences, singing songs in Korean and Japanese, with communication skills and looks undoubtedly playing a significant role. Once they secured a record contract, their lives could change dramatically. When Columbia chose to organize its own show nationwide, it did not announce any judging criteria. It wanted the audience to become involved and intended to use the momentum the shows built to sell records. The judges were mostly industry insiders, or at least part of an elite circle of music experts, and well aware of the commercial risk involved in voting against the unwritten criteria. By collaborating with major newspapers, the companies involved had nigh full control over the selection process and outcome. Audience members would have had their share of criticism but no public outlet for their voice. Since the few critical editorials that made it to print targeted no record company by name, they may have served to promote rather than discredit the shows that were still running.

After Liberation, music talent shows did not disappear, but those that ran did so without the involvement of any major record company or media outlet. Record sales were small, and the only radio station to frequently play pop music was that of the American Forces Korea Network (AFKN). Rather than using amateur radio shows as a springboard, aspiring artists would audition privately with the entertainment division of the Eighth United States Army in Korea (EUSAK), where good movement and showmanship outweighed musical skill. Successful entertainers could land a gig headlining the prestigious Walker Hill Shows (1962–2002) or appear on TBC's highly popular TV program *Show Show Show* (1964–1983). That the latter often featured talents from the military circuit was due to their ability to move well on stage and thus on camera.[59] Rather than good musicianship, therefore, from the 1960s Korean pop music began to prioritize good movement and showmanship, fostered partly by the expressiveness of the Western music genres popular on the military circuit. The cultural and political importance of the military entertainment circuit is exemplified by Korean pop idols the Kim Sisters migrating to the United States in the early 1960s in pursuit of the American Dream. It signaled an embrace of American culture and of a neoliberal, capitalist model of economic development that foregrounds individualism rather than defiance of any hegemonic superstructure. But Koreans would eventually develop a major, global entertainment industry of their own. And it is its hegemony that the industry's own talent shows are now meant to thwart.

Today's talent shows retain many of the elements of control: the lack of clear criteria, the record contract on the line, the momentum built over months of auditions, the involvement of major media outlets, and neoliberalist self-promotion by the artists. Among some of the new elements are the primacy of backstories and the selection of judges based on their ability to give strong, theatrical performances in supporting or critiquing performances.[60] While the sociopolitical conditions of today's shows are vastly different from those in the past, the notion of talent remains largely unquestioned. Despite criticism of commercial products and schemes being commonplace, the talent shows are supported by the backstories' evidence of authenticity and continue to compel viewers to participate in the voting process in the interest of preserving merit-based selection. However, the notion of "talent" still adheres merely to a skill set that "fits" a set of long-cultivated standards. While the desire to generate greater control over one's popular culture may be less than it was under colonial rule, deciding with many others on presumed authenticity and quality may allow voters to find unity in a common purpose, promote their fandom and ability for scrutiny, or compete with fans of other idols. It may be a neoliberalist trap, but the format does represent the voices and aesthetics of a majority and provide genuine business opportunities to individual artists. I suspect, therefore, that we may all be stuck to this man for some time yet.

Bibliography

Adorno, Theodor W. "On Popular Music." In John Storey (ed.), *Cultural Theory and Popular Culture: A Reader*, 197–209. Dorchester: Prentice Hall, 1998.
An, Ikjo. "Yuhaeng gasu jwadamhoe" (A discussion with popular singers). *Sinin munhak* 3 (December 1934): 92–97.
Bourdieu, Pierre. *Distinction: A Social Critique of the Judgement of Taste*. Cambridge, MA: Harvard University Press, 1984.

Choi, Hye Eun. "The Making of the Recording Industry in Colonial Korea, 1910–1945." PhD diss., University of Wisconsin-Madison, 2018.

Coulangeon, Philippe. "Social Mobility and Musical Tastes: A Reappraisal of the Social Meaning of Taste Eclecticism." *Poetics* 15 (2015): 54–68.

Couldry, Nick. *Why Voice Matters: Culture and Politics after Neoliberalism* (London: Sage, 2010).

Epstein, Stephen. "Fly the Flag (at Your Own Risk): Netizens, Nationalism and Celebrities between South Korea, Japan and Beyond." In Rumi Sakamoto and Stephen Epstein (eds.), *Popular Culture and Transformation of Japan-Korea Relations*, 167–181. London: Routledge, 2020.

Fiske, John. "The Cultural Economy of Fandom." In Lisa A. Lewis (ed.), *The Adoring Audience: Fan Culture and Popular Media)*, 30–49. London: Routledge, 1992.

Flew, Terry. "Six Theories of Neoliberalism." *Thesis Eleven* 122/1 (2014): 49–71.

Gilbert, Jeremy. "What Does Democracy Feel Like? Form, Function, Affect, and the Materiality of the Sign." In Lincoln Dahlberg and Sean Phelan (eds.), *Discourse Theory and Critical Media Politics*, 82–105. Basingstoke: Palgrave Macmillan, 2011.

Han, Hyeonu. "Odisyeon-gwa keompeotisyeon-ui chai" (The difference between an audition and a competition). *Joseon ilbo* (Korea Daily), April 18, 2013, A33.

Hill, Annette. *Restyling Factual TV: Audiences and News, Documentary and Reality Genres.* London: Routledge, 2007.

Jang, Yujeong. *Norae punggyeong: Jang Yujeong-ui eumak sanmunjip* (A Scenery of Songs: Essays on Music by Yujeong Jang). Seoul: Alma, 2013.
   Oppa-neun punggakchaengi-ya (My brother is a street singer). Seoul: Hwanggeumgaji, 2006.

Joo, Kyeongmi. "Gendered Differences in Modern Korea Toward Western Luxuries." In K. Pyun and Y. Wong (eds.), *Fashion, Identity, and Power in Modern Asia*, 143–166. Cham: Palgrave Macmillan, 2018.

Kang, Inkyu. "The Political Economy of Idols: South Korea's Neoliberal Restructuring and Its Impact on the Entertainment Labour Force." In Choi JungBong and Roald Maliangkay (eds.), *K-Pop: The International Rise of the Korean Music Industry*, 51–65. New York: Routledge, 2015.

Kim, Donghwan. "In'gi gasu jwadamhoe" (A discussion of noted singers). *Samcheolli* (Our land) 8 (January 1936): 130.

Kim, Sung Sik (Kim Seongsik), and Seung Mook Kang (Kang Seungmuk). "Odisyeon rieolliti syo 'Seuta odisyeon widaehan tansaeng'-gwa 'Syupeo seuta K2'-ui paendeom hyeonsang" (A study of the fandom of "Star Audition: The Great Birth" and "Superstar K2"). *Eollon gwahak yeon'gu* (Studies in Media Science) 12/3 (2012): 5–36.

Lee, Yongwoo. "Embedded Voices in between Empires: The Cultural Formation of Korean Popular Music in Modern Times." Doctoral thesis, McGill University, 2010.

Maliangkay, Roald. "Koreans Got Talent: Auditioning for U.S. Army Gigs in Korea." *Situations: Cultural Studies in the Asian Context* 11/1 (2018): 59–79.
   "New Symbolism and Retail Therapy: Advertising Novelties in Korea's Colonial Period." *East Asian History* 36 (2008): 47–48.

"Not a Habitus for the Have Nots: The Walker Hill Shows, 1962–2012." In Keith Howard and Catherine Ingram (eds.), *Presence through Sound: Music and Place in East Asia*, 148–161. London: Routledge SOAS Studies in Music Series, 2020.

"The Popularity of Individualism: The Seo Taiji Phenomenon in the 1990s." In Kyung Hyun Kim and Youngmin Choe (eds.), *The Korean Popular Culture Reader*, 296–313. Durham, NC: Duke University Press, 2014.

Nam, Im. "Gasu seonbal 'kongkul'-gwa keommeo-syallijeum" (The singer selection "concours" and commercialism). *Joseon Ilbo*, April 25, 1940, 4.

Oh, Jinseok, and Howard Kahm. "Selling Smiles: Emotional Labor and Labor-Management Relations in 1930s Colonial Korean Department Stores." *Journal of Korean Studies* 23/1 (2018): 3–24.

Pak, Chanho. *Han'guk gayosa* (A history of Korean popular songs), vol. 1. Seoul: Mizi Books, 2009.

Park, Yong-Gyu. "Han'guk tellebijeon eumak beoraieotisyo-ui seongsoe: TBC-TV-ui 'syosyosyo'-reul jungsim-euro" (The rise and fall of television musical variety shows in Korea: Focusing on TBC-TV's "Show Show Show"). *Han'guk kontencheu hakhoe nonmunji* (Journal of Korea Contents Association) 14/10 (2014): 51–63.

Song, Geumnyeong. "Geori-ui kanaria" (Street canary). *Joseon ilbo*, January 13, 1940, 4.

Storey, John. *An Introduction to Cultural Theory and Popular Culture*. Athens: University of Georgia Press, 1998.

Wada, Shigeyoshi. *Dai Keijō toshi daikan* [Overview of Greater Seoul]. Seoul: Chōsen shinbunsha, 1937.

Wong, Alyssa. *Luna Snow*, vol. 1. Marvel, 2019.

Yi, Dongsun. *Beonji eomneun jumak* [The tavern without a number]. Seoul: Seon, 2007.

"Iljemal gunguk gayo-ui balpyo hyeonhwang-gwa siltae" (Actual status and conditions of the release of military songs at the end of the period of Japanese colonial rule). *Hanminjok eomunhak* (Korean linguistics and literature studies) 59/59 (2011): 369 399.

Notes

1 Terry Flew, "Six Theories of Neoliberalism," *Thesis Eleven* 122/1 (2014): 51, 53–54.

2 Nick Couldry, *Why Voice Matters: Culture and Politics after Neoliberalism* (London: Sage, 2010), 11–12.

3 Couldry, *Why Voice Matters*, 13; see also 32, 34–35.

4 Inkyu Kang, "The Political Economy of Idols: South Korea's Neoliberal Restructuring and Its Impact on the Entertainment Labour Force," in Choi JungBong and Roald Maliangkay (eds.), *K-Pop: The International Rise of the Korean Music Industry* (New York: Routledge, 2015), 57, 59, 63.

5 See Stephen Epstein, "Fly the Flag (at Your Own Risk): Netizens, Nationalism and Celebrities between South Korea, Japan and Beyond," in Rumi Sakamoto and Stephen Epstein (eds.), *Popular Culture and Transformation of Japan-Korea Relations* (Routledge, 2020), 167–181.

6 Roald Maliangkay, "The Popularity of Individualism: The Seo Taiji Phenomenon in the 1990s," in Kyung Hyun Kim and Youngmin Choe (eds.), *The Korean Popular Culture Reader* (Durham, NC: Duke University Press, 2014), 296–313.

7 Alyssa Wong, *Luna Snow*, issue 1 (Marvel, 2019), 8.

8 Hyeonu Han, "Odisyeon-gwa keompeotisyeon-ui chai" (The difference between an audition and a competition), *Joseon ilbo* (Korea daily), April 18, 2013, A33.

9 See, for example, Jeremy Gilbert, "What Does Democracy Feel Like? Form, Function, Affect, and the Materiality of the Sign," in Lincoln Dahlberg and Sean Phelan (eds.), *Discourse Theory and Critical Media Politics* (Basingstoke: Palgrave Macmillan, 2011), 92–93, 99; Sung Sik Kim (Seongsik Kim) and Seung Mook Kang (Seungmuk Kang), "Odisyeon rieolliti syo 'Seuta odisyeon widaehan tansaeng'-gwa 'Syupeo seuta K2'-ui paendeom hyeonsang" (A study of the fandom of "Star Audition: The Great Birth" and "Superstar K2"), *Eollon gwahak yeon'gu* (Studies in Media Science) 12/3 (2012): 6, 9. See also Roald Maliangkay, "Koreans Got Talent: Auditioning for U.S. Army Gigs in Korea," *Situations: Cultural Studies in the Asian Context* 11/1 (2018): 59–79.

10 Gilbert, "What Does Democracy Feel Like?," 94.

11 Theodor W. Adorno, "On Popular Music," in John Storey (ed.), *Cultural Theory and Popular Culture: A Reader* (Dorchester: Prentice Hall, 1998), 203–204.

12 *The Straits Times*, June 1, 2020, C8.

13 John Fiske, "The Cultural Economy of Fandom," in Lisa A. Lewis (ed.), *The Adoring Audience: Fan Culture and Popular Media* (London: Routledge, 1992), 30.

14 *The Japan Times & Mail*, May 5, 1928, 1.

15 Yongwoo Lee, "Embedded Voices in between Empires: The Cultural Formation of Korean Popular Music in Modern Times" (doctoral thesis, McGill University, 2010), 77, 236.

16 Hye Eun Choi, "The Making of the Recording Industry in Colonial Korea, 1910–1945" (PhD diss., University of Wisconsin-Madison, 2018), 147.

17 Donghwan Kim, "In'gi gasu jwadamhoe" (A discussion of noted singers), *Samcheolli* (Our land) 8 (January 1936): 130; Choi, "The Making of the Recording Industry," 163.

18 *Busan nippō* (Busan daily), June 10, 1925, 7.

19 *Donga ilbo*, December 9, 1926, 5.

20 *Donga ilbo*, June 11, 1937, 2.

21 *Byeolgeongon* (Another world) (January 1930): 143.

22 *Donga ilbo*, April 25, 1934, 6.

23 *Donga ilbo*, June 22, 1935, 4.

24 Ikjo An, "Yuhaeng gasu jwadamhoe" (A discussion with popular singers), *Sinin munhak* 3 (December 1934), 94–95; Choi, "The Making of the Recording Industry," 124; Yujeong Jang, *Oppa-neun p'unggakchaengi-ya* (My brother is a street singer) (Seoul: Hwanggeumgaji, 2006), 202.

25 Geumnyeong Song, "Geori-ui kanaria" (Street canary), *Joseon ilbo*, January 13, 1940, 4.

26 Kyeongmi Joo, "Gendered Differences in Modern Korea toward Western Luxuries," in K. Pyun and Y. Wong (eds.), *Fashion, Identity, and Power in Modern Asia* (Cham: Palgrave Macmillan, 2018), 159.

27 Roald Maliangkay, "New Symbolism and Retail Therapy: Advertising Novelties in Korea's Colonial Period," *East Asian History* 36 (2008): 47–48.

28 *Maeil sinbo* (Daily report), September 19, 1936, 7.

29 *Japan Times & Advertiser*, April 24, 1936, 3. According to a report in the *Japan Chronicle* from May 1936, the radio amateur hour "craze" traveled from the United States to London. *The Japan Chronicle*, May 13, 1936, 2.

30 *Japan Times & Advertiser*, April 24, 1936, 3; *Japan Times & Advertiser*, March 4, 1941, 5; August 5, 1941, 3.

31 *South China Morning Post*, January 8, 1932, 10.

32 *The China Press*, November 12, 1935, 9.

33 Choi, "The Making of the Recording Industry," 162.

34 *Joseon ilbo*, February 15, 1934, 3; see also Choi, "The Making of the Recording Industry," 71–72.

35 Jang, *Oppa-neun punggakchaengi-ya*, 71; *Joseon ilbo*, February 10, 1934, 2.

36 Yujeong Jang, *Norae punggyeong: Jang Yujeong-ui eumak sanmunjip* (A scenery of songs: Essays on music by Jang Yujeong) (Seoul: Alma, 2013), 237–243.

37 *Joseon jungang ilbo* (Korea central daily), August 29, 1935, 3; *Donga ilbo*, May 29, 1936, 4; *Maeil sinbo*, February 23, 1939, 3.

38 *Joseon ilbo*, February 20, 1940, 3.

39 Chanho Pak, *Han'guk gayosa* (A history of Korean popular songs), vol. 1 (Seoul: Mizi Books, 2009), 239–240, 479.

40 *Joseon ilbo*, February 9, 1940, 3; *Donga ilbo*, May 1, 1940, 5; *Maeil sinbo*, October 2, 1940, 3.

41 *Maeil sinbo*, February 25, 1942, 4.

42 *Samcheolli* (Our land) 9/7 (October 1, 1935): 99; Jang, *Norae punggyeong*, 237–243; Dongsun Yi, *Beonji eomneun jumak* (The tavern without a number) (Seoul: Seon, 2007), 305.

43 Choi, "The Making of the Recording Industry," 122–123.

44 Choi, "The Making of the Recording Industry," 122–123.

45 *Samcheolli* 8/10 (August 1, 1938): 152; Jinseok Oh and Howard Kahm, "Selling Smiles: Emotional Labor and Labor-Management Relations in 1930s Colonial Korean Department Stores," *Journal of Korean Studies* 23/1 (2018): 11; see also Chanho Pak, *Han'guk gayosa*, 433.

46 *Joseon ilbo*, February 15, 1934, 3; *Maeil sinbo*, February 23, 1939, 3. The songs were sometimes preselected. See, for example, *Joseon ilbo*, February 9, 1940, 3.

47 Im Nam, "Gasu seonbal 'kongkul'-gwa keommeo-shallijeum" (The singer selection "concours" and commercialism), *Joseon Ilbo*, April 25, 1940, 4.

48 *Donga ilbo*, October 4, 1939, 7; *Joseon ilbo*, February 20, 1940, 3; Choi, "The Making of the Recording Industry," 162.

49 Gyusaeng Ssang, "Gasu seonbal-ui bangbeop munje" (Problems with the method of selecting singers), *Joseon ilbo*, May 19, 1940, 4.

50 *Maeil sinbo*, February 25, 1942, 4.

51 Dongsun Yi, "Iljemal gunguk gayo-ui balpyo hyeonhwang-gwa siltae (Actual status and conditions of the release of military songs at the end of the period of Japanese colonial rule), *Hanminjok eomunhak* (Korean linguistics and literature studies) 59/59 (2011): 374.

52 See Pierre Bourdieu, *Distinction: A Social Critique of the Judgement of Taste* (Cambridge, MA: Harvard University Press, 1984), 243.

53 Philippe Coulangeon, "Social Mobility and Musical Tastes: A Reappraisal of the Social Meaning of Taste Eclecticism," *Poetics* 15 (2015): 56.

54 Annette Hill, *Restyling Factual TV: Audiences and News, Documentary and Reality Genres* (London: Routledge, 2007), 15–16.

55 See also Choi, "The Making of the Recording Industry," 110–111.

56 *Maeil sinbo*, June 4, 1925, 2.

57 The percentage is relatively small compared to that of Chinese and Western music, which accounted for 10 and 12 percent, respectively. *The Japan Times & Mail*, February 5, 1940, 4.

58 *The Japan Times and Advertiser*, December 6, 1940, 3.

59 Roald Maliangkay, "Not a Habitus for the Have Nots: The Walker Hill Shows, 1962–2012," in Keith Howard and Catherine Ingram (eds.), *Presence through Sound: Music and Place in East Asia* (London: Routledge SOAS Studies in Music Series, 2020), 150, 153; Yong-Gyu Park, "Han'guk tellebijeon eumak beoraieotisyo-ui seongsoe: TBC-TV-ui 'syosyosyo'-reul jungsim-euro" (The rise and fall of television musical variety shows in Korea: Focusing on TBC-TV's "Show Show Show"), *Han'guk kontencheu hakhoe nonmunji* (Journal of the Korea Contents Association) 14/10 (2014): 52, 56; Maliangkay, "Koreans Got Talent," 67.

60 Hill, *Restyling Factual TV*, 16.

2 Itaewon Class, Gangnam Style, and Yeouido Star

The Industrial Revolution of Korean Pop in the 1990s

HYUNJOON SHIN

Kim Young-min (Gim Yeong-min), the former CEO of SM Entertainment, at a conference in 2015, remarked, "The business of SM Entertainment ranges from scouting and training talents, artist management, and promotion to music marketing and publishing, recording production and distribution, and concert production, etc." Then he turned to the audience with an improvised question without necessarily expecting meaningful responses: "What kind of company is SM?"[1] Even the impresarios of K-pop did not know how to define the specific characteristics of K-pop companies.

In fact, K-pop companies wear multiple hats, and their functions have evolved over several decades, shaping their versatile practices today. The main focus of this chapter is to provide a close study of the forms, characteristics, and operations of music-related companies during the 1990s, which paved the way for the current K-pop companies' global emergence and their star-making practices. Korean companies have insisted on their international outlook and labeled their products "global," although the organizations, functions, and business range of K-pop companies such as SM Entertainment differ significantly from those of their counterparts in North America, Europe, and Japan. Some scholars uncritically agree, dubbing K-pop a "global music genre."[2] Yet, given that the major K-pop companies widely known today entered the global music market only in the 2000s, there is need to examine how their predecessors, generally known as record companies (*eumbansa*), operated when the market for Korean pop was largely domestic.

In order to address the rapidly evolving Korean popular music industry of the 1990s, I first investigate various names that were used to address the industry participants and what they connoted in terms of power dynamics and working relations among them. The terms "K-pop" and "entertainment companies" here apply only to postmillennial Korean pop. The music producers in a literal sense were officially named "enterprise companies" (*gihoeksa*) and each company was called an "enterprise" (*gihoek*).[3] Sun Jung chose "entertainment planning company," which seems to be the direct translation of *yeonye gihoeksa*. But the word "planning" is not entirely suitable to reflect the nuances of *gihoek*. The producers even had a vernacular name, *jejakja*, which denotes "executive producer." I will adhere to "enterprise" as a way to respect how the constantly morphing business was addressed both officially and colloquially prior to the new millennium.

Of the major players in the music industry throughout the 1990s, I will focus on three artists and their companies that are arguably the precursors of present-day K-pop: Hyun Jin-young and Wawa, Kim Gun Mo, and Seo Taiji and Boys, who were managed by SM Enterprise (SM Gihoek), Line Enterprise (Line Gihoek), and Yoyo Enterprise (Yoyo Gihoek), respectively. After providing a general overview of these artists and companies, I will tease out distinctive characteristics of each company while paying particular attention to how prevalent metaphors used to describe today's K-pop industry, such as "machine," "factory," and "manufacturing," originated in the 1990s.

Thus, the focus of this chapter is on what kinds of business strategies, sounds, images, and performances actually worked (or not) in the Korean popular music industry of the 1990s, without being bogged down by the judgmental debate on the genre's aesthetic and moral valence. The chapter provides a critical discourse on how the Korean music industry evolved before the new millennium – in conjunction with the changing sociopolitical environment – that created the conditions for the present-day K-pop to emerge as a global phenomenon.

The 1990s: Big Shifts in the Music Industry

Referencing the 1990s as the time of changes might be redundant, since all periods are marked by changes either big or small. In the Korean popular music industry, however, the period bookended by the late 1980s and the early 1990s is remembered as a time of seismic shifts. The political democratization of the June Struggle in 1987 brought about directly elected state power, which then enabled the open-door policy (*gaebanghwa*) and globalization (*segyehwa*). In popular culture and mass media, deregulation took place in various fields. In the case of popular music, three noteworthy changes took place.

First, the multinational major music corporations, the so-called Big 6 (Universal, Sony, Warner Music, BMG, EMI, and Polygram), set up Korean branches in the late 1980s and early 1990s. Following soon after were the Korean conglomerates (*chaebol*), who ventured into manufacturing and distribution of records (CDs, VCDs, and LDs). The record market became wide open for a fierce competition among domestic and foreign labels, old and new business players, after the amendment of the Law on Records and Videos (*Eumban mit bidioe gwanhan beomnyul*) in 1991.

Second, a private terrestrial television and radio network, SBS, was set up in 1990, and several other radio stations emerged around the turn of the decade. Moreover, two cable television channels, Mnet and KMTV, started broadcasting by 1993. These newcomers challenged the virtual monopoly of two broadcasting corporations, the state-controlled KBS and the quasi-public MBC. As a result, music-related media became much more competitive during the 1990s, dubbed as the time of the multichannel and/or multimedia.

Third, the strict and notorious pre-censorship in the name of review by the Public Performance Ethics Committee (*Gongyeonyulliwiwonhoe*) was gradually losing its regulatory power and abolished in 1996. Although censorship by the Broadcasting Ethics Committee (*Bangsongyulliwiwonhoe*) continued, bans on record production and distribution were all lifted in 1996. Even moral regulations, such as the banning of the so-called undesirable artists on terrestrial television programs, were gradually disappearing throughout the 1990s.

It is reasonable to claim that foundational changes took place in three different instances in the circuits of culture: production, mediation, and regulation. Contrary to the assumption that they all collaborated in "neoliberal deregulation" in the global context, the political and cultural contexts in Korea differed from those in the so-called developed countries. While the deregulation policies often coincided with the processes of dismantling the public welfare regime in the developed countries, in the case of Korea, the deregulation policies were rather taken for granted and expected to reform the pervasive state-led authoritarian system.

However, a system based on the big shift toward deregulation can hardly be called a "free and fair market." Regarding the distinctive characteristics of the music industry in the 1990s, complicated power relations between the principal actors in the music industry need to be investigated more in detail.

Most of all, the broadcasting corporations, especially terrestrial television, still had strong power vis-à-vis record and production companies. Music-related companies were much smaller in terms of size, scale, and negotiating power. The rankings of top-of-the-chart programs on TV had been determined by a combination of fan voting ("electoral college") and expert voting ("selection committee"). That is why Lee Keewoong (Yi Gi-ung) argued that "hit charts were apparently based on public votes or requests; music awards were given to singers who were considered most popular that year."[4] Lee Jung-yup (Yi Jeong-yeop) also described popular music in the 1980s–1990s as "a television event."[5]

It is no secret that the selection committee composed of "experts" had the largest share of power.

I would like to call this the "television regime" – a term coined by Hiromu Nagahara in reference to the Japanese media regime in which "a single medium could rightfully boast of a truly national audience" for several decades in the mid- to late twentieth century.[6] Nagahara's term applies well to the Korean circumstances, except that the regime existed for a relatively shorter period because color television broadcasting had a late start in 1980. It was taken for granted that the record sales as well as the popularity of the singers heavily relied on their television appearances on not only music programs but also other entertainment programs. Considering that the television regime has already been replaced by a different regime (I will tentatively call it the "digital-mobile platforms regime"), the 1990s was the last period in which the nationwide mass media such as terrestrial television exerted its omnipotence.

On a practical level, the negotiating power of the managers depended on their formal and informal connections with the television industry, especially the entertainment producers (*yeneung PD*) of music programs. The prevalence of the television regime brought a considerable shift inside the music business. Managers for singers and musicians until the early 1980s basically focused on booking their talents. Most of them were self-employed small businesspeople who functioned as simple intermediaries among record companies and wholesalers, television and radio stations, and commercial live venues. After the mid-1980s, however, they became staff members of specialized companies that managed everything related to stars and their relationship with fans. In the late 1990s, neither multi-nationals nor domestic conglomerates turned out to be the winners. The true winners of the music industry were the managers working in the name of executive producers.

From the Power of Distribution to the Power of Management

The 1990s were the last decade to witness the power of the television regime as well as the physical sales of recorded music. The sales of records significantly contributed to the income of artists and their managers. Million-selling records appeared during the 1990s for the first time in the history of the Korean music industry, but the economic importance of record production and distribution during the period was much higher than in the following decades. This is related to another shifting power dynamic in the music industry: the relationship between record companies (and distributors) and artists (and managers). The companies that could manage several stars could have greater negotiating power vis-à-vis record companies, big or small, domestic or international. In the late 1980s, the exclusive contracts between record companies and artists became ineffective. Record companies did not choose artists and managers anymore; the reverse happened, with managers as intermediaries. At the end of the 1990s, the record companies had become nothing more than record distributors or manufacturing plants based on outsourcing and subcontracting.

Accompanying this shift in the music industry was a regulatory change: the virtual expiration of the aforementioned Law on Records and Videos, which required record companies to be the official owners of the production facilities, especially the recording studios and record-pressing plants. Starting in 1991, some cultural activists staged protests against the legal straitjacket, and as a result, on May 1993, Article 3 of the law was declared in violation of the Constitution. The record producers did not need to "own" the facilities any longer. The legal transition explains why numerous companies were officially "registered" as record companies in the 1990s. Most had been called independent record producers – "PD makers" in the industry jargon – since the mid-1980s, but some already had negotiating power vis-à-vis record distributors and wholesalers. A significant number of the record producers employed managers, the so-called road managers, as hired staff for the artists with whom they signed contracts.

Thus, Korean music enterprises filled the dual role of record production and artist management. These entities have been called talent agencies in the music industry in the developed world; their counterparts in Korea differ because they retain the publishing rights to the recorded music. One of the important tasks of the enterprises was (and is) organizing fan clubs and monetizing their activities.

Thus, it is understandable that companies' names transformed from "productions" to "enterprises" (*gihoek*). During the 1980s time of transition, the two were used interchangeably. For instance, the company that managed Cho Yong Pil (Jo Yong-pil), the 1980s male superstar, was Haeseon Enterprise (sometimes dubbed Pil Enterprise), while Na Mi, one of the iconic female singers of the same period, was managed by Samho Production.[7] Despite the interchangeability between "Ent." and "Pro," an abbreviation for "Production," during the 1980s, the two companies differed in one regard: while the star hired the producer-cum-manager in the former, the manager hired the star in the latter.

To sum up, the Korean music industry in the 1990s was reorganized around artist management or "star management."[8] Small companies consisting of five or six employees became the pioneers of the present-day

K-pop companies. These companies were not only passive intermediaries between the artists and media but also active "makers" of stars who recruited and trained them from obscurity. Not only singing stars but also acting stars were under their management – a business model captured in the vernacular expression of "total entertainment companies."

However, there has been virtually no significant shift in the dominant music genres of Korean pop since the 1990s. What John Lie awkwardly called "postdisco, post–Michael Jackson dance pop," locally and nationally branded as "the new generation dance pop" or "generation X dance pop," are the umbrella terms for the genre. Yet the changes in dominant music genres are not explained solely by the changes in the business model. The interactions between artistic creativity and the commercial business need to be examined in detail without reducing one to the other.

To explain the creation of dance pop, it is necessary to address the co-option of subculture by the mainstream culture. Throughout the 1980s, dancers and DJs at nightclubs across Seoul and other major cities emulated dance music from North America, Europe, and Japan, and constructed their own authentic genre by emulating African American dance music, notably new jack swing or rap dance, popular in the late 1980s and the early 1990s. The genre colloquially called "black dance music" was built on funky and syncopated beats and rhythm and was valued more highly than "Eurodance music" built on steadfast four-to-the-floor beats.

Among different areas in Seoul, Itaewon was definitely the most important place where DJs and dancers from all over the city gathered. The east edge of Yongsan Garrison and the physical center of metropolitan Seoul have demarcated the boundaries of Itaewon since the 1980s. One crummy dance club called Moon Night where dance battles were regularly performed has already become the legendary subject of a 2011 documentary drama series produced by cable channel Mnet – the most powerful broadcaster of Korean popular music.

Itaewon Class, the title of a 2020 Netflix drama, can be creatively applied to this subculture, although the drama is neither about music nor about the 1980s. "Itaewon class" denoted a high class in the subcultural scene of dancers and DJs but looked hopeless and futureless to the mainstream society. Ironically, the regulation of "decadent" nightclubs and discotheques starting in 1990 in the name of "the war on crime" and "the crackdown on overnight business" elevated this underground subculture into mainstream entertainment. The next destination for those who wanted to make a breakthrough in entertainment was definitely Yeouido, where TV broadcasters were clustered. The transformation of the subculture began in the late 1980s when dancers started their professional careers as backup dancers for the established singers in television programs.

Choe Jin-yeol, the former manager of Hyun and, later, Seo, noted, "Starting in the late 1980s, quite a few 'Itaewon families' moved on to the Yeouido scene either as singers, dancing teams, or choreographers in the broadcasting stations."[9] He even used the term "Yeouido pop scene" (*Yeouido gayogye*)"[10] and "Yeouido manager scene" (*Yeouido maenijeo segye*)"[11] to refer to these clusters of music industry workers.

Some DJs also appeared on those programs and performed live remixing, which was very unusual at that time. Some famous DJs dreamed of becoming record producers who created dance-oriented pop music, distinct from mixed and remixed sound played at nightclubs and also suitable for performance on television programs. Simply put, their ambition was to replace melody-centered pop ballads with rhythm-centered dance pop. As will be explored later in this chapter, the dichotomy is not clear-cut due to the genre diversification strategy consciously designed by the industry. Yet it is obvious that constructing, packaging, and branding dance pop as a new trend became effective by linking the genre with the (sub)cultural codes of the new generation (*sinsedae*) born in the 1970s.

SM Enterprise: The Rise of the "New Dance"

Hyun Jin-young and Wawa (sometimes spelled Wawaoowa!) was the pioneer of 1990s dance pop (see Figure 2.1). Son of a jazz pianist, Hyun grew up in the Itaewon area and began to make money by dancing in nightclubs in his teens. It is said that a rival was Lee Juno (Yi Juno), who would become one of the "boys" in Seo Taiji and Boys. His troubled and hopeless life as a nameless underground dancer ended when he was singled out by Lee Soo-man (Yi Su-man), who was not in the subculture but was interested in selling it to the wider public.

That is exactly the moment when Lee Soo-man officially founded SM Enterprise and built a house studio on the eastern fringe of the Gangnam area.

Figure 2.1 Record covers of three full-length albums by Hyun Jin-young produced by SM Enterprise in 1990, 1992, and 1993. Wawa disappeared from the second one.

Though a tiny company with three or four staff members, SM Enterprise showed the basic characteristics of the divisions within an entertainment company. Choe Jin-yeol, who had experience in the nightclub business throughout the 1980s, was schedule manager; Heo Jeong-hoe (aka DJ Kat), who worked as a DJ playing African American dance music at nightclubs in Itaewon, was recruited as house engineer; and Hong Jong-hwa, a talented musician and computer-savvy producer, worked as an exclusive songwriter even before the company was launched. The in-house production[12] and management that still characterize the gigantic K-pop companies were already nascent in the late 1980s, prior to Hyun's debut.

The format of Hyun Jin-young and Wawa was definitely similar to Bobby Brown backed by two dancers or Guy fronted by Teddy Riley. Brown and Riley were household names to those who were familiar with African American dance pop in the late 1980s, but they were not so well known to Korean pop fans, who were into balladeers and, to a lesser degree, rock bands.[13]

Wawa was not an anonymous dance duo backing the star singer but an organic part of the group that formed the dance pop trio. Even to those familiar with Korean pop in the 1990s, it was not well known that the first formation of Wawa evolved into Clon and its second formation into Deux, after they quit Wawa and signed with different management companies, respectively.

Hyun Jin-young and Wawa released their first full album in August 1990, the second in October 1992, and the third in September 1993. The song "You in the Faint Memory" (Heurin gieoksogui geudae) in particular was a smash hit around the time of the fourteenth presidential election in December 1992, when a civilian politician, Kim Young-sam (Gim Yeong-sam), took power, replacing the thirty-year military dictatorship. The song topped the chart at the weekly *Gayo Top 10* during December. It would not be an exaggeration to claim that the cultural transition epitomized by branding the music genre as "new dance" was symbolically associated with the political transition. Though not the focus of this chapter, it was also connected to the broader "new generation culture" (*sinsedae munhwa*) and its affluent and hedonistic protagonists called orange tribe (*orenji-jok*) or Apgujeong clan (*Apgujeong-pa*).

Yet Hyun could not continue to enjoy his success due to drug scandals. Even during his heyday, he was arrested at least twice due to the illegal use of drugs. The last arrest trailed the release of the third album and was regarded a serious offense due to his consumption of hard drugs. His sudden fall from grace badly affected SM's business, which was able to recover only after launching a male idol group, H.O.T., in 1996. A quintet boy group, H.O.T. flaunted a much more sanitized public image and was modeled on Japanese boy groups such as SMAP rather than American rap dance groups. The switch in the aesthetic and cultural codes of SM Enterprise became more visible when it signed a licensing deal with Avex Trax in 2000, which promoted S.E.S. and BoA for the Japanese market. These moves signaled the beginning of K-pop as we know it today. SM's pioneering moves included the change of its official name to SM Entertainment in 1995, just before the launching of H.O.T.

Returning to the second album of Hyun Jin-young and Wawa, two cover versions of Korean rock classics written by legendary figures Shin Joong-hyun (Sin Jung-hyeon) and Lee Jang-hee (Yi Jang-hi) were included. Lee had a career as a solo singer and vocalist in rock bands, and the inclusion of the rock songs in Hyun's album showcases the versatility of the budding K-pop genre. To this point, another song was cowritten by Kim Chang-hwan (Gim Chang-hwan) and Sin Jae-hong, who were the driving engine of Line Enterprise, the main subject of the next section, and had connections to both the dance music community and the rock music community in the 1980s.

SM's post–Hyun Jin-young and Wawa products were Major, a band branded as "easy rock," and a duo, J&J, branded as "guitar and dance." R&B singer-songwriter Yoo Young-Jin (Yu Yeong-jin), who would become a prolific house songwriter for SM Enterprise, also released records in the mid-1990s. Unfortunately, these SM Enterprise artists who debuted during the mid-1990s did not command much public attention. Contrary to the impression that SM has always been a successful industry leader, the company's trajectory spanning nearly thirty years was marked by trial and error as well as a series of crises. In this regard, the rhetoric of "success," which has frequently and uncritically been used in the K-pop discourse, needs to be carefully rectified.

SM retained old-type business practices of recording and distribution in the 1990s. Although the company presided over the entire process of recording, for manufacturing and distribution of the records, it relied on Seorabeol Records, one of the mainstays in the industry since the 1970s. In this sense, SM Enterprise before the launching of H.O.T. was definitely different from SM Entertainment as well as other K-pop companies after the millennium. It is no coincidence that "new dance" included layers of preceding pop genres such as folk, soul, and rock that had been highly indigenized during the 1970s–1980s (see Figure 2.2).

To sum up, SM in the early days developed a profitable model by selling a subculture to a wider mainstream audience. It was proved that the model would not be feasible without domesticating edgy subcultural elements. The future of then-emergent dance pop had to rely on recruiting boys and girls from nightclubs or from the street dance scene, but the recruits had to

Figure 2.2 The first "best albums" compiled by SM: Vol. 1 (left, 1994) and Vol. 2 (right, 2001). In Vol. 1, many songs are folk-tinged ballads performed by the artists who signed contracts with SM preceding Hyun Jin-young and Wawa's debut. Vol. 2 consists of recordings by SM idols such as H.O.T., S.E.S., Shinhwa, and BoA.

be disciplined by the company – an important hallmark of K-pop industry training.

In 2004, Lee Soo-man noted that "if Japan has forged J-pop by digesting [Anglo-]American rock, Korea has forged K-pop by digesting black [African American] music."[14] Although the SM music produced after Hyun hardly sounds "black," there are SM artists and producers who claim they pursued "black music." What did "black music" sound like when created and performed by Korean artists?

Line Enterprise: The Rise and Fall of the Empire of Genres

As of 2021, BTS has broken all music sales records by Korean artists. But before the age of BTS, there were two veteran artists who sold more than 10 million records: Shin Seung-hun (Sin Seung-hun) and Kim Gunmo (Gim Geon-mo). Kim's third regular album (1994) and Shin's fifth regular album (1996) in particular are estimated to have sold more than two million copies each.

These two chart-topping and multimillion-selling artists belonged to the same company, Line Enterprise, directed by Kim Chang-hwan, nicknamed KC Harmony (hereafter KCH). Having worked as a discotheque DJ in Seocho in the Greater Gangnam area throughout the 1980s, he transformed himself into a record producer of Shin, who was looking for the right person in the industry. Shin was followed by Kim, who was discovered by KCH during a visit to a live music venue where Kim was singing and playing the keyboard. All three of them were born in the 1960s.

Figure 2.3 Multimillion-selling records in the 1990s. The back cover of Kim's third album (left, 1994) and the front cover of Shin's fifth album (right, 1996). Kim's face color and fashion style are dark and playful, whereas Shin's appear light and dandy. Quite problematically, no criticism was directed at Kim's album image reminiscent of minstrel shows, although it appears that the artist and producers were unaware of potentially projecting a pejorative image of a black entertainer.

The genre and style of the two singers are (mis)labeled as pop ballad and dance pop, respectively. If we were to consider their megahit songs only, the labels would not be entirely wrong. But closer scrutiny reveals that their albums mixed pop ballad and dance pop in different proportions. While Shin recorded and performed some upbeat and danceable songs, Kim recorded and crooned some mid-tempo sentimental ballads. This is how Shin could differentiate himself from formulaic balladeers, and Kim from tawdry dance singers. Another strategy to diversify the two was to brand Kim's music as "black music" (*heugin eumak*) and Shin's music as generic pop. The two superstars were conventional to a certain extent, but definitely eclectic and versatile in ways that distinguished them from the rest (see Figure 2.3).

From the perspective of Line Enterprise, it was a part of the risk management strategy to diversify its portfolio. Line was by no means the only company that pursued this strategy, but its implementation was so unique and effective because KCH deployed what urbanist Ryan Centner called "spatial capital," or the "power to take place."[15] KCH and his colleagues represented the 1990s "Gangnam style": KCH hung out around Bangbae Café alley, worked as a DJ in the Seocho discotheque scene, and became a professional musician in his company located in Dogok, all of which are neighborhoods in the Gangnam area. He was not only a producer but also a songwriter who provided artists, including Kim, with quite a few songs that ended up becoming hits. Only Shin, a talented singer-songwriter, was not assisted by KCH's songwriting talent.

KCH created the pool of songwriters by mobilizing young and aspiring musicians, such as Sin Jae-hong, Bak Gwang-hyeon, and Kim Hyeong-seok, all of whom majored in music at prestigious universities in Seoul. What started as a personal network based on neighborhoods and schools transformed into a powerful force in the industry in a few years. It is well known that Gim Hyeong-seok taught songwriting and producing to Park Jin-young (Bak Jin-yeong), who would become JYP, one of the key impresarios of the K-pop industry today.

KCH's company started as Moa Enterprise, which was part of Dukyun Records, one of the latecomers to the industry in the mid-1980s. After breaking off from Dukyun in 1994, Moa Enterprise founded Line Sound as a record distribution company and Line Enterprise as a production company. Thus Line was a rare case that combined distribution and production under the same roof. Located in Dogok, a relatively quiet neighborhood in Gangnam, Line Enterprise featured a production system that was closer to the in-house production by K-pop companies in the new millennium than any other companies of its day.

Another act produced by Line Enterprise was Noise, a dance pop group led by talented artist Cheon Seong-il. As seen on the cover of their album, they were ambitious, perhaps too much so, to the extent that various genres – techno, rave, hip hop, and house – were mixed on one album. Moreover, each track proudly claimed the hybridity of the genres: rave dance, reggae house, European hip hop, slow dance, techno rave, disco house, new wave rock, funk bossa nova, and others (see Figure 2.4).

The proliferation of genres continued on other records produced by Line Enterprise. This included the platinum-selling record by Kim, featuring R&B ballad, reggae dance, jazz funky (*sic*), reggae ballad, hip hop, disco house, Latin funky (*sic*), a cappella, and twenty-four-beat funky (*sic*). This was not unusual for 1990s mainstream Korean pop, but Line was definitely

Figure 2.4 The front and back covers of the Noise debut album. "One genre for one song" is written on the back cover (right).

the pioneer of condensing various genres into one record album. The custom of "one genre for one song" persists after all those years, as can be gleaned from the liner notes of the recent BTS albums. I was among those music critics who at the time thought that it did not make sense at all and that the albums were far from authentic genre music. However, the "empire of genres" would be conceptualized as an extension of compressed globalization and digitalization: the wild, uncontrollable, and disjunctive global flows pushed by digital technology.

The subject of digitalization of popular music, particularly of 1990s Korean pop, is too wide of a topic to be discussed here. It could be summarized that the digital production of music was already due to appear way before the advent of digital distribution and consumption of music. Digital recording equipment (recorder and mixer) and digital musical instruments (synthesizer, sequencer, and sampler) began to be used heavily in the early 1990s by some early adopters in the industry.

Line Enterprise used the digital technology in an eclectic way by combining digital/"virtual" instruments with analog/"real" instruments, which explains the wide accessibility of the musical sounds produced. However, the innovative aspect of the sound lay in its heavy usage of digital beats and rhythms, which can be compared to Eurobeat in Japan – the invention of the famous producer Komuro Tetsuya and Avex divas such as Amuro Namie and Hamasaki Ayumi (see Figure 2.5). I will not go into detail on this delicate issue, but it is interesting that the highlight of Komuro's career in Japan evolved simultaneously with that of KCH in Korea.

Thus, the signature sound of Line Enterprise was represented by what the company called "disco house," which was epitomized by the megahit

Figure 2.5 Colloquially defined as "made in Europe for Japan," Eurobeat was invented and disseminated by Avex Trax through the compilation CD series. Avex Trax also released the "J-Euro" series, which compiled remixes of J-pop hits.

Figure 2.6 One of the compilation discs released by Valentine Music Korea in 1994 (left) and Made in Asia, released by Rock Records Korea in 1996 (right). The power of *guanxi* (Chinese-style connections)!

song "The Wrong Encounters" (Jalmotdoen mannam) by Kim Gunmo and other hits by a soulful dance diva, Bak Mi-gyeong, and a hip-hop–tinged dance pop duo, Clon. The soundscape of Line Enterprise's hit songs was based on heavy, machinic, and insistent kick drumbeats: Eurobeat or Eurodance or Eurodisco or Eurohouse. This eloquently shows that the spatial and temporal trajectories of K-pop cannot be simply and easily explained by "American influence" or "global flows." They were and remain much more complicated (see Figure 2.6).

Other influences and flows were discovered when Clon debuted in Taiwan in 1997. One of the intermediaries behind the process was Wang Bae-young, an ethnic Chinese businessman based in Korea. Before becoming the CEO of the Korean subsidiary of Valentine Music based in Singapore – an act followed by serving as the CEO of the Korean subsidiary of Taiwan-based Rock Records – he contributed to the club dance music scene in East Asia by importing and licensing records for DJs, including KCH. In the 1990s, he was skillful at releasing club dance music compilation discs and tried to make connections across East Asia. Clon was just one of the cases of then-emerging inter-Asia business connections, which exploded after the 2000s.

The Line empire did not last long because the CEO of Line Sound was charged with tax evasion and embezzlement in 1998, just a year after the financial crisis erupted in late 1997. After the crisis, Line Enterprise could not make a comeback in its own name, although KCH continued with a not-so-successful career as a producer and songwriter. But even before the financial crisis of 1997, there was a sign of crisis when Kim left the company in 1995. Line Enterprise was not big and solid enough to manage the million-selling superstar. The following section illustrates how "becoming a superstar overnight" was not so unusual in the 1990s, which eventually paved the way for the global explosion of K-pop in the new millennium.

Yoyo Enterprise: Of the President, by the President, and for the President

Very few will challenge that the most explosive artists to have emerged in the 1990s Korean pop scene were Seo Taiji and Boys. A dance pop trio, they debuted in April 1992 with the release of their eponymous album, which brought them an instant colossal success. They disbanded in January 1996[16] when they announced their retirement just two months after releasing their fourth full-length album. Throughout their career, which lasted three years and eight months, they stirred hysteria among fans, often referenced as "Taijimania," which is still used as a nickname for their fan club. It is safe to say that they radically transformed the existing modes of operation in the music industry in that short span of time.

The trio was formed on the ground of the aforementioned Itaewon-based subculture. However, Seo Taiji himself was not a core member of the subculture of dancers and DJs, but a bass player in the rock band Sinawi (aka Sinawe). His association with rock music was more visible than Hyun Jin-young's. Even on the debut album of Seo Taiji and Boys, his old bandmates Shin Daechul (Sin Dae-cheol) and Kim Jong-seo (Gim Jong-seo) were featured on guitar and as a guest vocalist, respectively, in recording sessions for some tracks. He also invited a rock guitarist and bassist to the studio when he self-produced the second album, *Seotaiji and Boys II* (1993), and third album, *Seotaiji and Boys III* (1994) (see Figure 2.7).

Figure 2.7 The transformation of Seo Taiji's image from a rebellious rock musician (left: Seo is the third from left) to a singer-cum-dancer in a B-boy style (right: Seo in middle). The right photo is a rare CD version.

Although the roots of rock were reprised more clearly in some recordings on the later albums, the trio rarely performed live backed even by a session band, let alone a nominal band. The recorded music came from North American rap (later transformed into hip hop) and European techno pop. In short, the blending of rock, rap, and techno in different proportions was their musical formula.

According to the record credits, the first album was produced by Yoo Dae-young (Yu Dae-yeong), who was then working as a mixing DJ in the broadcasting and record industries and was credited as "Scratch" on the first album by Hyun Jin-young and Wawa. However, he was fired by Seo Taiji just after two songs, "I Know" (Nan Arayo) and "You in the Fantasy" (Hwansang sogui geudae), became phenomenal megahits. He was replaced by Choe Jin-yeol, who formed Yoyo Enterprise after quitting his job at SM.

The least important actor in the process of making the Seo Taiji and Boys phenomenon was the record company Bando Records (Bandoeumban), signaling the shifting power dynamics between the recording companies and the enterprise companies involved in music production. Its role was limited to providing a "label" in the literal sense when the Law on Records and Videos was gradually phasing out to become only a nominal practice. Bando Records was one of the latecomers in the industry, officially registered as late as 1985, and did not have impressive hit records. This virtually unknown record company was consciously chosen by the artist as a way to minimize interference in his creativity. This was a harbinger of the shifting power relations between record companies and enterprise companies in the days to come.

What made this shift plausible was the digitalization of the recording process. Seo heavily used "synthesizer" and "computer programming" on the first album. Starting with the second album, he produced the whole sound in his home studio. The unrivaled position Seo occupied in Korean pop history was enabled by this shifting trend in music making toward widely employing digital technology. Pop music based on a rock idiom while also being heavily infused with rap and techno would not have been made before the 1990s. This new type of music suited well the format of television music shows that preferred playing prerecorded music to real-time live performance. Even lip-synching was legitimized in the chart programs, where different artists had to quickly rotate after performing one song.

There had been questions about the originality and authenticity of the recording and performances of Seo's group. Some even accused him of plagiarism ("unoriginality") and lip-syncing ("inauthenticity"). Rather than directly confronting the sensitive issue of originality and authenticity, I believe it is more productive to focus on Seo Taiji's music-making process. Seo Taiji's music was neither rock and heavy metal nor rap and hip hop. On the one hand, the recorded sound was different from conventional rock music because it was heavily based on computer programming and was difficult to perform live. On the other hand, the music style was not close to rap or hip hop, even though he frequently employed rapping skills, to the extent of creating a strange vernacular "rap song." It would not be an exaggeration to say that Seo Taiji and Boys' music is a savage anomaly constituting a genre unto itself.

After the disbanding of the group and the automatic relinquishing of Yoyo, two dancer "boys" started their respective businesses by launching their own enterprises: ING enterprise by Juno Lee, and Hyun Enterprise by Yang Hyun Suk (Yang Hyeon-seok). Neither of them minded the convention of television entertainment and enjoyed commercial success in the mid- to late 1990s. It is well known that Yang Hyun Suk transformed from a dancer into a record producer, eventually becoming one of the major impresarios of K-pop. His brainchild, YG Entertainment, positioned itself as a "hip hop label" and became a powerhouse of genre music.

Meanwhile, Seo made a comeback in 2000 by reinventing himself as a solo rock artist. Genius of both music making and music marketing, he ended up founding Seotaiji Company in 2001. It is not the only company that manages a single artist; superstars like Cho Yong-pil and Lee Seung-hwan (Yi Seung-hwan) also had their own companies exclusively in charge of their own careers. Yet Seotaiji Company is the most secretive in its business activities. It also failed to cross borders into other genres of music.

Thus is the history of the Korean popular music scene leading up to today's K-pop world. Yoyo Enterprise was a dream destination for artists who were artistically focused and commercially viable, but it did not provide any model for the next generation of artists and companies to emulate. In other words, the company, dominated by one person, became neither culturally subversive nor financially competitive. Seo neither restored his connections to the declining but still existent rock scene nor joined the wildly exploding hip-hop scene. To be fair, assuming leadership in the music scene was not part of Seo's agenda. He is often referred to as the "cultural president" (*munhwa daetongryeong*), but his presidential term was not renewed and lasted for only four years (1993–1997).

The last point about the case of Seo Taiji and Boys is that they had no substantial connections to the overseas music industry except the record release and concert tour in Japan. Yet the music and public image of the group mix American rap dance, European techno pop, and Japanese metal (often referred to as "visual rock"). Despite Seo's creativity in mixing heterogeneous sources, references from Milli Vanilli, a French-German R&B duo, and X-Japan, a Japanese rock band, are felt here and there in the group's soundscape and fashion choices. Here again, the "American influences" are not the only ones that matter, and multiple border-crossing cultural flows were already working in the early phase of globalization.

Many parallel circumstances existed between Korea and Taiwan. In the same year that Seo Taiji and Boys made their debut, another boy group, LA Boyz, emerged in Taiwan. Despite no direct connection, both groups were labeled the first rap group in their respective countries. But the latter was different from the former because the members were Taiwanese American returnees from Los Angeles. These overseas Taiwanese had close connections to Korean American returnees who debuted as Solid in 1993.

Solid was one of the rare boy groups that were highly regarded as creative artists, as the leader, Jae Chong (Jeong Jae-yun), wrote all the songs and produced all their records. The group was managed by Seoin Enterprise, another company set up by a former employee of Line Production, and signed a contract with Kim Gun Mo, who left Line in 1995. Too many complicated criss-crossings there may be, but that is characteristic of the pop entertainment industry in South Korea and East Asia at large.

Conclusion: The Road toward the K-Pop Companies

I hop across three places in Seoul that appear in the title of this chapter – Itaewon, Gangnam, and Yeouido – that have already proven their significance in the history that preceded today's K-pop world. Yeouido was the place to work for the promotion of stars, and Gangnam was the place for producing stars and music making. Itaewon, where youngsters hung out, was the place for the nightclub industry. Despite the variations among them, they all stand as pillars of the Seoul-based music industry.

The changes that took place after the 2000s are beyond the scope of this chapter, but I have no hesitation in calling the emergence of 1990s dance pop a revolution. However, there has been virtually no research on the industrial side of this revolution. While there are quite a few studies highlighting the cultural perspectives, this chapter has focused on the processes of music making that were symbiotically linked to the morphing relationship among creative artists, production-cum-management companies, and recording companies (or labels). Without any qualifications, the transformation of the discursive subculture based in nightclubs into a lucrative business associated with the music industry was revolutionary.

I assume that such a revolution would not have been possible in the countries in North America, Western Europe, or Japan. To my knowledge, in those regions with a highly consolidated music industry, breakthroughs by little-known pop singers or groups was (and still is) almost impossible without promotion and distribution by major labels. In South Korea in the 1990s, the enterprises operated on the principle of "high risk and high return." That is one reason some companies that dominated the market in the 1990s virtually disappeared in the midst of further digital disruption in the early to mid-2000s.

The enterprises had to further readjust themselves during and after the economic crisis of 1997–1998. Many changed their name once again to "entertainment companies." This reflected the increasing business volume, size of company facilities, and scope of their business activities. The winners in the music industry eventually went public on the stock market. As expected, they are what we call K-pop companies today and clearly take the form of multidivisional corporations that have established a distinct system of in-house production. As we know, the winners take it all and the losers have to fall.

However, even the big winners of K-pop are dubbed "indie"[17] in the global music industry, as evidenced by *Billboard*, which chose Bang Si-hyuk and Jimmy Jeong as two "2020 indie power players." If "indie" is simply defined as not part of the multinational majors, or the so-called Big 3 (Universal, Warner Music, Sony), then it makes sense at a global level. Yet, at least to South Koreans, it is hard to agree with the labeling, as the K-pop companies have never taken anticorporate stances and K-pop has got rid of "local" characteristics since the millennium. International illusion persists, and that is the "globe" we now live in.

If K-pop is the machine, there has been a ghost in the machine. The ghost was born in the early 1990s, and its protocol was formulated in the late 2000s and has kept evolving. That is the subject of other chapters in this volume.

Notes

1 Kim's presentation was a part of the special session "Korea-China Music Forum" at the conference organized by Korean Creative Content Agency (KOCCA). As his remarks come from my written memo on the conference booklet, my transcription is not exactly the same as what he said.

2 Ingyu Oh and Hyo-Jung Lee, "K-Pop in Korea: How the Pop Music Industry Is Changing a Post-Developmental Society," *Cross-Currents: East Asian History and Culture Review* 9 (2013): 72.

3 Sun Jung, *Korean Masculinities and Transcultural Consumption: Yonsama, Rain, Oldboy, K-Pop Idols* (Hong Kong: Hong Kong University Press), 85 and throughout the book.

4 Keewoong Lee, "Assembling Pop Records in Twentieth-Century Korea: A Double Is Twice as Good as a Single," in Hyunjoon Shin and Seung-ah Lee (eds.), *Made in Korea: Studies in Popular Music* (London: Routledge, 2017), 31.

5 Jung-yup Lee, "Broadcasting Media and Popular Music: Institutions, Technologies, and Power," in Shin and Lee (eds.), *Made in Korea*, 40.

6 Hiromu Nagahara, *Tokyo Boogie-Woogie: Japan's Pop Era and Its Discontents* (Cambridge, MA: Harvard University Press, 2017), 214.

7 See Hyunjoon Shin, "Love Will Keep Us Together … and Tear Us Apart: 1980s Fandom and Stardom in Korean Pop," paper presented at Association for Asian Studies Annual Conference, March 21–26, 2021.

8 The title of a local publication, *Seutareul mandeuneun saram* [People who make stars] (Seoul: Munyemadang, 1997), shows what the managers or the executive producers did in the 1990s. Hyunjoon Shin used "star manufacturing system" to describe idol production in the 2000s. Hyunjoon Shin, "Have You Ever Seen the Rain? And Who'll Stop the Rain?: The Globalizing Project of Korean Pop (K-pop)," *Inter-Asia Cultural Studies* 10/4 (2009): 5.

9 Choe Jin-yeol, *Taeji juno yanggungwa hamkke han 1036il* [One thousand and thirty-six days together with Taiji, Juno, and Yanggun] (Seoul: Myeongsang, 1999), 228.

10 Choe, *Taeji juno yanggungwa hamkke han 1036il*, 244.

11 Choe, *Taeji juno yanggungwa hamkke han 1036il*, 20.

12 For more details about the in-house system of K-pop production, see Shin, "Have You Ever Seen the Rain?," 510 and 519 (endnote).

13 The dominant genres in the 1980s and 1990s. See Keith Howard, "Exploding Ballads: The Transformation of Korean Pop Music," in Timothy J. Craig and Richard King (eds.), *Global Goes Local: Popular Culture in Asia* (Vancouver: University of British Columbia Press, 2002), 80–95.

14 Dong-uk Sin-Yun, "K-pop eun internaesyeoneolhada: SM chaegimja Yisumanssi inteobyu" [K-pop is international: Interview with Lee Sooman who is in charge of SM Entertainment], *The Hankyoreh* 21/530 (October 13, 2004).

15 Ryan Centner, "Places of Privileged Consumption Practices: Spatial Capital, the Dot-Com Habitus, and San Francisco's Internet Boom," *City & Community* 7/3 (2008): 198 and 216.

16 About the cultural significance of Seo Taiji and Boys, see Eun-young Jung, "Articulating Korean Youth Culture through Global Popular Music Styles: Seo Taiji's Use of Rap and Metal," in Keith Howard (ed.), *Korean Pop Music: Riding the Wave* (Folkestone: Global Oriental, 2006), 109–122; Roald Maliangkay, "The Popularity of Individualism: The Seo Taiji Phenomenon in the 1990s," in Kyung Hyun Kim and Youngmin Choe (eds.), *The Korean Popular Culture Reader* (Durham, NC: Duke University Press, 2014), 296–313.

17 "Revealed: Billboard's 2020 Indie Power Players," *Billboard*, June 15, 2020, www.billboard.com/articles/business/9400400/billboard-indie-power-players-executives-list-2020.

PART II

Sounding Out K-Pop

3 Finding the K in K-Pop Musically

A Stylistic History

J U N G - M I N   M I N A   L E E

Today's K-pop is a hybrid of cultural influences and musical styles. Popular music in Korea saw a definitive transformation in the 1990s, modernizing and internationalizing alongside South Korea's rapidly growing economy. Since then, K-pop as we know it – centering around idol stars trained by entertainment companies – has been guided by two main goals: to develop globally consumed cultural content and to satisfy domestic fans' taste for novelty and familiarity. This chapter explores how these goals have shaped K-pop's stylistic evolution, arguing that its musical styles are inseparable from the tension between the local and the global. To better explore this phenomenon, I use the term glocalization to capture the prevalent features and characteristics of K-pop. Glocalization refers to the considerations on both the local and global levels in developing a product or service, including the promotion of localized differences glob-ally.[1] K-pop has transformed global musical influences into unique local features, one of which is the recent trend of incorporating aspects of traditional Korean culture. This chapter shows that such global-local intersections challenge the widespread notion of the unidirectional influ-ence of Western popular music.

The focus of this chapter is on idol-driven K pop music that emerged in the mid-1990s. This discussion must begin by considering the validity of using the term "K-pop" as a genre designation. The expression "K-pop" was first used by Chinese and Japanese media in the late 1990s to refer to popular music originating from South Korea. In this early context, the designation denoted place of origin. More recently, as of April 2021, *Billboard* lists K-pop as an independent category, alongside pop, hip hop/R&B, dance, country, Latin, and rock. This choice indicates two possible rationales: It may imply that the primary consideration for K-pop is its linguistic and geographic orientation, or that K-pop is deemed to display musical qualities that are unique and allow it to stand as a separate genre. The former rationale can be misleading because the particular strand of Korean popular music known globally as "K-pop" is by no means inclusive of all genres and styles of popular music in Korea, which is called *daejung gayo* (or simply *gayo*) in Korean. As ethnomusicologist Michael

Fuhr notes, the discrepancy in the meaning of the term "K-pop" as used within and outside Korea reasserts "the significance of the nation as symbolic boundary market."[2] At the same time, the fact that many K-pop songs fall under the established genres or even mix different genres in a single track renders the task of genre identification even more complicated.

These considerations prompt the question: Can K-pop be considered a genre? That is, what musical characteristics, if any, distinguish it from other genres? To begin to answer these questions, this chapter traces K-pop's musical-stylistic development since its emergence in the 1990s. Fuhr has suggested, taking Adam Krims's genre classification for rap music as a conceptual model, that K-pop's mode of production, such as its casting and training systems and fan culture, is not only crucial but more relevant than musical features in understanding K-pop as a genre.[3] Agreeing with the notion that the mode of production is one of its most distinguishing features, this chapter also considers how the K-pop industry's global tendencies have had significant and direct influences on its musical and stylistic aesthetics – including the incorporation of traditional Korean music – which may hint at K-pop's unique genre identity.

The first part of the chapter provides a bird's-eye view of K-pop's stylistic evolution in three phases, delineated according to the extent of its global reach. The initial phase (1996–2006) saw K-pop's rise to popularity in Asia, and the second phase (2007–2017) was marked by K-pop's isolated successes in the West. The third and current phase (2018 to the present) is witnessing K-pop's consistent integration into global pop culture. The second part of the chapter discusses the incorporation of traditional Korean culture in K-pop, which began prominently around the late 2010s. More K-pop stars are now expressing their Korean heritage through music, music videos, and performances, as seen in the use of the Korean traditional clothing *hanbok* as the sartorial theme for BTS's "Idol" (2018) and BLACKPINK's "How You Like That" (2020), for instance. Thus, K-pop approaches globalization increasingly through local elements, which, given its current global popularity, may bring about changes in the traditional dynamics of influences between Western and Eastern popular culture.

Global Reach and Stylistic Evolutions

K-pop is a substantial component of *Hallyu*, or the "Korean Wave," a term that emerged in the 1990s to describe the popularity of various Korean cultural forms, including TV drama, film, and popular music, in China,

Japan, and other Asian countries.[4] *Hallyu* gained a new momentum around 2008 (sometimes called *Hallyu 2.0*), when Korean popular culture began spreading beyond Asia with the help of the digital infrastructure that the South Korean government had invested in since the 1990s and the bourgeoning global social media platforms.[5] Because K-pop and *Hallyu* inform each other, the three phases of K-pop outlined below coincide broadly with the *Hallyu* timeline, especially in terms of their global reach; however, the unique turns of events and stylistic trajectory of K-pop merit a separate discussion.[6]

Phase One (1996–2006)

Phase one saw the emergence of idol-driven popular music in Korea and its rise to popularity in other Asian countries. Some Korean music labels responded by building systems to further the music's global appeal, localizing K-pop acts to target markets while also embracing global musical trends. Genres such as R&B, hip hop, rap, and club dance music were integrated into Korean popular music that had been previously dominated by ballad, trot, and soft rock and formed the foundation of the sound of modern K-pop.[7]

K-pop's initial moment of global recognition was the explosive, unexpected popularity of the Korean boy band H.O.T. in China in the late 1990s. The band's first Chinese concert in Beijing in 2000 drew 13,000 fans, an unprecedented audience for a foreign group.[8] Subsequent Korean idol groups such as NRG, S.E.S., Fin.K.L, Baby V.O.X, and Shinhwa rose to popularity in other Asian countries, confirming K-pop as a cultural phenomenon. Because the popularity of K-pop was felt primarily within Asia during these years, many scholars have interpreted the success within the context of trans-Asian cultural traffic, inter-Asian relations, and the expansion of Asianism.[9] Others read the phenomenon through notions of cultural familiarity such as "geo-linguistic region" and "cultural proximity," both of which explain that consumers gravitate toward cultural products exhibiting linguistic or cultural similarities to their own.[10] However, by the early 2000s K-pop attracted fans from Turkey, Mexico, Egypt, Iraq, Europe, and the United States, albeit in a scattered manner.[11] The growing global fandom prompted the K-pop industry to draw blueprints to reach audiences beyond Asia.

One such plan came from SM Entertainment (SM hereafter), H.O.T.'s management company. In 1997, the company's CEO, Lee Soo-man, announced "cultural technology," a total management system inspired by a similar approach of Maurice Starr, producer of New Kids on the Block, and that of the Japanese talent agency Johnny & Associates.[12] SM's cultural technology system dictated every stage of artistic production, including casting, training, producing, marketing, and managing:

> The manual, which all S.M. employees are instructed to learn, explains when to bring in foreign composers, producers, and choreographers; what chord progressions to use in what country; the precise color of eyeshadow a performer should wear in a particular country; the exact hand gestures he or she should make; and the camera angles to be used in the videos (a three-hundred-and-sixty-degree group shot to open the video, followed by a montage of individual closeups).[13]

Essentially, the cultural technology system was designed to promote the artists through glocalization, customizing the music, music videos, and artists to the tastes and demands of the target audiences.

A good example of an early application of this system is the female singer BoA. Prior to her Japanese debut in 2001, SM put BoA through intensive Japanese lessons for more than two years, in addition to the usual training in singing and dancing. The company also formed a partnership with the major Japanese record label Avex Trax, who produced and promoted BoA's Japanese album. BoA was carefully positioned as a teenage singer (she was fourteen then) who could sing while performing hip-hop dances, thereby distinguishing her from other female singers in Japanese, many of whom did not showcase such a combination of singing and dancing. Her Japanese debut album, *ID; Peace B*, addressed Japanese audiences exclusively. Its title track had been released in Korea a year prior, but its lyrics were rewritten in Japanese. "Dreams Come True," from the same album, was written by a Japanese composer and a Japanese lyricist. Her subsequent album, *Listen to My Heart*, comprised fourteen Japanese-language tracks, eleven of which were composed by Japanese composers. All of BoA's Japanese releases – more than sixty in total, encompassing singles, compilations, and studio and live recordings – have been produced primarily by Japanese producers, lyricists, and composers, although the executive producer remained SM (and later BoA herself). As three of her albums became million sellers – an unmatched record for a foreign artist in Japan – BoA was fully integrated into the Japanese popular music scene.

When album production and promotion were managed from Korea, K-pop companies found ways to create a sense of cultural affinity for foreign audiences. For instance, for the boy group TVXQ, created in 2003 with the goal of making it the largest boy band in Asia, SM chose a name that would resonate as familiar to Chinese-speaking audiences. "TVXQ" is derived from the stylized phonetic expression of its Chinese name, 東方神起 (read *Tong Vfang Xien Qi*; 동방신기 in Korean, read *Dong Bang Shin Ki* and translated "The Rising Gods of the East"). In addition, although all members were Korean, some of them adopted more Chinese-sounding stage names (for example, Xia Junsu for Kim Junsu). By the end of the decade, it also became common for K-pop idol groups to comprise foreign-national members or members with foreign-language abilities.

Concurrent to these localization efforts, Korean popular music in the 1990s evolved as it embraced genres such as R&B, upbeat dance music, rap, and hip hop as part of its parlance. R&B was popularized foremost by the male-trio group Solid, active in 1993–1997. Emphasizing tuneful melody and rich harmony in their music, Solid appealed to Korean audiences' taste for melody-driven ballads. They added fluid rap or stylish dances to sentimental melodies, demonstrating genre mixing that is still an important aspect of K-pop.

Meanwhile, more energetic hip-hop music rose to popularity with SM's first act, Hyun Jin-young. His first full album, *New Dance 1* (1990), included tracks with raps, which he performed in baggy clothes and showcasing hip-hop (and the popular Roger Rabbit) dance. Lee Soo-man explained that with this album he wanted to create high-quality dance music in Korea: "People might think that the Rabbit dance and music came together, but I prioritized music."[14] Lee, who had just returned from his study in the United States, focused his new music business on creating well-produced dance music that he had heard there but deemed absent in Korea. By debuting Hyun, a seasoned hip-hop dancer, Lee successfully popularized new jack swing–style dance music in Korea.

Shortly after Hyun's debut, the three-member male band Seo Taiji and Boys took the Korean popular music scene by storm with their rap-heavy single "I Know" (1992). A blend of hip hop, metal, and electronic dance music, this track was far more powerful than any other dance music previously released in Korea. Their next, even more experimental hit, "Hayeoga" (1993), not only mixed heavy metal and hip hop but also incorporated the traditional Korean woodwind instrument *taepyeongso*, whose piercing sound blended seamlessly with other synthesizer and drum-and-bass sounds. The track also featured an unusual song structure, departing from the standard song scheme of intro-verse-(pre-chorus)-chorus-verse-(pre-chorus)-chorus-bridge-verse-chorus-outro (see Table 3.1).

"Hayeoga" has a three-part interlude, the second part of which includes a dramatic, amplified electric guitar solo lasting over a minute, underscoring the rock element of this track. Also, instead of the bridge, which is usually placed toward the end of a song and offers a moment of contrast, this track maintains high energy and drive throughout and then pushes the tempo even further in the final twenty seconds. With such experimental approach, Seo Taiji and Boys became synonymous with musical revolution in late 1990s Korea. Their groundbreaking music,

Table 3.1 *Formal structure of Seo Taiji and Boys's "Hayeoga"*

Time	Formal section	Musical features
0:00–0:30	Intro	Heavy-metal drum-and-guitar sound, beatbox, scratch
0:30–0:57	Verse 1	Rap, E–F#–E
0:58–1:33	Pre-chorus	Vocal (melody), E → Am, fast harmonic rhythm
1:34–1:52	Chorus	Rap, *taepyeongso* (folk melody), Am → E
1:53–1:59	Interlude I	Heavy metal drum-and-guitar sound, C#–F#–G
2:00–2:59	Interlude II	Electric guitar solo
3:00–3:24	Interlude III	Voice sampling ("Did you enjoy that"), material from intro (except first 5")
3:25–3:51	Verse 2	Rap, scratch effects, E–F#–E
3:52–4:26	Pre-chorus	Vocal (melody), E → Am
4:27–4:49	Chorus	Rap, *taepyeongso* (folk melody), Am → E
4:50–5:12	Postchorus	Fastest section of the track, E–(A-G-D)–E

along with their virtuosic dance and bold fashion, guided the K-pop scene in the years to follow.

After Seo Taiji and Boys's unexpected retirement in 1996, Korean music labels acted quickly to fill the void, producing similar single-gender idol groups one after another. These groups, equipped with striking visual appeal, targeted young audiences who were excited about dance music, hip hop, and rap. Idol music was thus often rhythm-driven, suitable for dynamic choreographed dances, and carried lyrics addressing issues such as the inner turmoil of youth or school culture, following the example of Seo Taiji and Boys's "Classroom Idea" (1995). Boy bands such as H.O.T., Sechs Kies, and Shinhwa (debuted in 1996, 1997, and 1998, respectively) made hits with such music and were subsequently regarded as the voices of teenagers. Girl groups such as S.E.S. (debuted in 1997) and Fin.K.L (debuted in 1998) similarly performed energetic choreographed dances, but their music tended to be more lighthearted and sentimental. For example, although S.E.S.'s dance pop hit "I'm Your Girl" (1997) gives a nod to hip hop with intense rap passages accompanied by scratch effects and heavy synth bass lines, the rest of the track is sprightly and light in texture, with R&B-style melodies, and the lyrics are about hope and promises of love.

Notably, the blending of dance, hip hop, and R&B exhibited in "I'm Your Girl" was comparable to new jack swing, which many Korean producers of the 1990s, including S.E.S.'s producer, Lee Soo-man, tried to bring to Korea. The dance and hip-hop elements of the genre fascinated Korean fans who were eager for new sounds and rhythms. At the same time, the use of soulful melodies also appealed to domestic listeners who already had a strong proclivity for the sumptuous melody and harmony that characterize ballad and trot songs, and the melodic and harmonic aspects of new jack swing were often further emphasized in K-pop songs to satisfy Korean consumers. Thus, the mix of dance beats, singable melodies, and rich harmony, which became one of the key characteristics of K-pop music, can be seen as a musical feature that resulted from glocalization.

While idol groups were emerging as key players in the Korean popular music scene, previously popular genres such as trot, ballad, and rock remained popular throughout the 1990s and in the early 2000s.[15] In fact, idol-driven K-pop experienced a relative lull in the early 2000s, when the first generation of idol groups retired with only a few new groups to fill the gap. Even so, the period was a pivotal moment in the history of Korean popular music, as everything surrounding idols – their music, performance style, production system, and fan culture – fundamentally changed the nature of popular music in Korea.

Phase Two (ca. 2007–ca. 2016)

If the first decade of K-pop was about recognizing its international potential and drawing the blueprint for further success, the second phase was the time of implementing that system in a fully fledged manner. The penetration into Japanese markets solidified with groups like BIGBANG and Kara, while the K-pop industry's reach expanded beyond Asia. Some general stylistic tendencies and approaches employed by SM, JYP, and YG – the top three K-pop management companies – included incorporating Western pop culture tropes while minimizing Korea-specific cultural references; using English words in song titles and lyrics, especially in song hooks; and collaborating with foreign, mostly European and American, composers and producers. These factors gave rise to two notable musical trends. One was extremely hook-driven music that became prominent in the mid- to late 2000s and continued to proliferate for almost a decade. The other was structurally complex, nearly modular music; this quality, which became noticeable around the mid-2010s, could be seen both as a development of the genre mixing witnessed in the first phase and as a reaction to the excessively repetitive hook music. As this section will show, both trends were closely tied to K-pop's globalizing tendencies.

Examples of strategic references to Western pop culture in K-pop of this phase are legion. In one such case, Wonder Girls's single hit "Tell Me" (2007) sampled parts of Stacey Q's "Two of Hearts" (1986), adapting the basic harmonic progressions and melodies of its verse, drumbeats, sound effects, and various filler phrases, such as "Oh no" and "No baby." The hook ("Tell me, tell me, te-te-te-te-te-tell me") of "Tell Me" is a twist on the opening words ("I-I-I-I-I-I need") of the older song. The music video of "Tell Me" similarly includes references to American popular culture. For instance, one member embodies the group's namesake fictional character Wonder Woman and protects other girls in various troublesome situations. More subtle references include high-five gestures (not a common celebratory gesture in Korea then), posters with English words on the stage set, visual effects reminiscent of Roy Lichtenstein's pop art, and American-style yellow school buses and school lockers. Wonder Girls's next hit, the retro-inspired "Nobody" (2008), drew from American popular culture, too. The track's music video features the five members as chorus girls performing on a Motown-style stage, garbed in sheath dresses, long white gloves, and coiffed hair, conjuring up images of 1960s girl groups such as the Supremes, the Shirelles, and the Ronettes.

Musically, this "cultural odorlessness" – an expression used by the sociologist Koichi Iwabuchi to denote the absence, in a product, of cultural references to the country of production – was matched by the rise of electronic dance music in K-pop.[16] The popularity of electronic dance music grew steadily in Korea throughout the 2000s. By the end of the decade, beat-driven music with tempos around 124–128 bpm, inundated with digital sound, dominated Korean charts. BIGBANG, whose members' musical identity is rooted in hip hop, debuted with an electronic dance track, "Lies" (2007), earning immediate mainstream popularity. Brown Eyed Girls, famous for their electronic dance "Abracadabra" (2009), originally debuted in 2006 as a R&B/ballad group but did not top Korean music charts until after releasing the electropop "L.O.V.E." (2007). Idol music of this time was inseparable from electronic dance music, giving rise to a somewhat homogenous sound world across K-pop in the 2000s.

The hook was another important feature of K-pop between the mid-2000s and early 2010s. Musicologist John Shepherd defines hooks as "musical and lyrical material through which the song remains in popular memory and is instantly recognizable in popular consciousness."[17] Whether a short melodic idea, lyrics, or instrumental riffs, hooks allow listeners to anchor a song to their memory. When the K-pop industry was expanding its global fandom, it was important to maximize such anchoring moments and render songs memorable. One of the first songs to start the hook trend was Wonder Girls's "Tell Me," whose hook, "Tell me, tell me, te-te-te-te-te-tell me," went viral in Korea and was parodied and adapted in numerous TV shows and dramas. This hook, short and catchy with its fun stuttering effect, is also made effective by repetition. In addition to repeating thirteen times between the chorus and the postchorus, the hook appears in varied forms in the interlude and as a melodic filler in other parts of the song. Moreover, its melody and harmony are designed to please: the melodies before the hook seldom land on the tonic pitch (the "do" of a scale), F#, even when the chord returns to the home key of F# minor, and the melody's arrival on F# at the beginning of the hook after the leap to the dominant C# gives the listener aural satisfaction as built-up tension is resolved (Figure 3.1).

Figure 3.1 Passage leading to the hook and the hook of Wonder Girls' "Tell Me," mm. 19–42.

One consequence of the sweeping success of "Tell Me" was K-pop songs being flooded with hooks with English words, which had several social and commercial advantages but not entirely favorable musical consequences. Linguist Jamie Shinhee Lee explains that in South Korea English references are generally associated with modernity, globality, and a new generation.[18] English lyrics can also operate as a discourse of resistance and greater artistic freedom, as musicians can use English to express notions that are considered too explicit in Korean.[19] Furthermore, mixing in English words can make K-pop songs more memorable to foreign listeners who do not understand Korean. For these reasons, simple hooks with English lyrics surfaced prominently in K-pop in the late 2000s and onward, often accompanied by English song titles (Table 3.2). The boy band Shinhwa's first album, released in 1998, had just one track with an English title, but nine out of fourteen tracks on their fifth album from 2004 had English titles (Korean titles were accompanied by English translations); by their tenth album of 2012, all eleven tracks had English titles. Although using English in titles and lyrics had apparent advantages for globally driven K-pop, English hooks were often rendered meaningless in efforts to maximize their phonetic or rhythmic effects, as in SHINee's "Ring Ding Dong" ("Ringdingdong, ringdingdong / Ringdiggy dingdiggy dingdingding") and Super Junior's "Sorry Sorry" ("Sorry sorry sorry sorry / Shawty shawty shawty shawty"). Such hooks certainly made K-pop songs catchy and memorable, but the repetitive music and the sometimes nearly nonsensical lyrics contributed to the reputation of idol music as being nonmusical or unsophisticated in these years.

Table 3.2 *English-language hooks in select K-pop songs from 2007 to 2013*

Release year	Artist	Song	Times hook repeats (variation)	Total hook time (including variations)/song length	Hook lyrics	Other hooklike materials
2007	Wonder Girls	"Tell Me"	13 (2)	55 seconds / 3:36	Tell me, tell me, te-te-te-te-te-tell me	None
2008	Wonder Girls	"Nobody"	7 (2)	42 seconds / 3:33	I want nobody nobody but you	None
2009	Girls' Generation	"Gee"	8	16 seconds (1 minute 36 seconds) / 3:20	Gee gee gee gee baby, baby	Variations and secondary hooks; four-chord track (AM7-F#m7-G#m7-C#m7 or AM7-F#m7-C#m7-C#m7)
2009	Super Junior	"Sorry Sorry"	8	56 seconds / 3:52	Sorry, Shawty (each ×4), followed by *naega, nege / michyeo, ppajyeo*	Single instrumental riff throughout
2009	T-ARA	"Bo Peep Bo Peep"	"Bo Peep" repeated 110 times	64 seconds / 3:43	Bo Peep (×7) Oh!	"Bo Peep" melody used as instrumental riff throughout
2009	SHINee	"Ring Ding Dong"	12	45 seconds /3:51	Ringdingdong (×2) Ring diggy ding diggy dingdingding	Secondary hook: "We wanna go rocka rocka rocka rocka rocka …"
2010	Super Junior	"Mr. Simple"	12	48 seconds / 4:00	*Bwara* Mr. (Miss) Simple, Simple	Instrumental riff throughout with minimal variations
2010	T-ARA	"Breaking Heart"	12	48 seconds / 3:14	Oh (×8) *Cheoreopge* (×7) *saldaga micheo* (Living foolishly makes me crazy)	Ostinato bass (Bb-Db-Gb-C-F(Cb, occasionally)) repetitive melody and lyrics throughout
2011	2NE1	"Naega jeil jal naga" (I am the best)	19	42 seconds / 3:29	*Naega jeil jal naga* (I am the best)	"Bam Ratatata Tatatatata Beat" (×8); single instrumental riff throughout
2011	T-ARA	"Roly Poly"	6	45 seconds / 3:34	Roly Poly Roly Roly Poly (plus two alternating Korean phrases)	Four-chord track (Am-F-C-G) except in the intro, interludes, and outro
2012	f(x)	"Electric Shock"	7 (1)	56 seconds /3:15	Na – Electric (×3) E-E-E-Electric Shock	Part of the hook appears at 0:03; full hook at 0:50
2012	Secret	"Poison"	8	40 seconds / 3:25	You are my poison	"Crazy crazy crazy love listen listen crazy love" (×4)
2013	Crayon Pop	"Bar Bar Bar"	Hook 1: 6 Hook 2: 15	1 minute 14 seconds / 3:00	Barbarbarbar (×2) / Jumping ye (×2) (everbody, *da gachi ttwieottwieo*)	Hook 1 first appears at 0:15; hook 2 first appears at 0:50
2013	EXO	"Growl"	12	30 seconds / 3:27	*Na eureureong* (×3) *dae* (I growl, growl, growl)	Instrumental riff (becomes chorus melody)

Global collaboration in music producing was another important aspect of this phase. In the early days of K-pop, when not many Korean composers were fluent in the vocabulary of dance pop music, Korean music labels often adapted and remade existing Western or Japanese pop songs (for instance, S.E.S.'s 1998 hit "Dreams Come True" was a remake of Nylon Beat's "Like a Fool"); this could be artistically limiting and legally complicated. Taking a step further with the glocalization efforts, around the mid-2000s, Korean management companies experimented with global collaboration, where foreign composers wrote original songs for K-pop idols and Korean composers mastered or arranged them according to the domestic listeners' tastes. In 2005, SM partnered with the Swedish producer Pelle Lidell, who had worked with pop stars such as Christina Aguilera, Madonna, and Celine Dion. Girls' Generation's iconic hit "Genie" (2009) was a result of this collaboration: Lidell and his roster of British and Scandinavian songwriters sent their original song to SM, to which the label's chief composer/producer Yoo Young-Jin added melodies that would appeal to Korean fans. By the early 2010s, SM also began collaborating with Teddy Riley, who brought back new jack swing through tracks such as Girls' Generation's "The Boys" (2011), Jay Park's "Demon" (2011), and EXO's "What Is Love" (2012). In addition, in 2013 SM established its own writer's camp and began inviting composers from around the world, completing its global music producing system. By the late 2010s, it became commonplace for K-pop albums to be produced by a team of Korean and foreign composers, an effective arrangement to create music that satisfies both domestic and international fans.

K-pop produced under the global system demonstrated a distinct set of musical characteristics, including memorable hooks, propulsive music conducive to dynamic dance, dense harmonies, richly melodic bridges, anthemic choruses, and the mixing of different musical styles. Because the market for K-pop was relatively young and responsive to external influences, it made an ideal place of experimentation for foreign composers. Moreover, K-pop's unique feature of having many members in one group required composers to write for many different vocal timbres, ranges of voice, and specializations (rap or singing), not only highlighting each member but also blending them into one cohesive ensemble. Taking all of these elements together, K-pop tracks became remarkably multifarious and maximalist, with frequent textual, timbral, and stylistic changes and constant aural stimulation matched by equally rich visual presentations.

Girl's Generation's "I Got a Boy" (2013) is a prime example of such experimental sound enabled by the global music-producing system. Composed by SM's Yoo Young-Jin and a team of composers from the Norway-based Dsign Music (Sarah Lundback, Anne Judith Wik, and Will

Simms), this five-minute track contains enough materials for at least three songs, cast in a complex and fragmented, yet tightly woven structure (Table 3.3).

The introduction alone has three parts, conveyed visually in the music video by three different sets. The song can be divided into two or three parts, depending on how the structural functions of the musical fragments are interpreted. The fragments include four verses (each with different music), two hooks, two interludes, and two bridges. There are also two tempo changes via short interludes, the first to shift to Broadway-style solo singing, announced with the words, "let me put it another way," and the second to "bring it back to 140." Notably, even in this kaleidoscopic music, hooks remain crucial: the track is held together by the two melodic hooks – the pre-chorus material (hook A; "Oh-oh-oh-oh") and the chorus music (hook B; "I got a boy") – that alternate throughout and come together in the postchorus. Finally, the track has elements from electropop, R&B, dubstep, rap, drum and bass, and bubblegum pop, like a potpourri of popular music genres. "I Got a Boy" takes K-pop's multi-genre approach to a nearly experimental level, transporting the listeners to a culturally nonspecific yet wonderfully surreal place. This innovative and maximalist music heralded a new phase of K-pop, characterized by great stylistic diversity.

Phase Three (2017 to present)

During its most recent phase, K-pop has experienced a heightened level of global attention and popularity. The landmark incident ushering in this new phase was BTS's winning the Billboard Social Artist Award in 2017, the first US mainstream recognition of any K-pop act. As the K-pop [...] rose to prominence, including HYBE (previously [...] ment; BTS's management) and Cube [...] and CLC). Many midsized and smaller [...] YG-SM-JYP triad, all established in the 1990s [...] diversification within the industry has [...] musical variety in K-pop. Stylistic diver- [...] ments of foreign composers, cultivation [...] producers, and more idols taking charge [...] eir own music.

[...] system introduced by SM in the previous phase has [...] ncing the entire K-pop industry. SM's system now consists of a [...] of over 500 producers, composers, and lyricists from around the [...], as well as robust songwriting camps.[20] Other labels have adopted SM's practice. For instance, Jellyfish Entertainment (management of VIXX), WM Entertainment (B1A4 and

Table 3.3 *Formal structure of Girls' Generation's "I Got a Boy"*

	Time	Function	Lyrics (starting phrase)	Musical features	Music video
Intro	0:00–0:30	Intro 1	(Diegetic sound: girls laughing, doorbell)	Instrumental music	Acting: Girls in a house, startled by a visit by a boy
	0:31–0:53	Intro 2	Ayo! GG! Yeah Yeah *Sijakae bolkka?*	Rap	Stage performance
	0:54–1:13	Intro 3	Ha Ha! Hey let me introduce myself! Here comes trouble o!	Introduces the pre-chorus hook: hook A ("Oh oh oh yeah oh")	Street performance
Part I	1:13–1:42	Verse 1	*Jiga mwonde? Utgyeo.*	Rap 1	Street performance and acting
	1:43–2:02	Pre-chorus	Oh oh oh yeah oh	Hook A	Street performance
	2:03–2:10	Interlude 1	Ayo, stop, let me put it another way	Tempo change; electronic dance music	Stage performance
	2:11–2:25	Chorus	I got a boy *meotjin,* I got a boy *chakan* …	Hook B	Stage performance and acting
	2:26–2:38	Verse 2	*A~ Nae wangjanim!*	Vocal (melody 1)	Stage performance
	2:39–2:53	Verse 3	*Na kkamjjang menbungiya*	Rap 2	Stage performance and street performance
	2:53–3:07	Pre-chorus	Oh oh oh yeah oh	Hook A	Street performance and stage performance
Part II	3:07–3:20	Verse 4	*Nae mal deureobwa geu ai neone alji?*	Vocal (melody 2)	Stage performance
	3:21–3:35	Pre-chorus	Oh oh oh yeah oh	Hook A	Stage performance and acting
	3:37–4:00	Bridge 1	*Nan jeongmal hwagana jukgesseo*	Tempo change to 98 bpm; Broadway-style singing	Stage performance (new stage setting)
	4:01–4:03	Interlude 2	"Don't stop! Let's bring it back to 140"	Narration, no accompaniment	Stage performance
	4:04–4:17	Chorus	I got a boy *meotjin,* I got a boy *chakan* …	Hook B	Stage performance and acting
	4:18–4:31	Bridge 2	*Eonjena nae gyeoten*	Vocal (melody 3)	Stage performance and acting
	4:32–4:45	Chorus	I got a boy *meotjin* … plus *A~ Nae wangjanim!*	Hook B + melody 1	Street performance and acting
	4:45–5:01	Postchorus	I got a boy *meotjin* … plus Oh oh oh yeah oh	Hook A + hook B + variation of melody 1 (as chorus material)	Stage performance and street performance

Oh My Girl), and DR Music (Rania) have partnered with foreign composers. HighGRND, the sublabel of YG, and JYP now run their own song camps, inviting both foreign and Korean composers. With such collaboration having become common practice in K-pop, more foreign musicians are producing, not only composing, in contrast to the early days of global producing when the songs provided by foreign composers were arranged and mastered by Korean producers. A famous example is BTS's 2000 hit, "Dynamite," composed by the British composers David Steward and Jessica Agombar and produced by David Steward; it was also the first K-pop track composed as an English song and performed that way.

Meanwhile, more Korean composers have cultivated their own sound for dance music: Yoo Young-Jin has been credited since K-pop's early days with SM's metal-inspired, beat-driven music combining dance, rap, and ballad singing, a style continued by the company's younger producer, Kenzi, who tends to create harmonically and texturally dense tracks. Producer/composer Teddy Park has been responsible for YG artists' music since 2006. JYP has a roster of Korean composers, including Sim Eun-jee and Hong Ji-sang; its composer audition programs help discover domestic composers. Black Eyed Pilseung, Hitchhiker, Monotree, Shinsadong Tiger, and Iggy/Youngbae are just some of the Korean composers active in K-pop.

Finally, more K-pop idols have been writing and producing their own music, adding to the stylistic diversity. BIGBANG's leader G-Dragon composed numerous hits for his band, including "Lies" (2007), "Heartbreaker" (2009), and "Fantastic Baby" (2012). Because K-pop management companies have traditionally exerted much control over their stars' artistic activities, and because the industry has long focused on the performance aspect of idol music, G-Dragon's producing his own music was a refreshing change. Moreover, he was among the first idols to refer to himself and his peer musicians as "artists," consciously rejecting their reputation as singing and dancing machines with only visual appeal and little artistic autonomy. Today, Mino of WINNER, Woozi of Seventeen, Hyunsik of BTOB, Soyeon of (G)I-DLE, and many others compose and produce their own music. The members of BTS also either compose or write lyrics for their songs; furthermore, RM, Suga, and J-Hope of BTS have released mixtapes as solo acts. Even established groups like Wonder Girls began producing later in their career, composing and producing nearly all of the tracks of their last two albums, *REBOOT* (2015) and *Why So Lonely* (2016).

With a greater number of competitive management companies, more robust global collaboration, a larger range of domestic composers, and increasing involvement of idols in the production of their own music, the stylistic spectrum of K-pop is now broader than ever. The following section discusses one notable feature that arose in this stylistic diversity: the borrowing of traditional Korean music in K-pop.

Traditional Korean Music in K-Pop

Traditional Korean culture began surfacing prominently in K-pop toward the end of the 2010s, indicating a change in the industry's approach to globalization.[21] In fact, throughout K-pop's history, musicians have experimented with incorporating traditional Korean music, through iconography, instrumentation, and lyrics, as shown in Table 3.4. However, only in recent years has it been happening in earnest and with notable frequency. The incorporation has thus not been monolithic, but rather involved diverse intentions and creative procedures, reflecting K-pop's evolving glocalization principles. The rest of this chapter examines three examples, TVXQ's "Maximum" (2011), Topp Dogg's "Arario" (2014), and Agust D's "Daechwita" (2020). They demonstrate different modes and extents of borrowing from traditional Korean culture, as well as their broader implications for listeners and musicians.

Table 3.4 *Select K-pop tracks released since the 1990s that borrow elements of traditional Korean music and/or culture*

Release year	Artist	Song title	Traditional elements
1993	Seo Taiji	"Hayeoga"	Title, sampling of *taepyeongso*
2000	1TYM	"Kwaejina chingching"*	Title, folk tune (*Kwaejina chingching*) in the chorus, *samul nori* performance, *Bukcheong saja*
2007	SG Wannabe	"Arirang"	Title, *gayageum* performance in the intro
2011	TVXQ	"Maximum"	Traditional drums, stage setup
2012	B.A.P	"No Mercy"	*Samul nori* (music only)
2012	Block B	"Nillili Mambo"	Title, samplings of traditional instruments and folk song in the intro
2013	G-Dragon	"Niliria"	Title, folk tune (*Niliria*)
2014	Topp Dogg	"Arario"*	Title, lyrics, costume, *samul nori*, *gayageum* performance, music video setting (props and background)
2017	VIXX	"Shangri-La"*	Title, *gayageum* (and *gayageum*-like electronic sound), props (fans), costume, MV setting
2018	BTS	"Ddaeng"	Lyrics, stage setting, costume
2018	BTS	"IDOL"	Lyrics, music video setting, costume
2018	Mino	"Financé"*	Lyrics, music video setting, costume (incorporation of trot)
2019	ONEUS	"LIT"*	Instruments, lyrics, costume, music video setting
2019	Sunmi	"Lalalay"	Sampling of *taepyeongso*
2020	Agust D (Suga)	"Daechwita"*	Title, sampling of *daechwita*, *taepyeongso*, costume, music video setting, narrative
2020	BLACKPINK	"How You Like That"	Costume

* Tracks adapting traditional Korean music or culture as primary visual or musical source.

TVXQ's "Maximum" (2011)

In TVXQ's "Maximum," references to traditional Korean music do not add up to a legible reading of Korean culture, but rather serve to create a vaguely East Asian feel. There are many borrowings from traditional Korean music in this idiosyncratically dense and beat- and synth-heavy song produced by SM. It opens with a brief solo passage by the traditional Korean zither instrument *gayageum*. The song's overall percussive sound intensifies as various traditional percussion instruments enter around mid-track, starting with the *jing* (gong) that bookends the interlude rap sections (1'23" and 1'45"). In the second half of the track, multiple electronic drum sounds are layered and culminate in the postchorus, when the jangling sound of the *kkwaenggwari* (small gong) is added (3'12"). This last section alludes to the traditional folk performance *pungmul* or *samul nori*, which includes drumming, dancing, and some singing. Also, throughout the song, the singers exclaim phrases like "urlssu" and "huh-ee," interjections used to express amusement and to encourage audience participation during traditional Korean performances.

However, these borrowed sounds from the traditional instruments are neither foregrounded nor instrumental in determining the narrative or structure of the song, but rather are subsumed into the layers of synthesizer drum sounds. Even the *gayageum* part of the opening is fleeting and atmospheric, serving as an incidental sound effect at best. Therefore, despite being a fresh case during a time when K-pop was generally preoccupied with hook-ridden dance music with the propensity to draw on Western culture, the referencing of traditional Korean music in "Maximum" achieves little beyond creating an exotic milieu in the context of Western musical procedures.

Topp Dogg's "Arario" (2014)

"Arario" by hip-hop band Topp Dogg (now Xeno-T) makes explicit and ubiquitous references to traditional Korean culture. The title is a variation of the word "Arirang," a famous Korean folk song. The lyrics of "Arario" are filled with direct quotations of words of folk songs and puns from Korean folklore. Furthermore, the words convey confidence about using Korean elements, a feature rarely seen in K-pop previously: "I don't know why people do such typical raps / I'll just say it, ours is the best."[22] The turn to Korean culture is communicated visually in the music video as well. Starting with an image of a *gayageum* player's hands in performance, the music video constantly juxtaposes performances of traditional instruments, such as *gayageum*, *buk* (drum), *Bukcheong sajanoreum* (lion mask dance), and *samulnori* (traditional percussion quartet), and those of Topp Dogg, whose costumes alternate between the traditional *hanbok* and clothes of hip-hop style. This conjoining of the two worlds culminates in the chorus, where all performers share the stage and take turns in displaying hybrid-style solo acts, as exemplified in one of the back dancers breakdancing while dressed in *hanbok*.

Ironically, the music itself does not match the extent of the expression of traditional Korean culture demonstrated in the music video and the lyrics. Except for at the very beginning and a brief moment in the final chorus, the traditional instruments are not actually heard, creating a disparity between the image and the sound whenever the music video shows performances of the instruments. Thus, despite the numerous references to traditional culture, there is little intermixing of traditional Korean music and hip-hop music. Even so, with both traditional Korean dance/music and hip hop and the lyrics filled with Korean idioms and references to Korean folklore, this track is an antithesis to the "culturally odorless" K-pop music commonly seen in the mid-2010s.

Agust D's "Daechwita" (2020)

"Daechwita" by Agust D (BTS member Suga's solo act name) stands as one of the boldest uses of traditional Korean culture and music in K-pop thus far. The track stylishly and effectively infuses elements of traditional Korean music, hip-hop and trap, reflecting the plot of the music video that weaves through Agust D's dual persona in two different temporal spaces, one as a king in the historic Joseon period (1392 1897) and the other as the rapper himself, somehow appearing in the historic period, disguised as a peasant and facing the king persona.

The title "Daechwita" is taken from the eponymous traditional Korean band music originating in the early seventeenth-century Joseon, performed for royal and military processions. *Chwi* means to blow, and *ta* means to strike; together, *chwita* refers to music performed by woodwind and percussion instruments, and *dae* translates to "grand," indicating the significance of the occasions where *daechwita* was performed. The instruments for traditional *daechwita* have changed over time, but the standard instrumentation in today's performances includes the woodwinds *nabal* (brass horn), *nagak* (seashell horn), and *taepyeongso* (shawm), and the percussion instruments *yongo* (drum), *jing* (gong), and *jabara* (small cymbals). The traditional performance begins with the band leader's command, "*myungeumilha daechwita harapshinda*" ("Hit the gong once and let *daechwita* begin"), to which the band responds by shouting, "Ye-I." To that, a strike on the gong and three hits on the side of *yongo* (drum) announce the start of the music, and the entire band commences.

Agust D's song borrows these iconic moments of *daechwita*, with modifications. Unlike the traditional performance, "Daechwita" begins with the gong, followed by the *taepyeongso* and the leader's command, delivered as a sung melody and accompanied by the gong and other drums. This intro rounds off with the band's response, "Ye-I," as done in a traditional performance. Notably, these sounds are sampled from a performance by the Court Music Orchestra of the National Gugak Center. The voice is that of the *piri* virtuoso Cheong Jae-guk, whose vocalization uses the *shigimsae* technique, melodic decorations involving microtonal bending, grace notes, or vibrations. Fittingly, this introduction, which adopts numerous elements of traditional *daechwita*, is matched visually in the music video by the image of Agust D's king character arising from his throne, followed by a view of the courtyard of a historical palace.

As the music transitions into the main verse and the music video shows Agust D's peasant (modern) persona strolling in an old marketplace, the traditional gong sound is re-created by the synthesizer. These shifts symbolize the intermixing of the tradition and the modern, on both musical and narrative levels. The sound of the *kkwaeggwari* (small handheld gong) introduced in this scene (0'31") could symbolize Agust D's peasant identity, since the instrument is not used in traditional *daechwita*, but in farmer's music, *nongak*. Musically, its jangling timbre perfectly depicts the boisterousness of the marketplace, while its high-pitched, metallic quality blends seamlessly with hi-hat and snare drums. Likewise, the gong, with its lengthy reverberation, mixes well with larger drums. Thus, the track effectively exploits the timbral similarities between traditional and electronic instruments to blend the two genres, which in turn informs the song's narrative.

Recurring pitch materials also help the two different genres mix with each other. For instance, the pitches from the commander's vocalization, the *taepyeongso* melody, and the pitch clusters created by the various instruments in the introduction are rich in microtonal bending and semitone relationships. The vocal bending and semitones serve as cohesive melodic ideas later in the track, as in the vocal chorus melody ("Daechwita-a-a, Daechwaita-a-a") that oscillates between the pitches C# and D. Additionally, the vocalization and the *taepyeongso* melody comprise the pitches G#, C#, D, D#, and F (slightly off pitch), which become part of the main melodic riff (spanning the pitches G#, C#, B, F#, and D) played against the drone on C# (first played at the appearance of the peasant Agust D) throughout the track. Through the cohesive use of pitch materials in both styles of music, "Daechwita" integrates two vastly different genres – traditional Korean music and hip hop – on structural, sonic, and narrative levels.

Overall, the musical, visual, and symbolic integration of traditional Korean music and culture in this track is by far more seamless and effective than in any other K-pop song. Such incorporation has had significant commercial implications, as illustrated by the popularity of "Daechwita" on YouTube (more than 318 million views as of July 2022, with 13 million likes). Given BTS's influence in the Korean popular music industry, the musical and commercial success of their engagement with traditional Korean music and culture may encourage other K-pop artists and management companies to continue to explore in this direction.

Conclusion

As this chapter has shown, K-pop's stylistic evolution has been guided largely by a search for a balance between the global and the local. Certain aspects of this dynamic have surfaced more prominently than others at different times. However, generally speaking, K-pop has progressed from a conscious resistance to Korea's local elements to a more willing and enthusiastic expression of them. K-pop artists – not only composers and producers but also choreographers and costume designers – are increasingly looking toward traditional Korean culture for fresh inspiration. One implication of this change is that K-pop as a whole is becoming more confident and assertive about expressing its Koreanness. At the same time, greater consumption of K-pop globally might signify changing dynamics of influence within the popular culture industries. Finally, this trend is symptomatic of the overall widening of the cultural spectrum in K-pop, as the incorporation of Korean traditional culture is counterbalanced by songs like BTS's "Dynamite" and "Butter," sung entirely in English.

Whether more K-pop idol musicians will continue to incorporate traditional Korean culture and music in their works is a matter of pure conjecture. However, it is certain that a greater number of international consumers have grown familiar with K-pop and other aspects of Korean culture, which might enable them to embrace K-pop's experimentation with traditional elements more readily. It will be worthwhile to investigate how this recent engagement with Korean tradition may impact the consumption of K-pop overseas, by Korean and non-Korean audiences, to understand the future direction of K-pop.

References

An, Yun-tae, and Hee-jun Kong. *I su-man pyeongjeon* (Lee Soo-man biography). Paju: Jeongbowa saram, 2012.

Chang, Yu-Jeong. "Trot and Ballad: Popular Genres of Korean Pop." In Hyunjoon Shin and Seung-Ah Lee (eds.), *Made in Korea: Studies in Popular Music*, 63–70. New York: Routledge, 2017.

Fuhr, Michael. *Globalization and Popular Music in South Korea: Sounding Out K-Pop*. New York: Routledge, 2016.

Howard, Keith. "Coming of Age: Korean Pop in the 1990s." In Keith Howard (ed.), *Korean Pop Music: Riding the Wave*, 82–98. Kent: Global Oriental, 2006.

Iwabuchi, Koichi. "From Western Gaze to Global Gaze." In Diana Crane, Nobuko Kawashima, and Kenichi Kawasaki (eds.), *Global Culture: Media, Arts, Policy and Globalization*, 256–273. New York: Routledge, 2002.

Jang, Soo Hyun. "The Korean Wave and Its Implications for the Korea-China Relationship." *Journal of International and Area Studies* 19/2 (2012): 97–113.

Jin, Dal Yong. "Critical Interpretation of Hybrid K-Pop: The Global-Local Paradigm of English Mixing in Lyrics." *Popular Music and Society* 37/2 (2014): 113–131.

New Korean Wave: Transnational Cultural Power in the Age of Social Media. Urbana: University of Illinois Press, 2016.

Kim, Pil Ho. "Korean Rock's Journey from Group Sound to Indie Punk." In Hyunjoon Shin and Seung-Ah Lee (eds.), *Made in Korea: Studies in Popular Music*, 71–82. New York: Routledge, 2017.

Kim, Seongmin. *Keipabui jageun yeoksa* (A short history of K-pop). Paju: Geulhangari, 2018.

Kim, Youna. "Globalization of Korean Media: Meanings and Significance." In Do kyun Kim and Min-sun Kim (eds.), *Hallyu: Influence of Korean Popular Culture in Asia and Beyond*, 132–154. Seoul: Seoul National University Press, 2011.

"Korean Media in a Digital Cosmopolitan World." In Youna Kim (ed.), *The Korean Wave: Korean Media Go Global*, 1–27. New York: Routledge, 2013.

"The Rising East Asian Wave: Korean Media Go Global." In Daya K. Thussu (ed.), *Media on the Move: Global Flow and Contra-Flow*, 121–135. New York: Routledge, 2007.

Kwon, Hyunseok. "Korean Pop Music and Korean Identities." In Hyunjoon Shin and Seung-Ah Lee (eds.), *Made in Korea: Studies in Popular Music*, 157–167. New York: Routledge, 2017.

Lee, Jamie Shinhee. "Linguistic Constructions of Modernity: English Mixing in Korean Television Commercials." *Language in Society* 35/1 (2006): 59–91.

"Linguistic Hybridization in K-Pop: Discourse of Self-Assertion and Resistance." *World Englishes* 23/3 (2004): 429–450.

Lee, Sangjoon. "Introduction. A Decade of Hallyu Scholarship: Toward a New Direction in Hallyu 2.0." In Sangjoon Lee and Abe Mark Nornes (eds.), *Hallyu 2.0: The Korean Wave in the Age of Social Media*, 1–27. Ann Arbor: University of Michigan Press, 2015.

Oh, Ingyu. "From Localization to Glocalization: Contriving Korean Pop Culture to Meet Glocal Demands." *Kritika Kultura* 29 (2017): 157–167.

Robertson, Roland. "Glocalization: Time-Space and Homogeneity-Heterogeneity." In Mike Featherstone, Scott M. Lash, and Roland Robertson (eds.), *Global Modernities*, 25–44. London: Sage Publications, 1995.

Seabrook, John. "Factory Girls." *The New Yorker*, October 1, 2012.

Shepherd, John (ed.). *Continuum Encyclopedia of Popular Music of the World: Part 1 Performance and Production*. New York: Bloomsbury, 2003.

Shim, Doobo. "Hybridity and the Rise of Korean Popular Culture in Asia." *Media, Culture & Society* 28/1 (2006): 28–31.

Shin, Hyunjoon. "K-Pop (Music) in the Emerging Cultural Economy of Asian Pop." *Journal of Communication Arts* 25/4 (2007): 1–11.

  "Reconsidering Transnational Cultural Flows of Popular Music in East Asia: Transbordering Musicians in Japan and Korea Searching for 'Asia.'" *Korean Studies* 33 (2009): 101–123.

Sinclair, John, "Culture and Trade: Some Theoretical and Practical Considerations," In Emile G. McAnany and Kenton T. Wilkinson (eds.), *Mass Media and Free Trade: NAFTA and the Cultural Industries*, 30–62. Austin: University of Texas Press, 1996.

Straubhaar, Joseph D. "Beyond Media Imperialism: Asymmetrical Interdependence and Cultural Proximity." *Critical Studies in Mass Communication* 8/1 (1991): 39–59.

Sun, Meicheng, and Kai Khiun Liew. "Analog Hallyu: Historicizing K-Pop Formations in China." *Global Media and China* 4/4 (2019): 419–436.

Sung, Sang-Yeon. "Digitization and Online Culture of the Korean Wave: 'East Asian' Virtual Community in Europe." In Youna Kim (ed.), *The Korean Wave: Korean Media Go Global*, 135–147. New York: Routledge, 2013.

Yoon, Tae-Jin, and Bora Kang. "Emergence, Evolution, and Extension of 'Hallyu Studies': What Have Scholars Found from Korean Pop Culture in the Last Twenty Years?" In Tae-Jin Yoon and Dal Yong Jin (eds.), *The Korean Wave: Evolution, Fandom, and Transnationality*, 3–21. Lanham, MD: Lexington Books, 2017.

Notes

1 Roland Robertson, "Glocalization: Time-Space and Homogeneity-Heterogeneity," in Mike Featherstone, Scott M. Lash, and Roland Robertson (eds.), *Global Modernities* (London: Sage Publications, 1995), 28–31. Also see Ingyu Oh, "From Localization to Glocalization: Contriving Korean Pop Culture to Meet Glocal Demands," *Kritika Kultura* 29 (2017): 157–167.

2 Michael Fuhr, *Globalization and Popular Music in South Korea: Sounding Out K-Pop* (New York: Routledge, 2016), 61.

3 Fuhr, *Globalization and Popular Music in South Korea*, 60.

4 Youna Kim, "The Rising East Asian Wave: Korean Media Go Global," in Daya K. Thussu (ed.), *Media on the Move: Global Flow and Contra-Flow* (London: Routledge, 2007), 121–135; Doobo Shim, "Hybridity and the Rise of Korean Popular Culture in Asia," *Media, Culture & Society* 28/1 (2006): 28–31.

5 Dal Yong Jin, *New Korean Wave: Transnational Cultural Power in the Age of Social Media* (Urbana: University of Illinois Press, 2016), 3–19; Sangjoon Lee, "Introduction. A Decade of Hallyu Scholarship: Toward a New Direction in Hallyu 2.0," in Sangjoon Lee and Abé Mark Nornes (eds.), *Hallyu 2.0: The Korean Wave in the Age of Social Media* (Ann Arbor: University of Michigan Press, 2015), 1–27.

6 See Meicheng Sun and Kai Khiun Liew, "Analog Hallyu: Historicizing K-pop Formations in China," *Global Media and China* 4/4 (2019): 419–436.

7 Trot is a genre of Korean popular music that emerged in the first half of the twentieth century. See Yu-Jeong Chang, "Trot and Ballad: Popular Genres of Korean Pop," in Hyunjoon Shin and Seung-Ah Lee (eds.), *Made in Korea: Studies in Popular Music* (New York: Routledge, 2017), 63–70; Pil Ho Kim, "Korean Rock's Journey from Group Sound to Indie Punk," in Shin and Lee (eds.), *Made in Korea*, 71–82.

8 Fuhr, *Globalization and Popular Music in South Korea*, 75.

9 Soo Hyun Jang, "The Korean Wave and Its Implications for the Korea-China Relationship," *Journal of International and Area Studies* 19/2 (2012): 97–113; Youna Kim, "Globalization of Korean Media: Meanings and Significance," in Do Kyun Kim and Min-sun Kim (eds.), *Hallyu: Influence of Korean Popular Culture in Asia and Beyond* (Seoul: Seoul National University Press, 2011), 132–154; Hyunjoon Shin, "Reconsidering Transnational Cultural Flows of Popular Music in East Asia: Transbordering Musicians in Japan and Korea Searching for 'Asia,'" *Korean Studies* 33 (2009): 101–123; Hyunjoon Shin, "K-Pop (Music) in the Emerging Cultural Economy of Asian Pop," *Journal of Communication Arts* 25/4 (2007): 1–11.

10 John Sinclair, "Culture and Trade: Some Theoretical and Practical Considerations," in Emile G. McAnany and Kenton T. Wilkinson (eds.), *Mass Media and Free Trade: NAFTA and the Cultural Industries* (Austin: University of Texas Press, 1996), 30–62; Joseph D. Straubhaar, "Beyond Media Imperialism: Asymmetrical Interdependence and Cultural Proximity," *Critical Studies in Mass Communication* 8/1 (1991): 39–59. For studies drawing on these concepts, see Tae-Jin Yoon and Bora Kang, "Emergence, Evolution, and Extension of 'Hallyu Studies': What Have Scholars Found from Korean Pop Culture in the Last Twenty Years?," in Tae-Jin Yoon and Dal Yong Jin (eds.), *The Korean Wave: Evolution, Fandom, and Transnationality* (Lanham, MD: Lexington Books, 2017), 3–21; Lee, "Introduction," in Lee and Mark (eds.), *Hallyu 2.0*, 1–27; Sang-Yeon Sung, "Digitization and Online Culture of the Korean Wave: 'East Asian' Virtual Community in Europe," in Youna Kim (ed.), *The Korean Wave: Korean Media Go Global* (New York: Routledge, 2013), 135–147.

11 Youna Kim, "Korean Media in a Digital Cosmopolitan World," in Kim (ed.), *The Korean Wave*, 1–27.

12 Seongmin Kim, *Keipabui jageun yeoksa* [A short history of K-Pop] (Paju: Geulhangari, 2018), 75–76.

13 John Seabrook, "Factory Girls," *The New Yorker*, October 1, 2012, www.newyorker.com/magazine/2012/10/08/factory-girls-2.

14 Lee Soo-man, interview, *Entertainment Weekly* (*Yeonyegajunggye*), aired June 30, 1990, on Korea Broadcasting System (KBS). Quoted in Yun-tae An and Hee-jun Kong, *I su-man pyeongjeon* [Lee Soo-man biography] (Paju: Jeongbowa saram, 2012), 214–215.

15 See Keith Howard, "Coming of Age: Korean Pop in the 1990s," in Keith Howard (ed.), *Korean Pop Music: Riding the Wave* (Kent: Global Oriental, 2006), 82–98.

16 Koichi Iwabuchi, "From Western Gaze to Global Gaze," in Diana Crane, Nobuko Kawashima, and Kenichi Kawasaki (eds.), *Global Culture: Media, Arts, Policy and Globalization* (New York: Routledge, 2002), 256–273.

17 John Shepherd (ed.), *Continuum Encyclopedia of Popular Music of the World: Part 1 Performance and Production* (New York: Bloomsbury, 2003), 563.

18 Jamie Shinhee Lee, "Linguistic Constructions of Modernity: English Mixing in Korean Television Commercials," *Language in Society* 35/1 (2006): 59–91. Also see Dal Yong Jin, "Critical Interpretation of Hybrid K-Pop: The Global-Local Paradigm of English Mixing in Lyrics," *Popular Music and Society* 37/2 (2014): 113–131.

19 Jamie Shinhee Lee, "Linguistic Hybridization in K-Pop: Discourse of Self-Assertion and Resistance," *World Englishes* 23/3 (2004): 429–450.

20 "Global Music Producing System," SM Entertainment Group, www.smentertainment.com/Entertainment/Music (accessed March 31, 2021).

21 See Hyunseok Kwon, "Korean Pop Music and Korean Identities," in Shin and Lee (eds.), *Made in Korea*, 157–167.

22 English translation mine.

4 Recording the Soundscape of K-Pop

HYE WON KIM

Timbre

EJAE (Kim Eun-jae), a rising singer-songwriter and producer, was in her car driving from Virginia to New York in December 2019 when she suddenly received an onslaught of direct messages from her Instagram account. Fans of the girl group Red Velvet were texting that her demo version of "Psycho" had been uploaded to YouTube. It was two days before SM Entertainment (hereafter SM), one of South Korea's largest entertainment conglomerates, was to release Red Velvet's song "Psycho," the title song of their next album, and the demo version, sung by EJAE and Cazzi Opeia, a singer-songwriter who cowrote the song, had been leaked. It immediately circulated as avid fans tracked down EJAE's SoundBetter account after Andrew Scott, the song's producer and other cowriter, had tagged her to promote the record before its worldwide release.

EJAE had accidently uploaded the demo for "Psycho" a few years before on SoundBetter, a music production marketplace, to connect with other musicians when she arrived in New York. In the SoundBetter portfolio, musicians post the SoundCloud link to their demo playlist, automatically loading all their songs onto the platform. She had uploaded several of her demos to promote her account and also had posted another demo identically titled "Psycho." Unaware that Red Velvet's version of "Psycho" had been uploaded to her song list, she had forgotten about the account. But the fans tracked her down. She immediately deleted her account and notified SM's A&R agent and EKKO Korea Music Rights publishing, to which she is signed. They advised her to report the unofficial uploads, so for the next two days, EJAE would report all leaks that came into her purview: "I've been reporting the leaked version all day long for the past two days. It was wildfire from then. There was nothing I could do other than to report endlessly."[1]

"Psycho," the title song for *The ReVe Festival: Finale* (2019) studio album, was met with extraordinary commercial and critical acclaim. It topped Korean and international music charts and won numerous accolades, including the prestigious Golden Disc Award's "Digital Single Award" in 2021. Ironically, it was EJAE's demo leak that sparked interest for me, apart from the fact that she is one of the few Asian and Asian

American women K-pop producers in the industry who has worked with women artists such as EXID's Hani, Suzy (former member of Miss A), and Taeyeon (Girls' Generation member). I was browsing the internet and clicked on the leaked demo, thinking it was the English version of "Psycho." I was surprised to find a well-polished, extremely well-sung song with catchy lyrics that would play in my ear for several days:

> You got me feeling like a psycho, psycho
> Got me chasing shots of Nyquil, Nyquil
> Without you got me dizzy and upset
> Got me so obsessed with you
> Look what you started, I'm psycho you're heartless.[2]

I was intrigued that EJAE was excluded from *The Korea Herald*'s article, which covered the production of Red Velvet's "Psycho." In-depth interviews were conducted with Scott and Cazzi Opeia, but not with EJAE. "Someone said something like being heartbroken is almost like feeling psycho. We then decided we wanted to write a song with beautiful chords that tells a story about this. And that's how 'Psycho' was born," Cazzi Opeia notes. But who was this *someone*? The article mentions that the song's inception took place at SM's songwriting camp in Seoul and that EJAE wrote the top line (melody) with Cazzi Opeia. Yet EJAE's name is unmentioned when the article recounts how the melody was developed, and only Cazzi Opeia is credited.[3] What happened during the production of the record or inside the recording studio?

Because many scholars contend that K-pop is driven by visual imperatives, such as Irene from Red Velvet, who seems to prove their point by singing that she is "original, visual" in "Psycho," academic analysis has been dominated by ocular-centric discussions while questions pertaining to K-pop as a sonic phenomenon have largely been neglected. Drawing on R. Murray Schafer's definition of "soundscape" – which treats sound as the combination of layers of culture, place, acoustic space, and technology – this chapter provides an overview of K-pop's soundscape with a particular emphasis on an aural turn in the discipline of K-pop studies. The industry's sonic practice has responded to new recording technologies and media, which are linked to particular temporal and spatial configurations. For instance, the technological mediation of sound in studio recording booths, where K-pop singers give literal voice to their self-expression, has become an integral component of the sonic form.

K-pop artists' recording methods drastically altered over the past decade with the advent of technologies such as smartphones, digital plug-ins, and music streaming platforms (Melon, Genie, and Spotify, to name a few), which facilitate portable music and make digital sound files effortlessly fungible. The soundscape of K-pop has expanded further into cyberspace as record production, vocal directing, and sound mixing are controlled remotely and synchronized with digital platforms, situating cyberspace as a form of recording studio produced by multiple participants and sound practices. Spaces of sonic performance are no longer confined to the recording studio but form part of the confluence of time and space in cyberspace. Once the demo for "Psycho" was cut for the album, Scott, who was based in Los Angeles, communicated with Yoo Young-jin, SM's in-house executive record producer in Seoul, to alter sound sources, instrumental stems, and chords, and to restructure sections to fit SM's sound design; Scott also worked with EJAE in New York and Cazzi Opeia in Sweden remotely to produce the bridge of the song, which was sent to Yoo for SM's approval. Technology has taken record production one step further, so that records are produced synchronously with digital platforms such as Audiomovers, where sound can be streamed, and mixed remotely in real time; the compressed time and space has accelerated and amplified K-pop's soundscape in ways that even COVID-19 cannot hinder.

From demo production to recording sessions, I address in this chapter a broad network of sonic practices in contemporary Korean music production, including through interviews with recording artists ranging from balladeers, singer-songwriters, rock stars, rappers, and idols to K-pop boy bands and girl groups. To contextualize their discursive practices, I also address the interventions of record producers, songwriters, sound engineers, A&R teams, and the CEOs of entertainment companies. With the aim of broadening the discourse of sound studies, I try to eavesdrop on how the soundscape of K-pop is recorded and how artists register their voices, both literally and figuratively, in music-making processes.

When I invoke "K-pop," a nebulous expression for Korean popular music, I refrain from limiting the term to boy bands and girl groups and expand it to encapsulate the spectrum of Korean popular music. In so doing, I focus on the intimate space of the recording studio and the performances of seminal figures who have built the platform for K-pop's global consumption. It is impossible to fully address the diverse sounds, genres, and presence of many celebrated personalities, but I have carefully selected recording artists and producers whose influences have most notably fashioned the K-pop industry. Finally, while listeners' multivalent reception (which one might call listener response) forms an integral part of K-pop's soundscape, for the purpose of this chapter I focus on the production of what Pierre Schaeffer has called "sound objects," or recorded sound.

Pulse

Sound studies in academia have gained traction in the past decade under the auspices of scholars such as Rey Chow, James A. Steintrager, Philip Auslander, Brian Kane, Jonathan Sterne, and Fred Moten, and the digital revolution has helped the discipline expand culturally, spatially, and theoretically.[4] Yet the fledging discipline of sound studies has produced a paucity of literature on Asia and none on K-pop. While Suk-Young Kim, Dal Young Jin, John Lie, and Youna Kim, to name a few, recently have published valuable research on K-pop, no scholar has focused on the production of sonic practices in the industry.[5] In this chapter, I situate the soundscape of K-pop, as a case study, from the perspective of sound studies.[6] I utilize sound theory to approach K-pop and elucidate its interplay between technological mediation and production, and attempt to intervene in the discourse of loss that treats sound as ephemeral, ineffable, and elusive. By rethinking K-pop and sound as categories of analysis, I aim to materialize a dimension that largely has been omitted in sound studies and the K-pop canon and offer new perspectives on the production and perception of sound.

In the physical world sound was captured and burned into objects such as CDs; in the digital world sound is archived in the data cloud, from which music is streamed. In sound studies, sound is conceived as an ephemeral and ineffable effect and is associated with loss, but that sense of capture and loss is interrupted by digital technology. Capture, in the age of digitized sound, as Chow and Steintrager explain, no longer involves loss; file formats such as the MP3 and MP4 positively connote plenitude, compactness, and pristineness that does not erode through repeated copying.[7] The grain of the voice is captured through sonic objectification (the objectified form of sound) in recordings whose copies all retain high-definition quality and clarity, so Chow and Steintrager postulate the need to revise the paradigm of sonic capture as mere loss and consider "sonic loss as gain."[8] I build on this stance but argue that sound is not ephemeral; sound capture does not primarily implicate the retention of what is lost. Instead, the ephemera of sound are always marked on the record and are distinctly material, even as they emanate from either the sonorous body (the larynx, vocal folds, palate) or the digital interface, where sound is activated through software with the touch of a human finger – sound remains.

Focusing on sound as what Chow and Steintrager termed an "object of sound" – or what Pierre Schaeffer coined as a "sound object" (*l'objet sonore*) – I highlight how these terms refer to the invisibility of what causes sound.[9] They situate sound no longer as the Other of vision and subvert the Western ideology of equating vision to rationality, science, and writing and sound to unscientific realms of affect and emotion.[10] Technological reproduction severs sound from source and audio from visual dimensions, and leaves us to perceive them on separated tracks. In so doing, recordings capture K-pop's tactility as an independent entity as sound waves touch and vibrate our bodies and the music becomes an object of sound. Yet most studies of musical recordings as objects of sound have centered on sound technology by underscoring technical mechanisms.[11] I instead examine the connection between human and nonhuman actors that generate the sound object by focusing equally on human interplay and recording technologies. As Brian Kane elaborates, "sounds and notes do not simply constitute a realm of essence detachable from their moment, sites of production, or reception. Rather, they need to be recognized as a sedimentation of historical and social forces."[12] For sound to become an object, the singers' voices, the musicians, and the producers' and engineers' mediation, inside and outside recording studios, form part of a complex and arduous collaboration that gives meaning to the sedimentation of sound. Within this trajectory, I utilize Schafer's concept of soundscape and introduce the soundscape of K-pop as a sound object tied to its geographical environment in its inception.[13]

I argue that sound objects are political statements embedded with multiple subjectivities; accordingly, K-pop is inextricably entangled with its temporal and spatial nature and is emblematic of the social, historical, political, and technological soundscape of the industry. The object of sound performs the "sedimented acts" of multiple agencies connected in the recording process. Chow brilliantly elucidates how a sound object can be translated as an embodied materiality via Mikhail Bakhtin's notions of double-voicedness and polyphony; "a word" appears in the form of "a singular vocal emission," but is consistently "underwritten (and under-spoken) by other voices; even when silent."[14] However inaudible the other voices are, they exert power in the emission and reception of the voice. For instance, with digital technology, the breathing of K-pop singers in between notes easily could be eliminated. Yet the silence is never an absence: the erasure of a K-pop singer's breath is a political act in itself in that power relations have been involved in the decision-making process. The creative choices of each actor in the network of songwriters, singers, musicians, producers, A&R people, sound engineers, and CEOs who participate in this process shape K-pop by burning themselves into the memory of a CD or writing data in binary numbers. Tracing the labor of multiple agencies in the manufacture of a sound object can disclose a web of power relations, and the sound object represents an imprint of the recording studio as a site of power relations.

Track 1. "Geunyeoui useumsorippun" 06:27, Written by Lee Young-hun and Kim Myung-gon

Prior to the rise of digital technology and the ensuing global consumption of K-pop, sound was produced in an analog recording system, by the interplay of human subjectivities in the recording studios in Seoul. In the 1980s, Lee Moon-sae, a multiplatinum solo recording artist who is regarded as the pioneer of K-pop ballads and pop aesthetics, recorded his songs with analog multitrack consoles. Lee debuted in 1978; released sixteen studio albums; was the recipient of numerous awards, ranging from the Golden Disc Award to the Presidential Commendation Award; and his ballads – such as "Yetsarang" (Old love), "Sarangi Jinagamyeon" (When love passes by), Gwanghwamun yeonga" (Gwanghwamun love song), "Geudaewa yeongwonhi" (Forever with you), and "Bulgeunnoeul" (Sunset glow) – are still popular and covered by contemporary artists. Lee is famous not only for his songs but also for his talent as an entertainer; he was the host of Munhwa Broadcasting Corporation (MBC)'s most popular radio show, *Byeori binnaneun bame* (On a starry night), from 1985 to 1996 and had several major TV music shows of his own. Lee's popularity gathered momentum with his third studio album, which was released by Seorabeol Records in November 1985 and sold 1.5 million copies. This marked the beginning of the vast popularity of *gayo*, which means Korean popular music, and the "ballad" genre. American popular music, trot music, and folk dominated Korea's music industry until M. Lee's third and fourth studio album in the mid-1980s. Lee's first single, "Nan ajik moreujanayo" (I still don't know), from his third album, peaked at number one on Korean Broadcasting System (KBS) TV's *Gayo Top 10* chart in June 1986, after seven months of promotion and gaining significant radio airplay. It also marked the beginning of his collaboration with Lee Young-hun, a songwriter who had just launched his professional career. K-pop balladeer M. Lee's subsequent albums also went platinum: His fourth studio album sold more than 2.85 million copies in 1987, making it the biggest seller in K-pop history (in the 1980s and 1990s, albums that sold more than 1 million copies were considered platinum); it also was the first studio album that entirely centered on M. Lee and Y. Lee's teamwork.

Recognizing their potential as a team, the duo developed a collaborative relationship for four consecutive albums. "While the singles from my fourth album reached number one on music charts, Y. Lee was already starting to write music for my next album," says M. Lee. He continues: "I was busy promoting the album, but all the while, my mind was occupied with my next album." During preproduction, the duo had long talks where they envisioned the direction of their highly anticipated album. Y. Lee preferred working on the piano and was far from spontaneous in writing his music and, in particular, his lyrics; he worked steadily and meticulously, selecting each word as he worked out his ideas for the characters, the narrative, and the sound design tailored to M. Lee's voice. He then presented the songs to M. Lee, who would select those that would best fit the concept of the album. "Mr. Young-hun Lee already had the lyrics naturally fused with the music; he was more than a lyricist – he was a poet," he explains.

> Once songs were confirmed, another six months was spent to practice and memorize the melody with the lyrics, and after extensive discussions on the exact kind of arrangement that reflected the precise mood of each song, it was during this time that we would record the demo on a reel-to-reel tape recorder to be delivered to the song arranger Kim Myung-gon.[15]

With only Y. Lee's piano and M. Lee's voice, the duo layered the polyphony of voices on the demo they desired to iterate on the master, and Kim, a renowned and prolific songwriter and arranger, would come in on the day of recording to capture their narrative into sound.

The production started with the recordings of instrumental sessions executed under Kim's guidance and was followed by vocal recording sessions: "I was always fully prepared, and my lyrics fully memorized by heart when I recorded my songs in the studio," recalls M. Lee. He adds, "I never brought in the lyrics with me when recording; it was a time when artists recorded songs with their eyes closed." During the 1980s, recording studios were equipped with analog multitrack consoles, the standard for Korea's music industry. Music was recorded to a master disc, reel-to-reel magnetic tapes referred to as "reel tapes" in the Korean vernacular. That decade was the era of the vinyl long-playing record (LP), the definitive analog sound storage format. Under those material and technical conditions, music was fully rehearsed and memorized before the artists entered the studio, because it was difficult to fix mistakes with the recording technology available. When collaborating on their fourth studio album in 1986, M. Lee as always was fully prepared to record "Geunyeoui useumsorippun" (Only her laughter), another hit song written as a gift to his loyal fans. The 6:27 duration was inappropriate for radio airplay, whose time limit was generally three to four minutes per song. "We didn't have Auto-Tune back then and couldn't alter a single note, so if you made a mistake, you had to sing it all over again," M. Lee recalled. By his own account, "To sing over six minutes straight, I could not even practice the song because my voice would go hoarse. So, to sing in the best condition possible, I had dinner, and after two hours of digestion in complete silence, I entered the studio, sang the whole song once, and the first take ended up in the album." (M. Lee did sing three backup versions.) In postproduction, the multitrack was delivered to the mixing engineer, who optimized the audio levels, and then pressed into LPs.

By 1992, recording studios had transitioned from using analog to digital multitrack recording consoles, and sound was manifested through visual displays of sound waves on the computer screen. M. Lee had started exploring other genres such as jazz, and collaborated with various musicians to expand his musical range, but the duo legend continued to work on pop ballads until Y. Lee's death in 2008. By 1992, the music industry had been transformed: three-member group Seo Taiji and Boys' debut in 1992 with "Nan Arayo," which utilized MIDI technology, popularized the incorporation of rap into K-pop, contributing to the K-pop idol songwriting formula, and galvanized the proliferation of dance music (electronic dance music, EDM) into mainstream popular culture. Dance music groups (including gender-mixed groups) and solo artists performing powerful choreography to dance music enjoyed immense popularity. With the exception of singer-songwriters and the rare dance music groups such as Seo Taiji and Boys and the two-member dance group Deux, where Taiji Seo and Lee Hyun-do were, respectively, song-writer and producer themselves, the efficient system of the compartmentalization of composers, lyricists, song arrangers, and producers took shape: Lyrics were rarely written before the melody; in extreme cases, they were written during recording sessions. Kim Hyun-chul, a producer and singer-songwriter, produced M. Lee's eighth studio album in 1993, and the modes of collaboration were very different from that with Y. Lee: Kim wrote the lyrics to the title single, "Jongwonege," in the recording studio, as M. Lee was in the booth recording the first phrase of the song, waiting for the lyrics to be handed to him. Demos were given to Lee in the form of cassette tapes with "dummy lyrics." The dummy lyrics were terrible, although they were fun to listen to. This compartmentalization of what used to be a holistic music production process was effective in a fast-paced neoliberal society such as Korea, and the collaborative format expanded drastically in the mid-1990s with the introduction of boy band and girl group idols such as H.O.T., S.E.S., Fin.K.L, and Sechs Kies, whose soundscape was buoyed by the advent of Auto-Tune. By the late 1990s, K-pop idols and music dance groups and solos depended heavily on Auto-Tune, software that corrects singers' pitch and added to the stereotype of K-pop automation.

Track 2. "Sangeo" 05:29, Written by Cho Kyu Chan

"이 앨범의 모든 수록곡은 **AUTO TUNE** 기능을 사용하지 않은 목소리로 녹음 되었습니다."
"All songs on this album were recorded with a voice that did not use the function of **AUTO TUNE**."
(bold letter emphasis in original)

Hip-hop artist Jay-Z released his single "D.O.A. (Death of Auto-Tune)" in 2009 to bash the overuse of voice-correction technology, but in Korea, already at the turn of the millennium, Cho Kyu Chan, a Korean Music Award winner, singer, songwriter, and producer, imprinted his anti–Auto-Tune statement at the end of the credits on his fifth studio album cover. Cho's position reflected the industry's overweening promotion of pop idols, boy bands and girl groups, and solo and dance group singers who were incapable of singing live on pitch and always lip-synched on TV due to their focus on presenting vigorous choreography.[16] Their voices were hypermediated in recording studios, and idol and dance groups were heavily criticized for their inability to sing live, except for their lead singers (such groups usually featured one capable singer). Most singers no longer needed to sing well, and it was no longer considered taboo to place a sheet of lyrics on a music stand when recording; the digitized manipulation of voices in recording studios manufactured timbre, tone, and pitch in an unprecedented fashion. Cho explains, "Nowadays, I do use Auto-Tune when necessary. It depends on the concept of the song, but back then, the tool was perceived negatively – it was a transitional period."[17]

This transitional period proceeded in tandem with rapid technological innovation – such as the invention of the MP3, a file-compression technology, and its free distribution on the internet – which affected the object of sound and the Korean music industry in multifarious ways. If the free distribution of the MP3 encoder impelled the inception of Napster in June 1999 in the United States, in Korea, there was Soribada, a Korean version of the free peer-to-peer MP3 file-sharing service that involved copyright infringement in May 2000. Free MP3 downloading had detrimental effects on the industry, with CD sales dropping drastically because players such as MPMan (the world's first MP3 player), Yepp, and Iriver made MP3s portable. It instigated a sharp decrease in sales of analog formats, such as compact discs (CDs), tapes, and vinyl, but also contributed to K-pop's stark shift from audio to visual culture. The shift was a survival strategy but also symbolized the resilience of the industry, since musicians had to provide listeners more than the sound component and needed to secure an alternative and innovative platform to CD sales. Still, the detrimental effects on singer-songwriters and balladeers were severe. By 2001, million-seller albums had disappeared, and technology also modified studio practices. When in 2001 Cho recorded his sixth studio album, on which he collaborated with R&B artist Brian McKnight on "Thank You for Saving My Life," the conversion to full-digitized recording, along with Pro Tools, an alternative editing software, allowed sound to be cut, pasted, and mended with simple mouse clicks. Even with advanced sound engineering, however, producers knew that consumers were listening to compressed MP3 files. After hours of mixing the tracks with the sound engineer, producers such as Cho and David Kang (Kang Hwa-seong) – a prominent record producer and songwriter who produced popular pop ballad albums for artists such as Sung Si-kyung, Naul, Brown Eyed Soul, and Fly to the Sky – would burn the final sound-mixed song to a CD and listen to it in their car on an average set of speakers, just as the casual listener would. Kang noted how sound mixing had changed: "sound was hypercompressed, and for idol albums, in particular, the low end was amplified where the bass sound was aggressively compressed for the MP3 listeners. At the time, there were rumors that SM Entertainment started to aggressively compress the low end during sound mixing to cater to listeners of the sound on MP3."[18] Today, Kang's statement attests to SM's standard sound-mixing practices, as producers use sources and mixing attuned to the industry's technological advances, such as the use of smartphones as music players.[19]

Cho is considered among the most important artists of Korea's popular music industry and epitomizes the era of K-pop's singer-songwriters of the 1990s and 2000s, which featured Kim Kwang-jin, Yoon Sang, Kim Hyun-chul, Yoo Hee-yeol, Lee Juck, Kim Dong-yul, Kim Yoon-Ah, and Paul Kim.[20] He is renowned as a "genius singer-songwriter," "a master vocalist," and "the king of chorus (backing vocals)"; Nam Tae-jung, an MBC radio producer and music critic, describes Cho as having a "microfiber voice" that captures "even the subtlest nuances, while musicians describe him as a true musician who is "the vocal producer for vocalists."[21] In 1989, Cho won the first Yoo Jae-ha Music Competition and made his solo debut with *Since 1993*; his first single, "Chueok #1," became a big hit. (The competition also produced popular singer-songwriters such as Sweet Sorrow, Yoo Hee-yeol, and Bang Si-hyuk, the founder of Big Hit Entertainment) In the 1990s, a plethora of dance music and pop ballads dominated mainstream Korean charts; however, Cho's nine studio albums explored diverse genres such as pop, rock, R&B, and jazz, and experimented with innovative sounds and vocal techniques that met with both commercial and critical acclaim. He plunged into R&B with his third studio album, *The Third Season*, which is regarded as having pioneered the most authentic yet Koreanized form of the R&B genre with songs such as "Baby You're the Lite," for which he used overdubs to enhance his R&B phrasing, turns, and falsettos. In 2010, Cho's ninth studio album received the Best Pop Album of the Year at the Korean Music Awards. Since receiving his MA in jazz studies at the University of Illinois at Urbana-Champaign, Cho has been teaching, performing, hosting his own radio show, producing records, and recently releasing one digital single each month for his tenth studio album.

Unlike artists and idols who do not write their own music, singer-songwriters such as Cho usually work alone, and Cho produces, writes, and arranges all his songs, although he occasionally collaborates with friends and colleagues. A multi-instrumentalist, he works with the piano or guitar to compose, depending on the concept and texture of the sound he needs. Cho begins with the chord progression, melody, and rhythmic idea, and transcribes them onto a lead sheet with rehearsal marks during preproduction. The initial creative process occurs in random places: his personal studio, his room, or the public bench in front of his house, where he wrote *K-Pop Star*'s season 3 winner Bernard Park's title song "Before the Rain" in one hour. Sometimes the lyrics come with the concept of the song, as he plays around with chords and melody, but for his records, the lyrics are fixed when he inscribes the concept on a lead sheet. If the arrangement requires additional programming, he works with a computer programmer, with the music score in hand. Cho sets the pulse (beats per minute, bpm) and plays all sound sources, including the groove (straight or swing), four rhythm (keyboards, drums, bass, and guitar), and synth source (a software interface called Virtual Studio Technology). He dubs when needed and makes selections on the tone, dynamics, and voicing of each digital instrument. Otherwise, he lays out the basic arrangement in his own studio with real-time or digital instruments and sound sources on his own iMac. For his own albums, he does not need demos, as he is his own client, but when he needs to send out demos for session musicians who will add real-time instruments, he sings the melody without words, providing just enough for the musicians to grasp the flow and atmosphere so that they have more freedom to develop their artistry.[22]

Track 3. "Byul" 02:40, Written by Sweetpea and Lee So-ra

The intimate space of the recording studio is a construction of the various agencies that are involved and registered in the sound objects of K-pop, and oftentimes, unplanned creative ideas take shape unrehearsed in the studio. Critics and musicians refer to Cho as the producer who has "influenced Lee So-ra to become the vocalist she is now."[23] Celebrated for her delicate musicianship, Lee is one of the most prominent female singer-songwriters of K-pop. In 2019 she collaborated with BTS member Suga on the hit single "Song Request," and she has worked with Cho on numerous albums since her solo debut in 1995. If Kim Hyun-chul helped her find her unique voice in the initial years of her career, Cho played the pivotal role in shaping her identity as a musician in later years. Since Lee's sixth studio album in 2004, Cho has served as the vocal producer. One fall night, they met at Booming studio in Daechi-dong, in the southern part of Seoul's Gangnam district, to discuss her forthcoming sixth studio album, *Nunsseupdal.* Lee writes only the lyrics to her songs and at the time had already selected potential songs written by other artists to accompany her lyrics. In the course of preproduction, the two sat side by side behind the control booth console, where Lee explained the overall concept to Cho. She played each demo with her handwritten lyrics in front of them, and Cho would listen carefully while Lee continued delineating the images and stories behind her lyrics. Since a different composer had written each song, Cho envisioned the need to develop an underlying narrative or dramatic arc in sound design and vocalization. Under Cho's direction, vocal technique, vocal chord progressions and patterns, sounds, ambience, melodic and harmonic ideas, delay, and reverb were all accurately planned, and on top of that instruments were dubbed with identical ambience; the musical concept also was applied to sound mixing.

The final recorded productions changed significantly because the demos contained only the skeletons of the songs; depending on the concept, the skeleton is often just the piano, guitar, and drum loop and at times added synthesizers. One song, "Byul" (Star), was written as a simple folk tune without any kind of ambience or vocal harmony. Before recording, the two sat in the control booth, where Lee sang the song with lyrics to Cho. Cho realized she sang with a lot of "scooping," a technique where the vocalist starts singing below the desired pitch and slides up to the intended pitch. The technique was her specialty, as it was a common vocalizing tactic in pop. Cho advised her to discard it and sing all notes straight, like Enya. They listened to Enya together, and following a long discussion, Cho's decision to alter Lee's vocalization elevated the spatialization (positioning a sound source, such as the vocals, in three-dimensional space) and mood of "Byul." That set the album's unequivocal narrative tone, which expanded into "Barami Bunda," for which a similar timbre, ambience, and spatialization were achieved by manipulating sound in the production and postproduction of sound mixing. Before entering the booth to record "Byul," Lee studied Cho's instructions and began to jot down musical notation in symbols, a method similar to Labanotation, a concept Rudolf von Laban developed in 1928 that now is used primarily to record dance movement in symbols. Lee documented all Cho's suggestions regarding the movement, crescendo, diminuendo, and vibrato wavelength of her voice, as well as the movement's duration, by means of symbols placed on each word or line of the freshly printed lyric sheet. Then she went into the booth, turned off all lights except for the thin pin light on the music stand, and started recording under Cho's direction.

The collaborative process was built on mutual respect and loyalty; Cho was the only vocal producer whom Lee trusted, in that she did not allow anyone in the studio other than the recording engineer – not even the songwriters or her manager. "Sisikolkolhan Iyagi" (Miscellaneous stories) was designed as a folk acoustic tune with a dry ambience, and Lee had written the lyrics as a monologue, which was a predictable concept. Most significantly, it wasn't pertinent to the narrative arc of the album Cho designed. Once again, Cho altered the concept and presented an additional persona, represented by an audible voice, in order to form part of the narrator's inner conversation. Lee adored this, and Cho wrote the additional melody and lyrics for the persona on the spot. While Lee was taking a break after recording the vocals, Cho jumped right into postproduction and manipulated the secondary voice by cutting off the lows and the high sound with the equalizer to open up the midsection and display the persona's voice, to make it sound as if they were on the phone and to separate the two personas. One "pro" (equivalent to a recording session in the United States) lasts three and a half to four hours, but would vary depending on Lee's condition and mood on the day of recording. They once recorded from four in the afternoon until eight the next morning. There was also an incident when they were recording at 2 a.m., and Lee was resting inside the booth; as Cho was editing the melodic phrase that Lee had just vocalized, he asked her via intercom to continue the next line and was met with silence. Lee had vanished into thin air. After an hour of waiting, Cho realized that she had gone home without telling him.

Track 4. "Psycho" 03:31, Written by Andrew Scott, EJAE, Cazzi Opeia, Druski, Yoo Young-jin, and Kensie

Rewinding to the intro da capo, I note that the leaked demo for "Psycho" was written at SM's songwriting camp in 2018, with EJAE, Scott, and Cazzi Opeia in SM's recording studio. "The melody was done in like thirty minutes," recalls EJAE as she starts to unravel the story of "Psycho."[24] At songwriting camp, musicians work with a number of producers; track makers, who construct the instrumental track, which includes the beat, chord progressions, loops, and sound samples; and topliners, who create the melody on top of the premade track with a set of English or Korean lyrics. For EJAE's session, Scott, the track producer, brought a list of full production tracks from which to choose. Cazzi Opeia chose a track, but one of SM's A&R people who managed the camp and with whom EJAE was acquainted through Andrew Choi, a singer-songwriter and prolific hit producer who won third place in *K-Pop Star* season 2, came in knowing that EJAE was in the session, and selected the "Psycho" track because she knew EJAE's preference for R&B and pop. On top of Scott's track, EJAE and Cazzi Opeia began to form melodic verses. EJAE's relationship with her boyfriend was tumultuous at the time and she was left with conflicting emotions of love, hatred, and despair that made her want to focus on relationships and mental health. The concept and chorus started to flow naturally. "Psycho" was a common English word in the Korean vernacular and easy to pronounce. Scott and Cazzi Opeia liked the concept, and Cazzi Opeia came up with the strong pre-chorus. Scott then sang a melody for the verse, which was later replaced with EJAE's, and EJAE wrote the hook (chorus) in a minute. EJAE observed, "For some reason I kept on saying 'Nyquil,' how I feel like a patient, and how your love makes me feel like I'm a sick person to your love and addicted to it." When the main hook was fixed, Scott selected additional melodic lines EJAE had composed and "Frankensteined" it together to form the chorus. EJAE also wrote the second hook at the end, "Hey now I'll be okay," and they inserted a rap section, which is mandatory for a K-pop idol group. A lot of the topline melodies selected were EJAE's ideas, such as the chorus, the post hook, and most of the second verse, and the process was a collaboration of the artists' creative choices. Interestingly, the demo was produced without Red Velvet in mind; during the listening session, the team thought about sending the demo to a pop artist such as Ariana Grande, and EJAE honestly did not think it would get cut for SM.

The concept and English lyrics for "Psycho" stem from personal experience. EJAE started as an SM trainee when she was eleven. She depicts the K-pop industry as "toxic" and reveals that the cultivation process was so traumatic that she still undergoes therapy for it. Each week, before she went on camera to show her progress in singing, dancing, and speaking Chinese, EJAE had to weigh herself in front of everyone. The staff would call out her weight in front of staff members and trainees. She was never good enough for SM's standards; they always gave her negative evaluations and told her that she was overweight. EJAE weighed 123 pounds at the time; SM asked her to lose 13 pounds – she stood 5'7" in middle school. A hardworking trainee who came to work before everyone else and was last to leave, she starved herself by eating only two sweet potatoes a day to maintain a 110-pound weight. "Honestly, the English lyrics have something to do with mental health," EJAE explains. "I wished the song could express that it's okay to be mentally ill. I hoped the Korean lyricist could express that. Everyone is at some point a psycho; being a psycho is part of being human." EJAE was set to debut her freshman year in college, but she chose to study at New York University's Clive Davis Institute of Recorded Music, and most of all she wanted to be a solo artist. EJAE still participated in training every summer at SM, but by the time she returned to Korea after graduation, she was twenty-three, which was considered too old by SM standards. Even so, artists such as Andrew Choi believed in her work and inspired EJAE to become who she is.

Because the recording process requires the performance of real-time physical instruments and sessions in expensive recording studios, nonidol artists, such as K-pop balladeers and singer-songwriters, usually have advance demos produced only once tracks are confirmed for placement on albums. K-pop idol groups follow a different trajectory. First-generation demo production from the 1990s to mid-2000s for idol groups such as S.E.S. and TTma was similar to that of nonidol singers, and live guitar sessions and orchestration proceeded once the demo was selected. But with the advent of electroacoustic music and digital instruments that had become more accessible and cost-efficient by the late 2000s, full-production demos became possible. Producers and songwriters could easily purchase a plenitude of reasonably priced analog emulation plug-ins and manipulate the sounds on their personal computers without having to learn how to play the instruments. Nowadays, the electroacoustic sound sources are of such high quality that the demos don't necessarily need full orchestration or real-time instruments such as guitars. For both demos and final recordings, technology enables producers freely to replace all digital sound passages, but altering real-time song arrangements requires re-recording acoustic instruments and string orchestration in recording studios, a process most record companies eschew to save money. In multiple contexts, digital instruments can replace acoustic instruments for dance music; but for balladeers and singer-songwriters, digital assemblage can never produce the ambience of real-time orchestration. I would have thought that the demo version of "Psycho" was the final English version if I hadn't known it was a leak. Yet EJAE notes that the "Psycho" demo is considered rough in the industry. To help me understand, she played the demo versions of her recent hits on Audiomovers from Virginia – Suzy's "SObeR" and Taeyeon's "Sorrow," both of which EJAE coproduced and sang in English. After listening to the two versions in Seoul, I could grasp what she meant – the demos for "SObeR" were immaculate; they sounded like official releases.

Track 5. GOT7 "Not by the Moon" 03:23, Written by Park Jin-young, Isaac Han, Aaron Kim, Jay & Rudy, Lee Seu-ran, and OKIRO

Isaac Han, a Los Angeles native who studied at Berklee College of Music, majoring in music business, is a preeminent record producer and songwriter, and cofounder and chief producer of 8PEX Company and Tech Arts Group; he has worked extensively in the K-pop industry, producing title records and hits for GOT7, Suzy, Super Junior, Nine Muses, Myteen, Day6, and many more. He started in 2012 with SM, where he wrote and produced acts for Super Junior, Super Junior-D&E, and Henry. At the time, Han was the main songwriter and idea maker in his teamwork with Neil Nallas, a Filipino American songwriter and rapper. When developing demos, Han always would start with a melodic idea: "I focus on the melody, melodic ideas, and conceptual ideas first and then I expand the idea with chords using a guitar, or the piano. That's how I build the skeleton of the song." The team would decide whether to move forward with the skeleton and proceed with the lyrics and the "concept," or theme of the song, to finalize the demo. But demo production for idol groups has undergone a radical transformation since 2012.

The process of recording studio demos for boy bands and girl groups is embedded in a network of power relations. When pitching records to A&R people and record executives, Han always chooses the lyrics and concepts, and produces full production demos to convey the concept of the song, meaning he executes a complete arrangement that includes sound mixing to get pristine quality. Even more than recording techniques, the contemporary production process resembles a factory line, where each role is compartmentalized. The record emerges within a scrupulously efficient system: the track maker constructs the track, usually on the standard pop song form: verse 1; pre-chorus; chorus (or hook); verse 2; pre-chorus; chorus; bridge; and back to chorus. The track is outsourced to topliners who create the melody and English lyrics (in rare cases Korean), and at times contribute to the vocal idea and concept. The track maker and/or the producer receives the topline and alters the production to fit the melody or vice versa; the producer then pitches the finalized demo to the record company A&R department; and, last, the demo is evaluated by the A&R board, in-house producers, and the owner of the company, who usually have the last say regardless of whether they are business-centric or musically inclined. Rarely is the demo cut if the company's CEO disapproves, unless it is for a high-profile celebrity such as Suzy. When she received the "SObeR" demo, Park Jin-young rejected it, but Suzy strongly advocated for the song and included the record in her second EP, *Faces of Love*. A cut demo selected as the title song rarely is approved as is, and the in-house A&R executives, producers, and executive producers or CEOs make subtle to extensive alterations to "domesticate" the track, tailoring it to the singer or group and adhering to the company's distinct style. Yet it can be inapt to compare K-pop production to that of a factory; a person must activate even digitized sound sources and physical devices (such as the interface), and the creative and personal choices of a network of competing agencies produce the sound object.

Although he works in diverse genres, Han's songwriting philosophy is similar to that of Kang, songwriter and producer for K-pop ballads: They both allow the melody to be the focal point, which is supported by the song arrangement; however, to keep pace with the music trends that rapidly change within K-pop's eclectic soundscape, Han converted to its compartmentalized music production system in 2015. With K-pop's global reach, innumerable musicians with newer and fresher sounds are continually pitching thousands of songs. The demo process for Super Junior-M's 2013 song "Go" was similar to that of a K-pop ballad or a new song by a singer-songwriter: Han would start with the track idea and then conceptualize melodic ideas. However, he explains, it has become impossible to do all the work himself: "I wouldn't say that I'm old, but in music years, especially in K-pop, trends change within months. Even this year, our team went through like multiple changes in trend from girl crush to dark trap, and at a certain point, we switched almost instantly to a city pop retro vibe."[25] For instance, when he worked in 2019 on the demo of the title hit single "Not by the Moon" by the boy band GOT7, of JYP Entertainment (hereafter JYP), for their eleventh EP, *Dye*, Han and Aaron Kim, cofounder and producer of 8PEX, outsourced their track to the Danish duo topliners Jay & Rudy, whom Han met during SM's songwriting camp in 2016. Similar to the way Cho used rough vocalization on demos for session musicians to embellish during live studio recordings, Han and Kim intentionally disbursed an unfinished preliminary track to give the topliners space to explore their melodic ideas. Afterward, the team would exchange comments by sending voice notes on Jay & Rudy's topline, and once Han received all their vocal stems and ideas, they expanded the track to fit the melody more engagingly. Han attests that Jay & Rudy's topline was perfect and explains how the postproduction of the mix and the process of infusing the track with the melody came after he picked up ideas from the topliners. With full sound mixing and quality sound, they pitched their complete demo, which was produced in three days, to JYP's A&R department. After JYP's distinct blind review process, where the board of A&R, producers, and Park Jin-young himself vote for potential demos with all song credits concealed, Han received an acceptance within two weeks.

Facilitating alterations to the demo has become standard practice for title songs at K-pop's major entertainment and record companies, such as SM, JYP, YG Entertainment, and Big Hit Music (Big Hit Entertainment in 2021 was restructured into HYBE Corporation, which manages many music labels including Big Hit Music). While productions such as "Psycho" and "Go" retained most of their found tracks, toplines, and concepts, including their English title, many songs, such as "Not by the Moon" by GOT7, were transposed substantially, allocating royalties to a long list of songwriters. That song's demo, originally titled "Paranoid," conceptualized a push-pull romance. However, because it was the title song for their EP, Park Jin-young (singer-songwriter, record producer, and founder of JYP) was heavily involved in the production, and the demo was revamped to "Not by the Moon." When Han received a call back from A&R, JYP saw the potential and requested numerous alterations that Han's team had to track out; they made twenty production changes to the demo. Once the track was finalized, Park Jin-young modified chords and bass lines, and thoroughly altered the concept. Han candidly remarks:

> I'm gonna say this in a way that's not negative at all, but ultimately, as Mr. JYP [Park Jin-young] came in and made changes to the song, I felt like the song was no longer ours anymore. The way he infused his color felt like I was being robbed, not in a bad way, though; it was more out of appreciation. He didn't even take that long, and [the changes] at first didn't feel like a big change, but over time, it came to the point where I was like, *I don't think this song is ours anymore.* He really laced the song together to make it come to life, and I have a lot of respect for that. He is one of the greatest K-pop producers of all time, and I could see why.

Best understanding each GOT7 member's vocal skills and talent, Park Jin-young presented an alternate narrative for Han, Kim, and Jay & Rudy's demo and applied a theatrical, Shakespearean approach to the song's storytelling. Moreover, Park Jin-young was involved in the sound-mixing process and outsourced the track to Manny Maroquin, an eight-time Grammy Award–winning mixing engineer based in Los Angeles.

Nonetheless, collaboration in K-pop's song production still occurs in a contested space of encounter. Most songwriters are comfortable with slight alterations to their work, but the intervention of revamping demos might be perceived as disrespectful. Yet, as is the case with SM, JYP, YG Entertainment, and Big Hit Music, in-house producers, group members, and owners "domesticate" all demos selected as title songs to fit the company's distinct timbre. Because the melody of a song is divided among the multiple members of a group, in-house producers and A&R agents find alterations essential, as their recording artists are trainees under their auspices. Although such instances are rare, the A&R agent and Park Jin-young can refrain from intervening in the recording process. In the production of "Before the Rain," Bernard Park's debut title song, written, produced, and vocal directed by Cho Kyu Chan, JYP was flexible and remitted full control to Cho as a gesture of respect, but also to imbue Park with Cho's aesthetic and songwriting artistry.

Although controversial, the domestication of the demos is comprehensible when we glimpse the recording process of idol groups who have numerous members in the studio. For Super Junior-M's "Go," the A&R executives scheduled each member's recording session and isolated different phrases, words, and lines of the lyrics, allocating some to each member. When Han and Kim orchestrated the vocals of GOT7's "Not by the Moon," the session went smoothly because each member's sessions had been scheduled beforehand. During the 1990s and early 2000s, all members of the first-generation idol groups, such as S.E.S. and TTma, had to stay in the recording studios. Eugene, a member of the first K-pop girl group, S.E.S., who is now a celebrated actor, recalled the recording process of her debut album: "Shoo, Bada, and I stayed in the recording studio even during other members' recording sessions for our debut album and its title, 'I'm Your Girl.'" Soy Kim, an actor, director, and singer-songwriter from the disbanded girl group TTMa, affirmed Eugene's statement: "It was mandatory and a way of showing each other support as a team."[26] Today, each member comes into the studio during their allotted time frame, and the vocal recording of the song takes about three "pros"; each singer is well prepared and professional but remains independent. Han tries to give each a two-hour slot to avoid wasting the company's and member's time. An extra session is mandatory for editing the vocal stems, and Han takes an extra session to Frankenstein and premix parts before delivering the multitrack to the mixing engineer.

Mastering

Mastering is the final edit in the postproduction process for a final mixed recording, from which the "master" (data storage device) is created to replicate manufactured copies for sales. The process involves devices such as an equalizer, dynamic range compressor, and amplifier to optimize the final sound. New forms of technology have contributed to and shaped K-pop's evolution, leaving distinctive marks on its soundscape. The complex layering and networking that occurs in the recording studios, where recording artists, musicians, producers, songwriters, A&R agents, and owners of record companies translate their creative choices into binary numbers or "bits," produce K-pop's sound object after a long process of production. The sedimentation of the arduous labor and multiple personal but creative choices by a network of agencies in record production is attached to a specific time and space in creating K-pop's sound objects as material forms. When I listened to Red Velvet's "Psycho" before I had access to the English demo, the Korean lyrics, written by SM's in-house producer and songwriter Kensie, emphasized a couple's relationship, which diverged from EJAE's initial concept; but I could hear what had been left unsaid in the final Korean lyrics. That is, I somehow traced the collective or "underwritten" remains of EJAE's English lyrics in the newly translated Korean lyrics. For instance, Kensie retained the word "psycho" in the English lyrics for the hook – "You got me feeling like a psycho, psycho," "I don't play the game" – and "I'm original visual," and modified "Hey now I'll be OK" to "Hey now we'll be OK." The initial concept was lost in translation, yet remained audible to me in the final Korean record. I could hear the unsaid words in the way the "Psycho" demo focused on mental illness.

K-pop's transformation of time and space altered the soundscape in a myriad of ways. Advances in technology and the conversion to full-digitized recording studios facilitated a method of collaboration that extends into cyberspace, allowing up to seven songwriters to collaborate on GOT7's "Not by the Moon." However, collaboration over the internet is nothing new: Cho met McKnight when he visited Korea after the recording of their duet "Thank You for Saving My Life"; they sang their parts separately and exchanged sound files via email. Even when M. Lee collaborated with Zion-T on "Snow" in 2017, they communicated through Kakaotalk messages and email and met in person only after the single was released.

I confront the presumption of the ideological construct of ocular-centrism associated with Western culture in K-pop's extreme emphasis on visual aesthetics, where the choreography and performance of boy bands and girl groups are the dominant narrative. This emphasis on the visual is closely associated with the marginalization of K-pop's soundscape. The devisualization of sound demonstrates the epistemology of K-pop's changing soundscape and presents opportunities to analyze the attending sounds in themselves as sonic phenomena. Technology has allowed us to capture nature's waves and make music mobile/portable, but K-pop as an object of sound cannot be ahistorical as it encapsulates multiple agencies involved in its production, where the distinctiveness of the temporal and spatial nature of sound is acknowledged. Rather than aiming to present fixed answers, I hope to have revealed a dimension of the process of recording this soundscape to broaden the discourse on K-pop within sound studies.

Notes

1 EJAE, interview with author, Seoul, Korea, December 29, 2020.
2 EJAE provided the demo lyrics.
3 Hyun-su Yim, "Why You Can't Stop Listening to Red Velvet's 'Psycho': The Masterminds behind the Track Explain How the Catchy Earworm Came to Be," *Korea Herald*, February 10, 2020, www.koreaherald.com/view.php?ud=20200210000280.

4 For an introduction to sound studies, see Jonathan Sterne, *The Audible Past: Cultural Origins of Sound Reproduction* (Durham, NC: Duke University Press, 2003); Rey Chow and James A. Steintrager (eds.), *Sound Objects* (Durham, NC: Duke University Press, 2019).

5 For books addressing the K-pop industry, see Suk-Young Kim, *K-Pop Live: Fans, Idols, and Multimedia Performance* (Stanford, CA: Stanford University Press, 2018); Dal Yong Jin and Hark Joon Lee (eds.), *K-Pop Idols: Popular Culture and the Emergence of the Korean Music Industry* (Lanham, MD: Lexington Books, 2019); JungBong Choi and Roald Maliangkay (eds.), *K-Pop: The International Rise of the Korean Music Industry* (New York: Routledge, 2015); John Lie, *K-Pop: Popular Music, Cultural Amnesia, and Economic Innovation in South Korea* (Berkeley: University of California Press, 2014); Gooyong Kim, *From Factory Girls to K-Pop Idol Girls: Cultural Politics of Developmentalism, Patriarchy, and Neoliberalism in South Korea's Popular Music Industry* (Lanham, MD: Lexington Books, 2019).

6 I utilize "music" and "sound" interchangeably, as they both emit sound waves, and I treat music as one domain of sound. But I do not limit the term to discrete pitches or rhythms. For a discussion of whether music is part of sound studies, see Leigh Landy, "But Is It (also) Music?," in M. Cobussen, V. Meelberg, and B. Truax (eds.), *The Routledge Companion to Sounding Art* (New York: Routledge), 17–26.

7 Rey Chow and James A. Steintrager, "In Pursuit of the Object of Sound: An Introduction," *Differences* 22 (2011): 5.

8 Chow and Steintrager, "In Pursuit of the Object of Sound," 6.

9 For the genealogy of the term "sound object," see Chow and Steintrager (eds.), *Sound Objects*, 1–19.

10 Sterne and Gavin Steingo and Jim Sykes explain how the audiovisual litany is prominent in the West and describe how the ideology is deeply inflected in Judeo-Christian theology. See Sterne, *The Audible Past*, 14–16; Gavin Steingo and Jim Sykes (eds.), *Remapping Sound Studies in the Global South* (Durham, NC: Duke University Press, 2019), 2–3.

11 Steven Feld, "I Hate 'Sound Studies,'" https://static1.squarespace.com/static/ 545aad98e4b0f1f9150ad5c3/t/55ef81ffe4b0e4ff182017bf/1441759743397/I+Hate.pdf (accessed August 1, 2020).

12 Brian Kane, *Sound Unseen: Acousmatic Sound in Theory and Practice* (New York: Oxford University Press, 2014), 38.

13 However, I disagree with Schafer's description of "schizophonia," a term that connotes the anxiety engendered when sound is severed from its source through electroacoustic reproduction, as well as his interpretation of the industrialized soundscape as sonic pollution. See Murray Schafer, *The Soundscape: Our Sonic Environment and the Tuning of the World* (Rochester, VT: Destiny Books, 1994), 90–91; for an overview of Schafer's coined term of soundscape, see Michael Bull, "Introduction: Sound Studies and the Art of Listening," in Michael Bull (ed.), *The Routledge Companion to Sound Studies* (New York: Routledge, 2018), xvii–xxxii.

14 Rey Chow, "Listening after 'Acousmaticity': Notes on a Transdisciplinary Problematic," in Chow and Steintrager (eds.), *Sound Objects*, 124.

15 All quotations from this section are from my interview with Lee Moon-sae, Seoul, Korea, December 14, 2020.

16 In 1997, KBS imposed a ban on lip-synching, requiring all singers to sing live until the early 2000s. Lip-synching was proof that you were not a "real" singer.

17 All quotations from this section are from my interview with Cho Kyu Chan, Seoul, Korea, January 5, 2021.

18 David Kang, interview with author, Seoul, Korea, December 8, 2020.

19 A recent text by Lee Soo-man to Red Velvet's Yeri confirms the rumor: S. Lee delineates how "Psycho," the lead single from *The ReVe Festival: Finale* studio album in 2019, was rearranged and remixed for smartphone listeners in ways that emphasized the gliding bass line. See Si-yun Jeon, "Redvelvet Yeri," *Star News*, January 13, 2020, https://entertain.naver.com/read?oid=108& aid=0002836065.

20 Bae Chul-soo, member of the band Songolmae and DJ of "Bae Chul-soo's Music Camp," compared Cho to Bob Dylan. See Rigveda Wiki, https://rigvedawiki.net/w/%EC%A1%B0%EA% B7%9C%EC%B0%AC#rfn8 (accessed January 6, 2021).

21 Woo Geun-hyang, "Jogyuchane geuksesa boiseu'," *Korea Economic Daily*, October 9, 2011, https://entertain.naver.com/read?oid=015&aid=0002555292; "Maeumeul Umjigineun norae … Jogyuchan," *YTN News*, January 19, 2012, www.ytn.co.kr/_ln/0106_201201191531009273.

22 Cho Kyuchan, interview with author, Seoul, Korea, January 5, 2021.

23 Woo Geun-hyan, "Jogyuchane geuksesa boiseu'."
24 All quotations from this section are from my interview with EJAE, Seoul, Korea, December 29, 2020.
25 All quotations from this section are from my interviews with Isaac Han, Seoul, Korea, December 16 and 19, 2020.
26 Eugene, interview with author, Seoul, Korea, January 26, 2021; Soy Kim, interview with author, Seoul, Korea, January 21, 2021.

and contemporary as well as classical and popular dance. The experimental style demonstrates how K-pop oscillates between manufactured homogenized and more authentic-looking aesthetics, an underground indie style that highlights artists' individuality. The hybrid style exhibits a complex layer of international collaboration, racial and ethnic identity, and ethics of cultural exchange in tourism and transnational digital dance.

K-Pop Dance: An Emerging Social and Popular Dance of the Global Youth

According to Julie Malnig, social dance refers to a local, vernacular dance tradition circulated in a community.[6] Cha-cha in a Cuban wedding ceremony and a folk music dance festival in Texas are examples. Frequently, a social dance becomes popularized and spreads beyond local contexts, and is then called popular dance, a type that becomes a "worldwide dance phenomen[on]," such as hip hop.[7] Nowadays, as dance easily circulates online a social media, it seems inevitable that the line between a vernacular social nce in a local context and a transnational popular dance is blurred.

Social and popular dance have traditionally been marginalized due to racialized elitism that prioritizes European and American concert e as high arts.[8] However, both social and popular dance are part of life and have served community members across the globe. In *The d Handbook of Dance and the Popular Screen*, Melissa Blanco Borelli hers examine sociopolitical and cultural implications of popular such as dance activism and the formation of racial and gender s, through in-depth analysis of dances in television, movies, music ocial media, and video games.[9] Sherril Dodds's groundbreaking discusses sexuality, race, gender, and diaspora by theorizing bes of popular dance in pop music, burlesque, Hollywood films, mental art.[10]

ance treads a slippery line between social dance and popular ough it started in South Korea as a local music and dance ame transnational and is now considered a global phenom- ave argued elsewhere, K-pop dance is an emerging "social- e of global youth" who perform alternative racial, ethnic, tic, and sexual identities through their localized adaptations e.[11] The visually stunning choreography with somewhat nce style has generated a sizable number of tutorial videos global fan-dancers who want to "be like" K-pop singers.[12] uses social and popular dance in an interchangeable way alized but transnational phenomenon of K-pop dance.

PART III

Dancing to K-Pop

5 K-Pop Dance Music Video Choreog

CHUYUN OH

In 2019, *CNN* reported that K-pop dance is
after hip hop.[1] K-pop is a dance-driven
polished idols' synchronized, sophistica'
transnational visibility of K-pop danc
dance fandom, and flashmobs, re
Intersecting performance studies, cri
ies, this chapter focuses on K-pop d
K-pop music videos over the pa
versions on the concert stage.

Employing descriptive anal
movement, sonic, and visual
videos by groups such
BLACKPINK, and TWICE
raphy. Movement analysi
directly embodies socioc
ment analysis in conjur
elements, such as clot
foundation for an au
type of choreograp
movement style,
to not only a s
expression, alo

This chap
dance in the
"social-po
social me
raphy
chorec
scho
exp
ar
s

pur
style exemp

An understanding of K-pop dance must consider the main platform where the performance is staged. Whether on a television station, YouTube, Tik Tok, or Instagram, K-pop is predominantly circulated via visual media, and thus choreography is arranged for the screen. It reflects what Dodds refers to as "popular screen dance."[13] When dance is created for and circulated on screen, a mediated digital body replaces a live body in a theater located in a fixed time and space.[14] K-pop dance predominantly emerges from music videos that highlight the visualization of music and sound. Above all, K-pop dance is a visual concept edited for the screen in the mainstream popular culture. The dancers/singers' appearance – what they wear, how their bodies look, how they move, how they wear makeup, what characters or personae they play on stage to highlight specific concepts – is as important as the music. The sleek, flawless, mediated dancing body in K-pop edited for screen with specific effects often exceeds ordinary human bodies' natural movement capability and visual presentation, akin to what Dodds calls "superbodies" in popular screen dance.[15]

Given that K-pop dance is specifically arranged for media platforms, "point choreography" becomes crucial. "Point choreography" refers to a short and iconic movement commonly placed in the chorus line.[16] PSY's horse dance in "Gangnam Style" (2012) is a prime example. A point choreography should reflect the general image, concept, and theme of the music video itself and boost the group's unique personae and characters onstage. More importantly, it should be highly eye catching, memorable with a clear structure, and, if possible, imitable for the fans who listen to and perform K-pop. Point choreography facilitates what Mark Franko called "democratization" of participatory dance today in social media.[17]

K-pop dance demonstrates a "participatory" dance culture in the twenty-first-century digital space.[18] In the digital age, social media in large part replace traditional theater. Many young people around the globe who have yet to see live theater have already watched K-pop music videos and dance tutorial videos on YouTube. Some have posted K-pop cover dances on YouTube, participated in K-pop flash mobs, or posted #Kpopdancechallege on TikTok and Instagram. As popular dance scholars have argued, pop dance has been a pivotal tool for young people to explore alternative cultural identities against the mainstream culture. The global K-pop dance fandom exemplifies how the global youth construct and physically perform alternative racial, gender, sexual, ethnic, and linguistic identities.

According to San San Kwan, contemporary dance refers to "the dance that is happening now" and includes not only concert dance but also contemporary commercial and contemporary world dance.[19] "World dance" means dance styles and practices outside the colonial logic of the "canonical" Western dance.[20] "'Asia' is yoked to 'traditional' and 'contemporary' is yoked to 'Western,'" Kwan writes, due to the pervasive Orientalism that perceives Asia as "historical" rather than "contemporary" – a notion predominantly held by Euro-American dance artists.[21] What is unique about K-pop dance is that it showcases a blend of both classical and popular dance as well as traditional and contemporary dance practices, not to mention Western and Asian dance styles. K-pop dance exemplifies what Kwan refers to as the characteristics of "contemporary Asian dance" in the world dance category.[22] To Kwan, contemporary Asian dance is an intercultural genre that incorporates Western contemporary dance into a local form with dancers' "hybrid bodily intelligence" and versatile training backgrounds.[23] As dance scholars have warned, however, it is essential to remember that such intercultural adaptation happens in both Asian and Western contexts in multidirectional ways, as demonstrated by prominent Western ballet, modern, and contemporary choreographers' and artists' cultural appropriations of the East and Asia and their significant effects on Western dance history.[24]

The production system of the K-pop industry suits well what Kwan calls "East-West blends" in contemporary Asian dance. The industry actively hires non-Korean musicians, dancers, and choreographers. Such transnational collaboration makes it challenging to define K-pop's identity as solely limited to geographical boundaries. K-pop dance is produced for commercial platforms, such as mainstream television shows, music programs, and dance competitions. Trainees go through the strict and disciplined process at entertainment agencies to learn dancing, singing, and often foreign languages. Many idols are formally trained in dance, including modern dance, ballet, and Korean dance. For example, BTS's Jimin, Cosmic Girls's Cheng Xiao, Gugudan's Kang Mi Na, and EXO's Kai graduated from conservatory arts schools and formally studied dance. K-pop dance has been turned into a formal subject in the South Korean education system, as it became part of popular and commercial dance classes offered at conservatory schools. K-pop dance not only challenges the line between social and popular dance but also blurs the low (pop dance) versus high (classical dance) art dichotomy.

Types of K-Pop Music Video Dance

The Schoolgirls and Schoolboys Concept

As Judith Butler noted, gender is a "stylized repetition of action" that is necessarily involved with repetitive bodily behaviors.[25] K-pop groups often emphasize conventional gender roles: either innocent, cute schoolgirls and schoolboys or seductive, sensual, and powerful figures. For the former, the choreographies commonly consist of bright smiles and light, cheerful, gestural movements to accompany happy, romantic, upbeat love songs. Cute and affectionate facial expressions and attitudes, called *aegyo* in Korean, emblematize the schoolgirls and schoolboys concept. Examples of *aegyo* can be a baby voice, a wink, or a duck face. It is also common in dance choreography, in movements such as girlish, restricted arm gestures, as if expressing shyness, and clenching fists next to the face, looking at the camera, and lightly rolling the fists, as if imitating toddlers or animals.

Space denotes gendered power dynamics. In her canonical essay "Throwing like a Girl: A Phenomenology of Feminine Body Comportment Motility and Spatiality," Iris Marion Young examined how physical space itself is gendered. For example, girls are expected to take up narrower and smaller space even when they engage in physical exercise, such as throwing a ball.[26] In order to match their shy, innocent schoolgirl personae, K-pop girl groups often tend to limit their spatial mobility. While performing, they often waddle, step side to side attentively, move their shoulders up and down like shrugging, flip their hands upward, then face their palms down. The width of both of their shoulder and leg movements is limited to an inward, narrow space. They also occasionally hold their hands behind their back as If they feel shy or intimidated. While their steps are ravishingly decorative and sophisticated, their choreographies do not execute an explicitly intense, powerful, or sexual movement. Neither do they take up a large space on stage. Even if some members who are mostly in charge of dance can execute more intricate and challenging movements, the level of power dynamics remains moderate so that they can maintain girlish appeal with light movements.

Maintaining a moderate level of sex appeal is the key to the schoolgirl concept and choreography. In TWICE's "Likey" (2017), between the chorus link, a member, Momo, does a solo dance to lively background music. She is clad in pink shorts and a white top. The garment reveals her body, but the color and style are bright, like clothing designed for teenage girls. She lifts and crosses her arms above her head, shakes her hips, and stylishly bends her arms near her face with multiple angles like voguing. Pushing her arms away from her body, she circles her hips backward and undulates and waves her chest, then seductively gazes at the camera, albeit briefly. When waving, she flips up her hand upward, like an animation character, pushing and facing her palm downward, lifting her fingertips upward. She does not forget to show an innocent smile so that the scene does not look dark or explicitly sexual. The backdrop is changed from an old alley with garbage bins to a colorful ice cream shop and bright yellow and pink alley. In contrast to the sensual lower body movement, her upper body communicates otherwise. Her hands flipping upward are accompanied by a joyful and naïve smile, and the bright backdrop resonates with a typical innocent, girlish manga character, which in turn reduces the sensual appeal of her lower body movement. With the choreographed use of space setting, costume choice, smile, and gaze, the solo maintains a delicate balance between being cute, if not chaste, and sexual.

Other visual elements match the choreography. The schoolgirls and schoolboys wear colorful but casual clothes or school uniforms such as pleated skirts and white blouses or navy pants and ties. Some of their videos have cartoonish edits, such as vivid color, modified size of the dancers like miniature figures vis-à-vis the environment, and imaginative and futuristic backgrounds and props that do not exist in reality. TWICE's "TT" (2017) presents a series of Halloween-themed cosplay scenes where the group members portray various characters such as the White Queen from *Alice*, Pinocchio, Tinker Bell, the Little Mermaid, and Elsa from *Frozen*. In "Signal" (2017), TWICE communicates with an extraterrestrial being and later turn themselves into aliens.

Girls' Generation is canonical in this category due to their delicate, balletic movements expressed through long and slim bodies and cute personae, which I term "hypergirlish femininity."[27] As they have grown older, the group has tried a nubile femme fatale image with sassy movements and even slightly androgynous, powerful choreography. In "Catch Me If You Can" (2015), they dance in what appears to be a construction site. They wear smoky eye makeup, cargo pants, and sporty ripped tank tops with gym gloves, and later short orange jumpsuits with white stripes. Instead of a shy smile, they show a confident, seductive gaze, staring directly at the camera. The point choreography consists of a headbanging, powerful body shake, a shimmy, rapidly shifting their torsos side to side, rhythmically crossing their knees, and spinning, stepping back and forth with controlled arm gestures to a low-pitched, upbeat electronic sound.

The choreography of the schoolboy concept is as gendered as that of the schoolgirls. An iconic example is boy band SHINee's "Replay" (2008), which stages innocent-looking young boys singing a sweet and bubbly love song. They place the back of their hands upward and sharply open their forearms horizontally, while also extending and drawing a circle with one leg on the floor, like a rond de jambe, and bending the other leg, lightly tilting their hips on the standing leg. Stamping their feet, they nimbly and lightly twist their shoulders side to side, lifting the chin rhythmically. Their lithe, youthful bodies complement the sprightly, light-footed, agile choreography. "Replay" is a love song to *nuna*, a term used by a man younger than the woman he refers to. On the other hand, *oppa* is a term used by women to refer to older men, frequently as a nickname, like "sweetie" or "honey." In "Replay," SHINee places themselves as younger boys occupying a less hierarchical position, at least in terms of age.

Pretty K-pop boys are called "flower boys" (*kkot-mi-nam* in Korean) who have androgynous, polished, sophisticated, often effeminate facial features. The flower boy syndrome signifies not only a new trend in men's physical appearance but also a changing image of ideal masculinity called "soft masculinity" and even gendered hypergamy.[28] In Korea, the number of older women/younger men couples has been increasing along with the rising level of education and economic empowerment of women, who expect less traditional gender norms and embrace more youthful and attractive men.[29]

Current examples of the bubbly schoolboy or flower boy concept include BTS's "Boy with Luv" (feat. Halsey) (2019), where they are clad in pastel-pink skinny jeans and T-shirts, dancing to a lively love song. The point choreography starts with the members' frisky jumping and kicking their legs in the air. Dancing to the chorus, "Oh my my my my," they twist their front feet briskly, as in disco, jiggling and bouncing their hips, cheerfully tapping their shoulders. Their hands dexterously pat down their chests and move to their lower abdomens, rippling their upper bodies as they cavort with bright smiles. The fast-paced, effervescent point choreography highlights the vivacity of the dancers.

The Beast Idols and Bad Girls Concept
The second prevalent type of K-pop music video choreography highlights mature sexual appeal. Compared to flower boys, "beast idols" (*jim seung dol* in Korean) refers to male idols who present tall, fit, muscular bodies and tough masculinity. To enhance their masculine appeal, they draw on various elements including gangster and macho images from energetic hip hop and breakdance as well as hypersexual (heterosexual) masculinity from strip dance, sometimes tearing apart their shirts to flaunt tanned abdominal muscles or dancing around a pole on stage. Their dance style consists of powerful, arduous movements and sharp, expeditious steps with swaggering and "beastly" facial expressions. Costumes are designed to match their staged masculinity and gendered choreography, often combined with black leather jackets and a dark, rebellious fashion style. BIGBANG, MONSTA X, 2PM, BEAST, and B.A.P are some of the representative groups of this category.

Nevertheless, the flower boys and beast idols are not necessarily dichotomized. Beast idols are not afraid of performing soft and cute masculinity by wearing pink skinny jeans and eyeshadow and even cross-dressing on variety television shows, at fan club gatherings, and in concerts. BIGBANG's rapper G-Dragon, for example, is known for his versatile persona ranging from an androgynous, funky, rebellious drunken boy in "Crooked" (2013) to a classy modern artist in "Untitled" (2014), a point elaborated further below in the experimental style section.

There is an equivalent term for K-pop girl groups who are admired because they evoke a "girl crush." Unlike the innocent, pure "good girl" image, those "bad girls" present a fierce, strong, sexy, independent, trendy "badass" image and have an equal amount of female fandom, if not more. 2NE1, ITZY, BLACKPINK, Red Velvet, and f(x) are known for their ferocity and individualistic characters who empower and inspire female fans across the globe. While they also stick to the conventional plaid schoolgirl skirts with a natural makeup look, the bad girls choose abrasive stylings too, such as black leather jackets, fishnet tights, smoky eye makeup, short haircuts, sports jerseys, and Doc Martens boots. ITZY, for example, is renowned for their mischievous lyrics, sassy choreography, and trendy gender-neutral outfits, such as funky faux fur coats, sweatpants with running shoes, and sports tops with mesh sleeves. Many of the girl crush groups' performances combine hip-hop and electronic music as well as vigorous, grounded urban and street dance movements.

BLACKPINK's record-breaking "Kill This Love" (2019) epitomizes the girl crush–type choreography. It became the fastest video to reach 100 million views on YouTube in roughly two days. The video starts with grandiose drum sounds like those of a marching band and the group's signature phrase, "BLACKPINK in your area." Taking a low-angle shot, the camera shows four members standing, hands on their hips, showing all their fingers in the front, a body gesture that often signifies dominance. Because of their elbows elevated to the side and lifted chins, they appear wider. They directly look at the camera like furious warriors without a smile. Combining the direct gaze, low angle, assertive gesture, and expressive music, they look dominant and authoritative.

The point choreography is featured in a gray setting that appears to be architectural ruins. Sunlight illuminates a broken white head of what resembles a Greek statue on the floor. The wall is covered with dust and ivy, and there are fallen leaves on the floor, which signifies the passage of time. The members are clad in mostly black tops, gloves, and leather boots, or fashion garters on their thighs. Combining both classy and modern appeal, they look like female secret agents or warrior goddesses. They stand facing sideways and fearlessly gaze at the camera, pointing and reaching out one arm while folding the other in front of their chests as if about to shoot a target. With the chorus lyrics, "Let's kill this love," they swiftly lift up and then push the front arm down, undulating and rolling their upper body backward. The movement is played in slow motion, enhancing the impact of the point choreography. There is an explosion behind them, which further accentuates the sharp movements of the scene. They then playfully twist their hips, slightly leaning back, swaying their arms back and forth, grimacing in a sassy manner resembling a smirk rather than a smile. They twirl one arm above their heads defiantly, looking over their shoulder and facing front, while placing the other hand on their hip. When they face the front, their flattened hands move by their foreheads, which resonates with saluting. Thrusting and circling their pelvis rhythmically, they whirl their arms above their heads as if cheering.

The rising popularity of the girl crush concept is related to the shifting gender dynamics in Korea, including an increasing feminist awareness of the Me Too movement.[30] Gender norms directly affect the body perception through which an individual internalizes socially acceptable and "proper" gendered behavior.[31] "Manspreading" exemplifies gendered politics in daily life, and how men have been traditionally allowed to take up a larger space in a public sphere with more power. As the body and its movements are a core site of reproducing power dynamics, they can simultaneously destabilize the norms embodied.[32] Certainly, the bad girl concept choreography has a limitation, as it mostly gains its power through the script of heteronormativity. Nonetheless, when female performers take up a large space with bold and purposefully boisterous movement patterns, the dancing bodies have the potential to question the ways female bodies have been traditionally disciplined to move and appear in certain ways, and thus challenge docile femininity pervasive in society. The girl crush groups' facial expressions are another sign suggesting a possibility of liberatory femininity. Many bad girl groups showcase boastful, intense eye contact without a sweet smile in their performance. Red Velvet is known for their smileless, cold, "haughty" faces along with "uncanny" and eerie album concepts.[33] The songs "Psycho" (2019) and "Monster" (2020) are some of the examples. The latter, for instance, features a devilish and queerish duet with member Irene and Seulgi clad in classy, extravagant, gothic garments. According to *Brunch* online magazine, Red Velvet's music videos often resonate with "horror movies."[34] Irene is particularly known as "a woman who does not smile." She is often criticized for her disinterested face, as she often refuses to smile or show *aegyo*. As exemplified in cheerleading dance, a smile is a gendered movement commonly associated with emotional labor – caring, supportive, and submissive femininity to please the male spectators or partners.[35] The girl crush groups' unsmiling facial expressions and cavalier attitudes in performance can reflect changing gender norms and power dynamics in contemporary Korea. Some female idols have been criticized for reading a feminist novel, *Kim Ji Young, Born 1982*, or participating in women's rights activism.

Some female singers further challenge the heteronormative gender stereotypes. Amber Liu, a Taiwanese American K-pop singer in f(x), is best known for her androgynous appeal. On her solo album, *Shake That Brass* (2015), she grooves to cheerful rap music in a cartoonish setting that features a basketball court and colorful graffiti. She has a short haircut and wears medium-length sporty jersey pants. Her male backup dancers are clad in baseball apparel. The point choreography comprises Liu stomping her feet to the side while punching her right arm forward. Holding her arm, she waves her upper body to the left, clenching her left fist positioned on her left thigh, and recovers her head to the center in a robotic manner. Featured in the music video is Girls' Generation's Taeyeon, whose typical feminine beauty and high-pitched voice contrast with Amber's androgynous looks and low, husky voice. Similar to the fluid gender performance between flower boys and beast idols, girl groups also present a wide range of personae on stage. As Suk-Young Kim explained in an interview with *Billboard* in 2020, there is a "conceptual versatility" of K-pop idols who "try on all kinds of concepts, from sexy to cute and innocent," for better profitability and relatability to a broader audience.[36]

Such fluidity in performing different characters is often restrained by gender and age. Gender fluidity seems more common in K-pop boy groups, who more freely traverse androgynous flower boys and macho beast idols, and even cross-dress. Contrarily, girl groups seem to have less choice other than presenting dark, robust, and sexy choreography as they mature, while innocent, cute, youthful concepts are mostly reserved for younger idols. For example, TWICE and Girls' Generation gradually switched their personae over time from innocent schoolgirls to more mature, seductive women. Yet it is quite common to see boy groups who debut with a strong, seductive (mature) image no matter how young they are, like 2PM and Stray Kids. Even with school uniforms, boy groups seem to have more options. In "Boy in Luv" (2014), BTS members wear school uniforms and dance in a space that appears to be a high school classroom. They present strong and rebellious characters with rigid movements accompanied by powerful braggadocio.

Surely, boy groups are not entirely free from this rubric of growing older and therefore resorting to a sexually mature image. On their first album, *Adore U* (2015), Seventeen features a jaunty dance, wearing school uniform–like white shirts and beige pants. In "Fear" (2019), they present seductive, mature masculinity, wearing tight black suits with dark makeup. The choreography contains dramatic facial expressions. A dancer gazes deeply at the camera, crossing his hands and touching his neck. Other dancers put on dreamy facial expressions and delicate hand gestures and smell their wrists as if they are mesmerized by the seductive scent. The point choreography consists of the dancers slightly leaning back, bending and spreading their legs to the side, gently putting their hands on their upper thighs. With their off-balance leaning, they look fragile and vulnerable. They repeat loosely rolling and waving their left and then right shoulder in an erotic manner, undulating their upper body to titillate the audience while seductively gazing at the camera.

Not just school uniforms but wearing uniforms in general is a trend that never fades away. Girl's Generation's "Genie" (2010) employs a navy-uniform concept with gold tassels and white shorts that stress their elongated balletic legs and intricate steps. BTS's "Dope" (2012) features uniforms of a police officer, soldier, office worker, car racer, and doctor. Uniforms are often fetishized, as they evoke certain types of gendered power dynamics. Maid and police officer costumes reflect such gendered fetishization divided into submissiveness and authoritarianism. Uniforms in K-pop dance match the disciplinary and synchronized movement style and at the same time serve the gendered appeal and perhaps enhance the sexual fantasy of K-pop groups.

The Dance-centric Style
The dance-centric style appears in the majority of K-pop music videos. Yet some stand out with their explicitly decorative, stunning choreographies that overshadow the other narratives, characters, and visual and even sonic elements. The dance-centric style is more common in boy groups' dances, as they tend to execute more intricate, powerful, and physically demanding choreographies. This is not to say that girl groups are less trained in dance. Instead, this trend reflects a gendered aspect of K-pop choreography where girls, with the exception of a few girl crush groups, are expected to remain "hypergirlish" for the most part and thus not to feature too explicitly strong or powerful dance. Such masking with hypergirlish femininity likely serves to hide athleticism, which, in the K-pop world, is traditionally seen as male property. Hyoyeon in Girls' Generation, for example, has not been given enough opportunity to showcase her powerful dance skills due to the group's chaste stage personae. Arguably, while light, fluid, airy balletic gestures are more popular among girl groups, sharp, grounded, energetic, and rigid movements are more prevalent in boy groups.

Boy group EXO epitomizes the dance-centric style. They are known for their flawless, intricate dance routines that underline the synchronization of group dance scenes. EXO's "Love Shot" (2018), "Call Me Baby" (2015), and "Monster" (2016) all have a relatively simple storyline. With minimalistic, futuristic backgrounds and costumes, the highlight of those music videos is synchronized, masculine, and eye-catching choreographies. For example, the point choreography of "Call Me Baby" begins with jostling with rigid and meticulous punching arm movements and stamping feet, bodies swaying horizontally. They put their feet together, stand straight facing the diagonal, and place one hand below their lower abdomen, waving and thrusting their pelvis in a sexually suggestive manner. They rhythmically shove their shoulders and step to the side, lightly moving their hips back and forth with the steps, tapping erotically the edges of their shoulders with delicately wiggling hands, gazing intensely at the camera and wearing alluring smiles, as if enticing the audiences to touch their bodies.

BTS also emblematizes the spectacular dance-driven style of K-pop music videos. Their "Fake Love" (2018) and "Blood, Sweat, & Tears" (2016) present vivid, seductive, decadent aesthetics through precise and dramatic choreographies. "'ON' Kinetic Manifesto Film: Come Prima" (2020), "Not Today" (2017), and "Black Swan" (2020), featured in an actual theater space, extend the spectrum of dance even further to appear nearly as conventional modern or contemporary dance films. They consist of vigorous footsteps and robust, dynamic choreographies with an agile rotation in space, nimble and effortless jumps, spectacular turns, smooth gliding, and floor movements. Further study is needed of those examples, particularly "Black Swan," as it signals a new chapter of K-pop choreography that seamlessly integrates the Western and Asian classical and popular dance venues, aesthetics, choreographic tools, and collaborations.

The Experimental Style

The experimental style employs less common camera work and video editing techniques, often departing from conventional aesthetics. G-Dragon's "Untitled" (2014) is an evocative piano ballad without percussion or beat. The video is set against a minimalistic backdrop with a sky that changes from poetic red to dreamy blue in between sunset and sunrise. The audience sees his silhouette in a dim light where his subtle, delicate gestures, and even stillness, become a dance. His body itself becomes a dance: his fragile neck, elongated fingers, legs moving to unpredictable and spontaneous rhythms of music, the decadent and nostalgic ambience, blurry silhouette of his movement, his disciplined but fearless voice, his face still youthful yet showing the traces of time, and his vulnerable yet centered gaze fully aware of the richness of his every move. It is a dance that does not need dance-like movements. Compared to his bubbly and childish character when BIGBANG first debuted in 2006, "Untitled," cowritten and produced by G-Dragon himself, explicates a journey of an idol who has grown as an artist.

Another BIGBANG member, Taeyang, also features an experimental approach in his "Eyes, Nose, Lips" (2014). The song is his second single cowritten by himself. The camerawork takes a long sequence shot. The video starts with an extreme close-up shot of the dancer's face and neck. Throughout the song, the camera gradually zooms out to show his bare chest and, eventually, his entire body and background. Everything remains the same other than the moving camera angle. The camera is so close that the audience can even see his body's slight movement. The body itself – facial wrinkles, sweaty pores, twitching muscles around the mouth, and chest that contracts and releases according to the music's tempo and tone – becomes part of the choreography.

BTS's "Save Me" (2016) appears to be a low-budget, independent-style music video. The dancers wear loose, casual T-shirts and ripped skinny black jeans with minimum makeup. They are featured in a deserted field filtered by a gloomy, bluish chromatic tone. They dance in the wind, which accentuates their powerful, airy movements. The relatively natural looks of the dancers enhance the sense of their vulnerability and the believability of the lyrics that highlight sad and desperate feelings of love. The point choreography consists of continual light kicking, stomping feet, and swirling along with endless jumping while turning. Their hair and T-shirts fly and wave with the wind flow, accentuating the choreography's free spirit. As many dance-centric choreographies highlight a nearly perfect level of synchronization and even homogeneity, from costume choices to movements, dancers often appear too artificial, like manufactured dancing machines. While "Save Me" certainly overlaps with the dance-centric style, it is distinguishable due to its indie aesthetics with more approachable characters, costumes, and background choices. This casualness might draw fans' attention even more, because the dancers seem more relatable and affable. BTS is known for their "boy-next-door" characters, especially their cordial and playful social media presence and active communication with fans.

Lee Hyori's "Seoul" (feat. Killagramz) (2017) makes a juxtaposition between Seoul and Jeju Island. The choreography has a similar movement pattern, such as her improvisational hair flipping and chest undulations, but it appears different depending on the spatial setting where the movement is presented: the highly modernized but monotonous city of Seoul at night versus the untouched, colorful nature of Jeju on a sunny day. In Seoul, a speeding car passing by resonates with her rigid, swift turn and twist of the upper body. Contrarily, a head circle and a relaxed body wave with natural hair flip in the breeze go with Jeju Island's natural scenery. In the climax, she lies down, glides, and spirals on the grass in Jeju, wearing socks without shoes. This scene appears to highlight the connection between nature and herself by physically getting closer to the earth. ZICO's "Any Song" (2020) portrays a casual house party where he gets bored. Wearing headphones, he starts dancing when everyone falls asleep after drinking. His movement appears improvisational, quirky, and spontaneous, consisting of idiosyncratic steps and self-focused wacky, dramatic facial expressions, such as playing an air guitar in an exaggerated motion.

All these examples compose another technique that makes the singers' works appear more authentic and less manufactured. The experimental style tends to depart from the emphasis on point choreography that molds the prototype of the mainstream music videos. This experimental style can range from a highly artistic manifestation with minimalistic aesthetics to indie, amateur-looking products that possibly increase fans' feelings of familiarity, emotional intimacy, and imaginary accessibility to the artists.

The Hybrid Style: International Collaboration and Korean Folk Dance

The last category focuses on hybridity by drawing examples from international collaborations and revivals of traditional Korean themes. Many of the collaborators are notable artists in the US music industry, so the collaboration itself often carries marketability. Examples are PSY's "Hangover" (feat. Snoop Dogg) (2014), Lady Gaga and BLACKPINK's "Sour Candy" (2020), BTS's "Boy with Luv (feat. Halsey) (2019), and J-Hope's "Chicken Noodle Soup" (feat. Becky G) (2019). In an interview on *Jimmy Kimmel Live*, PSY said that he and Snoop Dogg had never met before they shot the "Hangover" music video in South Korea.[37] They communicated virtually until they shot the video in Seoul, and the filming took only eighteen hours. Such a brief physical encounter would work in this collaboration because instead of using synchronized point choreography that would need ongoing physical training, the "hangover" concept can be illustrated with choreography that consists of simple, pedestrian movements with bouncy, swaggering, and often witty facial expressions and gestures. From a karaoke venue to an amusement park, the two singers lurch and teeter in a staggering manner, showing off their unique charisma and personalities. In *Jimmy Kimmel Live*, Snoop Dogg said that he always wanted to be in a martial arts movie, and he felt like a karate star in a kingdom while filming the video in Korea. His comment seems to resonate with a stereotypical understanding of Asia as a site of orientalist imagination. A limited exposure to each other's culture and history would be similar to that of PSY. Although he attended college in the United States, he did not necessarily spend years learning the collaborator's works and his cultural roots face to face.

While Snoop Dogg's charismatic presence is more than enough to draw the audience, his movements often seem alienated in the highly localized sites that directly generate specific, daily life movement patterns. Many of the scenes in "Hangover" are local places with specific cultural codes and customs of middle-aged Korean men, such as a men's hair salon, karaoke venue, spa, or drinking place. Some of Snoop Dogg's movements appear less natural and often awkward compared to PSY's, for example, in the scenes where they dance with and caress women in the karaoke bar or when they open a bottle of soju in a grilled shellfish bar. There are many different choreographed routines of opening a soju bottle among Koreans, which is considered a social skill to amuse people at a social gathering. Such site- and culture-specific actions should be familiar to PSY, who can easily embody the subtle nuances, attitudes, and even mood in it, which is not necessarily the case for Snoop Dogg. "Hangover" sheds light on how accessible an international collaboration can be in the digital era and, at the same time, how there is a danger of superficial understanding and presentation of a culture under the name of cultural exchange, without an embodied understanding of it.

The transnational circulation of and collaboration in K-pop illuminate issues of Koreanness. Scholars have often pointed out the "absence of Koreanness" in K-pop due to its hybridity, although hybridity itself is a characteristic of K-pop.[38] K-pop artists have hired and collaborated with international songwriters, producers, and choreographers. The ethnic and racial identities and citizenships of K-pop idols have become more diverse, including idols from the United States, Canada, New Zealand, Thailand, Taiwan, Hong Kong, China, Japan, Australia, and more. As Koichi Iwabuchi argued, cultural products can be de-ethnicized in the era of globalization, made "culturally odorless."[39] Global conglomerates Samsung, Sony, and Apple exemplify such transnationality. K-pop, too, as a manufactured performance, often traverses geographical, ethnic, and cultural boundaries.

As much as K-pop becomes hybridized through the increasing participation of foreign artists, it equally draws from traditional Korean aesthetics. BLACKPINK's "How You Like That" (2020) features a modernized version of *hanbok*, a traditional Korean garment. Their costumes have vivid colors and shorter open tops compared to the longer, traditional top with blouse closed with a ribbon. When BLACKPINK presented "How You Like That" on *The Tonight Show Starring Jimmy Fallon* on June 26, 2020, they had more than 210,000 views when the show was aired. The website of Danha, the clothing company that designed the *hanbok* BLACKPINK wore, had nearly 4,000 daily customers hailing from the United States, Asia, and Europe. This mischievous, modernized version matches BLACKPINK's luscious, feisty dance movements and mystical but cheerful onstage personae quite well. In "Refresh" (2020), Zico and Kang Daniel also wear modernized *hanbok* and dance in a space featuring traditional Korean architecture. Various dance styles are presented, including b-boying, breakdancing, and folk dance. Interestingly, the video was created in collaboration with and sponsored by Pepsi, and there are a couple of scenes where performers drink Pepsi after their dance.

In "IDOL" (2018), BTS dances against a computer-generated image of a yellow pavilion that resembles traditional Korean architecture, wearing modernized *hanbok* with black silky fabric embellished with gold. The music video includes visual images that reference traditional Korean folk painting and folk dance such as the fan dance (*buchaechum*) and lion mask dance (*sajachum*). Created by Korean folk dance master Kim Baek-bong in 1954, *bu-chae-chum* is a neoclassical fan dance inspired by shamanic ritual and folk dance as well as traditional court dance of the Joseon dynasty. Originating from ancient shamanic rituals, *sajachum* is a mask dance where performers are dressed as animals like lions and imitate their movements. BTS's performance of "IDOL" at the 2018 Melon Music Awards (MMA) – a major annual music awards show in South Korea – revived traditional elements on a live stage featuring lion puppets, a mask dance, and traditional instruments. The group wore flowery turquoise traditional garments with a modern touch.

Not only *hanbok* has become more visible in K-pop. BTS's Suga (or Agust D) recently released his solo song, "Daechwita" (2020), which adapts traditional Korean themes for the song's title, characters, costumes, background setting, and musical instruments. In the music video, he played two roles: a violent king and a boy who rebels against the king. "Daechwita" refers to the traditional Korean wind and percussion music reserved for a palace parade. The music video was filmed in Yongin Daejanggeum Park in Gyeonggi province, an outdoor film set and tourist attraction. The park is known for its traditional palaces built and commonly used for shooting Korean historical television dramas set in the Joseon dynasty. Suga wears stylish black *hanbok* with funky, dark makeup that shows a scar on his face. The traditional scene later overlaps with a contemporary one featuring typical hip-hop "gangster" imagery, wherein Suga wears a ripped green cargo jacket with silver accessories as he raps while surrounded by a group of men sitting on a car.

The revival of traditional Korean culture further fuels K-pop fans' interest. At MMA, Jimin performed a short solo of *buchaechum* (a neoclassical Korean fan dance), which reflects what I have theorized BTS as "Korean folk dancers."[40] BTS's Jimin attended the Busan High School of Arts and later graduated from the Korean Arts High School, where he learned both Western and Korean classical dances and popular dance. Although women commonly perform *buchaechum*, Jimin's performance was composed of all-male dancers. It incorporated urban and pop dance, such as breakdance and hybrid aesthetics, with vibrant multimedia as a backdrop. The Korean Cultural Center in China posted Jimin's fan dance video on Sina Weibo, the largest social media platform in China. Hashtagged as "#DanceKingJimin" by his fans, his video created overwhelming hype on social media. The fan dance video ranked second in the global real-time trend on Twitter. The transnational and real-time response opens a discussion on searching for a "new authenticity" in the global tourism industry reflected in the modernized traditions in K-pop.[41] Further, this example signifies the changing dynamics in dance reception and circulation in the era of social media without geographical and cultural barriers, where ordinary fans' voices and participation matter more than ever.

Conclusion

Discussing prominent types of K-pop music video choreography and its extension to concert stages and social media provides a glimpse of the transnational K-pop dance phenomenon. Currently, K-pop is the leading force of *Hallyu* (the international spread of Korean popular culture), and is nearly a national (dance) project sponsored by conglomerate agencies and the government. Examples are KCON, an annual Korean culture convention and K-pop concert across the world organized by CJ E&M, and the international K-pop Cover Dance Festival, an annual amateur dance competition hosted by the *Seoul Shinmun Daily* and sponsored by Korean Cultural Centers. From creation to distribution, K-pop dance is not a mere hobby or a short-lived trend but rather a sustained development of a particular dance style. While virtual communication facilitates international collaboration, it could also reinforce a superficial understanding of each culture. Digitization of dance in distribution, reception, and consumption opens up room for discussing the ethics of cultural exchange in neoliberal capitalism where culture can be cut and pasted, like a collage, without in-depth, embodied learning rooted in a local cultural context. Further studies are needed on facets of K-pop choreography such as copyright issues, creation process and structure, and dance education in the digital era. Moreover, given the rapidly emerging dance fandom, an in-depth discussion of ethics in intercultural adaptation regarding K-pop fan-dancers will further advance and illuminate social dance of the global youth, Korean pop culture, and popular dance studies.

Further Reading

Käng, Dredge Byung'chu. "Idols of Development: Transnational Transgender Performance in Thai K-Pop Cover Dance." *Transgender Studies Quarterly* 1/4 (2014): 559–571.

Khiun, Liew Kai. "K-Pop Dance Trackers and Cover Dancers." In Youna Kim (ed.), *The Korean Wave: Korean Media Go Global*, 165–182. Abingdon: Routledge, 2013.

Kim, Malborg. *Korean Dance*. Seoul: Ewha Womans University Press, 2005.

Kim, Suk-Young. *K-Pop Live: Fans, Idols, and Multimedia Performance*. Redwood City, CA: Stanford University Press, 2018.

Koeltzsch, Grit Kirstin. "Korean Popular Culture in Argentina." In *Oxford Research Encyclopedia of Latin American History* (2019). https://doi.org/10.1093/acrefore/9780199366439.013.766.

Oh, Chuyun. "From Seoul to Copenhagen: Migrating K-Pop Cover Dance and Performing Diasporic Youth in Social Media." *Dance Research Journal* 52/1 (2020): 20–32. https://doi.org/10.1017/S0149767720000030.

"Identity Passing in Intercultural Performance of K-Pop Cover Dance." *Journal of Intercultural Communication Research* 49/5 (2020): 472–483. https://doi.org/10.1080/17475759.2020.1803103.

K-Pop Dance: Fandoming Yourself on Social Media. New York: Routledge, 2022.

"Queering Spectatorship in K-Pop: The Androgynous Male Dancing Body and Western Female Fandom." *The Journal of Fandom Studies* 3/1 (2015): 59–78.

Oh, Chuyun, and David C. Oh. "Unmasking Queerness: Blurring and Solidifying Queer Lines through K-Pop Cross-Dressing." *Journal of Popular Culture* 50/1 (2017): 9–29.

Shin, Sang Mi. *Ingan-eun oe chum-eul chu-neun-ga. Inryu-ui chum munhwa ko-deu ilggi*. Seoul: Ewha Womans University Press, 2013.

Van Zile, Judy. *Perspectives on Korean Dance*. Middletown, CT: Wesleyan University Press, 2001.

Notes

1 Jeff Yang, "No, Simon Cowell, It's Not 'Time for UK-Pop,'" CNN, November 28, 2019, https://edition.cnn.com/2019/11/27/opinions/k-pop-groups-are-changing-music-and-world-yang/index.html.

2 Ann Dils and Ann Cooper Albright (eds.), *Moving History/Dancing Cultures: A Dance History Reader* (Middletown, CT: Wesleyan University Press, 2001).

3 Sherril Dodds and Colleen Hooper, "Faces, Close-Ups and Choreography: A Deleuzian Critique of *So You Think You Can Dance*," *The International Journal of Screendance* 4 (2014): 93–113.

4 Chuyun Oh, *K-Pop Dance: Fandoming Yourself on Social Media* (London: Routledge, 2022), 29.

5 Oh, *K-Pop Dance*, 34.

6 Julie Malnig (ed.), *Ballroom, Boogie, Shimmy Sham, Shake: A Social and Popular Dance Reader* (Champaign: University of Illinois Press, 2009), 5.

7 Malnig, *Ballroom, Boogie, Shimmy Sham, Shake*, 5.

8 Dodds and Hooper, "Faces, Close-Ups and Choreography," 402.

9 Melissa Blanco Borelli (ed.), *The Oxford Handbook of Dance and the Popular Screen* (Oxford: Oxford University Press, 2014), 2.

10 Sherril Dodds, *Dance on Screen: Genres and Media from Hollywood to Experimental Art* (New York: Springer, 2001).

11 Oh, *K-Pop Dance*, 29; Chuyun Oh, "Identity Passing in Intercultural Performance of K-Pop Cover Dance," *Journal of Intercultural Communication Research* 49/5 (2020): 472–483; "From Seoul to Copenhagen: Migrating K-Pop Cover Dance and Performing Diasporic Youth in Social Media," *Dance Research Journal* 52/1 (2020): 20–32.

12 Sun Jung, "K-Pop, Indonesian Fandom, and Social Media," *Transformative Works and Cultures* 8 (2011), https://doi.org/10.3983/twc.2011.0289.

13 Sherril Dodds, "Values in Motion: Reflections on Popular Screen Dance," in Melissa Blanco Borelli (ed.), *The Oxford Handbook of Dance and the Popular Screen* (Oxford: Oxford University Press, 2014), 445–454.

14 Douglas Rosenberg (ed.), *The Oxford Handbook of Screendance Studies* (Oxford: Oxford University Press, 2016).

15 Dodds, "Values in Motion," 448.

16 Oh, *K-Pop Dance*, 34.

17 Mark Franko, "Editor's Note: Taking (a) Part: Investigations into Participation," *Dance Research Journal* 45/3 (2013): 1.

18 Franko, "Editor's Note."

19 San San Kwan, "When Is Contemporary Dance?," *Dance Research Journal* 49/3 (2017): 39.

20 Susan Foster (ed.), *Worlding Dance* (New York: Springer, 2009); Joann Kealiinohomoku, "An Anthropologist Looks at Ballet as a Form of Ethnic Dance," *Impulse* 20 (1970): 24–33.

21 Kwan, "When Is Contemporary Dance?," 45. For Orientalism in the Western concert dance, also see Yutian Wong, *Choreographing Asian America* (Middletown, CT: Wesleyan University Press, 2010).

22 Wong, *Choreographing Asian America*.

23 Wong, *Choreographing Asian America*.

24 Priya Srinivasan, "The Bodies beneath the Smoke, or What's behind the Cigarette Poster: Unearthing Kinesthetic Connections in American Modern Dance," *Discourses in Dance* 4/1 (2007): 7–48; Vincent Warren, "Yearning for the Spiritual Ideal: The Influence of India on Western Dance 1626–2003," *Dance Research Journal* 38/1–2 (2006): 97–114; Wong, *Choreographing Asian America*.

25 Judith Butler, "Performative Acts and Gender Constitution: An Essay in Phenomenology and Feminist Theory," *Theatre Journal* 40/4 (1988): 519.

26 Iris Marion Young, "Throwing like a Girl: A Phenomenology of Feminine Body Comportment Motility and Spatiality," *Human Studies* 3/1 (1980): 137–156.

27 Chuyun Oh, "The Politics of the Dancing Body: Racialized and Gendered Femininity in Korean Pop," in Yasue Kuwahara (ed.), *The Korean Wave: Korean Popular Culture in Global Context* (New York: Palgrave Macmillan, 2014), 56.

28 Sun Jung, *Korean Masculinities and Transcultural Consumption: Yonsama, Rain, Oldboy, K-Pop Idols* (Hong Kong: Hong Kong University Press, 2010), 39; Jeehyun Jenny Lee, Rachel Kar Yee Lee, and Ji Hoon Park, "Unpacking K-Pop in America: The Subversive Potential of Male K-Pop Idols' Soft Masculinity," *International Journal of Communication* 14 (2020): 5904.

29 Sun-hwa Dong, "Younger Man, Older Woman Marriage – A Rising Tie-Up in Korea," *Korea Times*, November 20, 2018, www.koreatimes.co.kr/www/culture/2020/08/703_258991.html.

30 Jieun Lee and Hyangsoon Yi, "Ssen-Unni in K-Pop: The Makings of 'Strong Sisters' in South Korea," *Korea Journal* 60/1 (2020): 17–39.

31 Ursula Lutzky and Robert Lawson, "Gender Politics and Discourses of #mansplaining, #manspreading, and #manterruption on Twitter," *Social Media + Society* 5/3 (2019): 10.

32 Ann Cooper Albright, *Choreographing Difference: The Body and Identity in Contemporary Dance* (Middletown, CT: Wesleyan University Press, 2010), xxiii.

33 Melon, "Red Velvet 의 알 수 없는 호러 국내 뮤식 트렌드" (Red Velvet's unknowable horror domestic music trend), July 24, 2020, https://brunch.co.kr/@brunchmelon/218.

34 Melon, "Red Velvet."

35 Laura Grindstaff and Emily West, "Cheerleading and the Gendered Politics of Sport," *Social Problems* 53/4 (2006): 500–518.

36 Caitlin Kelley, "How 'Girl Crush' Hooked Female Fans and Grappled with Feminism as K-Pop Went Global," *Billboard*, December 27, 2018, www.billboard.com/articles/events/year-in-music-2018/8491604/girl-crush-k-pop-feminism-2018.

37 *Jimmy Kimmel Live*, "PSY & Snoop on Working Together," YouTube, June 8, 2014, www.youtube.com/watch?v=BhQxTr_ylBg.

38 Kyong Yoon, "Postcolonial Production and Consumption of Global K-Pop," in Dal Yong Jin and Tae-Jin Yoon (eds.), *The Korean Wave: Retrospect and Prospect* (Lanham, MD: Rowman & Littlefield, 2017), 3.

39 Koichi Iwabuchi, *Recentering Globalization: Popular Culture and Japanese Transnationalism* (Durham, NC: Duke University Press, 2002), 28.

40 Oh, *K-Pop Dance*, 93–95.

41 Bruce Prideaux, Dallen Timothy, and Kaye Chon (eds.), *Cultural and Heritage Tourism in Asia and the Pacific* (New York: Routledge, 2008), 7.

6 Embodying K-Pop Hits through Cover Dance Practices

CEDARBOUGH T. SAEJI

Before COVID-19, in large urban centers around the world, it was not unusual to spot a group of dancers re-creating the choreography showcased in live performances and music videos of K-pop. This eye-catching fan practice demonstrates the popularity of K-pop to the public who encounter dancers inside and outside shopping centers, in school playgrounds, in parking lots, and in public parks. Why is dance such a large part of K-pop, and of fan engagement with the music? What has motivated the participants? Where did the dance emphasis in international K-pop come from?

Live performances and music videos of K-pop are visually compelling in large part because of an emphasis on precise synchronized dance. Dance has become so essential to the performance of K-pop that certain groups and solo performers perform dance live while lip-synching to the music, in order to please the audience with perfect choreography unmarred by breathy vocal delivery.[1] This emphasis on dance is not new. In the *gogo* clubs of the 1970s and the nightclubs of the 1980s and onward, people listened to live music while dancing. Koreans also foregrounded dance in the way they spoke about pop music. From the late 1980s, before terms like *keipap* (K-pop) and *aidolpap* (idol pop), Koreans commonly divided popular music into two main types: *balladeu* (slow songs of love and heartbreak) and *daenseu eumak* (songs with a strong beat meant to dance to).[2] By the late 1980s, it was common for top artists to include a dance company performing behind them when they sang on Korean live television shows. Some singers participated in the dancing, like the undeniable darling of the time period, Wanseon Kim. In their 1992 debut, Seo Taiji and Boys, widely lauded as the first K-pop group,[3] incorporated choreographed hip hop–influenced dance moves into their performances, and such moves have since become the industry standard. As the years have passed, the dances performed by K-pop groups have become more prominent, and their precision, speed, and difficulty have increased.

For a country of 51 million, Korea has a surprisingly large amount of dance-focused activity, including societies to study dance, dance journals, university dance departments, dance performances, and festivals. International ballet companies have been recruiting Korean ballerinas for decades, and modern dance companies from Korea travel the world. Perhaps most important for elevating the quality of K-pop dance, however, was the explosion of hip-hop dance, or b-boy dance, that swept Korea in the early 2000s. Many Korean dance teams have won prestigious international dance competitions, including Gamblerz Crew, T.I.P. Crew, Rivers Crew, Jinjo Crew, and Morning of Owl. Individual Korean b-boys have also won top awards on the international competitive circuit. At the same time that K-pop has grown in Korea, a new era of dancers and dance-related businesses has emerged. The infamous after-school cram schools called *hagwon* now include studios teaching dance. Many crews and individual dancers run such dance studios, appear in advertisements, perform, and are contracted to develop choreography for K-pop stars.[4] Some of the more financially flush Korean *gihoeksa* (entertainment agencies) also contract with foreign choreographers to bring in new ideas.

All of this – the strong dance culture in Korea, the rise of Korean b-boys, and the incorporation of foreign choreographers – has shaped the type of dance shown in K-pop music videos and performances. How, then, did the dances of K-pop idol stars come to be transferred onto the bodies of K-pop audiences around the world? K-pop has a demonstrated ability to forge an affective transnational community; its hyper-emphasis on beauty, fashion, and self-presentation has made it ideal for sharing with large and diverse communities through visually rich social media platforms, and K-pop cover dance in particular allows participants to experiment with gender expression. Although passive, private fandom exists; participation through sharing content and reproducing the music is at the core of music fandom. Music videos are shared because of their visual elements – superior production quality, fabulous choreography, beautiful stars, and trending fashions. While performing the songs may be difficult because only a small population of non-Koreans possess the necessary language skills, international fan audiences often dance along. Although cover dance practices originated years earlier, PSY's "Gangnam Style" was particularly important in demonstrating to the world how much fun dancing along could be. With its relatively simple moves, it also convinced many that dance training was not a requirement for participation in the world of K-pop. Cover dance is a deeper engagement than simply listening to the music, and this vibrant participatory culture also plays a role in exposing new audiences to K-pop, as dancers practice in public spaces; perform at school talent shows, Korea-related events, and dance contests; and upload videos of their efforts.

This chapter provides an overview of the cover dance phenomenon, answering the following questions: What is cover dance, and who are the dancers? Why do they dance? What benefits do they find in cover dance?

Do they want to be stars? Cover dance is a confluence of dance practice, identity practice, and fan practice. As dance, it serves as a form of artistic expression, exercise, and self-care; as an identity practice, it allows dancers to embody something new – making room for play with gender and sexuality and even dreams of stardom. As a fan practice, it provides a way to come together with other fans to bond around beloved stars. Because cover dance can fulfill so many purposes, participation is robust and enthusiastic. Since 2010 – when I uploaded an online survey and conducted follow-up email interviews on K-pop dance – I have watched countless videos uploaded to YouTube and actively followed cover dance teams and solo dancers, some of whom are no longer active. I have attended classes on K-pop dance, learned K-pop choreography myself, and judged a cover dance competition on behalf of the Korean Consulate in Vancouver in 2017. In this chapter, observations from those experiences are supplemented by targeted interviews with cover dance contestants and over three dozen interviews with cover dancers conducted in person or via email between 2015 and 2021. Interviewees are identified by first name only or by a pseudonym, according to their preference.

What Is Cover Dance and Who Are the Dancers?

K-pop cover dance involves dancing to the infectious beats of popular K-pop songs, but beyond that, the variation is considerable – there is neither a right nor a wrong way to "do" cover dance. It can be either a faithful re-creation or a simplification (frequently), an improvement (arguably), or a reimagination of the official choreography. The context also varies: Cover dancers may dance alone, in a class (for fun, for exercise, with or without dreams of stardom), or as members of a club (open to members of the same school or community). The dancing may be observed in the form of a live performance or in a video made for upload. If a video is recorded, it can be done with advanced editing, lighting, and costuming or have minimal or no special effects; it may even be recorded as a single take. The participants can come from any ethnic or national background. Although the relatively recent popularity of K-pop fandom and the athletic moves mean that most cover dancers are relatively young, some are older. Dancers may have a decade of dance training encompassing ballet, modern, hip hop, tap, or a wide variety of other styles, or they may never have danced before.

Previous publications on K-pop cover dance address specific groups of cover dancers. Kai Khiun Liew (2013) focuses on the live rehearsals and performances of cover dancers in Singapore; Dredge Byung'chu Kang

(2018, 2014) examines cover dance in Thai subcultures; Chuyun Oh (2020) looks at YouTube uploads by cover dancers in Denmark; Sang-yeon Sung addresses K-pop participatory fan activities, such as cover dance, in Europe (2013); and I examined the participants in a government-sponsored contest in Korea (2020). Such contexts are highly visible, as dancers may be observed by nonparticipants in outdoor public spaces, on YouTube, and on television. But cover dance is not always executed to be viewed by others. For some, cover dance is an experience of doing, not being seen to do. Meanwhile, medical researchers in Korea have investigated the therapeutic effect of cover dance participation on troubled youth (Seo et al. 2015), and Hyeonju Im published a paper for the World Taekwondo Headquarters on combining K-pop cover dance and taekwondo in physical education classrooms (2019). In contrast to these more focused works, this chapter broadly characterizes and situates cover dance as an intercultural global participatory fan activity.

Most cover dancers are K-pop fans, but not all of them are. Some are interested in group dancing, friendship, or exercise – and they fall into K-pop fandom through exposure to the music via dance practice. Even if a cover dancer only dances, without recording and uploading, they learn, through embodying the same moves as the K-pop performers, to understand the art they see in a performance or music video on a deeper level. Apollo, an American university student, was introduced to K-pop by a friend. "I then went home and immediately searched back up the videos, and then YouTube decided to recommend me a TON of K-pop. After crying from these beautiful videos, I saw a random dance play video and discovered that fans dance, too. I was so excited [that] I immediately tried to dance myself."[5] Anyone who can watch a music video can begin to learn the dance moves, particularly with the help of tutorial videos, or by slowing the playback (a browser extension called MirrorTube allows users to mirror their screen and increase the speed of play 5 percent at a time). Cover dance does not have the same mystique or gatekeeping that surrounds many other dance forms. Jennifer, a working professional software developer, reminded me that idols are known to practice for many hours per day over several years before debuting: "The belief is that if you dedicate enough time and effort, you'll become good at something, such as dancing."[6] For Jennifer this meant that she, too, could eventually become a good dancer if she put in the time. For her, the idea that it was about effort, not natural talent, was liberating.

Table 6.1 shows some figures related to the production and popularity of fifteen cover dance YouTube channels that I have been tracking. All have a significant number of videos – enough output to be analytically interesting. The YouTube channels were created between 2008 (Sandy &

Table 6.1 *Examples of well-known cover groups (as of November 25, 2020)*

Cover group (country), date YouTube account opened	Subscribers	Total videos	Most viewed video	View count
Awesome Haeun (Korea), July 2014	4.95 million	435	2018 Melon Awards Best Dance Nominees	50.7 million
B-Wild (Vietnam), January 2017	688,000	218	BTS, "Boy with Luv"	8.5 million
East2West (Canada), November 2010	1.56 million	850	BTS, "Fake Love"	9.2 million
Haru Dance (USA), March 2012	876,000	316	BLACKPINK, "Forever Young"	6.8 million
Hive Dance Crew (France), August 2016	483,000	77	Momoland, "Boom Boom"	1.8 million
K-Boy Team (Thailand), May 2017	864,000	58	Momoland, "Boom Boom"	0.94 million
K-Tigers (Korea), December 2011	1.39 million	409	BTS, "Blood, Sweat, and Tears"	15 million
Kaotsun's Cover Dance Crew (KCDC) (Australia), January 2012	145,000	447	TWICE, "What Is Love?"	7.2 million
Kueendom & Kingsman (Malaysia), January 2012	511,000	157	GD x Taeyang, "Good Boy"	3.9 million
Risin' Crew (France), January 2015	474,000	281	BTS, "Go Go"	8.1 million
Sandy & Mandy (Taiwan), July 2008	1.25 million	231	Momoland, "Boom Boom"	5.1 million
St 319 Entertainment (Vietnam), January 2011	1.63 million	212	Aimee x B Ray, "Anh nha o dao the"*	110 million
Trainees Company (Venezuela), September 2013	39.2000	137	BTS, "On"	0.31 million
Waveya (Korea), January 2011	3.72 m	661	PSY, "Gangnam Style"	177 million
Yours Truly (Canada), September 2013	105 k	1,543	BTS, "Mic Drop"	2.3 million

* Original song, not a cover.

Mandy) and 2017 (B-Wild from Vietnam and K-Boy from Thailand). Each channel stands out – these are dominant cover groups in terms of geographic region, international contests, and channel popularity (by view count and by subscriber count). Interviewees in this chapter are associated with or discussing many of these channels. The channels range from having nearly five million subscribers (Awesome Haeun) to only 39,200 in the case of Trainees Company from Venezuela. K-Boy from Thailand has the fewest uploads – only 58 – while Yours Truly from Canada has the most, with over 1,500 videos on YouTube. Popular covers elicit a significant number of views, with popular channels able to secure viewing numbers comparable to original song releases by some idol groups. In comparison I offer the view count on four idol K-pop music videos released in November and December 2018.[7] EXO, a top K-pop group, has had 352 million views for "Love Shot." GOT7, a well-known K-pop group, released a mellow holiday ballad, "Miracle," that has had 40 million views. UP10TION has had 3.2 million views on "Blue Rose," and Lovelyz, who debuted in 2014, has had 3.5 million views with "Chaja gaseyo" from their fifth EP. Eleven of the fifteen YouTube channels I am tracking have at least one video with more views than the songs by UP10TION and Lovelyz, and three even had more than the track by GOT7. One of the highly successful channels is East2West, Montreal's premier cover group. It was founded by three friends who were part of a school club in 2009, just at the start of *Hallyu* (the international spread of Korean popular culture) popularity in Montreal. After graduating, they wanted to continue dancing, so they founded a group that evolved and grew, originally concentrating on live performance. Eventually they decided to make a YouTube channel and upload covers to share dancing with more people.

Why Do They Dance?

The formation of communities through fandom is not new or unique to K-pop.[8] Within K-pop, however, fandom cover dance provides an offline immersive experience that builds particularly strong community bonds. Consider the stories of Liliane, Miska, and Stephanie. Liliane has been a K-pop fan since 2006. She started dance classes while in high school in Taiwan and later enrolled in a K-pop dance class. When she entered university in Vancouver, Canada, she became active with a campus dance club, K-Wave, and danced with them for four years. Liliane explained the commitment, outlining how she would go to class all week, spend time with family on Saturday, wake up early on Sunday and go to church, then head directly to campus to practice for three hours. "It is something I like doing, but you have to invest time and effort. It was very mentally tiring on top of schoolwork."[9] As a member of K-Wave and a club executive, she participated regularly, week after week; there was no off season.

After graduation she joined a local club, Black Core, and this allowed her to continue to enjoy cover dance as an exercise activity with friends, but without the obligation to be part of every production. Instead, she could step in whenever there was a perception that her strengths matched a planned cover. Liliane explained, "K-Wave was very performance based, but with Black Core it is about getting together to film."[10] Like Liliane, many dancers participate in cover dancing casually, coming together with a group of other people who enjoy K-pop. In a follow-up email, Liliane articulated the type of friendship that drew her first to K-Wave and then to Black Core:

> The sort of connection you build with your fellow dancers (not like a group
> that started as a group of close friends) is kind of different from the type of
> connections you build with your close non-dancer friends. It almost feels like

you're coworkers in the sense that you have the same type of "expertise" or "professional jargon" when you communicate with each other and know what you're talking about with the whole insider type of talk.[11]

For her, leaving K-Wave meant losing this specific type of friendship that she had enjoyed for half a decade. Dancing with Black Core, then, was a natural next step. Many people stop dancing when they leave a school with a cover dance team not because they no longer enjoy K-pop or dancing, but because they are no longer interested in dancing without their community.

In early 2019, I interviewed Miska, a member of the Canadian group East2West, after she had returned from a performance at the finals of the Changwon K-Pop Cover Dance Festival. Miska had started listening to K-pop in 2008; a few years later, a friend took her to an East2West performance: "While they were performing, they were so united. I thought, 'Wow, this is so amazing, I'd love to be part of this,' and then after the show they announced when auditions were going to be held and I tried out and made it in."[12] In other words, it was the perception of community that attracted her to join the group, which had had a profound impact on her life. In 2019 she was already in her fifth year dancing with East2West, during which time the group had grown from fewer than 100,000 to more than a million YouTube subscribers. Miska felt proud of her role in this growth – to me, it seemed that the group and Miska had grown to maturity together. East2West has performed at Toronto and New York K-CON events and opened for two K-pop soloists: Hyuna in Montreal and Heize in Toronto. (After my interview with Miska, East2West was also invited to K-CON in Los Angeles.) Despite their success, and similar to other groups, East2West has no dedicated practice space and mostly relies on outdoor spaces for practice.

East2West illustrates the difficulty in converting cover dance to a career, or even having cover dancing support itself. Despite their impressive number of followers, East2West was to some degree funded by the members. They could earn more money if they uploaded videos that were not covers: Since covers use official audio, these videos are automatically monetized to the benefit of the idol artists. Their performance opportunities have not been a source of money either. When they went to K-CON in New York in 2017, they paid for their own transportation and lodging, receiving passes and tickets to some idol concerts in return; Miska wondered if a smaller group might have received more from K-CON. They have made some branded gear that they sell online and at events, and sometimes a video is sponsored by a company, such as the IZ*ONE "Violeta" cover.[13] After winning more than 1 million subscribers, they quit performing for free, but the funds they receive are used mainly to rent studio space to practice for shows.

Although Miska has no particular drive toward stardom, East2West has served her life in other ways. She credited East2West with helping her choose her major (communications) and giving her practical work experience (as part of the company's management team). She has her own YouTube channel and is active on other media (such as TikTok and Instagram). From her content, it is clear that cover dance has been part of her journey not just as a dancer but as a media creator who is increasingly comfortable in front of the camera. It has also brought her community – Miska described East2West's core values as those "of a family, a family that has a strong bond, and that makes us different than other groups and made us what we are today – relying on each other without external support."[14] East2West's performance at the K-Pop World Festival meant a free trip to Korea. A month after we talked, Miska began a semester as an exchange student at Kyunghee University in Seoul.

Many participants experience cover dance as a place of personal liberation. The dance scholar Chuyun Oh applied Edward W. Soja's idea of "thirdspace" to Danish women who used their cover dance practice to find a place where they felt liberated and could become themselves.[15] In many of my interviews, I heard echoes of this. K-pop cover dance seems to create an egalitarian space where dancers can come together and share their love of K-pop and of dance. Many live in regions where K-pop fandom may draw negative attention from classmates and coworkers. Through time spent practicing K-pop choreography with other fans, these dancers can find belonging and appreciation of shared interests that they otherwise might only have experienced online. Seeking connection and togetherness, they are finding it in Korean music and its associated fan culture. Stephanie, a cover dancer from Vancouver, explained what it was like to meet other friends who liked K-pop and join a cover dance group:

> This was possibly the first time I had felt like I found friends who had the same interests as me. I was able to talk about the things I was interested in with people that actually knew what I was talking about. In my opinion, the strongest thing about the cover dance community is that it's where people are able to express who they are and what they love.[16]

The K-pop fan communities in disparate locations around the globe are strengthened through active engagement with the music. As Liliane explained it:

> It's a very team-based activity. It becomes like a team sport, [with a] sense of team work. If I had to do solo covers I wouldn't enjoy it half as much.
> I would rather perform with multiple people than try to make my own name and perform on my own. We all want to make it look good.[17]

Figure 6.1 Miska (standing) with East2West performing BTS's "Not Today." The East2West cover has had more than 6 million views since March 2017. Still from www.youtube.com/watch?v=xu9rd7NsRmU (accessed November 25, 2020).

When groups come together to dance, they also support each other in other ways. In North America, many K-pop cover groups in cities like Vancouver with a large Asian population are the children of Asian immigrants or are immigrants themselves. K-pop provides them an alternative vision for their lives and support to resist a family-approved path. Stephanie, who recently returned from two post-university years in Korea, explained that for her, K-pop demonstrated that Asians could "be more than just doctors, lawyers, engineers, or whatever."[18] She remembered being nine and pivoting from saying that she would become a dentist to planning to become a dancer like BoA or TVXQ. In a follow-up email, Miska (see Figure 6.1) told me that cover dance "seems more welcoming because the idols that we 'copy' and that we look up to are Koreans, people of Asian descent, people who look like us. It's the Asian representativity that made us believe that we can do it too: be cool, be cute or be sexy!"[19] She remarked, "There's just a feeling of pure joy finding a place where you belong with a group of people who love and support you for who you are."[20] It is this intense feeling of community that has kept all three women involved in K-pop cover dance.

What Benefits Are Found in Cover Dance?

Sam from Venezuela is a fan of K-pop and a promoter of Korea-related activities, including cover dance, in Latin America. In his words,

> Most K-pop fans in our region come from middle-low to low income backgrounds, where multiple hardships are part of their everyday life. In such a scenario, [the] internet becomes their first source of entertaining; because

> K-pop is a digital phenomenon it's not rare that they encounter it sooner or later, through a video, meme, etc. K-pop aesthetic does a beautiful contrast with their daily life surroundings, while the diversity of idol masculinities becomes a point of empathy for LGBTQ+ males who feel somewhere in the world other men are living their masculinity the way we want to live it.[21]

Sam was not the only interviewee to mention both the inspiring beauty of the K-pop product and the space held within K-pop for fans to *perceive* gender expressions that might not be possible in their own country. On the one hand, K-pop cover dance, as a dance practice, is becoming more socially acceptable. From the perspective of Aydan, a young woman from the Brazilian cover group Opulence, men cover K-pop because the popular performers are also men. She noted that many choose to cover songs with a more "masculine" or "bad boy" concept. She also attributed male participation to simple popularity: "K-pop is way more popular nowadays and manages to get the attention of all sorts of people."[22] Lola, another Opulence member, remarked that the sexuality of men "isn't put on trial at all times" in K-pop cover dance, in contrast to ballet.[23] Fans may use the heteronormativity enacted by the male idols within an industry and society that creates a strong bifurcation between male and female as permission to engage in dance and a foil against any local implications that dance is not appropriate for men. In fact, K-pop cover dance sees substantial participation by men, and some teams are made up only of men.

Although a few outliers in the industry (such as Aquinas, Mrshll, and Holland) have proclaimed they are not heterosexual, the vast majority of K-pop idols maintain the cis-gender heterosexual norm, while fans celebrate gender and sexual inclusion. Some international viewers fixate on the relative freedom in gender expressions on stage, declaring K-pop queer-friendly. Anthropologist Dredge Byung'chu Kang has tracked how the LGBTQ+ population has long embraced K-pop cover dance practices in Thailand, where it is a social activity most commonly enjoyed in "gay dance clubs throughout Bangkok where patrons join in when their favorite K-pop songs are played."[24] In Korean gay clubs, there is a 2 a.m. K-pop dance break, where approximately five K-pop songs are played and the clubgoers perform the choreography from the videos. Stars also participate in crafting a queer-friendly reading for K-pop, for instance, performing "fan service," such as cuddling between two members of a group, which can at times encourage a gay fantasy interpretation of the celebrity text.[25] Idol stars are aware of their support from the LGBTQ+ population, and many idols have made statements supporting LGBTQ+ people in contexts ranging from fan meetings to BTS's first address to the United Nations. Collectively this has meant that men involved in K-pop fan spaces find greater latitude in self-expression.

Jostin, from Venezuela's Trainees Company, explained, "K-pop provides something that modern dance or ballet does not, freedom to not be judged for not being masculine in the way society wants."[26] Nini Destroy, a drag queen from Argentina who performs the dances of K-pop girl groups in drag, characterized the cover dance community as "inclusive of the queer community."[27] Nini Destroy and other international cover dancers may also have been emboldened by the cross-dressing of idol stars (on variety programs): "K-pop cross-dressing is a symbolic mask that allows the performance of queer identities, while at the same time shielding its performers from being perceived as queer."[28] If male idols can dress up and do girl group dances, why shouldn't fans do so as well? Whether an individual's dance practices are related to gender or sexuality or not, fans are empowered by the meanings they are creating from the media products and performed identity of the idols (see Figure 6.2).[29]

Krish, from the Philippines, explained the role of what she termed "reverse cover groups," or groups of female-presenting dancers who perform the dances of boy groups and especially groups of male-presenting dancers who perform the dances of girl groups. "To me, it seems as though most of the dancers I know that are in reverse cover groups use cover dancing as a way for them to express their gender identity, especially for biologically male dancers."[30] Even Korean cover dancers, such as those in Josh Kim's short documentary *Purple Night*, have found expressive freedom through learning reverse covers.[31] The young men Kim interviewed came to a regular K-pop dance class to learn girl group dances with other young men. The goal of their practice was

Figure 6.2 Hive Dance Crew (France) performing TWICE's "More and More." Still from www.youtube.com/watch?v=5Z3hO9_eVQA (accessed January 8, 2021).

not to dance in a competition or upload their dancing to YouTube; instead, it seemed related to enjoyment of the process and the community of like-minded individuals. In the documentary, the instructor, Gangmin, explains that when he began teaching, there were a lot of working women in his class, but nowadays a number of men are also attending. One of the students explains that the lyrics in girl group songs are more relatable, and another talks about learning to ignore those who might judge such an activity. The documentary implicitly emphasizes the importance of community – any of these men could learn by following along with YouTube at home, but group affirmation that learning the dances can bring happiness is clearly one reason they attend the class. The interviewee Minsuk explains, "My dream, like in dance class, is to always be honest with myself and express what I want. I want to live according to who I am and enjoy life like dance."[32] It seems clear that in covering girl groups, these young men find an acceptable way to express femininity while living in a culture that continues to pressure them to conform to a heterosexual norm.

A benefit to cover dance for non-Korean participants is the way it facilitates learning about Korea. Apollo, a senior majoring in East Asian Studies who has 63,000 followers on his K-pop cover dance TikTok account,[33] emailed me, "Before I became a K-pop dancer, I knew nothing about Korea or dancing," indicating just how important cover dance has been to his life trajectory.[34] From ordinary fan-level knowledge such as the names of groups and impressive dancers within the K-pop scene to comments about learning the language, past and future trips to Korea, and enrollment in Korea and East Asia–related coursework, it was clear that for my interviewees, cover dancing was not just about dancing. It was a factor (often a decisive or initiating factor) in learning about Korea more generally, and this process of learning serves the goals of the *gihoeksa*.

First, many fans learn about topics related to popular media. As Krish explained, "Cover group members' interest in Korea is primarily influenced by their consumption of K-pop/drama ... cover dancing serves as an avenue for cover group members to know more about selected aspects of Korea and relevant related industries such as beauty, fashion, and the like."[35] Liliane has visited Korea four times, with family and with friends. In the case of Hina, from Mexico, her family started to show interest in Korea and made plans to travel there because "I get up early each Saturday to rehearse, save up money and even get a job to buy my [dance] wardrobe, and currently I'm guiding my professional life toward being a dance cover teacher and classical arts or dance major."[36] Opulence's founder, Bells, wrote, "Cover dance opens the door to deeply studying Korean culture. You start because the songs are catchy, then one thing leads to another and when you least expect you're learning to speak Korean. Well done, Korea!"[37]

Film scholar Michelle Cho has pointed out that Korean celebrities are constantly negotiating self-presentation for both an international and a national audience.[38] In the same way, international fans of K-pop are constantly negotiating their non-Korean identity vis-à-vis their consciousness of K-pop as a Korean product. Each dancer, who may or may not have begun as a K-pop fan (some may have been looking for dance opportunities and come to fandom of specific artists later through exposure), conceptualizes their fandom as an act of engaging with Korean culture. Just as *doing things* with others (compared to doing something more passive, like watching movies or eating at a restaurant) involves a more active process of memory making and the release of more endorphins; the time young people spend together struggling to perfect choreography can produce vivid memories and tightly bonded communities. For foreign cover dancers, these experiences are interwoven with an awareness of K-pop as representative of Korea and Korean culture. Their dance practice conditions them to associate positive experiences with Korea.

Second, even the shallowest engagement inadvertently teaches the participant something beyond dance about Korea, Korean culture, and language. Many cover dancers agree that details such as lip-synching and appropriate facial expressions are as important as memorizing choreography. Eventually many cover dancers learn some Korean. Cover dancing often becomes inextricably linked to promoting K-pop and Korea more broadly. Cover dancers who practice or film themselves in public places demonstrate to local audiences the attractions of K-pop in a way that promotes a vision of grassroots popularity and musical vitality associated with Korea. The dancers become what I term "borrowed national bodies,"[39] enacting a love of Korea and extending the reach of Korean cultural products to new audiences. Because they seem to have no stake in Korean success, local audiences may find them more convincing than a slick, Korean government-funded project. After visiting Korea to perform in the Changwon World K-Pop Festival, Lindsay, from South Africa, was convinced that Korea was part of his future. His subsequent dance and performance-related activities in South Africa were designed to help him return.[40] This level of passion based on direct experience is infectious.

Do Cover Dancers Want to Be Stars?

Cover dancers who share their dance online learn a great deal about social media, such as YouTube, TikTok, and other platforms, and about videography and editing. They learn that YouTube channels are paid by Google AdSense, which tracks the views of advertisements that play before and sometimes during a YouTube video. To be monetized, a channel has to apply for monetization and have enough subscribers to qualify, but because funds are calculated based on thousands of views, a channel is not lucrative unless a large number of its monetizable videos gain a significant audience. Under YouTube's monetization policies, the view count and funds earned are assigned to the copyright holder. For example, Momoland receives all the benefits for the views of covers of their hit "Boom Boom."

In order to earn money from their YouTube channels and become part of the "K-pop adjacent industries," cover dancers have to appeal to their audience with content that does not include the copyrighted songs.[41] For example, Yours Truly uploads reactions; Awesome Haeun, a child model, shows clips of her life beyond K-pop dance; Sandy and Mandy appear as advertising spokesmodels; St 319 produces original music in Vietnamese; and Waveya directs fans to a subscription-based service, Member Me, for spicier cover dances. Other channels make no special effort to earn funds from cover dance or the popularity they have accrued, but demonstrate their commitment to teaching and performing (such as Kaotsun's Cover Dance Crew). Almost all the cover dance groups in Table 6.1 are popular enough to be considered secondary stars – in the area where they live, they may have multiple invitations to perform per year. Is that enough for them, or do they want something more?

There are a few stories of K-pop idols today who were once dancers, such as Kenta (JBJ95), who, before his *Produce 101* fostered stardom, was a well-known cover dancer in Japan with groups that were so successful that they released albums, sold merchandise, and collected ticket fees for their performances.[42] Soloist AleXa, Ashley Choi of Ladies Code, Dongpyo of X1, and Gowon of LOONA were also cover dancers before becoming idols.[43] In addition, most idols learn other artists' choreography as part of a training process, because choreography is "the foundation for performance for K-pop 'idol' artists."[44] Career arcs like those of Kenta, AleXa, Ashley, Dongpyo, and Gowon fuel the dreams of dancers everywhere, feeding a fantasy that one's cover dance practice could lead to greatness.

Interviewees from the Americas, although they expressed occasional wistful thoughts about the odds that people from their circle would become idols, seem to have entertained no real expectation that cover dance could be a stepping-stone to becoming an idol. For them it seemed that "success" in covering was connected to things like unique experiences and perhaps just enough income to offset costs. They aspired to have the type of audience commanded by the groups in Table 6.1, not the audience of an idol. Winning a contest and getting an all-expenses-paid trip to

Korea, as had happened for three of my interviewees, was most cover dancers' top goal.

Cover dance provides dancers an outlet for the side of themselves that longs for a stage. It can be a fulfilling hobby and even a major part of their lives, but it becomes harder to sustain after they enter the regular workforce. Out of the countless cover dance participants worldwide, only a select few keep dancing for more than a decade. A small fraction of participants move on to teach dance classes for profit or to join performance companies. Several interviewees mentioned that people stop covering when their life priorities change as they age – as they get a serious job and become busy. For example, in a follow-up interview conducted by email, Liliane explained that her participation in cover dance has been waning, following a string of small injuries, and was dampened by the social distancing restrictions of the pandemic in 2020.[45] Others move away from strictly dancing, like Jimin from Korea, who shifted to making videos of cover dancers and other performers to hone those skills, and began producing K-pop–related television programs.[46] Still others, like St 319 in Vietnam or K-Tigers in Korea, form their own companies and release original songs and videos. As participants age and their cohort of fellow dancers thins, participation drops off.

Melo characterized Singapore, where she lives, as having few opportunities for dance professionals: "Having been in this community for a long time, we have definitely seen so many of our friends pursue their dreams of becoming trainees and idols along the way. Some of them who have achieved some sort of acknowledgement include Tasha and Ferlyn from former Singapore-Korea girl group, SKarF, as well as Alfred Sng[47] who is currently still pursuing his aspirations to become an artist through programs in China."[48] Melo herself had landed paid performance opportunities, been invited to Korea to perform, and taught K-pop dance in one of Singapore's most recognized dance studios – which had a direct relationship with major Korean companies. However, now in her late twenties, she had also moved back into teaching dance part time, as neither she nor her parents saw it as a viable long-term career plan.

In Korea – where multiple dance studios have direct relationships with *gihoeksa* and are able to directly place their learners in auditions, or train dancers and place them in the same room with an artist – the situation is different. Paige is twenty-five and American. An avid dancer, she attends a *chwimi ban* (hobbyist class) in K-pop dance at a dance studio somewhat near her home in Seoul. Her class is not an *odisyeon ban* (audition preparatory class), but regular attendance twice a week for more than a year has allowed her to observe a range of other cover dancers and get to know some of her fellow students. Paige's experience is fairly typical for Korea – the difference between her and would-be auditioners is very clear, as she explained: "When a new song comes out at 6 pm one day, [audition students] will be already doing the choreography to that new track when I go in to dance at 8:30 pm."[49]

Several interviewees mentioned frustration with outside critiques of cover dance, which may be driven by an understanding that other forms of dance training are needed for professionals. Melo felt that many people leave cover dancing to move on to what she considered a more serious engagement with dance – she specifically mentioned popping, locking, and other forms of b-boy/b-girl dance.[50] Dancers with serious professional aspirations usually acquire additional skills, often through attending classes in other types of dance. For example, the studio where Paige practices, Reality 7, also offers classes in jazz, hip hop, and urban dance. However, those with dreams of stardom may do better to choose another studio.

1Million, one of Seoul's top studios, is closely associated with both K-pop and professional dance careers. Many, if not all, of its staff teachers have choreographed or performed as back-up dancers for idol stars. Major Korean stars like Jay Park, Uhm Junghwa, MFBTY, and Mamamoo have filmed themselves dancing in the 1Million studio, if the choreographer and backup dancers are from 1Million. 1Million also offers daily dance lessons at all levels and has become a destination for K-pop fans visiting Korea. In 2019 I visited, wading through fans who lined the stairwell waiting to sign up for a single lesson with the help of a receptionist who spoke by turns in Korean, English, Japanese, and Chinese. Stephanie, who regularly practiced at 1Million on the weekends while living in Korea, explained, "In my experience, 1Million is the place where if you're striving to become a prominent dancer in the entertainment world, you're at the right place if you're willing to put in the effort."[51] It is possible to become an idol or a professional dancer starting from cover dance, as in the case of the idols mentioned earlier, and entering the Korean professional sector is easier for young Koreans who begin training as tweens or teens. Living in Korea, a K-pop fan may have an opportunity to become a backup dancer or a "foreign dancing body" – a visibly non-Korean extra or even a love interest – in a music video,[52] but there are few opportunities to become an idol and many obstacles along the way.

How Do K-Pop Companies and the Korean Government Encourage Cover Dance?

Dancing to K-pop drives up social media statistics, YouTube-linked advertisements, and the power of K-pop videos as a site of embedded product placement – *gihoeksa* participate in encouraging cover dance not to facilitate learning about Korea but to achieve their bottom line. The view count on the dance practice videos by K-pop idols demonstrates how often they are watched. Although a fan may enjoy watching for a glimpse of a backstage moment, dancers watch such videos repeatedly, often mirrored, as they memorize the moves. Later, cover dancers may upload their own version of the dance, and by doing so, they further boost the popularity of the original song, choreography, and artist. Essentially, cover dance practices create a feedback loop that helps augment perceptions of song popularity. In addition, as already mentioned, each cover is copyrighted material of the original K-pop artists; therefore, the *gihoeksa* profit equally from YouTube views of music videos, dance practices, and covers.

To encourage participation and active engagement, K-pop groups and companies have taken to creating viral challenges, including the specific recording of "K-pop in public." Cover dance groups know that if they advance to the finals of a contest, there is a good chance the group they are covering will see them dance. K-Boy, a cover team from Thailand, participated in a contest for "Cherry Bomb," a song by NCT 127. Since they were one of the top three teams (East2West was another) in the contest, NCT 127 members filmed their reaction to the cover.[53] "K-Boy then uploaded a video to YouTube of their reaction to the reaction.[54] Later that year K-Boy was invited to Korea to perform the song at the *Seoul Music Awards*."[55] In another instance, IZ*ONE filmed their reactions to the top three teams in a cover contest of their song "Violeta"; East2West appears again, as well as B-Wild, a team from Vietnam that is also listed in Table 6.1.[56]

The Korean government invests deeply in projects that support and encourage cover dance, such as the annual Changwon World K-Pop Festival, which is actively supported by the Ministry of Foreign Affairs (since 2011), and the K-Pop Cover Dance Festival (since 2010), supported by the city of Seoul and the newspaper *Seoul Sinmun*. Similar opportunities for K-pop cover dancers to compete for a chance to perform in Korea, and maybe even meet their idols, are developed through partnerships between television stations, entertainment agencies, and regions seeking to boost local tourism. As Stephanie explained, for most cover dancers, "their main goal is that ticket to Korea. Cover dances, TikTok challenges, official government sponsored competitions. At the end of the day, fans just hope to get the attention of their favourite idols and to get their few minutes of fame."[57] A large amount of cover activity can be generated from even a single challenge like the "Cherry Bomb" and "Violeta" contests mentioned above, and each challenge is accompanied by more views of YouTube videos. Collectively those views and covers, per YouTube logistics and fan interest in metrics, increase earnings for the idols (and their *gihoeksa*) and the perception of the popularity of the idols and their songs.

Conclusion

Too often scholars dismiss these uploads to social media as sycophantic noise, an act of homage to the stars themselves. This assumption is not without a basis in reality – many K-pop cover groups only re-create choreography of the stars. Yet K-pop cover dance is so much more. Cover dancers, at least the successful ones, are watched – and the goal of their many uploads, as shown in Table 6.1, is to be watched. As they offer their participation in the K-pop space, they bring new ideas, challenges, and creativity to K-pop, adding juice and spice to an industry that needs to stay on its toes or risk losing its edge.

By moving their bodies together to the infectious beats of K-pop, these cover dancers share their passion and create tightly bonded communities that sustain them emotionally, even (and perhaps particularly) if they are also resisting societal or familial expectations. K-pop fandom is a seed that, if nurtured, can change the fans' expected life trajectory, leading them to new classes, new majors, new linguistic abilities, a new travel destination, or even a new home. The connection between Korean celebrities and diverse dance lovers from around the world seems to be a remaking of a cultural pole, the creation of a new set of aspirations. No longer constantly looking to America as the origin of cultural trends, cover dance demonstrates that K-pop permeates not just the headphones but also the muscles, tendons, and ligaments of young people around the world.

Acknowledgments

The names of many interviewees appear in this chapter. All of them took time out of their days to meet with me or email me their thoughts. I am grateful to all of them, and especially Liliane, Stephanie, Miska, and Sam, who helped me contact other dancers, answered follow-up queries, and in Stephanie's case gave feedback on a draft. In addition, former TAs Youngji Kim and Elliott Y. N. Cheung helped me to formulate my thoughts on cover dance, and my former student Augusta Wong emailed valuable observations that appear here. Conversations with Hwang Dae-gyun (Virus of T.I.P. Crew) and dance scholar Haeree Choi were key to setting up the background of this chapter. Volume editor Suk-Young Kim, as well as Jena Barchas-Lichtenstein and Allison Van Deventer, provided useful editing advice. Each conference presentation and each class where I discussed cover dance helped me to refine my ideas on this topic. Thank you to those audiences and students, particularly those who asked questions and gave feedback.

Bibliography

Anderson, Crystal S. *Soul in Seoul: African American Popular Music and K-Pop.* Jackson: University Press of Mississippi, 2020.

Cho, Michelle. "Domestic Hallyu: K-Pop Metatexts and the Media's Self-Reflexive Gesture." *International Journal of Communication* 11 (2017): 2308–2331.

Hinck, Ashley. *Politics for the Love of Fandom: Fan-Based Citizenship in a Digital World.* Baton Rouge: Louisiana State University Press, 2019.

Im, Hyeonju. "Taekwondowa kei-pap daenseu yunghapsueoge daehan yebicheyuk gyosaui gyeongheomgwa insik" (Perceptions and experiences of teacher trainees on integrating taekwondo and K-pop dance in PE classrooms). *Gukgiwon taekwondo yeon-guso* (Journal of the World Taekwondo Headquarters) 10/2 (2019): 111–131.

Jung, Eun-Young. "Articulating Korean Youth Culture through Global Popular Music Styles: Seo Taiji's Use of Rap and Metal." In *Korean Pop Music: Riding the Wave*, 109–122. Kent: Global Oriental, 2006.

"The Place of Sentimental Song in Contemporary Korean Musical Life." *Korean Studies* 35 (2011): 71–92.

Kang, Dredge Byung'chu. "Idols of Development: Transnational Transgender Performance in Thai K-Pop Cover Dance." *Transgender Studies Quarterly* 1/4 (2014): 559–571.

"Surfing the Korean Wave: Wonder Gays and the Crisis of Thai Masculinity." *Visual Anthropology* 31/1–2 (2018): 45–65.

Kim, Suk-Young. *K-Pop Live: Fans, Idols, and Multimedia Performance.* Stanford, CA: Stanford University Press, 2018.

Kwon, Jungmin. *Straight Korean Female Fans and Their Gay Fantasies.* Iowa City: University of Iowa Press, 2018.

Liew, Kai Khiun. "K-Pop Dance Trackers and Cover Dancers: Global Cosmopolitanization and Local Spatialization." In Youna Kim (ed.), *The Korean Wave: Korean Media Go Global*, 165–181. London: Routledge, 2013.

Maliangkay, Roald. "The Popularity of Individualism: The Seo Taiji Phenomenon in the 1990s." In Kyung Hyun Kim and Youngmin Choe (eds.), *The Korean Popular Culture Reader*, 296–313. Durham, NC: Duke University Press, 2014.

Oh, Chuyun. "From Seoul to Copenhagen: Migrating K-Pop Cover Dance and Performing Diasporic Youth in Social Media." *Dance Research Journal* 52/1 (2020): 20–32.

Oh, Chuyun, and David C. Oh. "Unmasking Queerness: Blurring and Solidifying Queer Lines through K-Pop Cross-Dressing." *The Journal of Popular Culture* 50/1 (2017): 9–29.

Saeji, CedarBough T. "Borrowed National Bodies: Ideological Conditioning and Idol-Logical Practices of K-Pop Cover Dance." *Transactions of the Royal Asiatic Society, Korea Branch* 94/1 (2020): 43–68.

"Cosmopolitan Strivings and Racialization: The Foreign Dancing Body in Korean Popular Music Videos." In Andrew David Jackson and Colette Balmain (eds.), *Korean Screen Cultures: Interrogating Cinema, TV, Music and Online Games*, 257–292. Oxford: Peter Lang, 2016.

Seo Taebeom, Gim Yeongsuk, Gim Yumi, Gang Minjeong, Seo Gyeongho, and Bak Haechan. "Kei-pap keobeodaenseu undongi cheonsonyeon pokryeok gwanryeon simni byeonin mit byeoljung horeumon nongdoe michineun yeonghyang" (Effect of K-pop cover dance on violence-related psychological factors, blood hormones, and neurotransmitters in adolescents). *Han-guk saenghwal hwan-gyeong hakhoe* (The Korean Living Environmental Society) 22/5 (2015): 739–746.

Song, Myoung-sun. *Hanguk Hip Hop: Global Rap in South Korea*. Cham: Palgrave Macmillan, 2019.

Sung, Sang-yeon. "K-Pop Reception and Participatory Fan Culture in Austria." *Cross Currents: East Asian History and Culture Review* 9 (December 2013): 90–104.

Notes

1 Suk-Young Kim, *K-Pop Live: Fans, Idols, and Multimedia Performance* (Stanford, CA: Stanford University Press, 2018), 16.
2 Eun-Young Jung, "The Place of Sentimental Song in Contemporary Korean Musical Life," *Korean Studies* 35 (2011): 77.
3 Roald Maliangkay, "The Popularity of Individualism: The Seo Taiji Phenomenon in the 1990s," in Kyung Hyun Kim and Youngmin Choe (eds.), *The Korean Popular Culture Reader* (Durham, NC: Duke University Press, 2014), 296–313; Eun-Young Jung, "Articulating Korean Youth Culture through Global Popular Music Styles: Seo Taiji's Use of Rap and Metal," in *Korean Pop Music: Riding the Wave* (Kent: Global Oriental, 2006), 109–122; Myoung-sun Song, *Hanguk Hip Hop: Global Rap in South Korea* (Cham: Palgrave Macmillan, 2019), 8–10; Crystal S. Anderson, *Soul in Seoul: African American Popular Music and K-Pop* (Jackson: University Press of Mississippi, 2020), 44–46.
4 http://beyondhallyu.com/k-pop/5-talented-korean-choreographers-happen-work-k-pop/, accessed May 25, 2014.
5 Apollo, email interview, August 7, 2020.
6 Jennifer, email interview, August 5, 2020.
7 "Love Shot" is available at www.youtube.com/watch?v=pSudEWBAYRE; "Miracle" is available at www.youtube.com/watch?v=RtRtLf84I2M; "Blue Rose," is available at www.youtube.com/watch?v=1ESlM8D_fds; "Chaja gascyo" is available at www.youtube.com/watch?v=ZUYvvuaZnoI. Videos accessed on and view count from December 23, 2020.
8 Fan communities are discussed at length in recent works like *Politics for the Love of Fandom* by Ashley Hinck (2019).
9 Liliane, personal interview, March 28, 2018.
10 Liliane, personal interview, March 28, 2018.
11 Liliane, email interview, January 6, 2021.
12 Miska, live video call interview, February 21, 2019.
13 www.youtube.com/watch?v=Ij9P7LYHhig (accessed January 8, 2021).
14 Miska, live video call interview, February 21, 2019.
15 Chuyun Oh, "From Seoul to Copenhagen: Migrating K-Pop Cover Dance and Performing Diasporic Youth in Social Media," *Dance Research Journal* 52/1 (2020): 27–28.
16 Stephanie, email interview, January 8, 2021.
17 Liliane, personal interview, March 28, 2018.
18 Stephanie, email interview, January 08, 2021.
19 Miska, email interview, January 12, 2021.
20 Stephanie, email interview, January 08, 2021.
21 Sam, email interview, July 29, 2020.
22 Aydan, email interview, August 4, 2020.
23 Lola, email interview, August 4, 2020.

24 Dredge Byung'chu Kang, "Idols of Development: Transnational Transgender Performance in Thai K-Pop Cover Dance," *Transgender Studies Quarterly* 1/4 (2014): 562.

25 Jungmin Kwon, *Straight Korean Female Fans and Their Gay Fantasies* (Iowa City: University of Iowa Press, 2018).

26 Jostin, email interview, August 3, 2020.

27 Nini Destroy, email interview, August 4, 2020.

28 Chuyun Oh and David C. Oh, "Unmasking Queerness: Blurring and Solidifying Queer Lines through K-Pop Cross-Dressing," *The Journal of Popular Culture* 50/1 (2017): 11.

29 Stephanie, email interview, January 8, 2021.

30 Krish, email interview, July 30, 2020.

31 *Purple Night*, dir. Josh Kim, https://youtu.be/L7FiZeaj5Xc (accessed November 24, 2020).

32 Minseok expresses this idea in *Purple Night*, dir. Josh Kim, starting at https://youtu.be/L7FiZeaj5Xc?t=141.

33 Apollo's Tik Tok is available at www.tiktok.com/@apolloeon?lang=en (accessed January 6, 2021).

34 Apollo, email interview, August 7, 2020.

35 Krish, email interview, July 30, 2020.

36 Hina, email interview, August 2, 2020.

37 Bells, email interview, August 4, 2020.

38 Michelle Cho, "Domestic Hallyu: K-Pop Metatexts and the Media's Self-Reflexive Gesture." *International Journal of Communication* 11 (2017): 2309.

39 CedarBough T. Saeji, "Borrowed National Bodies: Ideological Conditioning and Idol-Logical Practices of K-Pop Cover Dance," *Transactions of the Royal Asiatic Society, Korea Branch* 94/1 (2020): 43–68.

40 Lindsay, video call interview, March 3, 2019.

41 Saeji, "Borrowed National Bodies," 50.

42 For more on Kenta, see https://channel-korea.com/takada-kenta-profile/ (accessed November 25, 2020).

43 AleXa has discussed her background doing covers on DIVE studio's podcast with Jae from Day6; see www.youtube.com/watch?v=1E20M8W617A&feature=emb_logo, accessed January 8, 2021. Ashley's cover dance past appears in most online bios; see https://ladiescode.fandom.com/wiki/Ashley#:~:text=%EC%B5%9C%EB%B9%9B%EB%82%98%20(Eng%3A%20Choi%20Bitna%2C, the%20leader%20of%20LADIES'%20CODE. Dongpyo used to be part of the Korean dance group ARTBEAT; https://kprofiles.com/x1-member-profile/. Gowon's fandom and her past as a cover dancer were highlighted, for example, in the *Weekly Idol* (TV program) clip at www.youtube.com/watch?v=E0VKVAm3VqM&feature=emb_logo (accessed January 8, 2021).

44 Anderson, *Soul in Seoul*, 68.

45 Liliane, email interview, November 23, 2020.

46 Jimin, personal interview, Seoul, March 18, 2016.

47 https://hypeandstuff.com/alfred-sng-k-pop-hopefuls-alpha-auditions-interview-singapore/, accessed January 14, 2021.

48 Melo, email interview, November 7, 2020.

49 Paige, email interview, August 12, 2020.

50 Melo, email interview, November 17, 2020.

51 Stephanie, email interview, January 8, 2021.

52 CedarBough T. Saeji, "Cosmopolitan Strivings and Racialization: The Foreign Dancing Body in Korean Popular Music Videos," in Andrew David Jackson and Colette Balmain (eds.), *Korean Screen Cultures: Interrogating Cinema, TV, Music and Online Games* (Oxford: Peter Lang, 2016), 257–292.

53 https://youtu.be/5Vp-FqpzjlI, accessed May 7, 2020.

54 https://youtu.be/hn5FuAcfcpI, accessed May 7, 2020.

55 https://youtu.be/y_D25_jD7qU, accessed May 8, 2020. Saeji, "Borrowed National Bodies," 53-54.

56 www.youtube.com/watch?v=xH4–dcWhQY, accessed January 8, 2021.

57 Stephanie, email interview, January 8, 2021.

PART IV

The Making of Idols

7 K-Pop Idols

Media Commodities, Affective Laborers, and Cultural Capitalists

STEPHANIE CHOI

The K-pop industry is one of the fastest-expanding industries in the world. Unlike the global music markets that have faced consistent decreases in album sales, the South Korean market has had a gradual increase since 2014 – its album sales exceeded 10 million in 2016; 16.9 million in 2017; 22.8 million in 2018; and 25 million in 2019 – thanks to K-pop fans, who have strategically and competitively consumed their idols' music.[1] K-pop groups are dominating international music charts – EXO Baekhyun's *Delight* (2020) ranked No. 1 on iTunes charts in sixty-nine countries, and EXO's *OBSESSION* (2019) and BLACKPINK's "How You like That" (2020) in sixty. In 2020, BTS released four number-one albums faster than any other group since the Beatles, and their song "Black Swan" reached number one on iTunes in 103 countries – more than any song in history.[2] By the end of the 2010s, K-pop had become even more saturated, with millions of aspiring performers hoping to become the next BoA and BTS.

If aspiring idols were inspired by the rags-to-riches stories of BoA and BTS, numerous investors saw K-pop idols as a one-time jackpot. The flow of reckless investments has resulted in small companies producing the same style of idol groups, going into financial peril, and disbanding the groups within a few years. These companies are often denigrated as "idol factories" that force teenagers to look and act in certain ways, sacrificing their privacy, education, family life, friendships, and romances to maintain a loyal fan base.[3]

Western media have continued to describe K-pop stars' limited agency as "the dark side of K-pop."[4] However, the Western counterparts also suffer from chronic structural problems of unfair contracts, sexual abuse, and exploitation behind the commercial myth of musical authenticity. Among the examples are Brian Epstein's molding of the Beatles's image, Michael Jackson's childhood history of abuse, Ke$ha's sexual assault lawsuit against her producer Dr. Luke, Lauren Jauregui's leaked audio that described her group Fifth Harmony as "literal slaves," and Scooter Braun's legal ownership of Taylor Swift's music catalogue. Attempts to control artists' agency are endemic in the global music industry.[5]

The goal of this chapter is not to perpetuate the myth of K-pop as magical and/or abusive but rather to reveal the complexity and fluidity of human relations in the popular music industry. Keith Negus's study of genre cultures in the British music business of the 1970s and early 1980s is critical of defining culture industries in Fordist terms, because that ignores the historical specificities that contextualize the development of the music business.[6] He also points out the impossibility of theorizing cultural production in general terms, due to differences in "aesthetic form, content, working practices, means of financing and modes of reception and consumption" in each industry, because "all industries are cultural."[7] It will be productive, then, to discuss the K-pop industry not as a standardized culture built on a Fordist business model but as a critical site in which diverse social relations are created, subverted, and negotiated.

This is why field research is important in examining an industry as culture. On the one hand, trained experts sustain the industrial system; on the other hand, there are always thinkers who question capitalist principles that alienate laborers and reject human-essential capacities, discuss the laborers' calling and raison d'être in economic activities, and take actions within and beyond the given social structure of the industry. While the former is readily noticeable through top-down, media-based cultural studies, listening to the latter requires participant observation, interviews, and personal networks in the field. From 2015 to 2018, I interviewed more than seventy people, including K-pop idols and trainees; entertainment company CEOs; workers in A&R, marketing, and casting divisions; TV show producers; music video directors; reporters and journalists in Korean and American media; academics; and fans from Korea and around the world. All the interviewees are active in the K-pop industry and wished to remain anonymous because they discussed sensitive issues that might affect their employment status or public image. For this reason, I have replaced their names with letters (e.g., Worker A, Idol B, Rapper C, Company D).

I identified four groups of participants and institutions in the K-pop world: the K-pop industry (i.e., Korean entertainment companies and the mass media), the South Korean government, idol singers, and fans. In an industry where idols' bodies serve as unstandardized products through volatile media (re)presentations, how do entertainment companies produce idols? How do idols manage their multiple roles and expectations as media commodities, affective laborers, and cultural capitalists? How does the government intervene in this global trade of affective commodities like K-pop, protect the human rights of the idols, but also benefit from the soft power that the idols produce as national icons? Last, how do fan communities circulate this commodified intimacy and make themselves de facto shareholders of entertainment companies? Although I have categorized actors in the K-pop world, I will explore how K-pop is sustained as a culture formed through interactive communications, conflicts, and negotiations.

Idol Recruitment and Contract

The idea of idols as puppets of the industry derives from idols' limited agency, especially in the first three to four years after their debut. They are not simply musicians but also affective laborers who perform "fan service" – that is, verbal, physical, textual, and/or musical performances that offer pleasure – and work ceaselessly to maintain a close relationship with their fans. For this reason, entertainment companies select idol trainees based on several factors, such as appearance, *kki* (aura or stage presence, including charisma and sex appeal), talent (singing, dancing, and/or rapping), *inseong* (politeness, kindness, and sincerity), and teamwork.

Prospective idols must be extraordinarily attractive or talented to pass the audition. Once they are selected as trainees, they are expected to demonstrate *inseong* and cooperative teamwork until they join a debut team. Some private institutes (*hagwon*) for vocal and dance training partner with entertainment companies and send their students to company auditions, while other aspiring idols make their debuts through television audition shows. Most companies hold weekly auditions at their building while the cast division goes on an audition tour inside and outside Seoul, or even overseas. The casting division often goes to middle and high schools, singing/dancing contests, and K-pop festivals to discover good-looking and talented teenagers. It is common for companies to sign non-Korean idols who can speak other languages so that the idols can speak for their group without a translator at overseas promotions.[8]

Entertainment companies occasionally recruit trainees solely based on their appearance. Some companies host beauty pageants for preteen girls and boys in order to track potential idols for several years. Worker C at the new artist development department at Company D explains that if the potential idols are too young, casting managers will maintain contact with them without signing a trainee contract. Even though they are not under contract, the managers give an impression that the company is interested in them, by regularly contacting and asking them to inform the company if they receive an offer from another company.[9] Once the preteens enter adolescence, the company will sign a contract with discretion after evaluating how their appearance will change as they mature.

Worker C explains how the casting managers take profile pictures of audition applicants:

> We take photos of the entire body, then divide the parts into knees, the waist, then the bust. Next, a full shot of the face. Then we divide the face into the forehead and the nose. Then we take photos of their profile and repeat the same process. Next, we tell them to uncover their ears and take photos of their ears. Then we take another photo, from the ears to the forehead. After that, we tell them to turn around while saying "ee" to check the dental interlocking, because as kids grow up, their bones grow as well. There is the possibility that their faces will become asymmetrical. Especially in boys' case, their chin and cheekbones will grow, so if they have a slightly asymmetrical [face] then they have to correct their habits or have orthodontics. We also report which parts they should modify and supplement – for instance, if [the applicant's] jaw is too sharp, then we report that they need to reshape the jaw lines [through cosmetic surgery], or that they should have their cheekbones sculpted, or that they need eye-length extension surgery. Correcting a body shape is nearly impossible. You just have to make them exercise, but there's no way to fix it. Bow legs may be fixed, but it takes a long time.[10]

Both female and male idols are under pressure to look attractive through diet and cosmetic surgery. After four years of rigorous training, JinE made her debut in 2015 as a member of Oh My Girl, although soon after, she went on hiatus for a year due to extreme weight loss, anorexia nervosa, amenorrhea, hypothermia, and hypotension. In 2017, she left the group. It is common for idols of both genders to share their diets with their fans. BTS member Jin states that he was once on a crash diet where for an entire year he ate only two packs of chicken breast a day: "I was told to take vitamins, but I refused to do so to lose more weight, so I eventually suffered from malnutrition."[11] Another BTS member, Jungkook, was not allowed to bulk up before he became an adult, because his company wanted him to "maintain a boyish image."[12]

Idol C states that liposuction is the most common surgery that female idols undergo, as they are compelled – by both the company and their own fans – to be thin. According to her, an idol with a height of 160 centimeters (about 5'3") must maintain a weight of 40 kilograms (about 88 pounds).[13] Idol B says he was 180 centimeters (about 5'9") tall and weighed 60 kilograms (about 132 pounds) right after the debut, as he had "tuna sandwiches and chicken breasts every day – the company told us to do so. We had to do whatever they ordered, so I just did whatever they wanted me to do."[14] Fans and the public do not hesitate to tell idols to lose weight or undergo cosmetic surgery. Idol B recalls the online comments he received in his early career: "Now I don't get hurt by people saying that I'm ugly. But back then, it was so hurtful when they said I was ugly. 'How dare you make a debut as an idol [with such an appearance]?' There were definitely many fans among those who criticized my appearance."[15]

A flirtatious aura, or *kki*, is also a significant asset. Worker A at a cast division states that Idol N, whom she scouted simply because she found him cute, was a flirt: "[Idol N] was annoying while I was setting up an audition schedules for him. He didn't arrive on time, asked irrelevant questions, and kept saying things like, 'I can't go today.' But later I realized that those annoying kids were often good at flirting with their fans."[16] Appearance and flirting skills are important, but performing techniques must also reach an acceptable level before the trainees come onto the market as idols. Once they have been recruited, entertainment companies teach them singing, dancing, foreign languages, etiquette, and other skills. Based on each trainee's personality and talents, the company assigns them a role as a vocalist, rapper, or dancer.

Education curricula generally include singing, dancing, foreign languages, courtesy and manners, elocution, and acting. Some companies cover expenses for music (composition and instrument) lessons, mental health care, academic tutoring, and Korean language for foreign trainees.[17] Because most trainees are teenagers, they practice after school, and some quit school to dedicate themselves to training. Kim Sung-eun stresses her role not only as a vocal trainer but also as a life mentor of the trainees: "[Vocal training] is not just about singing. You should keep an eye on how the trainees' personalities and potentials are shaped as individuals, because you never know how this will lead to growth, just like Seokjin [BTS's Jin]. I never knew Seokjin would listen to and study music to such a deep level.... If we build a good foundation for [the trainees], they'll perceive themselves as singers and will study music by themselves. How meaningful and fun would that be?"[18] Kim argues, "One's retirement as an idol shouldn't be the end of one's singing career. Even after they retire as an idol, you should help them survive as a musician."[19]

Trainees practice singing and dancing for several hours a day and take weekly and monthly exams that determine whether or not they will remain in the program. Among dozens of trainees, the company selects a group for the so-called debut team (*debwi tim*). Big companies like SM Entertainment, YG Entertainment, JYP Entertainment, and HYBE reveal their new idol candidates on television audition programs to promote them before the debut. In the meantime, the producers (in-house producers and some CEOs) decide the group's "concept" (*keonsep*) and "worldview" (*segyegwan*), an alternate universe that undergirds the group's concept. For example, EXO's concept and worldview are "aliens with supernatural powers who came from the exoplanet." BTS's early concept was "hip hop-dol" (idols who perform hip hop), whose worldview was to "secure their music and values from social prejudice and suppression for those in their teens and twenties."

Last, *inseong* and teamwork are important properties for an idol. Worker A explains that it is possible to check trainees' sincere attitudes or *inseong*: "There are kids who are kicked out just because of their *inseong*. There are kids who drive a wedge between trainees and cause drama, or date other trainees and get caught after taking weird photos. There is a lot of drama happening here."[20] When idols are suspected of school violence, drug use, prostitution, or other types of crimes, television and radio stations immediately cancel their appearance on shows to avoid complaints from the audience.

There are two types of contract: one for trainees and the other for idols. Trainee contracts may last for one to two years or may be connected to the idol contract and remain in effect for seven years. In this case, the trainee cannot move to another company but should wait until the current company schedules the debut. The trainee contract requires the company to pay for the trainee's lessons, meals, and lodging, and the company has the right to end the contract if the trainee makes "trouble," fails to improve their singing and dancing skills, or does not pass the monthly exam. "Trouble" may consist of conflicts with other people in the company, dating scandals, and/or crimes.

Once the trainees have been chosen to debut as an idol group, they sign a seven-year idol contract. The company first pays all expenses during the promotion period, such as hairstyling, makeup, and skincare treatment, in addition to lessons, meals, and lodging.[21] However, the majority of small companies sign a contract that compels the idols to pay back the expenses for training, music production, and promotion. As a result, idols from these small companies earn no profits in the first three to four years of their careers, until they pay the "debt" (*bit*). Then they can receive their portion of the profits earned.[22]

By 2015, the amount of investment for debuting an average idol group – of five members who underwent two years of traineeship – reached 940,000,000 KRW (approximately US$830,000). According to the Ministry of Culture, Sports and Tourism, the average period of traineeship was 25.6 months. The expenses for a debuting idol group are shown in Table 7.1.[23]

Although the K-pop training course is known for its rigor, it also becomes an important source of fans' love for their idols, because they understand how demanding and difficult the training is. Presuming K-pop idols as puppets of their companies also neglects the latter phase of the idol career. As I will address later in this chapter, idols gain more voice and power in the production process as they develop their career and establish a larger fan base.

Table 7.1 *Expenses for a debuting idol group*

Type of expense	Total
Lessons (15 million/month × 24 months)	360 million KRW
Trainers from overseas (20 million (two times) × 2 years)	40 million KRW
Lodging (5 million/month × 24 months)	120 million KRW
Meals, etc. (5 million/month × 24 months)	120 million KRW
Album production	50 million KRW
Music video production	50 million KRW
Marketing and promotion	100 million KRW
Costumes, hairstyling, etc.	100 million KRW
Grand total	**940 million KRW**

The South Korean Government's Role in the K-Pop Business

In the early 2000s, the South Korean government and the entertainment industry began discussing the "slave contract" between entertainment companies and entertainers.[24] Three months after actress Jang Ja-yeon died by suicide (her company allegedly forced her into sexual service), the Korea Fair Trade Commission finalized the Standard Form of the Exclusive Contract (*pyojunjeonsoggyeyakseo*) for entertainers, based on the guidelines provided by the Korea Entertainment Producers' Association in June 2009. The contract period for singers was limited to seven years, taking into consideration the long training period.[25]

In March 2017, the Korea Fair Trade Commission released the Improvement of Unfair Trading Convention between Entertainment Companies and Affiliated Trainees after evaluating the trainee contracts of SM Entertainment, LOEN Entertainment, JYP Entertainment, FNC Entertainment, YG Entertainment, Cube Entertainment, Jellyfish Entertainment, and DSP Media. The commission amended six articles from the previous contracts, and all eight companies revised their trainee contracts to include the changes shown in Table 7.2.[26]

Because most idols and idol trainees are minors, entertainment companies are bound by the "Protection of Children and Teenagers," Article 18 of the Standard Form of the Exclusive Contract for Entertainers (Singers) in Popular Culture provided by the Korea Fair Trade Commission:

1. [The production company] guarantees the child/teenage entertainer's fundamental human rights such as physical/mental health, right to learn, right to personal freedom, right to sleep, right to rest, and freedom of choice.
2. When [the production company] concludes a contract for entertainment management, it must check the age of the entertainer, and in case of a child/teenager, it cannot request indecent exposure of [the entertainer's] body or excessively suggestive performances for the purpose of profit or popularity.
3. [The production company] cannot demand popular cultural art labor for an excessive amount of time from the child/teenage entertainer.[27]

Table 7.2 *Revisions after release of the Improvement of Unfair Trading Convention between Entertainment Companies and Affiliated Trainees*

Before the improvement	After the improvement	Reasons (selected)
When the trainee violates the contract, the trainee must pay a penalty equal to double or triple the amount invested by the company for training. (Valid at YG, JYP, FNC, Cube, Jellyfish, and DSP)	When the company cancels the contract, it may demand a penalty equal to the amount invested for training.	• It is unfair to force the trainees to bear such financial pressures. • Considering the economic status of trainees, they are not capable of rejecting or negotiating excessive penalties.
After the trainee contract is terminated, the trainee is responsible for signing an exclusive contract with the company. However, even before the trainee contract ends, the trainee must sign an exclusive contract with the company upon request. (Valid at JYP, Cube, and DSP)	After the trainee period designated in the trainee contract is terminated, the trainee will prioritize the company for contract renewal or an exclusive contract.	• This article forces the trainee to sign an exclusive contract and thus unfairly restricts the trainee from signing a contract with a third party and unreasonably restricts the trainee's legal rights. • Since the trainee contract is separate from the entertainer contract, under the principle of contract freedom, the trainee should be able to freely determine which entertainment company's contract they will sign following the termination of the trainee contract.
The company may cancel the contract via written notice anytime during the contract period. (Valid at LOEN, JYP, YG, Cube, and DSP)	When the company wishes to cancel the contract due to the trainee's fault, the company must inform the trainee, and the contract can then be terminated thirty days from the day the trainee was informed.	• This article unreasonably deprives the trainee of the benefits during the cancellation period, and may be unfairly disadvantageous to the trainee by loosening the requirements for the company's contract cancellation rights.
The trainee must not demonstrate behavior that demeans popular cultural artists or negatively impacts their entertainment activities, and must not demonstrate behavior that harms the dignity or credibility of the company or its affiliated entertainers. (Valid at SM, FNC, and DSP; SM Entertainment followed the Standard Form of the Exclusive Contract, although since this article has unfair clauses, the commission plans to revise the article on the Standard Form.)	Removed.	• The article sets a duty that is too abstract and vague and allows the company to cancel the contract whenever it determines that the trainees have disobeyed its rules; thus it is unfairly disadvantageous to the trainees. • Since contract cancellation is beneficial to the contracting party's interest, the reason must be valid and detailed. • When determining abstract factors such as the damage to the company's dignity or credibility as the trainees' obligation, it is difficult to verify the trainees' performance of this duty, and thus is disadvantageous to the trainees and may create a legal dispute. • Contract cancellation due to the violation of an abstract and unclear duty makes up the largest portion (28.5%) of legal disputes over artist contracts.

Table 7.2 (*cont.*)

Before the improvement	After the improvement	Reasons (selected)
The trainee must immediately pay any penalty to the company. (Valid at YG and LOEN)	Removed.	• This article unreasonably restricts the trainees' legal rights by forcing them to pay penalties without negotiation.
In case of a legal dispute over the current contract between the company and the trainee, the court with exclusive jurisdiction will be the Seoul Central District Court. (Valid at YG, FNC, LOEN, Cube, Jellyfish, and DSP)	In case of a legal dispute over the current contract between the company and the trainee, both parties will make an effort to reach an amicable agreement with trust and sincerity; if they cannot, they will resolve the dispute based on the fundamental principles of the Civil Procedure Code.	• The article is unfair to the trainees in terms of the agreement over trial jurisdiction.

While some companies use a standard contract, an industry executive states, "Honestly, the standard form of the (exclusive) contract is disadvantageous for the companies, so what company would observe all [of the articles]? No one cares whether they observe it or not."[28] Although the South Korean government continues to set and revise criteria for the rights of idols and idol trainees, the criteria remain on an advisory level.

Because of the performers' young age and subordinate position in the industry, the company CEO and idols' relationship is often described as paternalistic. John David Ebert, in his biography of Michael Jackson, states that Diana Ross and Berry Gordy were "displaced parental figures of Michael, and thus played roles in the very ancient myth of the birth of the hero, in which the hero's original parents are swapped out for a new set who happened to stumble on the child in the wilderness, where he has been abandoned and then raised him."[29] Typical K-pop stars, as seen in dozens of documentaries and interviews, tell a similar story: Idols are passionate youths who are so diligent and desperate that it would seem unfair if they were not to succeed. Yet they seem to be financially naïve, because they care only about becoming a singer. Then they find the "right" CEO, who can give them that opportunity. The CEO is not merely a business partner but also a father figure who cares about his idols' welfare.

This paternalistic relationship can also be abusive. In October 2018, eighteen-year-old Lee Seok-cheol and sixteen-year-old Lee Seung-hyun, two members of East Light, revealed that they had been exposed to four years of assault, verbal abuse, and death threats from Moon Yeong-il, the in-house producer of Media Line Entertainment. Lee and Lee's lawyer stated, "Until now, Media Line has controlled the members by making them surveil one another. Because all members were minors, they were worried that the executives of Media Line would find out if they discussed the abuse with their parents."[30] The members were beaten with baseball bats and microphone stands, forced to smoke cigarettes, and choked with guitar strings. They stated that they had not reported the abuse because of their "dream and fear that [they] might not be able to continue performing music once [they] were kicked out of here."[31]

Ideally, once the parents sign the contract and send their children to the company dorm, the company executives should take on the parenting role for teenage idols and trainees. BLACKPINK's Rosé states that YG Entertainment's in-house producer Teddy supports her group as an experienced friend and mentor.[32] Girls' Generation's Tiffany also recalls, "I was fifteen, I didn't have parents around me in Korea, I didn't speak Korean fluently at the time, so I was scared … trying to blend in but still have my own opinions and be around K-pop parents [the company executives].… My bandmates were at the label starting at ten, so their lives are based around, like, going to practice and rehearse and then going to school and kind of maintaining it all at the same time as ten-year-olds. Yeah, you do need [company executives as] parents to manage that."[33] JYP Entertainment, for instance, offers mental health and sex education for its trainees and terminates the contract when the trainees get failing grades for two semesters in a row.[34]

Controlling Self-Expression, Human Relationships, and Affective Outcome

To be commercially successful, idols must tolerate several restrictions. As Rapper E, who gave rap lessons to idol trainees and wrote songs for idols at Company S, recalls,

Rapper E: [The idol trainees] were good [at rap], but their attitudes and behaviors were a lot different from those of other rappers their age. I could strongly feel that they were controlled – or mature, to describe it in a good way. They were extremely polite, and I could feel that they were censoring themselves. But it was not like they were suppressed; I rather felt like they were educated to be immaculate persons – you know how Company S pursues that kind of image. The A&R team also told me that I should avoid writing lyrics that are too sexual or political. In sum, the musicians [at Company S] were very decent, well-educated, well-disciplined people.

Author: I also felt that the idols [at Company S] were already business-minded. It was not like the company was forcibly suppressing or controlling free spirits.

Rapper E: I think the idols are aware of how big the reward is. The company's previous achievements tell them what they will get later. They are aware of the fact that they will get bigger freedom and rewards once they go through struggles and restrictions.[35]

When I asked what Idol B thinks about fan complaints against the punishingly hectic schedules managed by his company, he replied, "Some say the company is abusing us, but honestly, we are in the same boat, and the company is obviously trying to treat us well. After all, it's fans who will leave us if we don't appear often [on the media]."[36] It is common for companies to control the idols' behavior, relationships, and online activities, especially in their early career before they have a fan base.

The company and fans take a special interest in an idol's friendship with other members of the band, outdoor activities, and love life. Through analyses of idols' interactions with each other on television shows, social media, real-time chats, and fan-filmed videos, fans constantly evaluate friendships among the idols. Almost all of the fans I interviewed told me stories about their idol's best friend in the group. Based on the chemistry between two members, fans develop a "shipping" relationship that becomes a primary source of fan fiction (see Chapter 13 in this book). Then successful idols must be capable of controlling their relationships. Idols explain that they learn how to display their friendship in public in the most natural way. During my interview with Idol A, we watched a television interview of his group. Idol A observed that his group members were intentionally touching each other, although the touch seemed completely natural and habitual to me – it was a way of displaying a shared homo-erotic or homosocial connection with each other before their fans.[37]

It is difficult to maintain a solid fan base when idols are caught dating, drinking, smoking, or doing any other type of "misdemeanor" outside the dorm. Fans do allow their idols to go outside but urge them to take responsibility for what they do. Because fans are the ones who are paying the "debt" – by buying concert tickets and merchandise – idols must show gratitude and appreciation by "working hard," not by dating in public or going out to bars and clubs. For our interview, Idol B met me at 2 o'clock in the morning, to avoid both his fans and his managers, who wouldn't let him go out. His manager eventually called him around 4:30 a.m. To avoid giving the wrong impression to any fan who might be watching, we kept a distance of ten to twenty feet from each other.

A company will ask its idols to be kept informed of their romances, in case of dating scandals and rumors. Super Junior member Heechul states that his company, SM Entertainment, encourages its idols to date each other, because it is more convenient to handle dating scandals within the company.[38] Meanwhile, small companies try to prevent idols from dating by confiscating their cell phones, although the idols will eventually contact others via social media.[39]

Idols' Roles and Agency in the Production

In the early stage of their career, idols' musical tastes and opinions are rarely taken into consideration. A company will recruit the broadest pool of idol trainees, choose a concept, and select the trainees who best fit that concept. Those who fail to join the debut team may wait for another chance or leave the company. Due to the lack of debut opportunities, trainees often make their debut with a concept or worldview that does not reflect their musical taste and artistic preference. Idol C, who left his group after a seven-year contract, states, "My company wanted to make an idol version of a hip hop crew. I like hip hop, so the plan sounded nice to me, but the company really worked with no plan. After all, the production had changed after the company collected random tracks via acquaintances. Because [the company people] recklessly received songs from their friends or famous people, our group's music eventually became more similar to Japanese rock sound than to hip hop."[40]

As they develop their careers and establish a fan base, idols engage in making music, selecting themes, and expressing their individuality in music production. Girls' Generation's Tiffany states, "Because there are so many things to juggle, I've got to be really hands-on in terms of the creative direction, like, what kind of music and what kind of fashion and videos.... I'm just very passionate and expressive, and they were just like, 'No one loves this more than you, no one loves us more than you, we trust you!' and it led to me taking control and also being able to create a subunit out of it."[41] Albums by a solo artist or a subunit group (a smaller group within the group) can give idols a great opportunity to showcase their musical virtuosity, artistic sensibility, and thoughts. Idol D explains, "For a group album, I make music based on our concept and stories that need to be added to the album. There's a certain theme set up [for the group], so sometimes we cover something trendy. When I make music alone, I don't think about my group. I just find a subject that pops up in my head … because that's most genuine, as if your unconscious mind is reflected in your dream. I try to make my music only when I have such intuitive moments."[42]

As multimedia entertainers, idols also develop their talents in art and fashion. SHINee's Key, for example, helped design the stage costumes for the group's single, "View" (2015). K-pop male idols used to customarily wear tailor-made suits on stage. However, Key pointed out that suits do not match the sounds of deep house and suggested that his members wear off-the-rack clothes – this style later became a new norm in K-pop.[43] Key also prepared a thirty-five-page PowerPoint presentation to explain his ideas on stage costumes to the company and coordinated the costumes for SHINee's 2015 and 2016 concert tours.

Fan Management

As much as idols are subject to meet the demands of their fans, fans are also expected to follow the rules set up by their idols and entertainment companies. During the era of the first-generation idols (between the late 1990s and early 2000s), fan clubs were run by fan club executives who volunteered. They were the liaison between the company and fans, managing food and transportation and delivering gifts from fans to the company. In return, the fan club executives stayed in touch with idol managers, acquired advance information about the idols' schedules, and met idols when they made their deliveries to the company. Only those who were well known in the fandom through active, long-term participation in offline events could be elected to fan club executive positions.[44]

With the debuts of the second-generation idols (between the mid-2000s and early 2010s), entertainment companies started creating in-house fan club management divisions. As soon as a company debuts a new idol group, it recruits members for its fan club. To join, fans pay annual membership fees and will receive a gift box that contains a photo book with messages from the idols; access to the idols' exclusive messages, photos, and videos; and priority when purchasing concert tickets. Meanwhile, idols' schedules are announced to the public on the official website.

In-house fan management brought several changes to the idol-fan relationship. Removing the hierarchy between the fan club executives and nonexecutive fans standardized the proximity to idols across the fandom. Fans are now able to communicate with idols directly through social media under the company's fan management. Maintaining fair access to idols has become one of the most important values in the K-pop business. For this reason, neither idols nor fans consider *sasaeng* (people who hack idols' cell phones, follow their private schedules, or trespass on their property) "fans," because respecting idols' privacy is one way of maintaining a healthy and respectful idol-fan relationship.

Conclusion

In an active participatory culture, such as K-pop fandom, celebrities assume several roles: Their mediated images circulate as textual commodities; they please their fans through "fan service" performances as affective laborers; and their publicity and music productions transform into cultural influence that allows them to accumulate more cultural and economic capital. While K-pop idols have many obligations and restrictions, music offers them a space of empowerment through which to express their thoughts and build a reputation, wealth, and relationships. Fans are also active consumers and promoters of K-pop productions. Through active interactions with idols and other fans, K-pop fans learn how to maintain a healthy idol-fan relationship. "True" fans respect idols' privacy, maintain ideal idol-fan relationships, and sustain the K-pop economy; those who do not will be expelled from fandom and lose company fan club membership.

When BTS's J-Hope was asked, "How do you measure success?" he answered, "When I see people around me smile in any situation."[45] The K-pop industry is easily labeled as a machine, but despite its fast-paced, profit-oriented nature, there is endless effort, caring, and support by people who value each other's hard work, personal growth, and labor rights. If there is a "dark side" in K-pop, there should be a "bright side" as well, because all industries are intertwined in the complex affective flows and multidirectional cultural dynamics.

Notes

1 Gaon Music Chart, "2019 Annual Chart Review," www.gaonchart.co.kr/main/section/article/m .view.gaon?idx=16313 (accessed July 10, 2020).

2 Hugh McIntyre, "BTS Has Charted Four No. 1 Albums Faster than Any Group since the Beatles," *Forbes*, March 6, 2020. Also see Bryan Rolli, "BTS Just Shattered a Major iTunes Record Formerly Held by Adele," *Forbes*, July 6, 2020.

3 See John Seabrook, "Factory Girls," *The New Yorker*, October 1, 2012. Also see Jessica Wong, "The Punishing Pressures behind K-Pop Perfection," *CBC News*, February 24, 2018.

4 Matthew Campbell and Sohee Kim, "The Dark Side of K-Pop: Assault, Prostitution, Suicide, and Spycams," *Bloomberg Businessweek*, November 6, 2019.

5 See Matt Stahl, *Unfree Masters: Recording Artists and the Politics of Work* (Durham, NC: Duke University Press, 2013).

6 Keith Negus, *Music Genres and Corporate Cultures* (London: Routledge, 1999), 17.

7 Negus, *Music Genres and Corporate Cultures*, 22–23.

8 Tiffany Young, "Tiffany Young Talks over My Skin, Girls' Generation & One Direction," https:// youtu.be/1McYk39AnvI (accessed April 8, 2021).

9 Worker C, interview by author, Seoul, September 28, 2016.

10 Worker C interview.

11 Jin, "Naengjanggoreul Butakhae 153 Hoe" (Please take care of my refrigerator ep. 153), https:// youtu.be/6j0OUjmCuZI (accessed April 8, 2021).

12 Ban Kyung-Rim, "Bangtansonyeondan Jeongguk, 'Hwanggeummagnae' In Iyu" (Why BTS Jungkook is the golden *maknae*), *Viewers*, December 21, 2020.

13 Idol C, telephone interview by author, November 29, 2017.

14 Idol B, interview by author, Seoul, August 21, 2015.

15 Idol B interview.

16 Worker A, interview by author, Seoul, September 15, 2016.

17 Forty-seven idol trainees participated in the survey, and the percentage represents the number who received each lesson. Sim Jae-geol, "2 nyeone 10 eok, 'eok' sori naneun aidol yukseong biyong" (1 billion won in two years, idol training expenses that cost billions), *Sporbiz*, June 2, 2015.

18 Hee-A Park, *Idol Maker* (Seoul: Media Sam, 2019), 45.

19 Park, *Idol Maker*, 53.

20 Worker A interview.

21 Song Jae-Ho, "Aidoreui gyeyakjogeone daehae allyeodeurigetsumnida" (I will tell you about the contract conditions for idols), www.youtube.com/watch?v=mOduguKcYBs (accessed October 30, 2018).

22 Idol A, interview by author, Seoul, July 3, 2017.

23 Sim, "2 Nyeone 10 Eok."

24 Kwon Hyuk-Ju, "Yeonyein hyeondaepan nobimunseo bulgongjeong panjeong" (Entertainer's modern version of slave contract is judged to be unfair), *Nocut News*, June 17, 2004.

25 Park Yu-Young, "Idal mal yeonyein pyojungyeyakseo naonda" (The standard contract form for entertainers will be released by the end of this month), *Newsis*, June 22, 2009.

26 The Korea Fair Trade Commission, "Yeonye Gihweksawa Sosok Yeonseupsaenggan Bulgongjeong Gyeyak Gwanhaeng Gaeseon" (Improvement of Unfair Trading Convention between Entertainment Companies and Affiliated Trainees), www.korea.kr/common/download.do?fileId=184821188&tblKey=GMN (accessed October 7, 2018).

27 Korea Creative Content Agency, "Gasu jungsim pyojunjeonsokkyeyakseo" (Standard Form of the Exclusive Contract for Entertainers (Singers) in Popular Culture), https://ent.kocca.kr/UID/BBS/U007/contract.do (accessed November 13, 2018).

28 Lee Yu-Jin, "'Anjikyeodo geuman,' heo-ulppunin pyojun-gyeyakseo-e meongdeuneun 'yeonyein inkwon'" ("Doesn't matter if we don't observe it," "entertainers' rights" are not protected under the gloss of the Standard Form of the Exclusive Contract), *The Kyunghyang*, October 23, 2018.

29 John David Ebert, *Dead Celebrities, Living Icons: Tragedy and Fame in the Age of the Multimedia Superstar* (Santa Barbara, CA: Praeger), 191.

30 Choe Gyu-Hwan, "Deo Iseuteu Laiteu-ga balkin Midia Lain 4 nyeon pokhaeng jeonmal ... 'jeongsan, chugeobi jiwondo mu'" (The East Light's full account on Media Line's four-year assault ... "no payment nor rent support provided either"), *Chosun Ilbo*, October 19, 2018.

31 Choe, "Deo Iseuteu Laiteu-ga balkin Midia Lain 4 nyeon pokhaeng jeonmal."

32 Rosé, "Rosé Talks on the Ground, 'R', Blackpink & Hank," https://youtu.be/RXqysZ6Bqno (accessed April 3, 2021).

33 Young, "Tiffany Young Talks over My Skin, Girls' Generation & One Direction."

34 Eun-Gu Kim, "'Peurodyuseu 101' ro deureonan yeonseupsaeng 100 manmyeong sidae-eui 'sukje'" (The "homework" revealed on "Produce 101" in the era of 1 million idol trainees), *Edaily*, April 22, 2016.

35 Rapper E, interview by author, Seoul, August 22, 2017.

36 Idol B interview.

37 Idol A, interview by author, Seoul, July 18, 2017.

38 Lee Seung-Mi, "Taeyeon-Backhyun 'yeoraeseol' ... Kim Hi-cheol 'Yi Suman, sanaeyeonae gwonjang" (Taeyeon and Backhyun's dating scandal ... Kim Heechul says, "Lee Soo-man encourages his company's idols to date other idols in the company"), *JTBC News*, June 19, 2014.

39 Idol C interview.

40 Idol C interview.

41 Young, "Tiffany Young Talks over My Skin."

42 Idol D, interview by author, Seoul, August 25, 2015.

43 MMTG, "I Invited SHINee Because of VIEW, Why Are We Talking about a Different Song? / [MMTG ep. 181]," https://youtu.be/siAsCLpgZTI (accessed April 24, 2021).

44 Kim Jakka, "Igeosi han-guk paenkeullop saengtaegye" (This is the nature of Korean fan clubs), *The Hankyoreh*, February 17, 2011.

45 J-Hope, "BTS Interview," https://youtu.be/Hk2_A-rh7IM (accessed May 1, 2021).

8 From K-Pop to Z-Pop

The Pan-Asian Production, Consumption, and Circulation of Idols

SO-RIM LEE

Seven girls elegantly walk toward a large, magnificent door. Light pours onto their anticipating faces as the door opens to reveal a small box. A girl opens the small box and beholds a shiny, silver medallion in her bejeweled hands. Engraved in a futuristic font with the letter Z, this round object is revealed as the source of emanating light. Beats and colors roll in to the dynamic tempo of Z-Girls' debut song, "What You Waiting For"; the camera cuts to juxtaposition between two sequences – close-ups of each girl holding fresh flowers up to her face in bright light, and the girls dancing in a synchronized formation to sleek backdrops of an indoor set. They are the Z-Girls: Bell, Queen, Vanya, Priyanka, Carlyn, Mahiro, and Joanne, who won the first season of *Z-POP Dream*, a 2018 pan-Asian audition competition televised and held across seven countries from which each member respectively hails: Thailand, Vietnam, Indonesia, India, the Philippines, Japan, and Taiwan. Under the combined name "Z-Stars," the seven Z-Girls and seven Z-Boys – their equally transnational male counterparts – made their official South Korea debut in February 2019 with a sizable concert at Seoul's Jamsil Arena, featuring as guests the prominent K-pop stars A.Pink, Monsta X, Rain, and Chungha. While the South Korean media primarily took note of the Z-stars as curiosity K-pop acts "with no Korean members," more welcome awaited the groups in Indonesia, Vietnam, and the Philippines in March 2019 showcases; Vietnam's POPS Worldwide even awarded them the "Best Idol Debut Award" for the year. Later that year, Zenith Media Contents (ZMC), their former management agency,[1] held the second season of *Z-POP Dream* auditions in Thailand, Taiwan, Japan, Indonesia, Vietnam, the Philippines, and India.

The Z-Girls released their music video of "What You Waiting For" on February 21, 2019; it had garnered 8.1 million views on YouTube by March 2021, making it the most popular song by Z-stars.[2] The stylish up-tempo number is also a transnational endeavor, written by Japanese songwriter Kanata Okajima, English songwriter Abi F Jones, and Swedish producer Dejo. Its music video features the visual and auditory formula familiar to a trained K-pop audience – catchy riffs and hooks, organized choreography, sartorial style, elaborate camera work, and computer-generated graphics – with one major difference: the girls sing entirely in English. At a press show in Seoul's Gangnam district in August 2019, Jun Kang, the founder and executive producer of ZMC, revealed that the issue of language was indeed a major hurdle for Z-Girls and Z-Boys in trying to break into the K-pop industry. In an interview with *Korea JoongAng Daily*, Kang said that K-pop music shows refused to feature Z-Girls and Z-Boys on their programs: "I've been working in the industry for 30 years and have many connections, but music shows tell us that they want K-pop and Korean songs and that our groups don't fit in."[3] When asked about his vision for the two groups, Kang replied: "to create a K-pop project based on cultural exchanges with many countries."[4]

The 2010s saw K-pop's rapid globalization in the US-dominant international pop music industry; the World Economic Forum noted that K-pop's global revenue in 2016 reached $4.7 billion,[5] while the *New York Post* reported that BTS alone brought $3.6 billion a year to South Korea.[6] If the nascent era of *Hallyu* ("Korean Wave") of the early 2000s beckoned scholars and the general public alike to ask the ontological question, "What is K-pop?" by 2020, K-pop's transnational impact and niche within the global pop music industry had shifted the question to "What counts as K-pop?" or "*Who* gets to do K-pop?" An early controversial public debate on these questions came from the 2014 debut of EXP Edition, a "K-pop boy group" composed of four American men, three of them white-passing.[7] A most vehement criticism against EXP Edition came from American K-pop fans from the point of view of US racial politics, disappointed to witness "white men" take over yet another nonwhite, "niche" popular culture. And in April 2020, the first London-based K-pop girl group, KAACHI, debuted as an international, multiethnic group of four, managed by FrontRow Records, of the United Kingdom – generating perplexed reactions and debates about cultural appropriation from online K-pop fans on yet another K-pop act from the so-called First World. Such debate on "who gets to do K-pop," then, is more relevant now than ever. Alecsandra Tubiera of the *South China Morning Post* asks whether it is fair for anyone to determine the legitimacy of certain K-pop artists on the basis of their nationality.[8] I argue that the deeper issue underlying this debate has to do with complex tensions concerning inter-Asia politics, the rhetoric of technology (which is part and parcel of K-pop as a "Korean" cultural export), and the perceptions of a hierarchically racialized world ordered by the logic of global capitalism. This is evident in the anonymized comment section of Jun Kang's interview featured on the popular English-language K-pop blogs Allkpop and Kpopmap, where users questioned the fairness of how K-pop music shows seemed to allow only certain artists to be on K-pop music stages.

CHUCK_T: So they can have Christina Aguilera, Usher, Westlife on Inkigayo.... Lady Gaga on M Countdown ... Ryan Reynolds on Masked Singer ... Charlie Puth on Genie Music Awards and Janet Jackson on MAMA.... ALL these people "not Korean" but they have a problem with Z-Boys and Girls.

YEHN: Knetz [Korean internet users] are very ethnocentric. I wonder why they always use the term global girl/boy group but their mindset is not even global.[9]

"Chuck_T" on Allkpop pointed out how famous non-Korean-speaking Euro-American pop stars were invited to perform on numerous shows that rejected Z-Stars. Beyond the obvious fact that American media imperialism has considerable effect on the regional music markets in Asia, this comment allows us to rethink the exclusion of Z-Girls and Z-Boys from the shows as less about their foreignness per se than about their "minor" presence as South and Southeast Asians in the global hierarchy of racial capitalism, in which the export-oriented K-pop industry is imbricated. In other words, are Z-stars too "third world" for Korean television? "Yehn" on Kpopmap calls out the "ethnocentrism" of "Knetz," accusing domestic K-pop fans (rather than the industry personnel) for being proud of the "global" popularity of K-pop yet having a closed mindset in maintaining a purist definition of who counts as a K-pop artist in terms of race and ethnicity.

To be clear, the partial nature of anonymous online comment threads cautions us against assuming that such opinions are a majority voice of international K-pop fans; nor is there any substantial evidence that proves Korean internet users to be more "ethnocentric" than non-Korean ones. That said, these comments demonstrate that the K-pop industry's reluctance to accept Z-pop into its arena is an urgent yet underexplored subject, especially given that the K-pop industry famously touts globalization and transnationalism as signature qualities as it expands into the South and Southeast Asian markets. This strategy resonates with how Ingyu Oh redefines "glocalization" – from its original use as *dochakuka* (global localization), a buzzword in the 1980s Japanese business sector – as "high quality localization that is meant to be re-exported to other countries due to a small domestic market."[10] Lee Soo-man, the founding chair of one of K-pop's big companies, SM Entertainment, actively uses glocalization to make K-pop an international enterprise. SM Entertainment has been branding their K-pop enterprise as a system of cultural technology that combines recruiting idols across Asia and "re-localizing" them to the preferences of local consumers. This rhetoric of K-pop as technology has become their signature strategy to produce apparently multiethnic, multi-national K-pop groups for markets in and beyond South Korea.

The prevalence of such glocalization, however, should not be mistakenly translated into a celebration of diversity. The K-pop music scene is a cutthroat neoliberal market, with far too many performers with far too short careers. Even those who become successful, Suk-Young Kim notes, have an "an extremely short life span, usually five years or so," due to the "high pressure of the industry that cultivates the insatiable appetite for newer and younger idols."[11] This, coupled with years of training and financial investment put into the idols-in-making, compels the industry to run on tested formulas of success in producing new idols. In other words, that an idol group has never been entirely non-Korean and primarily English-speaking and produced by a non-Korean management company is anomalous enough to make Z-stars instantly dubious as potential K-pop idols.

Z-pop fans' calling out what they perceive as the K-pop industry's hypocrisy, then, becomes a critical point of interrogation into where K-pop as well as K-pop studies stand in 2020, nearly a decade since PSY's "Gangnam Style" became a worldwide YouTube sensation in 2012. Globalization positions its subjects in a system of hierarchies, whose logic "materializes in a worldwide grid of strategic places" to form what Saskia Sassen called a new geography of centrality and marginality.[12] This geography certainly informs K-pop's relationship to American pop and U.S. media imperialism, as K-pop scholars have analyzed in the past decade, from PSY to BTS – most recently in the nuanced interrogations of K-pop's fraught relationship with Black American culture.[13] But it also informs K-pop's – and by proxy, South Korea's – status as a neo-imperial cultural hegemon in relation to the regional markets across Asia, often overlooked as "peripheral" to the "metropoles" in the globalization grid. Zooming in on the significance of South and Southeast Asian performers in K-pop thus aligns with François Lionnet and Shu-mei Shih's argument[14] for the need to see beyond the homogenizing logic of globalization by focusing on "minor transnational" actors, who complicate these processes in the interstitial spaces of cultural clashes and transactions.

Using Z-pop as a case study, this chapter reconsiders the complex relationship among technology, globalization, and K-pop in inter-Asia contexts. First, I trace how the discourse of techno-nationalism undergirded South Korea's economic development and accelerated the globalization of the K-pop cultural industry. Next, I explore the significance of Z-pop's tapping into the South and Southeast Asian consumer base – specifically, how the management company (Divtone) and fans (GalaxZ) use the idealized rhetoric of a transnational "One Asia." Interpreting the GalaxZ's adoption of English as lingua franca and the Z-stars' resistance to what I call "K-pop visuality," I extend the question of "Who gets to do K-pop?" to the K-pop producers and consumers alike. In my discussion of Z-pop, I join Soo Ryon Yoon's call to rethink how we see and interpret the directions of cultural circulation in Asia to avoid situating the West as "the final destination of K-pop's ultimate arrival."[15] So doing also takes up Kuan-Hsing Chen's framework of "Asia as method,"[16] a self-reflexive intellectual movement that interrogates how we study Asia by addressing globalization with the aim of de-imperialization. As Koichi Iwabuchi noted, inter-Asia referencing as a process of de-Westernizing the interpretation of media cultures in Asia can make possible "hitherto underexplored intra-regional or inter-Asian" comparisons based on "shared experiences of 'forced' modernization and less hierarchical relationships than a prevailing West-Asia comparison that is based on assumed temporal distance between them."[17] Embracing such theorizations, I align with the vibrant research community that Chua Beng Huat calls transnational East Asia pop culture studies.[18]

Culture, Techno-Nationalism, and K-Pop

The Z-POP Dream project specifies its primary audience as Asia's Generation Z, the demographic cohort born into the most widespread use of digital technology in history. Born between roughly the mid-1990s and the early 2010s, these digital natives tend to spend "six hours or more a day on their phones," and "more time on social media than does any other age cohort in Asia."[19] Fittingly, the project has maintained an active web and social media presence through the formative three years since its launch in 2018 – so much so that it even had a now-defunct "start-up pitch" site for tech-industry collaborators and financial sponsors. This website included a freely downloadable twenty-seven-page white paper delineating the Z-pop project as a brand new model of technology venture and "the first global entertainment ecosystem" comprising three parts: audition competition show, idol training system, and fan-based digital community platform through a smartphone mobile app. This ecosystem, it stated, would employ Ethereum-based blockchain technology to let fans purchase "Z-pop coins" to vote for the idol trainee of their choice; blockchain ledgers were to create tamper-proof election returns integral to building a trustworthy digital community critical to its transnational business.[20] When the newly minted and Singapore-based Divtone Entertainment took over the Z-POP Dream project from ZMC in 2020, the company also wasted no time emphasizing the technological innovations it would bring; its fluorescent-colored website introduces itself as "the world's first Entertainment Technology ('Enter-Tech') enterprise, harnessing the latest technology to deliver electrifying, interactive experiences that transport fans into a breathtaking virtual world."[21] This rhetoric of a technology-driven futurism is what undergirds the Z-POP Dream project as a business venture akin to K-pop.

Significantly, the discourse of technology is what launched the globalization of K-pop. In the wake of the 1997 crisis, the Kim Dae-jung administration invested in information technology to resuscitate the nation through neoliberal economic reforms. Noting how the financial crisis thus led to a government-sponsored promotion of broadband and the birth of PC *bangs* (internet cafés) as "test beds for the high-speed Internet" around this time, Inkyu Kang argues that "it was the symbolic value [of new technologies] rather than the practical one that motivated young Koreans to learn to use them."[22] Engaging with digital technology soon became a cultural, if not neoliberal ethos, reinforced by "positive associations" of progress, innovation, ability to use English, savviness, youth, and upward mobility. Not coincidentally, "culture" itself – or more specifically, the culture industry – was also inducted into the realm of technology in 1994 by Kwangyun Wohn of the Korea Advanced Institute of Science and Technology (KAIST), who used the term *munhwa gisul* (culture technology) to refer to the content-based, multimodal set of technologies involved in the industrial production of film, drama, animations, characters, music, performing arts, games, and theme parks. With the establishment of the Korea Creative Content Agency (KOCCA) within the Ministry of Culture, Sports and Tourism in 2001, *munhwa keon-tenchcu gisul* (cultural content technology) became one of six official government-promoted technology initiatives alongside biotechnology, energy/environmental technology, information technology, nanotechnology, and space technology. Taking the 1997 financial crisis as a turning point, then, South Korea refashioned itself into a veritable technocultural superpower at the turn of the millennium.

In the world of K-pop, it was also around 1997 that SM Entertainment's Lee Soo-man trademarked the corporation's in-house idol-training system as Culture Technology™ to refer to the fourfold process of recruiting, training, producing, and marketing K-pop idols worldwide. In 2016, in a hologram-incorporated presentation, Lee performed his first large-scale "product launch" of what he called New Culture Technology, introducing the latest platforms, content, and eponymous idol group (NCT) developed by SM Entertainment. It was there that he introduced the plan to "glocalize" the K-pop industry by building a system to locally source (recruit) idol trainees from across the globe[23] and manufacture (train) them into K-pop idols, thus rhizomatically expanding the K-pop industry. Rendering K-pop as a technology thus redefines its idols as transnational biocapital embodying the formula of their own creation. Also apparent in this system is the symbiosis of the technocentric state and the culture industry embedded in the globalization of K-pop.

Lessening the gap between culture and technology also denotes a desire to bridge the core values that entail each notion – such as creativity and innovation – within the neoliberal nexus of individualism and nationalism: to quote Suk-Young Kim, "Creativity and innovation were now heralded simultaneously as both individual achievements and national virtues – the two pillars that sustain South Korea's brand of neoliberalism."[24] In other words, K-pop's success resonates from within and beyond the affective register of technonationalist, or the mechanism by which the developmental narrative of nation building, government sponsorship of technology, and nationalist pride amalgamate into a cultural ethos. Tae-Ho Kim points out that such nationalist rhetoric is "so subtle and abstract that it can be compared to the transparent and multi-colored cloak"[25] that the K-pop industry dexterously mobilizes to promote the excellence of idols in the global music market. This is closely related to what Doobo Shim observed: "Koreans heartily welcome the fruits of the Korean Wave in the midst of recovery from the 1997 economic crisis, and the subsequent International Monetary Fund (IMF)-directed economic restructuring, which they often refer to as 'national humiliation.'"[26] In other words, the *Hallyu* globalization echoes the affective cadence of a technonationalist victory embedded in South Korea's crisis management through a neoliberal turn.

The victory of technonationalism, then, celebrates not only the artistry of the idols' individual performances – perfectly symmetric choreography, flawless vocals, and an overall visual excellence – but also the artisanry that exemplifies the innovative technology behind their making. The idols are larger-than-life products and proud "faces" of South Korea's national exports – from soju, electronics, beauty products, and cars to the Korean Tourism Bureau and, by proxy, South Korea itself. As such, they renegotiate the relationship not only between the corporation and the state but also between culture and technology.

The Möbius strip of K-pop and technonationalism also informs how the Euro-American media often treat K-pop as a genre of music with Korea as the single site of origin. In August 2019, for instance, the MTV Video Music Awards gave BTS the first win in the Best K-Pop Group category, excluding them from the marquee awards like Video of the Year or Artist of the Year. Putting K-pop into its own basket – one that *Variety*'s Jae-Ha Kim quipped is an "exile" into a "nationality-based category"[27] – well illuminates what the American media sees as a threat to its long-standing global media empire. The threat is rapidly expanding, as the K-pop-contingent industries of K-dramas, K-beauty, K-food, and other cultural exports synergistically continue to amplify the total revenue generated by Culture Technology. In short, K-pop is very much a national venture that goes far beyond the category of music; it is a revenue-generating mode of "soft power" that the MTV VMAs decided to keep in check – perhaps reminiscent of how the Trump administration banned Huawei products and raised tariffs on imported washing machines in 2019.

If K-pop's technonationalist expansion poses a threat to the American media empire, it poses a different, perhaps more imminent threat in South and Southeast Asia, where South Korea has become a veritable cultural hegemon. In the late 1990s and early 2000s *Hallyu* first gained traction in Vietnam, Malaysia, Thailand, Myanmar, Indonesia, and the Philippines through the cultural products of Korean dramas and films. Chung-Sok Suh et al. trace this process through the analytical framework of "cultural proximity" – not only a measure of cultural similarities and differences in societal values, languages, and living standards but also a rubric for a more dynamic mapping of historical, political, economic, and sociocultural interactions between South Korea and the aforementioned regions.[28]

On using this explanation to draw out a broader "inter-Asia cultural affinity" across the region, however, Mary J. Ainslie astutely warns against reductively homogenizing Southeast Asia "in a similar way to that of the older European colonialist project," flattening the complexities of how each nation interacts with *Hallyu* in different ways.[29] She delineates how the relatively less developed ASEAN nations referred to as CLMV countries (Cambodia, Laos, Myanmar, and Vietnam) experienced a concentrated South Korean investment, with Laos as a case study, where *Hallyu* as a project of "pan-Asian urban modernity" is frequently accompanied by exploitative representational rhetoric portraying the underdeveloped nation to Korean audiences as "uncivilized."[30]

While acknowledging such discourses of power carried out through South Korea's national branding and cultural diplomacy, Peichi Chung also reminds us to see the spread of *Hallyu* in Southeast Asia as a "regional cultural phenomenon that has a bottom-up, audience-centered approach connecting to pan-Asian consumerism and fan-based communities."[31] This, Chung notes, is keenly tied to the rapid digitalization of the region, resulting in skyrocketing consumption of global social media services like Facebook and Twitter having a direct impact on the region's market power for *Hallyu* producers by the early 2010s.

One instance of digitalization includes the widespread practice of "fan-subbing" (online fan subtitling) Korean content into multiple languages, leading to the increased visibility of *Hallyu* content such as the South Korean variety television show *Running Man* (2010 to present).[32] Initially gaining a huge cult following in the Southeast Asian region through fansubs, *Running Man* began airing on local television networks in Cambodia, China, Hong Kong, Indonesia, Japan, Malaysia, Singapore, Taiwan, and Thailand. Often dubbed the most successful *Hallyu* television show in Southeast Asia, it has spawned a franchise industry with coproduced spin-offs with local television producers in China, Vietnam, Indonesia, and the Philippines. Such online and on-air proliferation of *Hallyu* content, in turn, generated a steady increase in the consumption of "made in Korea" lifestyle products in urban city centers across the ASEAN nations. Lotte Shopping has been expanding the number of department stores and supermarkets in Hanoi and Jakarta since 2008, and in 2019, the BT21 Store – a global franchise from Line Friends selling lifestyle goods designed by the members of the K-pop group BTS – opened two offline locations in Manila.

Unsurprisingly, the ubiquitous presence of *Hallyu* soon generated antipathy toward it. Analyzing the emerging discourse of the *Hallyu* backlash from interviews with eighty consumers in Thailand, Malaysia, and the Philippines, Ainslie et al. offer a nuanced analysis of varied reasons. A significant chunk of *Hallyu* criticism came from the explicit rhetoric of Korean technonationalism perceived to put on a "very naked show" of Korean superiority through echoes of cultural imperialism not lost on the consumers of the region so fraught with histories of colonialism:

> For some Southeast Asian consumers *hallyu* and its aggressive promotion reinforces a colonial mentality, and points to the usurping of local culture as well as the construction of Southeast Asia as a poorer Asian "Other" next to the superior Korea. Instead of challenging Western hegemony (as was a major source of attraction for Asian consumers in early years), the promotion of *hallyu* then actually functions to reinforce a colonial mentality in which it is positioned as usurping local culture.[33]

Ainslie et al. carefully delineate how the rhetoric of technonationalism embedded in the export industry of *Hallyu*/K-pop insinuates a colonial mentality, a term that social psychologists E. J. R. David and Sumie Okazaki apply to characterize how Filipino Americans internalized "a perception of ethnic or cultural inferiority that is … a specific consequence of centuries of colonization under Spain and the U.S."[34] This does applies not only to the obsolete West versus non-West binary; Kuan-Hsing Chen reminds us of the urgency of deimperialization amid inter-Asia imperial structures. Chen particularly illuminates the thin valence between globalization and neocolonial imperialism, "a form of structural domination in which a country with more global power uses political and economic interventions in other countries to influence policy and exercise control over markets."[35] South Korea, an ex-colony and "Tiger economy," has become a veritable subempire simultaneously dependent on the United States, while politically, economically, and culturally dominating the "third world" countries of the Association of South East Asian Nations (ASEAN) (currently, ten member states: Brunei, Cambodia, Indonesia, Laos, Malaysia, Myanmar, the Philippines, Singapore, Thailand, and Vietnam). Reports continually surface of the multinational South Korean conglomerate Samsung's violation of "minimum wage and probationary worker laws, forced labor, unfair termination, and verbal abuse" in its electronics factories in India, Vietnam, and Indonesia.[36] And in South Korea proper, ample documentation attests to how migrant workers (the majority from China, Vietnam, Uzbekistan, Cambodia, Nepal, and the Philippines) and foreign brides (the majority from Vietnam, China, Thailand, and the Philippines) face rampant racism and xenophobia on the basis of their economic status and darker skin.[37] Considering that the ASEAN region is K-pop's critical consumer base responsible for the highest number of K-pop streams on YouTube from 2018 to 2019,[38] the unidirectional flow of *Hallyu* products – which Ainslie et al. called "modern day mercantilism" – reinforces the hierarchical logic of capitalism.

How, then, can we interpret Z-pop's piggybacking on the K-pop industry's globalization model – especially when Divtone Entertainment, a non-Korean newcomer to the K-pop industry, fully takes up the fraught discourse of cultural technology used in K-pop's expansion into South and Southeast Asia? As I discuss in the next section, Divtone differentiates Z-pop from K-pop through a rhetoric of transnational community building across Asia. Yet the compound relationship among technology, technonationalism, and the inter-Asia dynamic complicate Divtone's motives as but another neo-imperialist enterprise tapping into the "under-explored" ASEAN region. This is even further complicated by Divtone's own corporate structure composed of transnational capitalists. CEO Norimitsu Kameshima is a Japanese entrepreneur based in Singapore; his team includes Euro-American private equity investors and Silicon Valley tech entrepreneurs; and the company's parent corporation ("holding company"), Divtone Group, is located in Luxembourg. Our earlier question, "Who gets to do K-pop?," then, should be not solely about non-Korean individual performers but extended to the industry bigwigs with the financial stakes.

To be clear, the K-pop industry is always already situated in a curiously ambivalent space; on the one hand, it is a globalizing enterprise run by the logic of global capitalism; yet on the other hand, these globalizing processes of K-pop enable transnational interactions and hybrid popular cultures generated on the local and individual levels of interactions and frictions. How can we navigate the slippery and ill-defined labels of K-pop and Z-pop, not from the top-down perspective but from that of the fans?

"Welcome to Our GalaxZ"

Fans of Z-stars call themselves "GalaxZ," based on an apt visual metaphor of the world reimagined as a galaxy of Z-pop; this interstellar community consists of present and future Z-stars as well as constellations of fans strewn across the globe. Digital and social media are the gravitational attraction that holds this galaxy together – Facebook, Instagram, YouTube, Twitter, Line, WhatsApp, and Glitsy. As of August 2020, the GalaxZ remained an unofficial group rather than a coherently mobilized club with membership dues and benefits, their size and demographic hence largely unknown. Like most social media–based K-pop fandom, the members of GalaxZ organically coalesce on the platforms to share their love for the Z-stars; unlike most K-pop fandom, however, the GalaxZ is more than a community "stanning" their idols; it also empowers members to join the idols by becoming the next Z-star. In the world of Z-pop, fans aspiring to do so are called Dreamers. On Glitsy, a smartphone app designed exclusively for the Z-POP Dream project, Dreamers are actively encouraged to upload thirty-second videos of themselves singing, dancing, or playing musical instruments to pre-audition for the next season of *Z-POP Dream*. The more "likes" they receive from other users on the app, the more experience points they receive, and high-ranking Dreamers have a better chance at being selected for auditions. They are also encouraged to collect points by streaming Z-stars' reality TV features, past seasons of Z-pop auditions, and "how to" videos on K-pop dancing techniques taught by the Singaporean choreographer Alif Archo. Shortly after the launch of the Glitsy app in Apple Store and Google Play in June 2019, *Z-POP Dream*'s season 2 auditions took place; Dreamers pre-auditioned by uploading their thirty-second videos until July 15, and those selected were invited to in-person auditions held in Thailand, Taiwan, Japan, Indonesia, Vietnam, the Philippines, and India for the final round.

For the Dreamers, the Z-Girls and Z-Boys serve as role models who actively remind their fans that dreams of becoming a K-pop idol can come true; these stars share their daily adventures in Seoul through reality television shows that chronicle their K-pop training ("Z-Pop School A to Z") and Korean culture education sessions ("Annyeong Korea"). As yet

K-pop "underdogs," the Z-stars also share videos of themselves cover dancing famous K-pop groups as well as "busking" – performing unannounced in Seoul's various public spaces. Many of those who auditioned for *Z-POP Dream* in 2017 had been longtime K-pop fans dedicated to singing and cover dancing their favorite idols while active as pop starlets in the local music industries. For instance, Vanya, Carlyn, and Mahiro had debuted in girl groups in Indonesia, the Philippines, and Japan, respectively; Priyanka won the Excellent Vocals award by singing Park Bom's song "You and I" at the 2016 K-Pop World Festival organized by South Korea's Ministry of Foreign Affairs. In 2018, as soon as fourteen Z-Girls and Z-Boys were selected, the producers flew them to Seoul to begin training in the K-pop trade: singing, dancing, grooming, language learning (English, Korean), interacting with fans, and learning to embody a level of intercultural competence by cohabiting with one another. Going from performing their favorite idols' repertoire to becoming a K-pop star, then, is the ultimate dream-come-true narrative at the heart of *Z-POP Dream*.

Hence, unlike in most K-pop fandoms, fans and idols alike are Dreamers who compose GalaxZ – a community that the idols simultaneously belong to and represent. In a memorable scene from a 2019 YouTube documentary on the Z-POP Dream project, Jun Kang of ZMC speaks heartily to the Z-stars ahead of their debut: "On the stage you will meet the best K-pop stars. When they're looking at you guys, I don't want them to look down [on you] like, 'Oh, they just want to cover dance for me.' No, you are our true artists."[39] This remark encapsulates the underdog sensibility shared by the GalaxZ, while also foreshadowing the dismissal of Z-stars by the K-pop music shows. Perhaps most critically, "you are our true artists" encapsulates a sense of upward mobility critical to the Z-POP Dream project, the sense that Z-pop is about telling future idol hopefuls who have not been noticed by the conventional K-pop system, "You too can be one of us."

To put things a little differently, the exclusion from the K-pop industry ironically informs Z-pop's transnational aim of "One Asia." Sid, an Indian member of the Z-Boys, told the *Philippine Star* during a 2019 Manila press conference: "We share a special bond with each other because we come from seven different countries. It's really innovative, a new feel of how people of different cultures come together and present [music]."[40] Z-Girls' Priyanka, who comes from Assam, India, told the *Indo-Asian News Service* in 2020: "Our goal is to unite Asia and be one Asia. We not only plan to sing in English but also in as many languages as possible. We can be the cultural bridge through music in the world."[41] Many of the Z-stars' YouTube and Glitsy videos also demonstrate their emphasis on intercultural adventures; besides learning Korean culture together through their reality TV show, the Z-stars chronicled their travels to Vietnam, India, and the Philippines. For many, it was a brand-new experience; they learned Hindi slang and Bollywood songs from Priyanka and Sid and tried Filipino, Indonesian, and Vietnamese snacks introduced by respective local members. Many YouTube comment threads show the GalaxZ's enthusiasm for representation, including a comment from "Sanchita Sahana" liked by 14,000 others: "Zstars teaches us 'Unity in Diversity.'"[42]

Critically, not only the Z-stars' intercultural adventures but also the GalaxZ's YouTube comments are exclusively in English. In fact, "GALAXZ," an active Z-pop Facebook group with 4,900 members, restricts posts to English to facilitate open communication among fans logging in from all over the world. Robert Philipson famously criticized the globalization of English as lingua franca as a form of linguistic imperialism "asserted and maintained through the establishment and continuous reconstitution of structural and cultural inequalities between English and other languages."[43] This view was further complicated by the 2009 sanctioning of English as a common language by the ten ASEAN nations, with varying historical, postcolonial, politico-economic, and sociocultural contexts and relationships to multilingualism. Simply defining English as a form of linguistic hegemony does not adequately address its use as an intercultural method of communication among nonnative speakers coming from varying postcolonial contexts; nor does it address the diverse forms of English spoken by the Z-stars through their respective dialects and vocabularies – many come from countries with multiple languages that Andy Kirkpatrick calls "regional lingua franca" other than English.[44] Thus, if not using Korean was a major reason the Z-stars found themselves unwelcomed by South Korean music shows, and for their disrupting the K-pop industry in general, using English acknowledged their audience as less defined by nationalities and including any technology-savvy citizen from the digital "galaxy." In other words, if English carried within it a symbolic value of progress and innovation pivotal to the development of technonationalism in South Korea, English used by GalaxZ is a nod to the digital technology that undergirds the formation of this imagined community.

What perhaps ultimately redefines the Z-POP Dream project's identity from one of many "K-pop inspired" acts to "the first Z-pop" act is their unapologetic self-propulsion into the K-pop production as brown-skinned South and Southeast Asians from outside the industry. When asked about the negative comments she received online upon her debut in 2019, Priyanka answered, "There were a lot of people who said, 'She doesn't deserve to be an idol because she's brown, she doesn't look Korean.'"[45] The comment alludes to what Timothy Laurie described as the K-pop industry's enforcing of "a subtle code of racial belonging that places uneven burdens on performers relative to their (perceived) skin tone."[46] In other words, Priyanka's exotic appearance – marked by deep-set eyes, high cheekbones, and visibly darker complexion – accentuates the unspoken rule undergirding an imagined sense of physiognomic homogeneity of what I call "K-pop visuality." Although many non-Korean idols hail from different national, ethnic, and cultural backgrounds, they are recruited, trained, and groomed according to K-pop's visual rubric to look and perform in a stylized way, "from vocalization to choreography, to even how to 'manage your gaze' when facing the cameras."[47] Maaike Bleeker defines the term "visuality" as an intersubjective experience arising from the relationship between the seeing and the seen, constructed according to social, cultural, and historical conventions.[48] K-pop visuality, then, is a theatrical situation co-constructed by the K-pop idol's performance rubric to be seen – attractive physical traits; makeup and sartorial choices; styles of gesture, air, and mien; charisma; and general likability characterized by a cadence of humility – and by the subjective identities and expectations of the fans who do the seeing.

Priyanka's minoritized image simultaneously disrupts and accentuates the K-pop visuality built on the values of unity and synchronicity (see Figure 8.1). Her perceived brownness among the Z-Girls, while perhaps too easily singled out as "Other," defiantly resists the symbolic value embedded into the K-pop idol's body as idealized capital that is made, rather than born. If anything, the Z-stars fully acknowledge their nonconformity to the "industry standard" of idols' physiognomies that John Seabrook of *The New Yorker* bitingly characterizes as "chiseled, sculpted, and tapering to a sharp point at the chin, Na'vi style," produced out of the "S.M.-style factory system."[49] When asked about the possibility of plastic

Figure 8.1 Priyanka's visual performance diverges from the perceived Korean physiognomy.

surgery – yet another *Hallyu*-contingent industry in South Korea by way of state-sponsored medical tourism – Priyanka shook her head and stated in a reassured voice, "Grooming is also part of our training, and we are taught how to manage ourselves."[50] Priyanka's nonconventional presence, coupled with a quietly self-assured demeanor and skillful onstage performances, all pointedly renegotiate the norms of K-pop visuality. If anything, Priyanka's perfectly synchronized dance performances blending into the unity of the whole demonstrate a dexterous reappropriation of the K-pop visuality – channeled into a visual discourse of "One Asia" – while each close-up resists homogeneity.

Thus repurposing K-pop's cultural technology as only they can, the Z-stars and GalaxZ have just begun calling for more representational diversity in K-pop.

Coda: Looking Ahead

The Z-POP Dream project takes up K-pop's technonationalism and repurposes it to create a pan-Asian cultural community for a generation of digital nomads. Through their slogan "One Asia," Divtone Entertainment claims that Z-pop brings innovation to the K-pop industry by using cutting-edge information technology for more ethnically and culturally diverse representation in K-pop. However, this technocentric rhetoric based on global capitalism is perhaps the very thing that undermines its premise of innovation; if applying technology to "source" and to "bringing" underrepresented nationalities and ethnicities into an established cultural industry sounds ominously familiar, it is because of the apparent power imbalance and imperialistic rhetoric that Ainslie et al. argue have generated a *Hallyu* backlash in Southeast Asia.

That said, the fans and supporters of the Z-stars were quick to call out the foibles of the Z-POP Dream project. Pointing out the irony of Divtone's inclusion of but seven countries in "One Asia," many members of the GalaxZ took to social media in 2020 to criticize the exclusionist pre-audition rubric that specified rigid criteria of age, gender, height, language ability, and nationality (fifteen to twenty-three years old, female or male, over 160 cm [5′3″] for females and 170 cm [5′7″] for males, native or fluent English speakers, and citizens of the seven designated countries). Using technology to claim agency and mobilize their nascent digital community, the GalaxZ reminds us that the outdated mode of unidirectional K-pop circulation no longer has relevance. This became most evident when an unprecedented global pandemic hit the world in 2020 and made digital technology the sole mode of sustaining the K-pop community. The GalaxZ have been virtually mobilizing a monthly "Z-Stars Mention Party" on Twitter in order to keep the Z-stars visible in the public media, in addition to "Mass DM [direct messaging] and Email Party" to demand that Divtone provide more updates on the performers' suspended schedules.

But one year since the official debut of the first generation of Z-stars in 2019, the Z-POP Dream project as a whole leaves many questions for future research. What is at stake in the treatment of K-pop as a mode of technology that can be "applied" to non-Korean performers hailing from different cultures, ethnicities, and nations? How does the rhetoric of technology simultaneously legitimize and undermine the South Korean corporatized monopoly of K-pop? Last but not least, how can we expand upon the question of "Who gets to do K-pop" in the face of an industry rapidly being reshaped by an increasing number of non-Korean idols and corporate entities? The answers to these questions will contribute to further situating K-pop within a discourse of transnational pop culture studies interrogating the political economy of consumption, representation, and inclusion.

Further Reading

Ainslie, Mary J. "Korean Overseas Investment and Soft Power: Hallyu in Laos." *Korea Journal* 56/3 (2016): 5–32.

Ainslie, Mary J., Sarah Domingo Lipura, and Joanne B. Y. Lim. "Understanding the Hallyu Backlash in Southeast Asia: A Case Study of Consumers in Thailand, Malaysia and Philippines." *Kritika Kultura* 28 (2017): 63–91.

Kim, Suk-Young. "Disastrously Creative: K-Pop, Virtual Nation, and the Rebirth of Culture Technology." *TDR: The Drama Review* 64/1 (2020): 22–35.

Shin, Solee I. "How K-Pop Went Global: Digitization and the Market-Making of Korean Entertainment Houses." In S. Heijin Lee, Monika Mehta, and Robert Ji-Song Ku (eds.), *Pop Empires: Transnational and Diasporic Flows of India and Korea*, 268–281. Honolulu: University of Hawai'i Press, 2019.

Yoon, Soo Ryon. "'Gangnam Style' in Dhaka and Inter-Asian Refraction." *Inter-Asia Cultural Studies* 19/2 (2018): 162–179.

Notes

1 In May 2020, Divtone Entertainment took over the management of the Z-POP Dream project from Zenith Media Contents.

2 www.youtube.com/watch?v=MouqjZJnwqA (accessed March 2, 2021).

3 Eun-Jin Kim, "Z-pop Dream Project Gives K-Pop a Global Spin: Members of Z-Girls and Z-Boys Hail from across Asia but Are Based in Korea," *Korea JoongAng Daily*, August 9, 2019, https://koreajoongangdaily.joins.com/news/article/article.aspx?aid=3066593.

4 Eun-Jin Kim, "Z-Pop Dream Project Gives K-Pop a Global Spin."

5 Tommy Soesmanto, "Here's What Other Nations Can Learn from Korea's Pop Music Industry," *World Economic Forum*, December 10, 2018, www.weforum.org/agenda/2018/12/k-popnomics-how-indonesia-and-other-nations-can-learn-from-korean-pop-music-industry/.

6 Christian Gollayan, "K-Pop Band BTS Brings $3.6 Billion a Year to South Korea," *New York Post*, December 18, 2018, https://nypost.com/2018/12/18/k-pop-band-bts-brings-3-6-billion-a-year-to-south-korea/.

7 The four members of EXP Edition are Hunter Kohl, Frankie DaPonte (Portuguese American), Sime Kosta (Croatian American), and Koki Tomlinson (Japanese/German American).

8 Alecsandra Tubiera, "Are Non-Korean K-pop Groups like EXP Edition, Kaachi and 5High Cultural Appropriation – or Is 'K-Pop Is Only for Koreans' Racist?," *South China Morning Post*, July 2, 2020, www.scmp.com/magazines/style/news-trends/article/3091538/are-non-korean-k-pop-groups-exp-edition-kaachi-and.

9 These are comment threads from two 2019 articles: "Are Non-Korean K-Pop Groups, Z-GIRLS & Z-BOYS, Going to Be like EXP Edition?," Kpopmap, February 22, 2019, www.kpopmap.com/are-non-korean-kpop-groups-z-girls-z-boys-going-to-be-like-exp-edition/; and "Z-Girls and Z-Boys' Producer Says the Groups Aren't Being Invited to Music Shows," Allkpop, August 14, 2019, www.allkpop.com/article/2019/08/z-girls-and-z-boys-producer-says-the-groups-arent-being-invited-to-music-shows.

10 Ingyu Oh, "From Localization to Glocalization: Contriving Korean Pop Culture to Meet Glocal Demands," *Kritika Kultura* 29 (2017): 160.

11 Suk-Young Kim, "Black K-Pop: Racial Surplus and Global Consumption," *TDR: The Drama Review* 64/2 (2020): 91.

12 Saskia Sassen, *Globalization and Its Discontents* (New York: New Press, 1998), xxv.

13 Kim, "Black K-Pop"; Crystal S. Anderson, *Soul in Seoul: African American Popular Music and K-Pop* (Jackson: University Press of Mississippi, 2020).

14 François Lionnet and Shu-mei Shih, *Minor Transnationalism* (Durham, NC: Duke University Press, 2005).

15 Soo Ryon Yoon, "'Gangnam Style' in Dhaka and Inter-Asian Refraction," *Inter-Asia Cultural Studies* 19/2 (2018): 167.

16 Kuan-Hsing Chen, *Asia as Method: Toward Deimperialization* (Durham, NC: Duke University Press, 2010).

17 Koichi Iwabuchi, "Korean Wave and Inter-Asian Referencing," in Youna Kim (ed.), *The Korean Wave: Korean Media Go Global* (London: Routledge, 2013), 43–57.

18 Beng Huat Chua, "Engendering an East Asia Pop Culture Research Community," *Inter-Asia Cultural Studies* 11/2 (2010): 202–206.

19 Thomas Rüdiger and Naomi Yamakawa, "Asia's Generation Z Comes of Age," *McKinsey & Company* (2020), www.mckinsey.com/industries/retail/our-insights/asias-generation-z-comes-of-age.

20 "Z-POP DREAM Project: White Paper" Version 2.1.0 on the now-defunct website z-popdream.io/docs/whitepapers/zpopdream-whitepaper-en.pdf (accessed November 13, 2019).

21 Available at divtone.com (accessed March 11, 2021).

22 Inkyu Kang, "It All Started with a Bang: The Role of PC Bangs in South Korea's Cybercultures," in Kyung Hyun Kim and Youngmin Choe (eds.), *The Korean Popular Culture Reader* (Durham, NC: Duke University Press, 2013), 58.

23 www.youtube.com/watch?v=Ky5NvWsXnn8&t=1s (accessed March 8, 2021).

24 Suk-Young Kim, "Disastrously Creative: K-Pop, Virtual Nation, and the Rebirth of Culture Technology," *TDR: The Drama Review* 64/1 (2020): 27.

25 Tae-Ho Kim, "How Could a Scientist Become a National Celebrity? Nationalism and Hwang Woo-Suk Scandal," *East Asian Science, Technology and Society: An International Journal* 2/1 (2008): 43.

26 Doobo Shim, "Hybridity and the Rise of Korean Popular Culture in Asia," *Media, Culture & Society* 28/1 (2006): 31.

27 Jae-Ha Kim, "BTS Wins First VMA in Controversial K-Pop Category," *Variety*, August 26, 2019, variety.com/2019/music/news/bts-vmas-kpop-category-mtv-1203314934/.

28 Chung-Sok Suh, Seung-Ho Kwan, and Tae Young Choi, "An Analysis of the Korean Wave and Cultural Proximity in Southeast Asia," Korea-Australasia Research Centre (University of New South Wales), 2006.

29 Mary J. Ainslie, "Korean Overseas Investment and Soft Power: Hallyu in Laos," *Korea Journal* 56/3 (2016): 8–9.

30 Thuy Linh Nguyen Tu, "White like Koreans: The Skin of the New Vietnam," in S. Heijin Lee, Christina H. Moon, and Thuy Linh Nguyen Tu (eds.), *Fashion and Beauty in the Time of Asia* (New York: New York University Press, 2019), 29.

31 Peichi Chung, "Co-Creating Korean Wave in Southeast Asia: Digital Convergence and Asia's Media Regionalization," *Journal of Creative Communications* 8 (2013): 199.

32 Grace Danbi Hong, "'Running Man' Subbed in Many Languages Amazes Korean Fans," *MWAVE*, May 31, 2012, web.archive.org/web/20140216140843/http://mwave.interest.me/enewsworld/en/article/7364/running-man-subbed-in-many-languages-amazes-korean-fans/.

33 Mary J. Ainslie, Sarah Domingo Lipura, and Joanne B. Y. Lim, "Understanding the Hallyu Backlash in Southeast Asia: A Case Study of Consumers in Thailand, Malaysia and Philippines," *Kritika Kultura* 28 (2017): 75–76.

34 E. J. R. David and Sumie Okazaki, "The Colonial Mentality Scale for Filipino Americans: Scale Construction and Psychological Implications," *Journal of Counseling Psychology* 53 (2006): 241.

35 Chen, *Asia as Method*, 18.

36 Kee-won Ock and Lee Jae-yeon, "Samsung's Labor Violations Gone Global," *Hankyoreh*, June 23, 2019, english.hani.co.kr/arti/english_edition/e_international/898950.html.

37 Statistics Korea, "Survey on Immigrants' Living Conditions and Labour Force," December 19, 2019, kostat.go.kr/portal/korea/kor_nw/1/3/4/index.board.

38 www.kpop-radar.com/brief/34 (accessed March 8, 2021).

39 Z-POP Dream, "Making Film: Z-POP Dream Documentary," YouTube, February 21, 2019, www.youtube.com/watch?v=2AF7gKYo6Do&t=164s.

40 Natalie Tomada, "Z-Pop's Dreams of 'One Asia,'" *The Philippine Star*, April 1, 2019, www.philstar.com/entertainment/2019/04/01/1906144/z-pops-dreams-one-asia.

41 Natalia Ningthoujam, "K-Pop Inspired Group Z-Stars All about 'One Asia,'" *Indo-Asian News Service*, March 4, 2020, www.outlookindia.com/newsscroll/paytm-offices-shut-after-employee-tested-positive-for-coronavirus/1752035?scroll.

42 Z-POP Dream, "Happy Lunar New Year!," YouTube, January 24, 2020, www.youtube.com/watch?v=wB16RyRfOLs.

43 Robert Phillipson, *Linguistic Imperialism* (Oxford: Oxford University Press, 1992), 47.

44 Andy Kirkpatrick, *English as a Lingua Franca in ASEAN: A Multilingual Model* (Hong Kong: Hong Kong University Press, 2010), xi.

45 Asian Boss, "Meet the First Indian K-Pop Idols (feat. Z-Stars)," YouTube, May 18, 2019, www.youtube.com/watch?v=fW9xHlEPkgU&feature=share.

46 Timothy Laurie, "Towards a Gendered Aesthetics of K-Pop," in Ian Chapman and Henry Johnson (eds.), *Global Glam and Popular Music Style and Spectacle from the 1970s to the 2000s* (London: Routledge, 2016), 219.

47 Tomada, "Z-Pop's Dreams of 'One Asia.'"

48 Maaike Bleeker, *Visuality in the Theatre: The Locus of Looking* (Basingstoke: Palgrave Macmillan, 2008).

49 John Seabrook, "Factory Girls: Cultural Technology and the Making of K-Pop," *The New Yorker*. October 8, 2012, www.newyorkcr.com/magazine/2012/10/08/factory-girls-2.

50 Ningthoujam, "K-Pop Inspired Group Z-Stars All about 'One Asia.'"

PART V

The Band That Surprised the World

9 BTS, Transmedia, and Hip Hop

KYUNG HYUN KIM

The Name in Transmedia Storytelling

Seo Taiji and Boys' single "Nan arayo" (I know), released in 1992, may have not been the first rap song recorded in Korea, but it is still remembered by many Koreans, after close to three decades since its release, as the first Korean rap song they ever heard. Seo Taiji was undoubtedly an icon of the youth culture in the Korean popular music scene of the 1990s, and it was not coincidental that he found hip hop to be the music genre most appealing to the emerging youth in the era of postmilitary dictatorship, eager for cosmopolitan style and sensibility. Ever since Seo Taiji and Boys, hip hop has sustained its popularity in the Korean popular music scene, and most K-pop idol groups today include at least one member who can rap. BTS, arguably the world's most popular group active today, features three members who rap. When the group, initially known for its underdog spirit, first started out in 2013, it identified hip hop as its most influential music genre.

Ever since Elvis Presley and the Beatles emerged as global superstars in the 1950s and 1960s, respectively, pop music has actively exploited various transmedia formats in order to commercialize stardom and sell more albums. Well before Henry Jenkins coined the term "transmedia storytelling,"[1] and in the days before user-generated content (UGC) on the internet – on sites such as YouTube and Facebook – allowed consumers and fans to express their own creative views through fan fiction, the idol musicians of the twentieth century were marketed not only through their music played on radio and vinyl but also through fantasy tales. Many pop artists, such as David Bowie, conceptualized fantasy story lines that would blur the lines between real-life performances and stage personae, such as Ziggy Stardust. Before Bowie, Elvis played larger-than-life characters in movies, ranging from a convicted murderer (*Jailhouse Rock*, 1957) to a biracial cowboy caught in a racial conflict in a Western (*Flaming Star*, 1960) to a boxer (*Kid Galahad*, 1962), and a Hawaiian GI returning from a tour of duty (*Blue Hawaii*, 1961). Not to be outdone, John, Paul, George, and Ringo packaged themselves into Sergeant Pepper animation characters, rode a yellow submarine, and donned enormous walrus and other costumes, all in order to create better points of convergence with their fans.

These dreamlike fantasy characters stoked the imaginations of young consumers beyond their enjoyment of the music of their idols. Although the fantasy tales featured less-than-real scenarios, they became central visual images of cool America and mod Britain and worked their way into millions of homes in the postwar "free world." This transmedia storytelling was every bit as important as the musical tunes themselves, as film, television, radio, publishing, and tabloid culture, and even toy and stationery merchandisers, collaborated with the music industry in fueling the fantasies of consumers who sought to tell their own stories around the stars they adored.

During the 1980s and 1990s fantasy based on transmedia storytelling continued to play an important role in films, and then in music videos; it became popular in the age of MTV, even becoming bigger than the music itself. Music giants such as Michael Jackson, Prince, and Madonna all crossed over various media of motion picture, music videos, television, fashion, and even amusement park rides to appeal to their fans. Albums that were explosively popular with fans, such as *Thriller* (1982), *Purple Rain* (1984), and *Like a Virgin* (1984), were not only supported by music videos and theme park–like stadium tours but also heavily promoted by feature or concept films in which the artists starred (*Michael Jackson's Thriller* video, *Purple Rain* starring Prince, and *Desperately Seeking Susan* starring Madonna, among others). Music was just one element among a confluence of *other* star-making ingredients that were equally if not more powerful in the world of fandom that craved ever more fantasy stories, fashion trends, and viral dance moves.

However, starting around the 2000s, fantasy stories began to wane in the music industry. There are two reasons for this. First, popular television music audition programs, such as *American Idol,* which began in 2002, groomed their new musical talents into stardom by touting autobiographical stories rather than fantasies. After being nearly destroyed by Napster and other free music-sharing services, the music studios needed to regroup, and did so by forging alliances with television and its growing demand for reality content to rebound from its own ratings crisis. Second, the hip-hop industry, which was hitting its stride after several decades of ascent, had likewise taken an autobiographical turn, focusing on rappers' real-life stories steeped in Black urban ghettos, and this emphasis on authenticity became far more important than selling stories based on fantasy re-creations of zombies, virgin myths, and cartoon characters. Although, ironically, the genre of hip hop put into practice a postmodern blurring of distinction between the "authentic" and the "copy" – by narrowing the gap between production and consumption via empowering DJs who endlessly looped, sampled, and appropriated original R&B songs on their turntables – hip hop also prioritized what Achille Mbembe has referred to as the "becoming black of the world," that is, the postured rearticulation of an authenticated "I" rooted in social hardship and street culture and known for its fights against the establishment.[2] My explanation of "becoming black" here is deliberately complicated, because from N.W.A.'s West Coast gangsta rap to Jay-Z's East Coast hustler rap, the "keep it real" image of hip hop, as marketed throughout the past several decades, is mediated by blurring the line between dramatization and street reality.

Complete debunking of the authenticity argument of hip hop, which stresses the importance of Blackness at its origin, as a bankrupt essentialist enterprise, can often exempt egregious and offensive misappropriation of African American cultural practices from being critiqued. Hip hop became a vehicle for a public art forum on sensitive topics about racism and police brutality around many global urban centers one or two decades after the genre was born in the streets of Bronx during the 1970s. As Andy Bennett notes in his research on hip hop in Frankfurt, Germany, and Newcastle, United Kingdom, what began as experimental street music in New York City in the 1970s successfully expanded to both racialized minority and white youths in Europe. However, even though the global mobility of hip hop has proven to be expedient, popular, and effective, many cases of non-Black localization and appropriation have to be cautiously approached and theorized. Even Bennett argues, after having studied hip hop in Newcastle, a predominantly white, working-class city in the 1990s, that the "use of black music and style on the part of the white working-class youth [in the UK] becomes a particular form of lived sensibility; a reflexive lifestyle 'strategy.'"[3] In other words, without the recognition of affinity with African Americans' struggles, hip hop performed by non-Blacks and minority groups can reinscribe the danger of foreclosing the dialogue with the African Americans who innovated and continue to innovate this novel cultural experience.

Cynthia Fuchs argues in discussing Jay-Z's music video "Hard Knock Life" that the 'hood depicted in the hustler-cum-rapper's video is "a specific and imaginative construction ... simultaneously diurnal and sensational, depressed and sanguine, a dramatization of the dreams ignited by such an environment."[4] Although the representation of the 'hood in rap songs is inevitably overdramatized, the emergence of hip hop suddenly allowed the American public to see real, unfiltered images of Black ghettos for the first time. Just as the early rock stars mentioned above carved fantasy alter egos from the concept images of their albums or films, many rappers had to shuffle between two identities: an illegitimate street identity and a second identity unencumbered by street reputation. Both Dr. Dre and Jay-Z play with their real names in songs (Andre Young and Shawn Carter, respectively) as if they possessed multiple subjectivities. These rappers' dual identities are not only self-mocking, playful acts put on by the performers themselves but also punctuated by the historical oppression of African Americans that made renaming a necessity.

Not unlike these American rap stars, about half of the members of the Korean idol septet BTS, which started as a rap group, feature double identities. For instance, RM (previously Rap Monster) also uses his birth name (Kim Nam-joon) when he reverts to his everyday "normal" persona. However, this is where the comparison between Korean and African American rapper self-naming conventions ends. Unlike Black rappers, whose nicknames, dual identities, and near obsession with reclaiming a new sense of self are due to their illegitimate street identities from the 'hood, the dual identities of Korean rappers lack political depths of nomenclature. The self-effacing fogginess, legal caginess, and complexity of birth origin embedded in the naming of American rappers could be traced back to the beginnings of African American history and slavery in the United States, none of which can be applied to the background of the names given to Korean artists. Korean rappers can at best approximate the kind of political manifestation sought by Black rappers' name shuffling, which also subverts numerous binaries, including home versus exile, sobriety versus addiction, and freedom versus incarceration. In American rapper names, what began as a recognition of power enfranchisement and disenfranchisement – materialized in legal troubles, bouts with alcohol and drug addiction, incarcerations, and police harassment – can only be mimicked in the Korean pop world, where the experience and concept of the ethnic 'hood is largely absent. The names of BTS's rappers, such as RM and Suga, provoke swag and cuteness with little underlying substance. Only the rapper members of BTS have adopted stage names that bear no resemblance to their original names (RM, Suga, and J-Hope), whereas the group's vocalists (Jin, Jimin, and Jungkook) have retained at least part of their birth names. The seventh and second-youngest member of the group, V, remains the only outlier, but once again, his name simply stands for a common and trite term, "victory."

The purpose of this chapter is not to raise the specter of the debate over authenticity in relation to race and Blackness. Every ethnic community around the globe is producing its own rap culture and has created its own version of the "Black man." In major cosmopolitan sectors, not only Korean but also Puerto Rican, Indian, and Arabic youth communities, for instance, distinguish themselves from the mainstream corporate industry by producing their own hip-hop music and culture. As I have stated above, the debate about authenticity and the appropriation of the African

American origin of hip hop continues to unravel not only outside but also still in the United States. For instance, during the mid-2010s, pioneering rapper Q-Tip's public outburst of displeasure with the white rapper Iggy Azalea and her ignorance of the historical origins of hip hop exhibited the difficulty of resolving the debate well into the twenty-first century. Also, during a hip-hop panel I moderated in October 2019, when asked how he feels about the strong connection between hip hop and the "criminalized Black body," the legendary Korean rapper Tiger JK refrained from directly engaging with the question, only to show frustration privately, for the question implied that his hip hop was less than legitimate because he does not possess a "Black body." But even he lamented that today's rappers in Korea know very little about the African American origin of hip hop. I wish to ask how K-pop, and more specifically BTS, makes or unmakes its own ethnic identity in a way that becomes emblematic of its hard work on self-cultivation and that may then approximate a connection to Blackness. To rephrase this question, in what specific ways does K-pop propose the sense of "home" (*gohyang*) that African American musicians have used in portraying the complexity of the 'hood that is so deeply entrenched in the visual landscapes of hip-hop expression? If hip-hop sound not only gave rise to the style and music of African Americans but also served to reimagine the 'hood for Black musicians who found their way to the global mainstream, where can K-pop's reclamation of its own 'hood be? Given that transmedia storytelling strategies have paid enormous dividends for BTS, what kind of shared spatial identification has this K-pop group been able to conjecture for both itself and its fans? What interests me is the question of how BTS's transmedia storytelling campaign enables the group's members to solidly link their identities with their fans in order to forge a sense of collective spatial belonging that serves as a postethnic, postnational, and postlinguistic home. What comes into play in these music videos is a manufactured sense of place, ranging from encounters on harsh streets to an alternate-reality universe existing only in cyberspace, all of which is designed to appeal to global fans.[5] In 2015, for instance, Big Hit Entertainment scored big with an image of fictive blue flowers that was featured on a music video by BTS. When these flowers provoked curiosity, Big Hit gave them the name "smeraldo" and opened a blog on the Korean portal site Naver.com called "Flower Smeraldo," which posts random newsletters on the manufactured history of the flowers and, to a larger extent, a sense of cyber habitat for the invented flora.

BTS was the first and only K-pop idol group to "train" in one of the *bonto*s (homelands) of hip hop, the African American neighborhood of Los Angeles, for the Mnet reality-television program *American Hustle Life* (*AHL*). The program aired weekly and had been specifically designed for

BTS. In watching *AHL*, I am fascinated by BTS's self-deprecation and how its members engage almost in self-mockery to project themselves as underdog heroes struggling in the land of hip hop. As they attempt to impress rap mentors from the 'hood, such as Coolio and Warren G, their efforts to earn legitimacy in K-pop history by making a pilgrimage to the *bonto* of hip hop actually expose the impossibility of bridging the gap between K-pop and Black hip hop. After initial attempts to launch BTS as a hip-hop idol group failed, largely because of the different genealogies of the two music genres, the septet moved away from hip hop and took a step toward a more mainstream pop sound. It was around the same time that the group also created Bangtan Universe (BU), a multimedia fictional realm of music videos and short films, books, a game app, and a webtoon. After my discussion of *AHL*, I propose a reading of the images of BU, productively drawing on Kay Dickinson's theory of synesthetic possibility, which refers to the effects of music videos that appeal to the senses of both sight and sound. The sense of visual space that BTS promotes through BU is a kind of neither-here-nor-there fluidity, which can both strongly invoke visual significations open to creative reinterpretation on the part of fans and overwhelm viewers with the force of neoliberal globalization, where every space unfortunately becomes gentrified for the sake of promoting universality. BU, the fictive space of BTS – not unlike its fictive "smeraldo" flower shop – ends up restoring a sense of universal belonging, but in the process it also denies a sense of material belonging that could potentially tap into a Korean idea of the 'hood. Music in the era of social media has become a metamusical enterprise, appealing to a young global audience less preoccupied with a shared sense of history, language, and racial bonding raised in melody and lyrics. Instead of the actual offline 'hood affinity and lived sensibility that have been critical in building bonds around African American cultural history, BTS through BU offers an identifiable spirit of "telling stories of underdog experience" that is deeply felt by its fans through the social media space. Whether or not online spaces such as BU could actually rearticulate a lived, affective experience of either *bonto* or *gohyang*, which may sound old-school, they nevertheless firmly carve out an emotional space from a material and historical sense of place.

American Hustle Life

The transmedia storytelling that came into vogue with the first boy band, the Beatles, has reached a new level of heightened interactivity between stars and fans during the contemporary social media era. As Tamar Herman has argued, "K-pop has long utilized transmedia as a way to promote its stars across different mediums and to maximize revenue."[6]

Just like many other K-pop idols who have maximized their interaction with fans in order to further their careers beyond their identity as musicians, BTS members often become performers on different platforms such as stage, television, film, YouTube channels, celebrity travel shows, and advertisements. As social media have begun to demand more candid images from celebrities, K-pop stars have been unable to keep their private lives entirely separate from their fans, and the boundaries that separate public and personal image have begun to erode. The need to come up with stories and content beyond music posed a new challenge, especially for BTS, known since its early days both for its bold association with hip hop and for its effort to maintain close fan ties. Tight choreography, flashy colors, and youthful energy have never been lacking over the course of the group's young career. However, beyond their performances, how could the personal histories of its members be revealed in a way that would forge even stronger bonds with their fandom? BTS did manage to identify its early music alliance with hip hop, featuring no fewer than three rappers (RM, Suga, and J-Hope) and employing a dance routine steeped in b-boy choreography. However, as evident in the footage from *AHL*, there were still various barriers beyond skin color that prevented these young Korean musicians from achieving their identification with the hip-hop genre. Even as BTS's global fame has risen, hip-hop fame remains a distant reach. In the band's early efforts to bond with hip hop, its members were encouraged to reauthenticate their "real" stories of pain, hardship, and depression by traveling to Los Angeles in 2014. For many members of the group, this was their first trip to the United States.

The eight-part reality television show *AHL* begins in the worst way possible. In the first episode, almost immediately after the septet arrives at LAX from Korea, they are "kidnapped" by a group of "dark men" from an unattended parking lot when their road manager and driver exit their van. The young Koreans, who have had hardly any contact with people outside Asia up to this point, are struck by panic and fear, all captured by a hidden camera. They are subsequently taken to an empty house in a seedy section of Los Angeles that will become the setting for their reality television performance. The house is bare, with the exception of one room filled with seven prison-like steel bunk beds and a set of tawdry sofas. Unable to communicate with their Black captors about what is going on, they have been installed in an undisclosed Skid Row location. *AHL* thereby begins with images that evoke typical racist stereotypes, playing off the fear of Black men, people living on the street, and the inner city. Unfortunately, this image of African American culture and people, despite the supposed closeness that the group later establishes with their "captors," persists awkwardly throughout the program, which never manages to bridge the gap between the aspiring hip-hop group and the West Coast mecca of American hip hop.

Although the members of BTS should have realized that their "kidnapping" was part of a scheme concocted by the producers of Mnet, they are nevertheless portrayed as a fearful bunch unaware of the multiethnic makeup of American culture. Even though veteran Korean rappers Tiger JK and Epik High have made efforts to publicize the significance of African American history, stemming from their youth spent in the United States, and although many hip-hop critics in Korea have emphasized the importance of hip hop's Black roots, the young K-pop idols of BTS, with the exception of the two main rappers, RM and Suga, have shown very little passion about learning this history.

The next day, a special guest arrives at the house where the Korean group is staying. It's Coolio, with his signature cornrow pigtails sticking up from his head. Although he is quite possibly twenty years past his prime, with no memorable musical success since his breakout hit "Gangsta Paradise" in 1995, Coolio will serve as a mentor to the young Korean musicians. The aging rap star starts by asking them basic questions about American hip hop. At a rapid clip, he asks, "How and where did hip hop start?" "What was the first rap single that went platinum?" and "Which group is Chuck D from?" Even RM, the only BTS member who speaks fluent English, has trouble understanding him, much less the others, who do not speak English. As Jimin proceeds to admit in a later interview inserted during the quiz, he had no idea who Coolio was nor any knowledge of the material he was being quizzed about. To be fair, Jimin is not one of BTS's rappers – rapping duties are shared mostly between RM and Suga – but because he is a member of a group known at the time for its hip hop, his professed unawareness underscores his naivete and ignorance of history. And of course, their unawareness could be rearticulated into an accusation that K-pop is merely a copycat music genre that imitates American styles and music without necessarily understanding the history and the struggles beneath their surface and swag.

To be sure, the program's characterization of BTS's members as unaware of the history of their own music genre may be too harsh. Many young rappers in present-day America may also be ignorant of the influence of Run DMC or Kurtis Blow; nor would they care much about the genealogy of rap music other than the fact that it started in the streets of the Bronx and Compton. Furthermore, Coolio likely had no knowledge of the history of the Korean hip-hop scene. BTS, to its credit, once paid tribute to Seo Taiji, one of the pioneering figures in Korean hip hop. In a 2017 concert by Seo, every member of BTS joined him on stage, performing several of his signature songs from the 1990s, including

"Class Ideology" and "Come Back Home." Clearly, BTS is willing to donate their time to pay respect to the history of Korean hip hop, which, especially now with the ascent of K-pop within global pop music, may well be considered as important as any other global hip-hop tradition outside the United States. Despite the growing distance between BTS and hip hop over the past five years, when *AHL* was shot in the mid-2010s, the members openly discussed that they wanted to be a lot more than just a copycat hip-hop group. The language barrier certainly also played a part in creating the awkwardness between the interrogator Coolio and his baffled Korean mentees.

Although the beginning of *AHL* is rough, the show does rebound somewhat from its initially shocking racist tones. Coolio, for instance, shows himself to be a caring mentor who offers useful advice to the young rappers, validates their own experiences, offers feedback on their performances of earlier hip-hop songs such as "Rapper's Delight," and also teaches them how to cook. He turns out to be as adept with the kitchen stove as he is with his verses. The boys from the K-pop group also walk the streets of Compton (and, later, Hollywood), attempting to impress random African American residents and visitors with their singing skills and dance moves. This was all shot in 2014, several years before BTS became a worldwide sensation, scoring hit after hit. Viewed half a decade later, the images of members of a now ridiculously famous septet desperately attempting to impress anonymous pedestrians on the streets of Los Angeles (although there is some speculation that the latter are professional actors paid to play prearranged roles for the show) are charming and novel, for they could never do the same today. The eight-episode show ends with a splash when BTS performs on stage with Iris Stevenson, the African American inner-city high school choir director whose real-life story inspired *Sister Act 2* (dir. Bill Duke, 1993). Stevenson teaches Black gospel songs for BTS to perform as part of their repertoire in the finale concert at the LA club Troubadour, where they first realized that they actually had a small, yet loyal fan base in the United States. BTS's encounter with Black culture in Los Angeles did help them write a couple of songs for their next album, *Dark and Wild*. This 2014 studio album features a song entitled "Hip-Hop Phile" (Hiphapseongaeja), which celebrates the historical roots of both African American and Korean hip hop. As if to compensate for their failure to come up with satisfying answers to Coolio while in Los Angeles, the song features the group naming all of the Black (and Korean) rappers, such as Jay Z, Snoop Dogg, J. Cole, and Epik High, among those who have influenced them. Suga's rap verses in this song also feature personal lyrics such as "going to a studio in Daegu, Namsandong . . . to throw myself and work the dull tip of a pen all night long" in a rare acknowledgment of his Korean 'hood that became the soil for his success.

While *American Hustle Life* may be a goofy reality television program and a self-deprecating joke about a Korean hip-hop group, it nonetheless manages to ask fundamental questions about K-pop and the approval it seeks from American progenitors. Because contemporary Korean popular music in large part emerged from military *sho-dan* (entertainment troupe) musicians performing for American military personnel after the country's liberation from Japanese colonial rule, its focus was not changing the world so that Koreans would one day occupy the position of the center; it was more observing the hierarchical order. Even though Black music and "Blackness" were often at odds with the power of the white establishment, to most Koreans even hip hop was still aligned within the bounds of Western supremacy embodied in the American military presence in Korea. No matter how immaculately they execute their razor-sharp and athletic dance kicks or utter their rapid rap verses, Korean hip-hop stars' acts can never be compared to those of Michael Jackson or the Notorious B.I.G., for these Black stars have, until now, never had to create their own choreography or their signature rap styles.

Performance studies scholar Judith Hamera argues that "[Michael] Jackson's virtuosity is inexplicably linked to place and race: the socio-economic landscapes from which it emerged or, as the popular mythos has it, the places from and to which he 'escaped.'"[7] Not only do many of Jackson's songs pay homage to the rhythms and melodies of "Black folk," but his dance moves also quote many brilliant African American prede-cessors such as James Brown and Josephine Baker, to name a few. Although Jackson was raised in the industrial Midwestern town of Gary, Indiana, the songs of Southern Black sharecroppers narrating the toils of farm work were planted in his brain from early childhood. Even though the automated dance music genre called EDM has maintained its staying power mainly in clubs over the past two decades, what drives even the most contemporary popular music amalgamated from country, rock, hip hop, musical ballads, and other genres is a sense of home and of linguistic and melodic belonging, which builds a broad cultural base among listeners. Despite the earnest efforts of *AHL*'s coproducers, Mnet channel and Bang Si-hyuk, the leader of Big Hit Entertainment, to bridge the gap between the K-pop idols and the home of American hip hop, it was very clear that BTS would never manage to claim the dilapidated, barren streets of Compton as their musical home. *AHL* shows that the linguistic and cultural gap between American hip hop and K-pop, in addition to the difference between racial histories in the United States and Korea, proves to be as wide as the Grand Canyon. Aside from the intimacy built between the BTS members and their mentors, Coolio and Warren G, the question remains: What kind of *bonto* ('hood) or *gohyang* (home) can BTS members imagine for themselves and their fans?

Bangtan Universe as a Sense of Home

BTS has one mighty ambassador: the ARMY, which may be the most significant fan club that has ever existed in the history of pop music. One might even claim that this fandom, which is actually more forcefully articulated in territories outside Korea than within the country, serves as BTS's real home. If the sense of belonging that rappers Coolio and Warren G sought within their creative space was located within the parameters of the African American neighborhood of Compton – just as the declining mills along the Midwestern riverfront cities of Minneapolis and Detroit served for Prince and Madonna, respectively – online fandom is where BTS would claim its home. The group lives and breathes through its fans, as members tweet, post updates, and maintain their own active social network channel on V Live, a live streaming service operated by Naver. com that provides frequent opportunities to interact with their fans. V Live is also where BTS releases special promotional videos, such as concert documentaries and reality television content for paid consumers.

Having no actual physical home base has allowed BTS to go further and cultivate the online space as its asylum. The group was ambitious in its launch of Bangtan Universe (BU), a shared fictional cyber universe that helped it acquire a hard-edged identity and served as a useful tool for building the superstardom that the group would eventually achieve in the mid-2010s. The internet is the base from which BU – a fictive yet nonetheless unique entity for the group itself and its fandom – has been created. In many ways, the internet offers both a reverie and a concrete home for artists like BTS, who are definitely from a specific country called Korea. But in the context of the American-dominated Western pop world they are essentially without a home insofar as Korea is mapped as a nondescript place lacking hip-hop roots and tradition. It was probably not coincidental that BTS's mainstream success came only *after* it began to drop its official affiliation with hip hop. Although RM and Suga continue to serve as the group's rappers and many of BTS's songs continue to be rooted in rap, the boy band ensemble has become undeniably more pop since its albums in *The Most Beautiful Moment in Life* series became global hits in 2015 and 2016 and subsequently served as the launching pad for BU. Unlike even bands such as Backstreet Boys, whose members were recruited from the Orlando, Florida, area, K-pop largely lacks the distinction of place. Though fans may be able to remember the hometowns of members of, for instance, BTS or TWICE, these groups can hardly be claimed as "home-brewed." Members are individually selected through various auditions held by an entertainment company that combs through the Korean countryside and even abroad in search of young new talent. BTS was no exception, as every member of the group was recruited from near and far corners of Korea by Big Hit Entertainment in the early 2010s. This meant that the members' identities would be homogeneously Korean yet lack a strong centripetal force that would allow them to claim a singularly common home in the sense of the Bronx or Compton – in a nation full of possible such homes, whether the Gangnam neighborhood in Seoul, well known for its nouveaux riches; Hongdae, on the other side of the nation's capital, known for its underground culture and arts; or even various rural areas in Korea known for the pristine beauty of their paddy farms, mountains, or scenic beaches. It could be argued that many places featured in BU or the travel reality show called *Bon Voyage* that the BTS members themselves make instantaneously become what Youngmin Choe has defined as "affective sites" that blur boundaries between history, memory, and consumerism in *Hallyu* cinema (Choe 2016). These sites, however, offer at best a fleeting sense of affinities. In other words, they may become tourist attractions for BTS fans but can never assume a sense of a home (*gohyang*) or an African American–style 'hood (*bonto*), which is deeply entrenched in the sociopolitical landscape of Korea that has yet to recover from its traumas of the twentieth century. Because BTS lacked both a musical genre home and a physical home, it may have been easier to craft what essentially became a cyber home called BU.

A dizzying array of reality television programs, podcasts, music videos, webtoons, and vignette story inserts for their CD albums (since *The Beautiful Moment in Life* in 2015) have given BTS's fans opportunities to interactively participate in creating narratives for BU. With the release of "I Need U" – the first single from *The Beautiful Moment in Life*, which would eventually become one of the group's biggest hits and change its direction toward a more pop sound – BTS also produced a music video that spearheaded a departure from its early aesthetic. Videos for their songs prior to "I Need U" featured visuals that almost exactly mirrored the templates of other K-pop groups (band members lip-synching and executing perfectly choreographed dance moves to upbeat songs in excessively colorful sets), but BTS found a new aesthetic that would accompany several music videos and even short films, unaffiliated with any of the songs on the album, that would later be constituted as BU.

Because there are so many accessible interpretations of BU, and particularly with the final summary of the narrative becoming available through the 2019 webtoon *Save Me*, perhaps only a brief summary of "I Need U" suffices here. In this music video, all the BTS members are seen, mostly apart from each other, as they roam or struggle through spaces including dark alleys, foggy bathrooms, and abandoned train tracks. Jungkook gets beaten up by a group of thugs; J-Hope collapses in broad daylight crossing the bridge over the River Han; Jimin shivers alone in the bathroom next to a tub filled to the brim; RM pumps gas at a gas station; and V ends up stabbing an older man who appears to be his father, after the latter has violently beaten up V's sister. Along with these disturbing images, fire is seen being set in an anonymous location. Interspersed with flashback clips of the seven members collectively having a good time on an otherwise empty, desolate beach, this music video, like twenty or so other BU music videos and short films equally somber in tone, definitely veers away from the sense of *heung* (excitement or playful energy, or liveness) that Suk-Young Kim has defined as the force "forged around K-pop performances."[8] With neither dance nor singing performances, "I Need U" conveys a message of "hurt": a manufactured, desperate sense of collective longing to be with friends or loved ones with whom one may never be able to reunite.

If the 'hood that is projected in rap videos stands as a strong metaphor for the economic hardship and systemic racism that continually strike at the heart of the universal popular imagination, the images featured in BU open up postmetaphoric and metonymic significations that facilitate anational, postethnic, and post-traumatic figurations that have a greater degree of malleable, mentally illogical, and unmappable locations. Just like the fictive "smeraldo" flower of Italian origin (and a fiction narrative about an "international smeraldo federation" that putatively hosts a meeting every year), with its Naver.com blog site on which fake unrequited love stories are posted and announced, no real sense of history or place can be substantiated through these images on BU. Now, to rant that an image or sound from a K-pop video completely exceeds any particular historical and linguistic domain is perhaps not all that novel. BU is capable of becoming a positive, open-ended text. I am particularly drawn here to Kay Dickinson's notion that music videos strongly invoke a synesthetic response in which the aural and the visual "inform each other, cross each other's tracks, and most importantly, embody both a singularity and the potential to merge."[9] BU respects no linguistic fixity where the mouths of the singers are synched to the lyrics; no corporeal movement in which the idol's bodies are synchronized to the beats of the songs; and no history behind the geographical locations of the sets featured in the music videos. The abstraction and flatness of the images allow fans across many national and linguistic identities to creatively reassemble the signs being rendered. In so doing, BU's images and music open up what I call a "synesthetic liminality" that realigns metaphors in order to rezone them in what Gilles Deleuze and Félix Guattari once termed "deterritorialized assemblages" that might block the trappings of metaphors and instead inspire viewers to rewrite the meanings of these images and music with more authority. Indeed, a quick search for "BTS Universe" on the internet will generate endless blogs and video channels by BTS fans who have voluntarily reordered, rewritten, and reauthorized the narratives of BU in a parallel, alternative universe separately engineered by fan fiction.[10]

BU does take a definitive step toward conceptualizing a sensorial framework that fully extends the utopian belief in the synesthetic metaphor that builds on the potential irreconcilable cross between music and visuals. Many of the visuals from the "certified 22 BTS videos" (some are music videos, others are short films with no songs) that officially constitute BU feature BTS members playing with each other in an alternate, somber reality. Alcohol abuse, violent fathers, drug addiction, suicidal anxiety, and depression are strong themes with which each and every member of BTS is associated. These traumatic themes raised in BU can benefit teenager fans struggling with mental anguish by encouraging them to share their stories in a more fluid manner, reconstructing them to blend narratives of both idols and fans. Imagining stories and sharing them with people who have undergone similar experiences can, of course, be therapeutic and productive.

However, this is not to suggest that BU operates outside the promotional machinery of the global capitalist enterprise. BU is no different from the many documentary short films, online fan meetings, and even the serialized travel show *Bon Voyage*, all featuring BTS members, that are craftily produced and distributed by Big Hit Entertainment and yield streams of revenue and profit. Particularly with regard to the mobile game BTS World released in fall 2020 – which piggybacks on BU by allowing players to construct their own stories loosely based on the BU setting and share them with other players – the entire enterprise can be seen as a shrewd consumer marketing strategy that is capable of packaging and commercializing even a subject of hurt. BU is similar to other streaming content and kitsch commercial products released by media empires such as Marvel Cinematic Universe or the Star Wars franchise or even Hello Kitty products, which even before BU also had success with their transmedia storytelling platforms for consumers in the age of social media.

Conclusion: Can K-Pop Rap?

It is astounding that a K-pop group consisting of young men who appear neither white nor Black has achieved a popularity level equal to, if not greater than, that of Elvis or the Beatles, largely thanks to the fact that the internet has a broader reach than television did a little more than half a century ago. Given that their ethnic identities continue to be aligned with anational and posthistorical ones, it is perhaps not surprising that BTS's "universe" also still remains largely nondescript or hazy. Although obviously shot in Korea, most of the videos use settings that carefully avoid referencing any specific locations in Korea. Their abstraction of space expands the capacity of the various metaphors they employ, such as flowers, a bathtub, mirrors, and abandoned buildings and alleyways, into an open-ended signification that allows worldwide fans to reinterpret them. Yet in this process of reauthoring, what is lost are linguistic origins and ethnic historiographies that metaphors and poetic significations usually undergird.

Like it or not, we live in a world where ethnic violence, national strife, and gender wars continue to rage. The immense popularity that African American artists have enjoyed in the music world – much more so than in any other popular art form – was probably not coincidental. It is a lot more difficult to censor and ban what cannot be seen. Despite the ongoing discrimination that Black artists in the United States have had to face over the past century and earlier, they have almost certainly achieved greater representation in the music industry than in film and television. Their success, especially during the 1990s when music videos and hip hop were both in their heyday, meant that African American 'hoods, like it or not, acquired a greater force of expression. Exciting synesthetic figurations between sound and image continue to be achieved by Black artists today. Videos for Jay-Z's "4:44" and Kendrick Lamar's "Humble" challenge viewers to sensually feel the music through powerful spatial metaphors and the tension caught between them. By breaking down the barriers between image and sound, between language and music, and between images of the present and those from the past, the virtuosity of these artists is reconfirmed and the history of the people they represent can be rediscovered. K-pop's problem, despite the increasing visibility of groups like BTS in US social media, celebrity news, and talk shows, is that the visual counterparts of its music continue to foreground an unrecognizable and almost unidentifiable sense of physical and historical belonging, and this lost sense of place may eventually undercut the music's "universal" appeal. Though the places featured in BU may become popular tourist sites (see Chapter 14 in this book for more on K-pop tourism), the music content deliberately erases people, historical landmarks, and other mnemonic references that could allow viewers access to the sites' localization. In music, abstraction alone does not make great art. For true musical ingenuity to be recognized – and particularly for a song to claim authority in hip hop, or in any other genre of music – it must, despite the rise of EDM or DJ music that deliberately features no sense of linguistic or national origin, orchestrate a sense of cultural roots, spatial belonging, and linguistic locality. It remains to be seen whether the idealistic, abstract projection of a group such as BTS – remaining ahistorical, aspatial, and, in particular, color-blind – can continue to inspire an asignifying metaphorical assemblage that welcomes "everyone." Unlike superheroes in Marvel comic books, R2-D2 of *Star Wars*, or Mario Brothers in video games, BTS members are real humans who will soon outgrow their youth and advance into a midlife where they may be required to look back on their own roots and history. Can K-pop rap? Of course it can. But can it rap songs in videos that synesthetically reference a historically dense space called Korea and its underlying real traumas? The jury is still out on that question.

Works Cited

Bennett, Andy. "Hip-Hop am Main, Rappin' on the Tyne: Hip-Hop Culture as a Local Construct in Two European Cities." In Murray Forman and Mark Anthony Neal (eds.), *That's the Joint!: The Hip-Hop Studies Reader*, 177–200. New York: Routledge, 2004.

Choe, Youngmin. *Tourist Distractions: Traveling and Feeling in Transnational Hallyu Cinema*. Durham, NC: Duke University Press, 2016.

Dickinson, Kay. "Music Video and Synaesthetic Possibility." In Roger Beebe and Jason Middleton (eds.), *Medium Cool: Music Videos from Soundies to Cellphones*, 13–29. Durham, NC: Duke University Press, 2007.

Fuchs, Cynthia. "'I'm from Rags to Riches': The Death of Jay-Z." In Roger Beebe and Jason Middleton (eds.), *Medium Cool: Music Videos from Soundies to Cellphones*, 290–302. Durham, NC: Duke University Press, 2007.

Hamera, Judith. "The Labors of Michael Jackson: Virtuosity, Deindustrialization, and Dancing Work." *PMLA* 127/4 (2012): 751–765.

Han, Sobeom. "Jal Goochukhan 'Universe,' bangtan sonyeondan-eul segyejeok star-ro mandeuleokda" (Well-established universe has made BTS into a global star). *Hanguk ilbo*, August 17, 2020. www.elitedaily.com/p/heres-every-bts-video-thats-in-the-bangtan-universe-so-you-can-catch-up-22618079.

Herman, Tamar. *BTS: Blood, Sweat & Tears*. San Francisco, CA: Viz Media, 2020.

Jenkins, Henry. "Transmedia Storytelling 101." March 21, 2007, http://henryjenkins.org/blog/2007/03/transmedia_storytelling_101.html.

Kim, Kyung Hyun. *Hegemonic Mimicry: Korean Popular Culture of the 21st Century*. Durham, NC: Duke University Press, 2021.

Kim, Suk-Young. *K-Pop Live: Fans, Idols, and Multimedia Performance*. Stanford, CA: Stanford University Press, 2018.

Mbembe, Achille. *Critique of Black Reason*. Trans. Laurent DuBois. Durham, NC: Duke University Press, 2017.

Naver.com. "Flower Smeraldo," https://m.blog.naver.com/PostList.nhn?blogId=testesso&categoryNo=0¤tPage=1.

Tiger JK, Bizzy, and Kurtis Blow. "Conversation on History of Hip-Hop." Panel discussion at Korean Hip-Hop and New Explorations of Afro-Asian Identity Conference, University of California Irvine, October 7, 2019.

Notes

I wish to acknowledge Imelda Ibarra, the CEO and Founder of US BTS ARMY, who generously gave her time to talk about the subject of BTS Universe (BU) on several occasions – first at George Washington University in November 2019 and then again on Zoom in June 2020.

1 Henry Jenkins, "Transmedia Storytelling 101," March 21, 2007, http://henryjenkins.org/blog/2007/03/transmedia_storytelling_101.html.
2 Achille Mbembe, *Critique of Black Reason*, translated by Laurent DuBois (Durham, NC: Duke University Press, 2017), 6. See also Kyung Hyun Kim, *Hegemonic Mimicry: Korean Popular Culture of the 21st Century* (Durham, NC: Duke University Press, 2021).
3 Andy Bennett, "Hip-Hop am Main, Rappin' on the Tyne: Hip-Hop Culture as a Local Construct in Two European Cities," in Murray Forman and Mark Anthony Neal (eds.), *That's the Joint!: The Hip-Hop Studies Reader* (New York: Routledge, 2004), 190.
4 Cynthia Fuchs, "'I'm from Rags to Riches': The Death of Jay-Z," in Roger Beebe and Jason Middleton (eds.), *Medium Cool: Music Videos from Soundies to Cellphones* (Durham, NC: Duke University Press, 2007), 293.
5 See Naver.com, "Flower Smeraldo," https://m.blog.naver.com/PostList.nhn?blogId=testesso&categoryNo=0¤tPage=1.
6 Tamar Herman, *BTS: Blood, Sweat & Tears* (San Francisco, CA: Viz Media, 2020), 32.
7 Judith Hamera, "The Labors of Michael Jackson: Virtuosity, Deindustrialization, and Dancing Work," *PMLA* 127/4 (2012): 756.
8 Suk-Young Kim, *K-Pop Live: Fans, Idols, and Multimedia Performance* (Stanford, CA: Stanford University Press, 2018), 12.
9 Kay Dickinson, "Music Video and Synaesthetic Possibility," in Roger Beebe and Jason Middleton (eds.), *Medium Cool: Music Videos from Soundies to Cellphones* (Durham, NC: Duke University Press, 2007), 15.
10 Han Sobeom, "Jal Goochukhan 'Universe,' bangtan sonyeondan-eul segyejeok star-ro mandeuleokda" (Well-established universe has made BTS into a global star), *Hanguk ilbo*, August 17, 2020, www.elitedaily.com/p/heres-every-bts-video-thats-in-the-bangtan-universe-so-you-can-catch-up-22618079.

10 The BTS Phenomenon

SUK-YOUNG KIM AND YOUNGDAE KIM

Igniting the hearts of global fans with their chimeric personas – angelic, mournful, intellectual, mischievous, suave, approachable, and tempestuous all at once – the seven members of BTS have become some of the most sensational figures in millennial pop culture. Since they debuted as up-and-coming underdogs to the K-pop establishment in 2013, BTS has not only become the most successful group in the history of K-pop but also emerged as a major force to be reckoned with on the global music scene. With every release of their songs and albums, BTS has started a new chapter in the K-pop history book: They were sought-after guests attracting an army of cheering fans at major music award ceremonies in recent years, and in 2021, they reached a new height by becoming the first K-pop group nominated for a Grammy Award. That year was also notable for the group because they topped the Billboard Hot 100 chart for ten consecutive weeks with their single "Butter." How did the band step into such unprecedented prominence for K-pop idols while defying the conventional rules of the K-pop industry?

Of the multitude of elements that drive BTS's phenomenal success, authentic storytelling may be the most crucial. Before the rise of BTS, the pursuit of authenticity for idols was not regarded as the usual pathway to success. Since Korean popular music was introduced to the global music market under the banner of "K-pop," the conventional strategy widely deployed by K-pop groups was to "localize" their production and marketing approach to adapt to foreign markets with distinctive cultural specificity and sensibility. BTS's route to success had nothing to do with this model. The absence of the localization strategy resulted in the ironic situation of the reception and consumption of BTS appearing rather uniform and streamlined across the diverse nations and cultural blocs where their music circulated. BTS's case proves that success in pop music is not simply attained by carefully calculated commercial strategy; rather, it shows that we need to look into more profound emotional rapport and relatability between the band and their fandom to understand the BTS phenomenon.

Authenticity is a concept that often evades close scrutiny and critical assessment, but on a basic level, it is closely related to the notion of the "real" (as opposed to "fake"). In the world of popular music in the West, the term has been specially associated with the genre of rock in the post–World War II era. As music historian Elija Wald has noted,

> From the beginning, though, one of the appeals of rock 'n' roll was its air of authenticity, the idea ... that there was something "honest" about the voices of young black urbanites or rural Southerners that was missing from the polished studio hits that Mitch Miller and his peers [produced].... This was, after all, the era of Marlon Brando and James Dean, who moved young fans with the sincerity of their moody, inarticulate performances. When Miller argued that singers should project passion with technical expertise rather than feeling it personally, he was taking the same position as older actors who disdained the emotion-driven "method," and teenagers preferred Elvis to the mainstream pop singers for much the same reasons they preferred Dean to the more traditionally glamorous movie stars.[1]

Wald's comparison between technically polished musicians and the rugged but sincere-sounding Elvis Presley – or to paraphrase it in terms of acting, between suave actors and sincere method actors – resonates closely with Richard Middleton's idea that "what distinguished authenticity in rock music was its emphasis on spontaneity and improvisation."[2] It is also quite akin to John Lennon's often-cited 1971 *Rolling Stone* interview:

> Rock and roll then [when I was fifteen] was real, everything else was unreal. The thing about rock and roll, good rock and roll – whatever good means and all that shit – is that it's real and realism gets through to you despite yourself. You recognize something in it which is true, like all true art. Whatever art is, readers. OK. If it's real, it's simple usually, and if it's simple, it's true. Something like that.[3]

The legendary figure's definition of rock authenticity of the 1950s West was in large part owned by the postwar generation, whose existential crisis in the popular cultural realm championed rugged and real heroes as champions of the time.

This dichotomy between authentic and manufactured pop may be analogous to the distinction between the ingenuous quality of BTS and supremely polished K-pop idols. Many fans find BTS's lyrics to be authentic, as they are imbued with philosophical depth that allows for contemplation of the precarities of life – the quality for which the band was dubbed "the voice of the millennial reality."

In the world of classical music, authenticity may be gauged by how closely the given performance actualizes the canonical performance style, whereas in folk music, the local flavor of folklore and the rootedness of the people who inhabit that culture endow the genre with authenticity. The claim to musical authenticity can be made by aligning a new emergent genre with the preexisting one regarded as authentic. According to Wald, such was the case in rock 'n' roll's association with folk: "By the mid-1960s, folk music was overtaking classical music as the favored listening for serious young intellectuals, so when rock 'n' roll was described as a folk style (by Belz, among others), that was a claim of roots and authenticity, not an invitation to transform it into something more elevated."[4]

Pop music, on the other hand, has different ways of cultivating an authentic aura, namely along the lines of whether the reality in which the artist resides is well communicated or not. Unlike the popular perception of BTS as a grassroots band that naturally emerged, the conventional wisdom surrounding most K-pop groups' origin is distanced from the notion of authenticity. The usual debut process for K-pop idols begins with their discovery by talent scouts, followed by rigorous training and performance production facilitated by entertainment companies. Such meticulously planned debuts create an impression that K-pop idols are not authentic artists. Especially in the United States, where the authenticity of rock, hip hop, and folk music comprises the absolute core value of popular music, K-pop idols inevitably face challenges when attempting to win the hearts and minds of the audience.

To be clear, BTS is not entirely an outlier to the K-pop industry standards; they share much with other successful K-pop groups in that they emphasize singing skills, visual presentation of their music, and captivating performances. Nonetheless, they managed to expand the parameters of K-pop. What sets BTS apart in particular is their lyrics. As writers of their own lyrics, the members of BTS sincerely express their struggle as students, celebrities, and Korean youth while exposing societal failures that hinder the younger generation from succeeding. Without any pretense, in a highly personal voice, they share who they are and where they come from. BTS may be the first K-pop group to have become a mainstream sensation in the world, and their relentless pursuit of authenticity has made them the most globally successful K-pop band.

In further exploring BTS's authenticity, their use of locally specific dialect revealing the place of their origin is noteworthy. Invoking an association with a genuine place is essential for grounding the band in realness, as musicologists Chris Gibson and John Connell once proclaimed.

> Cultural origins for a scene or style can often be traced to particular groups of musicians, producers and audiences – specific contexts from which a "sound" develops and disseminates. The Motown sound relied on entrepreneurs like Berry Gordy and a specific set of songwriters and performers, as did Seattle grunge (with Sub Pop Records) and San Francisco psychedelia. Such "authenticity" in music begins with individual musicians and performers, who are seen as credible if they can trace their roots back to organic, local scenes.[5]

BTS trace their roots mostly through their adoption of "regional dialect rap (*saturi raep*)." A case in point, "Paldo Gangsan" (2013) – directly translated as "Rivers and Mountains of Eight Provinces," a well-known poetic moniker for Korea – is their representative song relying on the distinctive charm of "regional dialect rap."

> Gaga gaga? I-reon ma-reun ana?
> Gaeng-sang-do-neun eok-sidago? Nuga geu-kano? (meo-ra-ke-ssat-no?)
> Gaeng-sang-do jeong-ha-mo! Anabada gateun-geo-ji!
> Mo niga jikjeop waseo
> Hanbeon bwa-ra! (A dae-ddama!)
> Daegu meo-seu-ma-ra-seo! Du mal an-han-da-kai!
> Hamo! Hamo! Gaeng-sang-do jwuik-in-da! A-in-gyo? (A-jura ma!)
> Uriga eo-di nam-in-gyo!
>
> Gaga gaga, do you know this expression?
> You say Gyeongsang Province is rough? Who says so? (What are you taking about?)
> Gyeongsang Province, *jeong-ha-mo*! It's like "*anabada*."[6]
> Well, why don't you visit
> And see it for yourself! (Well, forget it!)
> Boys of Daegu! They don't need qualifications!
> Wonderful, wonderful! Gyeongsang Province is the best! Isn't that the case? (Give it to the kids!)
> Don't say we are strangers!

The distinctive dialect of Gyeongsang Province, from which four members of BTS (Jimin, V, Suga, and Jeongguk) hail, is not easily translatable, as the pungent flavor of locality will inevitably be lost in the process. For Seoulites whose local dialect provides the notion of a standard Korean language, the original lyrics in Gyeongsang dialect exude humorous as well as exotic provinciality. In Korean hip-hop tradition, closely aligned with urbanity rather than distinctive regional characteristics, it is rare to come across regional dialects as in "Paldo Gangsan." In this regard, BTS's refreshing play with regional dialect simulates the "long-term historical continuity of performance as involved in folk and country music" or even the strategies of "the most commercial performers such as Bruce Springsteen, [who] cherished continuity with earlier popular music and evoked a sense of place."[7] It intensifies the notion of their rootedness.

Much like Korean hip hop, mainstream K-pop music driven by idols shuns regional dialects, which are regarded as antithetical to the cosmopolitan and sophisticated image the K-pop industry strives to cultivate. But in the global tradition of hip hop, introducing the place of origin is an indispensable aspect of establishing the artists' authenticity, as they become crucial vectors for addressing the central questions of identity.

BTS's deployment of regional dialect means that they are not shy about revealing their place of origin (Gyeongsang Province in this case) and their identity as Koreans. Much as with global hip-hop artists, various identitarian markers, including regional identity, anchor the foundation of BTS's music, which in turn closely resonates with their central themes of "Love Yourself" and "The Map of the Soul."

Hardly the only point of BTS's relatability, the linguistic charm embedded in the rich use of dialect is augmented by their storytelling ability. The magnetic power of BTS lies in how they present relatable stories of their journey as underdogs rising to the top through their sheer talent, hard work, camaraderie, and fan support. The construction of a powerful narrative and storytelling is not just an age-old device harking back to the age of oral tradition but a significant technique and asset needed in the age of digital communication.

The centrality of narrative power has been explored by economist Robert J. Shiller, whose thesis sheds light on how media contagion can take place on digital and social networks through influential storytelling. In *Narrative Economics*, Shiller advanced the notion that such storytelling is central to economic success. To ignore economic viability would be a disingenuous denial of the K-pop industry's main concerns, and in this regard, Shiller's work on the economic power of effective narratives presents notable insights for gauging BTS's success. Shiller posits that effective economic narratives defined by viral and contagious stories can alter people's economic planning. He elaborates further, emphasizing the significance of successful storytelling by (1) offering a story the audience can retell, (2) including a vivid visual image to tease out the main ideas of a story so that it sticks with the listeners, and (3) valuing what the audience values.[8]

BTS's storytelling technique embodies these various aspects of creating a relatable and unforgettable narrative. To be more precise, the inclusion of vivid images is a widely shared practice in the K-pop industry, where much energy is directed toward the creation of high-quality music videos and stage performances aided by spectacular choreography, fancy makeup, and fashion statements. Prioritization of vivid images is also symptomatic of the broader digital culture and not a particular practice of BTS, but the band's qualitatively different strength lies in their ability to offer stories the audience can retell while valuing what the audience values.

BTS's famous epithet, "the voice of millennial reality,"[9] indicates the band's empathetic ability to provide audiences with stories. Their voicing of the anxieties of youth living in an uncertain world scarred by depression, suicidal thoughts, and bleak visions of the future while finding beauty, hope, and the courage to love oneself reflects widely shared sentiments among the younger generation. BTS's critically accepted music video "Spring Day" (2017) is a case in point.

> I miss you, miss you even more now that I say it.
> Even as I stare at your photo, I miss you . . .
> Like little dust motes floating in the air
> If I were snow scattered from the sky
> I could reach you sooner . . .
> How much waiting, how many sleepless nights
> Must pass before we meet again?

The lyrics may at first present romantic longing for the other, but "Spring Day" is hardly an ordinary love croon. Its narrative is steeped in grave tragedy, which provides a context for plumbing the depth of its lyrics. As Suk-Young Kim has previously commented,

> Many fans and critics have noted that this highly acclaimed music video presented a haunting allegory of the MV *Sewol* disaster on April 16, 2014, when 306 passengers, among them 246 high school students, lost their lives as the ferry sank deep into the ocean off the southwest coast of the Korean Peninsula. Multiple factors caused this calamity, including: careless navigation by the captain and his crew; the company's greed and lack of safety measures that resulted in overloaded cargo; and the lack of immediate rescue response by the government, epitomized by the fact that then South Korean President Park Geun-hye could not be accounted for during more than seven hours after the ferry started to capsize. The catastrophic event – especially in terms of how the older generation failed so many young lives – left deep wounds in the minds of Koreans, painfully haunting the collective psyche to this day.[10]

Indeed, the majority of BTS fans are of similar age as the students who perished, and the narrative of "Spring Day" is an elegy dedicated to a friend who has crossed the boundary of life and death. BTS represents the pain and loss of the young generation by offering sublimated narratives that will be retold by those whom the group represents. This circular echoing and fusing are at the heart of valuing what the audience values. The documentarian truth of their lyrics and the poetic sublimation of the tragedy anchor the authenticity of BTS.

From Idols to Artists

In a 2012 article on the reasons behind the meteoric rise of K-pop around the globe, journalist Jonathan Seabrook offered one of the most memorable monikers of K-pop idols: "factory girls." Lurking behind the term was the idea that K-pop idols are highly manufactured products quite similar to factory-made items: artificial and lacking in authenticity. Although manu-factured stardom is also a hallmark of the Motown music scene and therefore it is problematic to bracket only Korean pop as manufactured music, Seabrook's judgment is fair to a certain degree, given that the K-pop industry has a substantial track record of suppressing the diverse talents of individual performers as it has evolved around the prioritization of fantas-tic visual spectacles central to establishing each band's identity.

BTS's success is in large part due to their defiance of such industry standards. The authenticity of the group's music stems primarily from the fact that, since their debut, the members have been deeply involved in songwriting, composing lyrics, arranging, and producing. Self-producing in the pop music industry often serves as a litmus test for the authenticity of artists – a quality not always easy to come by in the K-pop world. Although BTS was made to be idols, due to their self-production, they are perceived differently because they are seen as artists with creative autonomy. Such is the vision cultivated by BTS producer Bang Si-hyuk, who intended to create hip-hop idols – in part due to the mainstream commercial success of hip hop music in the 2010s, but more due to his belief that the hip-hop genre would allow idols to reveal their true selves as artists. Whether Bang's choice was based on commercial or artistic reasons, it proved highly successful. BTS embraced a direct and undecor-ated storytelling technique, which created the new model of idols as artists.

The hybridity of idol and artist is fully embraced in the 2018 song "IDOL." Rather than coyly alluding to their double identity, they confront it with full-on honesty in the song's lyrics.

> You can call me artist (artist)! You can call me idol (idol).
> Whatever you call me, I don't care! I don't care! I'm proud of it (proud of it)!
> I'm free (free)! No more irony (irony)! I was always myself.
> Point fingers at me (yeah yeah yeah yeah), I don't care at all! No matter what
> reason you blame me for! I know what I am (I know what I am)! I know what
> I want (I know what I want)! I never gon' change (I never gon' change)!
> I never gon' trade! (Trade off)

Their self-proclaimed identity as both artist and idol is shared without any sense of sarcasm or irony. BTS in effect is creating a narrative archetype of uninhibited youth who can go on to love and be proud of themselves.

BTS on the World Stage

One defining difference between BTS and most other K-pop groups can be found in where their careers first took off. Unlike other K-pop groups who became popular in Asia first and then went to Europe and America, BTS first became popular in the United States, which attracted the attention of the Korean audience. As a so-called reverse import to Korea, BTS is unique in that they made it in the US music market, arguably the most challenging to penetrate. From the late 1990s, Korean popular music started to take the world stage under the banner of "K-pop." The primary target at that time was Japan and East Asia, which shared many cultural similarities with Korea. K-pop overcame the insularity of the Japanese popular music market catering to mostly domestic audiences and became successful through its localization strategy. It remained successful in Japan by either recruiting artists already fluent in Japanese or training artists to be fluent in Japanese as well as casting Japanese members. In this regard, it would be no exaggeration to state that K-pop has become an integral part of Japanese popular culture.

Nonetheless, the barrier to entering the market in the United States and European countries remained high. As the epicenter of contemporary popular music, the mainstream US music market is not an easy place for foreign artists to land. More than anything else, K-pop artists had to rise above their anonymous status. Individual artists were unknown in the United States; moreover, the West did not know that South Korea had a thriving pop music industry. For instance, in the early 2000s in the United States, one had to be a hardcore music aficionado to know of BoA, then the leading female solo artist in the K-pop world. Around 2006 the popularization of YouTube became a significant game changer; nonetheless, K-pop artists were much less known than American indie artists. Rain, who was the leading Asian pop star in the 2000s, was invited by reputable American record companies to have a showcase in the United States, only to be met with harsh criticism that his music was outdated. Wonder Girls, then the top K-pop girl group, was relegated to opening for the Jonas Brothers and toured around the United States under challenging circumstances. But the power dynamics between the K-pop industry and the US music industry was so lopsided that K-pop idols had to be grateful for these opportunities. When their songs occasionally made the Billboard chart, it was a result of a targeted marketing strategy focusing on Korean American and Asian American communities. But the situation gradually started to shift at the end of the 2000s, with SM idols performing at New York's Madison Square Garden and bands such as Girls' Generation, Super Junior, BIGBANG, and 2NE1 garnering major success on world stages. This expansive outreach of K-pop culminated in the truly global success of BTS.

The path to the present moment, however, has not been a smooth one. The United States has a more than 200-year history of popular music with three tracks: (1) Eurocentric music, which constitutes the mainstream; (2) equally influential African American music; and (3) Latinx music. Youngdae Kim noted that "these trends fused throughout history to create the U.S. music culture that has come to dominate the global pop scene."[11] Even in this melting pot of cultural influences, Asian artists had difficulty entering the mainstream music scene. Asians in the United States in particular were faced with the added challenge of having to confront negative images. While jazz and classical music place much emphasis on performance technique and artistic virtuosity, ethnic music places much emphasis on the authenticity of the ethnically specific experience. Different from these genres, popular music often appeals through the attractiveness – including sexual attractiveness – of the artists. Such tendencies presented particularly challenging conditions for Asian artists, since Asian men were stereotypically projected as asexual by the US media.

The current K-pop industry led by BTS is directly challenging the stereotypical notions surrounding Asian male artists. BTS could be successful in the US market because they defied such Asian male stereotypes and presented themselves as attractive and sophisticated youths, which appealed to the mainstream audience. In this regard, the success of BTS presents a different model than PSY's breakout song, "Gangnam Style." While both artists have benefited tremendously from their presence on social media, there is a foundational gulf between the two: PSY's "Gangnam Style" was a typical viral video made with comical dance at an entertaining cadence that stood as a one-time hit. PSY's success model bears no resemblance to those of either BTS or other K-pop idols who have been present on the world stage since the 2000s. Neither did it come from K-pop's training or production system; rather, it had everything to do with his personality and the song's individual appeal. PSY in a way appealed to a Western audience by reaffirming the preexisting stereotypes about Asians, very similar to how Asian American comedians have operated on the US media circuit. BTS's approach is different in that they do not rely on any stereotypes or fantasies about Koreans, Asians, or exotic foreigners but operate much the same way that mainstream artists in the West do.

Another way BTS's success differs from that of PSY or other Asian pop stars is that their power stems from robust fandom rather than virality on social media or systematic promotion in the mainstream music industry. In the past, foreign pop artists' success was based on their viral hits, as was the case with PSY. In other words, success depended on several songs going viral; therefore, the artists enjoyed only temporary popularity rather than enduring fame supported by their loyal fans. From the early stage of BTS's career, a small group of extremely loyal fans organized themselves and led a grassroots movement to shepherd the group to stardom. Once BTS became top artists, their fan base grew exponentially into the most visible and phenomenal fandom in the world of pop music. Historically, global-scale fandom used to exist only for Euro-American pop or rock stars, but BTS is writing history as the first Asian pop stars to command a global audience.

Awards are by no means the only yardstick to measure the success of artists, but they are significant indicators of visibility on the world stage. On May 23, 2021, Billboard Music Awards announced that BTS had been nominated in four categories: top duo/group, social artists, top-selling song, and song sales artists, all of which they eventually won. This was by no means the first time BTS appeared on Billboard's award roster; they had previously won the top social artist (2017–2020) award and top duo/ group artist award (2019–2020). Regardless of the results, BTS's high-flying streak as Asian artists at the Billboard Awards carries particular significance. Since the 2000s, K-pop has attempted to become successful in the United States, but for the most part, it has remained a subcultural fascination. BTS's presence in the music award ceremonies marked a turning point: K-pop is now regarded as mainstream in the United States. BTS's proven success is the reason behind major US record labels' willingness to collaborate with Korean companies to produce or distribute K-pop. The fact that BTS released a globally circulated English-language hit song like "Dynamite" and consistently win major music awards is creating a new global cultural phenomenon where Asian artists are reaching unprecedented stature.

The 2021 Billboard Music Awards proved to be special in this regard. Out of five groups nominated in the top social artist category, three were K-pop groups: in addition to BTS, widely popular K-pop girl group BLACKPINK and another popular boyband, Seventeen, made the list. Also noteworthy is the Filipino boyband SB19. What does it mean to have so many Asian nominees for mainstream awards like the Billboard Music Awards? How much weight does the top social artist award carry when it is based on online voting and given to the group whose fans have the largest social media presence? These are questions that do not yield simple answers, but obviously the system of judging popularity is changing. In the past, the popularity of artists was generally measured by album sales and the frequency of TV and radio appearances, making high-selling music and frequently visible artists popular. But nowadays, "music enjoyed by everyone" no longer carries the same weight; significant changes in popularity came with changes in the way music is shared and how the fandom coheres around their shared agenda. Popular music no longer is propagated via traditional media such as radio or broadcast TV networks.

Listeners now use streaming services to access the music of their favorite artists and tend to listen to their favorites repeatedly – a trend that prioritizes interpersonal social media communication more than broadcasting systems. Social media platforms are where users reveal their personal tastes and share their interests with like-minded people. Social media also serve as a forum to freely express fandom affiliations. It is a place for high-frequency users with intense emotional involvement, "serving as the space to showcase the popularity of artists in the most primal sense."[12]

Popularity in the age of social media networks differs significantly from conventional notions. The social index is not just a casual sign of fleeting curiosity; more likely, it is a reflection of conscious fan engagement in an attempt to promote their favorite artists. While the vast majority of listeners stream their favorite songs several times at most, hardcore fans actively engage in promoting their favorite artists' songs via hashtag bombardments. One might have difficulties accepting the buzz created by such activities, akin to a political campaign, as genuine popularity, and it is still debatable which makes a broader statement about the artist's popularity: a large number of silent and passive fans or a smaller number of hyperactive and visible fans.

To be clear, the top social artist award was not created in anticipation of K-pop's rise and global prominence. Rather, it was established in 2011 to reflect the rapidly changing patterns of pop music consumption. Since its inception, pop idol Justin Bieber won the top social artist award for six consecutive years, but in 2017, the winning streak came to a halt when BTS won. The year 2021 marked the fourth consecutive year BTS was chosen. As a group with a hyperactive fandom on social media, BTS is changing the concept of popularity against the backdrop of the rapidly shifting media landscape.

In contrast to Billboard's top social artist award, which reflects the latest popular trend, BTS's Grammy nomination in 2021 registers the band's significance in a different manner. In this regard, BTS marks a new chapter in Grammy history with their presence in the popular music category – a category that is not defined by a particular music genre but rather signals "the nominees' popularity and recognizability in the popular music arena."[13]

This was the first time Asian pop artists had been nominated in the category. Before BTS's nomination, Asian nominees or winners of the Grammy had been either classical musicians or technical engineers. Therefore, BTS's entry marked a tidal shift in not only the K-pop/Asian pop industry but also US popular culture. Having worked outside the US music industry and reached the height of global prominence on their own, BTS is enjoying success not simply as an individual band but as a symbol that started to create cracks in the existing order in the US-centric music business. Despite the announcement in June 2022 that the group's activities will be temporarily halted, BTS will continue to cast a long shadow in the times to come.

A Shift in the K-Pop Music Industry

The year 2021 saw a paradigm shift in the globalization of the K-pop industry. As if it had been previously agreed upon, the top three representatives of K-pop companies announced projects that appeared different on the surface but in essence shared much in common. In February, HYBE Corporation (formerly Big Hit Entertainment) announced that it would create a joint label and groom new K-pop groups based in North America in collaboration with Geffen Records, a subsidiary of the largest record label, Universal Music Group. According to Carolina Malis, a K-pop journalist, "Both Big Hit and Universal have something to add to the mix, and it makes sense that they're partnering up for this new challenge instead of trying to make it happen separately." Malis added that Big Hit had expertise in artist development and engaging fans, while Geffen and UMG could take care of marketing, production, and distribution.[14]

It is likely that this joint label will follow the time-honored idol recruiting system: hosting a reality audition show to discover future stars, who will be produced and promoted by the joint label. Although there has been a case in the past where SM Entertainment collaborated with Capitol Records to launch SuperM, an all-star boy band comprising the shiniest stars of SM Entertainment, the HYBE-UMG joint venture presents a unique opportunity for the K-pop industry in that a major US label will entrust a Korean partner with total control over producing a new K-pop group for the US audience.

Three months after the announcement, CJ ENM and SM Entertainment announced similar plans. CJ ENM will collaborate with HBO Max to produce a Latin American K-pop band, while SM Entertainment will work with MGM Television to audition members for NCT Hollywood, a North American unit of the group NCT. All three projects share a common objective of creating a "localized" group based in North America. Although such developments would have been simply unimaginable just a few years ago, localization projects are nothing new to the K-pop industry. Since K-pop's early attempts at globalization, producers' ultimate aim was to make it in the West, especially in the United States. But only a few believed that it would be realistic to set such a goal. Many believed that the success of K-pop would be restricted to Asia due to linguistic and cultural differences between Korea and other countries outside the region. Current developments in the music industry belie such a prognosis, since not only is the K-pop industry striving to reach a broader global audience, but also Euro-American music markets are actively courting K-pop acts.

To date, efforts to globalize K-pop have evolved in the following steps. Often known as "cultural technology," the conventional production and marketing strategy developed sequentially around (1) Korean musicians' debut in the foreign music market after mastering foreign languages and customs, (2) the formation of global groups by incorporating foreign or overseas Korean members, and (3) establishing a joint venture with foreign companies or debuting a group consisting entirely of foreign members in a foreign market. The previous two stages garnered a degree of success, but they were also faced with risks and limitations. For this reason, only the third stage was regarded as the solid model to realize the K-pop industry's ultimate dream.

The third stage has already had its trial in Japan and China, respectively, with JYP Entertainment's Japan-based group Nizhu and SM Entertainment's China-based WayV. The big question is whether this model will work in North and South America. Time will tell, but the present industry consensus points to an optimistic outlook that now is the right time to launch such projects. The fact that three similar projects were announced almost simultaneously by HYBE, CJ ENM, and SM Entertainment proves the point.

BTS's success must be one of the reasons for the optimistic attitude. Especially for producers with financial means, BTS's surpassing of native artists must have been a motivator to invest in fostering new groups. It is noteworthy that the US music industry started to pay attention to the commercial potential of the Korean-style system of producing idols; for instance, the audition reality show that CJ ENM and HBO Max prepared was but another rendition of *Produce 101*, the most popular idol audition show that CJ ENM previously produced. The NCT Hollywood project by SM Entertainment would not have been realized had it not been for their American partner's trust in SM's "culture technology" – a term coined by SM's chief producer in reference to the systematic recruitment, training, and promotion of idols.

As many cultural critics note, the future of the music industry depends on how successfully it can build fandom. In this regard, K-pop has an unparalleled culture of catering to fans. When it comes to communicating with fandom and understanding the fans' desire, it has long surpassed the teen pop industry in the United States. Korea has dominated the teen pop genre – mainly idol music geared to young fans – across the globe by the sheer visibility of their fandom in social media spaces, providing an incentive for US labels to forge partnerships with K-pop companies.

Another notable event of 2021 was the news that HYBE Corporation planned to merge with Ithaca Holdings. Ithaca Holdings was founded by Scooter Braun, who, with subsidiary artist management companies such as SB Project, discovered and produced teen idols such as Justin Bieber and secured contracts with top stars such as Ariana Grande. The fact that Braun sold his shares to HYBE is an indication of how this major player in the US pop industry intended to become a player in the future of K-pop. The merger signaled HYBE's ambition to go beyond the status of K-pop entertainment company and transform itself into a multi-entertainment company on a global stage.

K-pop today is perceived as the only viable music industry to measure up to the dominance of the Euro-American pop music industry, but there remains something unique about the path BTS has taken thus far. BTS is larger than the K-pop industry itself, and without their phenomenal success and visibility, major media outlets in the United States would not have launched collaborative projects with K-pop bands. From the US perspective, rather than approaching K-pop in abstract terms, it is much more attractive to create a "post-BTS" phenomenon.

Into the Storm: Racial Prejudice, Racial Solidarity

With the K-pop industry's global reach, the world in which K-pop idols dwell has and will continue to become ever more multiracial and diverse in cultural sensibilities. Both bright and dark moments of K-pop will inevitably become more visible with the genre's growing global presence.

In February 2021, Bayern 3 Radio host Matthias Matuschik's racialized remarks on BTS proved the point. Early in 2021, BTS covered the British rock band Coldplay's hit song "Fix You" for *MTV Unplugged.* This performance ignited a vitriolic response from the German host of Bayern 3 Radio, who used "blasphemy" to express his discontent with the performance. Comparing BTS to a virus, Matuschik invoked North Korea as well as South Korea–manufactured cars out of context, exposing a long-standing prejudice Westerners hold against Asians. Only when confronted with a protest by the BTS fanclub ARMY from all over the world, including ARMY members based in Germany, did the station make an apology and set out to alleviate the situation. But the incident exposed a deep-seated prejudice against Asian performers.

To be sure, racial insults against BTS take a slightly different tone compared to, say, widespread racism against Blacks in the United States or widespread antiforeign sentiment in the West. The Bayern 3 Radio host's remarks were more akin to the sentiment against the shifting order in popular culture. More precisely, they came as a snappy response to the rising influence of what is considered a threat to the preexisting order in the music industry. Underlying such a sentiment are the belief in rock superiority, pop imperialism, and derision of Asian popular music. This is by no means an isolated case. Ever since BTS claimed the top band position on global charts and in awards, innate conflict percolating for a long time below the surface has been erupting in full force.

The German radio host could not stomach the fact that, as he saw it, rock authenticity was being tarnished by BTS, an Asian boy band hailing from the margins of the music industry. In the minds of this host and many others in the Western audience, these Asian pop stars thrive on saccharine melodies and childish tunes, to the adulation of girl fans who are hardly music connoisseurs. Rock music represents artistic authenticity, intellectual force, and machismo, which prioritizes agency of artists over popularity of idols. It must have been difficult to accept that *MTV Unplugged*, where rock legends such as Eric Clapton and Nirvana performed, gave its stage to a Korean boy band. The case with the German radio host is just one realization of such sentiments, which still saturate the industry, ready to resurface at any moment.

It is highly possible that BTS as well as K-pop at large will enter the pages of history as a curious cultural phenomenon of social media–obsessed GenZ or Gen Alpha. But BTS is breaking the conventions of the pop imperialism that thrived under the notions of cosmopolitanism or modernity. What makes the group a formidable counterforce to the previous order is their engaged fandom, ARMY, which is making inroads into political activism, voicing their concerns about racism, gender equality, and advocacy for youth. The most striking incident to date came during the 2020 presidential campaign, when K-pop fans, many of whom were members of ARMY, sabotaged Donald Trump's political rally in Tulsa, Oklahoma. They deployed their social media skills to reserve a large number of tickets to the rally with no intention of participating, leaving gaping holes in the seating area to ruin Trump's photo op.

Following the eruption of racist violence with the murder of George Floyd and other people of color, the online and offline activism involving #BlackLivesMatter in 2020 was ripe with a broader stream of people willing to participate in the movement against long-standing racial violence in the United States. K-pop fans, as seen in the Tulsa rally, were one such group, as analyzed by Suk-Young Kim:

K-pop's strong hip hop basis appeals to racially diverse music fans, and K-pop performers' seemingly gender-fluid looks attract the attention of the LGBTQ+ community. The majority of K-pop fandom in the U.S. are women and people of color, who are more likely to stay attuned to significant social shifts such as BlackLivesMatter and the MeToo movement. It is no wonder they have earned monikers such as "online vigilantes" or "digital warriors" who use their tech savviness to act upon outrageous political events in a time of lockdown.[15]

The online presence of K-pop fans, most prominently illustrated by ARMY, is creating a substantial voice in social activism, presenting themselves as a force to be reckoned with. Pop stars of today are more influential social organizers than simple entertainers, and an Asian group such as BTS has become a rallying point where traditionally marginalized people can voice their concerns in the world. This, too, is a crucial aspect of BTS's authenticity.

Notes

1 Elija Wald, *How the Beatles Destroyed Rock 'n' Roll: An Alternative History of American Popular Music* (Oxford: Oxford University Press, 2009), 179.

2 Richard Middleton, *Studying Popular Music* (Philadelphia: Open University Press, 1990), 53.

3 Jann S. Wenner, "John Lennon Remembers, Part One," Rolling Stone.com, January 21, 1971, www.rollingstone.com/music/music-news/lennon-remembers-part-one-186693/.

4 Wald, *How the Beatles Destroyed Rock 'n' Roll*, 236.

5 Chris Gibson and John Connell, *Soundtracks: Popular Music, Identity, and Place* (New York: Routledge, 2003), 122.

6 "*Anabada*" is a neologism from the late 1990s that refers to the post-IMF sentiment in South Korea to live frugally and economize on everything. *Anabada* is an abbreviation of four verbs: *a* from the verb *akkida* (to economize); *na* from the verb *nanwo sseuda* (to share); *ba* from the verb *bakkwo-sseuda* (to exchange); *da* from the verb *dashi-sseuda* (to reuse).

7 Gibson and Connell, *Soundtracks*, 54.

8 Robert J. Shiller, *Narrative Economics: How Stories Go Viral and Drive Major Economic Events* (Princeton, NJ: Princeton University Press, 2019), part I.

9 Tamar Herman, "A Guide to BTS, and 7 Other Korean Boy Bands Making Waves in the U.S.," Vulture.com, November 13, 2017, www. vulture.com/2017/11/your-guide-to-the-latest-wave-of-k-pop-boy-bands.html.

10 Suk-Young Kim, "Beauty and the Waste: Fashioning Idols and the Ethics of Recycling in Korean Pop Music Videos," *Fashion Theory* (March 2019): 11.

11 Youngdae Kim, *Idols as Artists in the K-Pop Era* (Seoul: Munhak Dongnae, 2021), 256.

12 Kim, *Idols as Artists in the K-Pop Era*, 266.

13 Kim, *Idols as Artists in the K-Pop Era*, 258.

14 "BTS Label Big Hit and Universal Seek Next Boy Band," BBC News, February 18, 2021, www.bbc.com/news/business-56107527.

15 Suk-Young Kim, "K-Pop Stans' Anti-Trump, Black Lives Matter Activism Reveals Their Progressive Evolution," *NBC Think*, June 28, 2020, www.nbcnews.com/think/opinion/k-pop-stans-anti-trump-black-lives-matter-activism-reveals-ncna1232327/.

11 Transcultural Fandom

BTS and ARMY

CANDACE EPPS-ROBERTSON

It is almost impossible to mention the name of any Korean pop group or idol without acknowledging their fandoms: BTS has ARMY, TXT has MOA, TWICE has ONCE, and BLACKPINK has BLINK. Although these groups and their fandoms might be recognizable to many, stereotypes abound about the relationships between fandoms and artists, fandom activities, and the individuals who make up fandom communities. Fans and fandoms play a significant role in bringing success and attention to the artists and, arguably, the music industry. However, there is a delicate relationship between fandoms and artists. Some perspectives in popular media might lead one to believe that fans are mindless consumers who will do anything to promote their "faves." These broad strokes miss (or completely ignore) that many fans are driven by the deep connection felt with the music and other fans. Additionally, if we fail to account for the role of fans, we risk continuing the tradition of "seeing fans as 'other,' non-intellectuals drawn to mindless entertainment."[1] Understanding popular music must include the importance of fans and fandoms.[2]

Fandoms can wield a great deal of power and influence, but there can also be a great deal of mystery surrounding how they operate and their motives for particular actions. It can be challenging for those not part of fandoms or operating with their own biases to recognize them as complex networks made up of individuals who bring a host of interests, beliefs, and experiences and want to support a group of artists. For many fans of Korean popular music, the stereotypes and assumptions – often rooted in misogynistic and xenophobic ideologies – do not represent their lived fandom experiences. Further, because most accounts of Korean popular music focus on the collective fandom identity, it can be challenging to understand that fandoms and fan experiences are as personal and individual as they are public and collective expressions.

The purpose of this chapter is to examine the role fandom plays for Korean popular music through an exemplary example of BTS's fandom, ARMY. This transcultural fandom has worked to support BTS, the fandom community, and communities not even related to the fandom. There are many fandoms, each with their unique histories, stories, and practices, but, arguably, ARMY has risen to the top as one of the most visible for their online and offline presence.[3] Fans who identify as part of ARMY may differ in nationality and span a wide age demographic, along with other identity markers, but what connects them is their appreciation and enjoyment of BTS. For many BTS fans, being part of ARMY is more than purchasing music or merchandise; it is about supporting the band and the ARMY community. Furthermore, fandoms are continuously changing in response to historical and material conditions.[4]

This chapter begins with a brief history of fandom as understood within the context of fandom histories at large and Korean popular music. Certainly, it would be impossible to offer one history that encompasses all fandoms. This chapter shows fandoms' role for both artists and the industry by looking at practices that are most readily identifiable across Korean popular music fandoms: fan support for music, fandom philanthropy efforts, education, social justice, and community uplift. How fans carry out these practices varies widely given the social and material conditions of artists and fans. These practices remain some of the most recognizable (and possibly misunderstood) by those not familiar with Korean popular music. This chapter uses ARMY as an illustrative example of these characteristics.

To understand Korean popular music fandoms, we must put their history within the larger context of both fandom and K-pop history. While fandom communities vary widely, scholars have identified shared characteristics that often shape fandom spaces. Fandoms consist of people who are passionate about their object of fandom; there is a shared cohesion not only with the object of fandom but also among others in the community, and these spaces share their own cultures and traditions.[5] The same characteristics are reflected across K-pop fandom communities.[6] The history of the very term "fan" gives us some perspective into why this term and phenomenon often signals people to think negatively. Media studies and cultural studies scholar Mark Duffett traces the etymology of the word "fan" back to "fanatic," first used in the seventeenth century in England; it was associated with a person considered to be a "religious zealot."[7] Similarly, Henry Jenkins describes how the term "fan" not only carried a religious connotation but also came to be used to describe those with "political zealotry, false beliefs, orgiastic excess, possession, and madness."[8] The term continued to develop new associations regarding enthusiasm for sports teams and other cultural phenomena, but the negative connotations often remained. Early fan studies research sought to counter the negative stereotypes and offer a more robust understanding of how these communities function as active, engaged, and creative spaces where people develop their own culture in conversation with popular cultural objects.

While research in fan and fandom studies has moved away from continually defending fans, negative stereotypes associated with particular types of fandoms and fans, such as those with large numbers of women, girls, or members of BIPOC communities, continue. Concerning popular music in particular, there is a long history of reducing female fans to being obsessive, shallow, and hysterical. These stereotypes point to a long legacy of dismissing things that women enjoy.[9] K-pop fandoms especially have faced negative branding from popular media, where they are often described as being full of "hysterical teenagers" or women with "excessive obsessions."[10] The significant demographic of women and BIPOC present in these fandoms, alongside the xenophobia around Korean idols and idol groups, have continued misconceptions and a lack of critical engagement about these communities' practices and traditions.[11] The stereotypes and misconceptions fail to notice that K-pop fans and fandoms are often highly organized, multifaceted communities that not only act in response to their desire to support the artists but also show their frequent commitments to helping the fandom community in ways that are not readily connected back to the artists or K-pop at all. This is not to suggest that fandoms are without their own issues. Fans can bring their own biases into these spaces, and, unfortunately, negative expressions, like bullying, can be part of the fandom experience.

Where Are the Fans? The Globalization of K-Pop Fandom

Research has demonstrated that K-pop fandoms are pretty diverse across demographics such as race, gender, location, and age (Anderson 2013; J. Lee 2019). K-pop fandom research continues to document the growth of these fandoms around the world, in Asia (Siriyuvasak and Shin 2007; Jung and Shim 2014), Latin America (Han 2017; Min, Jin, and Han 2019), the Middle East (Otmazgin and Lyan 2014; E. Lee 2017), and North America (Yoon 2017; McLaren and Jin 2020). While much research points to diversity in terms of nationality and ethnicity, K-pop fandoms can also be understood as both transnational and transcultural spaces. Media and fan studies scholars Bertha Chin and Lori Morimoto posit that using the term transcultural helps in examining "border-crossing fandoms" where "the nation is but one in a constellation of contexts that inflect and influence their rise and spread."[12] Even among similar regions, the fandom community's experiences and expectations may vary widely because of each fan's social and cultural background.

In part, understanding K-pop fans must be done with attention to the general spread of Korean popular culture globally through the Korean cultural wave, or *Hallyu*. The export of Korean popular culture is not relegated solely to music but also includes film, drama, food, clothing, beauty products, games, and other products. While there is often debate over exact dates, scholars most often demarcate the Korean Wave by phases or generations.[13] Seo Taeji and Boys are heralded as the group that marked the beginning of K-pop and K-pop fandom as we know it. Blending hip hop and choreography with traditional Korean music, they ushered in a new music sound and style in Korea in the early 1990s. Notably, concerning fandom, one of the marks of this group is that their fans stressed the importance of performance and visuals through music videos.[14] In the first phase of *Hallyu*, from the mid-1990s to the early 2000s, K-pop was aimed at countries throughout Asia. During this time, first-generation idol groups like H.O.T., Shinhwa, and Baby V.O.X. saw popularity (and fandom growth) in China and Japan.[15] From the mid-2000s through the early 2010s, the second phase of *Hallyu* saw increased attention to Korean boy and girl groups, with stars such as BIGBANG and Girls' Generation popular with fans in Asia, Latin America, and the Middle East. With the rise of the internet, entertainment companies increasingly turned to digital technologies and social media to spread their music and messages and engage with global audiences. Third-generation groups continued to build upon these practices, utilizing Twitter, YouTube, and apps that allow for artist-fan communication and multimedia content. Like BTS, BLACKPINK and Seventeen have maintained global fandoms. While recognizing these artists' trajectories as managed by their entertainment companies and the technological forces that influenced the spread of Korean popular music is important, studying the music and messages of these artists is equally important for understanding their fandom.

K-Pop Fandom Structure and Design

K-pop fandoms have existed since the industry's inception, and entertainment companies have long invested in developing and sustaining them.[16] In most instances, the concept for the fandom begins with the artists' label. Companies may name the fandom and give it a representative color and associated logos that appear on merchandise. Companies do extensive market research to inform the decisions made about creating experiences for fans to enjoy the music and artists, such as concerts and fan meets, and designing spaces for fans to interact with each other and the artists online. These platforms can shape the ways fans interact and experience the music, the artist, and being in a community with other fans. For example, V Live is a South Korean streaming service used explicitly by celebrities to communicate with their fans. In addition to acting as a streaming service for videos, it provides celebrities with the ability to go "live" via video feed and allows fans to view and comment during these sessions. The entertainment companies certainly play a role in creating a fandom brand and experience; fans and idols have crucial roles in developing and sustaining the community.

The artists' music is often the first point of entry or interest for fans. Whether recommended by a friend or an algorithm on a streaming service, listening to a song is how fans come to feel invited to learn more about a group. While the mainstream media have often claimed that K-pop produces manufactured music and performances, this is not a truth for all artists. In the case of BTS, fans often comment on the authenticity present in the music and messages.[17] This authenticity is connected to the observation that BTS writes many of their own songs, allowing them to address topics in their lyrics that reflect their own experiences. Opportunities to communicate with and see the artists offstage often shape the kind of connections fans think they can have with the artist, which influences the fandom community. This suggests that social media does not have the sole role in developing the relationship between a fan and artists and complicates claims that seem to fixate on social media as the sole reason for an artists' popularity. Fans can learn more about the artists' personalities through social media such as V Live, social media posts, interviews, and vlogs. These are ways for fans to learn more about the dynamics between members of the group and the artists' personalities. The encounters may shape how fans then feel connected to the artists, but ultimately the music and content are what keep fans engaged. For those who may have experienced these groups only via YouTube or shared media recordings of performances, such encounters are often the only "live" experiences they will have to get to know who these idols are offstage.[18]

Entertainment companies often establish official fan clubs that carry annual membership fees and offer incentives such as raffles, unique concert ticket sale offerings, or access to the artists themselves through fan meets. For some fans, membership may be an important marker of belonging to the fandom community. However, one does not have to be part of an official club to participate in all fandom activities. Fandoms have coalesced online without the necessity of official membership because of the global popularity of K-pop. Access to official K-pop fandom communities was difficult for those who neither speak Korean nor reside in Korea. Fan cafés, digital clubs that allowed for artist-fan connection through message boards, forums, and other content, were most often all in Korean. The internet enabled fans to organize themselves and connect with others without fan clubs organized by entertainment companies, which was especially useful for those outside Korea. These unofficial sites are often housed or run through Twitter, Facebook, or Tumblr. They are integral to providing resources, such as translation content into other languages, fan meetup opportunities, and other community-building activities.[19]

Many K-pop fandoms are diffuse in terms of structure and organization, without designated or official leaders. Still, most are highly organized, with the ability to share news, resources, and goals for supporting their respective pop artists through social media. Twitter, Instagram, and Facebook allow fandoms to quickly organize and share information.[20] Some scholars have noted that for Korean popular music fandoms outside Korea, this diffuse structure is different from Korean fandom experiences, which tend to be more hierarchical.

Fandoms often have regional bases for each country (and also regions within a country). Additionally, social media accounts often monitor music charting, track fan voting efforts for fan-driven awards and philanthropy efforts, monitor and share news about the artists, and provide translations across languages. While companies may create and initially provide fandom identity markers such as names, colors, and even online spaces for fans to connect, once fans start to interact with the artists, content, and other fans, how these fandoms take shape and evolve is unique to each.

Fandom Practices: Supporting One's Faves and One's Fandom

A core value of many K-pop fandoms is the desire to support the performers and enjoy music and content with other fans. If there is a central shared characteristic, it is that most in these communities see their primary mission as supporting the work of the artists. How this manifests can look different for each fan. For some, participating in voting for fan-driven awards and streaming music for charting purposes takes precedence. For others, it may be participating in offline fan events such as meetups or celebrations in honor of a group's anniversary or artist's birthday. Still, for others, the work of doing online PR through actions such as trending hashtags, vlogging reaction videos to music or performances, writing reviews, or providing a translation of content from Korea to other languages is essential. All of this fan labor is a means to provide positive attention and support to the artists.

There are many ways that fans may show support and increase visibility for artists. Perhaps the most recognized and talked about is streaming and purchasing music to help artists succeed on music charts and break records. While some awards, charts, and radio play might be region-specific in that they are limited to participation from fans from a specific area, fans work together to support one another through sharing resources about goals, metrics, and details on what the process looks like for specific charts. For example, music charts, such as the Billboard Hot 100, are ranked according to radio play, streaming across music platforms, and sales in the United States. Social network spaces provide ground for fans to organize efforts around charting, streaming, and voting to promote the music and artists. Although practices such as streaming may seem to suggest an uncritical engagement with the music, these actions often reflect fans' desire to be more engaged listeners who want not only to support the artist but also to exercise control over their music choices on these platforms. They may use streaming (and charting music) as a means to respond to what some fans perceive as bias toward music from groups like BTS.[21]

Fandoms can also create and sustain visibility and attention to a group or performer in other ways. Fans make and trend hashtags to bring attention to a new song or album, in some instances creating their own digital content to boost awareness of a group. On YouTube, fans upload reaction videos to reflect on a performance or music video, expressing that they are watching the content for the first time to capture an alive and honest response. These videos often show "excessive delight, a structure of feeling that might characterize fandom."[22] For example, a YouTube channel with over 210,000 subscribers, "WhatchaGot2Say," offers BTS reaction video content. Three creators watch BTS content and provide commentary and reviews. Their reaction videos, which range from reactions to BTS performances to music videos, often include laughter, joy, and commentary that expresses excitement. These videos, as Cho argues, also build community among fans and viewers online, drawing attention to the artists and offering a shared sense of community as fans can watch others experience the same thing they enjoy.[23] Many of this channel's reaction videos see over 200,000 views with comments that range from agreeing with what the creators make to fans sharing their own reflections on the video or content being reviewed. Another YouTube creator, xCeleste, with a channel that has over 313,000 subscribers, creates and posts videos with a range of BTS content, from introduction videos aimed at newcomers to the group and their fandom to reaction videos of performances. xCeleste's "This Is BTS: Introduction," posted on August 19, 2020, has just over 398,000 views as of this writing. The 15:37 video presents a montage of video clips that give a history of BTS's career trajectory, highlighting both their success and their hardships.[24] Videos such as these also serve as a way to document history for fans.

Fans are aware of the bias often present against K-pop in mainstream media and what had been a lack of coverage until 2018.[25] It is perhaps from this awareness and a desire to communicate within the community that fan-driven publications can be spaces for fandom news, band news, and other types of content. Sometimes these publications focus on more news-oriented content about the artist, such as reporting on milestones or achievements like awards and new music. In contrast, others provide creative writing, essays, fan art, and scholarly articles. Before the rise of social media, fandoms circulated information via fliers or within local community meetups through word of mouth.[26] Now, internet spaces allow fans to create blogs, vlogs, and even extended Twitter threads to circulate news and creative responses.

In addition to providing publicity for the artists, perhaps one of the most recognized and appreciated acts of labor by fans in K-pop fandom is translators' work. While there may be subtitles provided for some K-pop music videos and interviews, this is not always the case. Translation accounts abound on Twitter, where many fans post real-time translations when artists share tweets or livestreams in Korean. Most translators operate for a specific artist, and accounts can be managed by one person or an entire team.[27] It is often because of the work of fan translators that fans have access to K-pop song lyrics in other languages. Some translators also share news related to Korea and Korean entertainment that affects the focal artists.[28] K-pop's global spread means that there are often articles and interviews written about artists across languages. While translations from Korean to other languages are necessary, so is translation of content from other languages into Korean for Korean-speaking fans.[29] Translators act as a bridge for the community. HYBE Corporation (the Korean entertainment company that manages BTS) created an education division, HYBE EDU, in which part of the focus has been to develop Korean-language books and materials to help fans learn Korean.[30] Even with these resources and subtitles on official content, the role of translators remains integral for sharing information.

Activism and philanthropic efforts have long been part of K-pop fandom communities, from fan groups organizing to support specific charities or causes to speaking out about policies in the entertainment industry that affect artists and communities outside the artist-fandom relationship. At times activism has meant fans organizing and calling attention to mistreatment by the entertainment companies on behalf of the artists. In some instances, fans have managed to bring attention to perceived issues with idols or other unfair treatment contracts. In 2009, the members of the fandom for JYJ (a former K-pop group) organized to show support for the members who filed a lawsuit against an unfair contract through petitions and boycotts of SM Entertainment, the management group.[31] Such actions have changed industry practices.[32] While there are positive aspects to this kind of fan involvement, it has been examined and critiqued for the problems it can cause when fans try to intervene on behalf of artists but lack understanding of the full context for the issue they are trying to address.[33]

Artists can sometimes spur or encourage fan activity around social and humanitarian causes. For example, a K-pop group or its members might use social media to promote a fundraising cause, spurring fandom to provide their support. BTS's anti-violence campaign, Love MYSELF, began in 2017 in partnership with the United Nations Children's Fund (UNICEF). This campaign has raised 4.5B KRW as of December 2021.[34] As will be discussed, it also served as the impetus for a group of ARMY to establish One in an ARMY (OIAA), a fan-driven philanthropic organization. K-pop artist IU donated to the Korean Foundation for Support of the Senior Citizen in both her name and the fandom's name, who provided gifts and inspirations to her philanthropy project.[35]

Other actions are more grassroots, coming directly from fans who organize initiatives and give to a charity of their own choice in the name of a group or an artist. One of the earliest mentions of fandom philanthropy is from Shinhwa fans who sent rice donations to a charity to mark Shin Hye-sung's first solo concert.[36] In 2012 fans of Seo Taiji and Boys helped celebrate the twentieth anniversary of the group's debut by raising enough money to create the "Seo Taiji Forest" in Brazil.[37] An artist's birthday or landmark group anniversary may be the occasion for such actions and result in donations to support the building of schools, scholarships, and a variety of charitable organizations. As will be discussed later in this chapter, some fandoms have dedicated charity fanbases that run campaigns.

The political and racial protests in the United States during the summer of 2020 saw a great deal of media attention given to K-pop fandom activism. From donations raised in support of the Black Lives Matter movement (#BLM) by ARMY that totaled $1 million to spamming a police scanner app for Dallas, Texas, with fancams (a short video clip of an artist or group) to jam the app, media coverage began a narrative about K-pop fandoms that shifted from the stereotypes of "screaming teenagers" to question to what extent they could influence politics.[38] While it is true that activism has long been part of K-pop communities, for some fans, these actions stem not from their identity as fans of K-pop but rather from the commitments and beliefs they bring with them into these spaces. As one K-pop fan said in response to her online activism during the summer 2020 #BLM protests: "I'm Black before I'm a K-pop stan . . . the main point of why we were fighting was for the Black Lives Matter cause, not to get recognized [as K-pop fans]."[39]

A Case Study in Fandom: The Presence and Growth of the BTS ARMY Fandom

BTS is one of the most successful international K-pop groups of the twenty-first century, with one of the world's largest fandoms. As of October 2021, BTS had 40.5 million followers on Twitter and just over 13 million subscribers on the Weverse app. Sales for touring also demonstrate their popularity and fandom size; BTS was the first Asian act to sell out Wembley Stadium in London twice and touted viewership of 775,000 during one of their pandemic online concerts, "Bang Bang Con: The Live."[40] Since debuting with Big Hit Entertainment (now under HYBE) in June 2013, they have seen steady success across multiple fronts: breaking records on the music charts, earning music awards globally, selling out worldwide stadium tours, and serving as invited speakers for international organizations such as the United Nations General Assembly. While BTS has garnered steady attention for their artistry and ability to break records, their fandom has received attention for their creativity and innovation in supporting BTS. Scholars and music critics have cited many factors that have led to their success and massive global fanbase: their music, authenticity, history, and a wide variety of engaging content.[41]

The acronym ARMY stands for Adorable Representative M.C. for Youth. The fandom receives attention for their ability to sell out stadiums, help BTS chart their way to a Billboard #1 hit for both English and Korean songs, and consistently place BTS as winners for the Billboard Top Social Artist award (as of October 2021 they have won every year since 2017). While those achievements directly impact the group, the synergistic relationship between BTS and ARMY must be put into context with BTS's history and music. Korean media did not give BTS as much attention as other groups because Big Hit was not a significant entertainment company when BTS debuted. Accordingly, Big Hit did not have the same resources as more established entertainment companies to garner access to media and invitations for idol groups to appear on variety shows or engage in circuits that would have helped build their reputation. Members of BTS used social media to connect with fans, telling their own stories to build relationships. Early vlogs described their struggles as trainees preparing for debut and scenes from their daily lives (cooking, practicing their music and dance, and simply spending time with one another). These more personal interactions would help fans feel more connected to the members.

Rather than feel as if they were getting to know BTS members onstage or through performances only, viewers came to know them in more personal and intimate settings.

Jeeheng Lee posits that BTS coming from a small company influenced the way their fandom formed: "Unlike idols from large agencies – who gain exposure and grow a fan base via TV appearances – BTS barely benefited from broadcasting opportunities and compensated by diligently uploading behind-the-scenes footage and their daily lives online."[42] The disadvantages BTS encountered made the relationship between BTS and ARMY stronger. Members of the fandom saw themselves as BTS's only allies, which motivated them to give them the support and recognition they believed the band deserved. BTS's unique history among K-pop groups has relied on this strong relationship in particular ways. Most groups' popularity and fandom grew in Korea before gaining attention abroad, but BTS's initial stronghold with fans began in the United States. Music critic Youngdae Kim describes the reason behind this: "In the early 2010s, none of the Korean media paid attention to this group of unknown boys as the 'next big thing' in the middle of the cutthroat competition among idol groups. Instead, American fans and the media that harbored less prejudice against BTS recognized their potential first. They were not large in number, but their existence was nonetheless critical."[43] It is important to acknowledge that even with these early challenges and steady rise of fandom outside Korea, BTS had a dedicated Korean fanbase that was supportive as well.

In addition to the initial conditions that laid the groundwork for BTS and Big Hit to develop their fanbase, the strategies that sustain a dedicated fanbase are also essential to understand. Big Hit has cultivated countless opportunities for fans to enjoy BTS's music and content and become part of the group's story. While BTS's core way of connecting with fans has been through their music (much of which they write themselves), there are other avenues, such as V Lives, in which the members spend time with fans, sometimes after important events like concerts or awards shows. For example, after the 2021 Grammy Awards show (in which they were nominated for Best Pop Duo/Group Performance), BTS had a live event in which they reassured fans that while disappointed about their loss, they were grateful for the opportunity and would continue to work hard. It is also not uncommon for members to respond to viewer comments during these livestreams. They might wish a fan happy birthday, offer advice, or pass on kind words in general.

Scholars have talked at length about celebrity-fan relations through the framework of parasocial relationships.[44] The connections established between artists and fans often emerge from a collective experience, such as BTS fans enjoying content together. This can take many forms, from celebrating countdowns on Twitter in anticipation of new music releases to fans creating games or other nonofficial content as a way to connect. Most fans do not have an illusive perception that they actually "know" the artists. Instead, fans may feel that they know the message and philosophy of the group well enough to recognize the parts of the personalities that artists do show. Social media also offer fans a way to feel connected. The BTS members' joint Twitter feed and individual Instagram accounts provide fans with photos, music clips, recommendations, and other messages. Similarly, Weverse allows members to post messages and pictures to fans, and through these encounters, fans may come to feel that they do get to learn about a member's personality. For example, RM (Kim Nam-joon) frequently posts pictures of his museum visits. An avid art collector, he has inspired many fans to visit the same galleries.[45] On Weverse, members will often respond to fan posts, further establishing the connection fans feel. In addition to these traditional K-pop ways of establishing a relationship between fans and artists, Big Hit has taken on more innovative means. In 2020, as part of BTS's *Map of the Soul: 7* album, the company hosted an international global art show, *Connect, BTS*. Although hindered in some ways by the COVID-19 pandemic, this program spanned five cities and featured over twenty artists. It invited both fans and the general public to experience art exhibitions that resonated with BTS's philosophy of making art and music accessible to all. Big Hit has also used transmedia storytelling across platforms that encourage fans to theorize and build connections across content. This began with BTS's 2015 album, *The Most Beautiful Moment in Life, Part 1*. A narrative began to construct the Bangtan Universe – a complex conglomerate of fictional stories centering around the members' characters and woven across albums, music videos, and a webtoon. Bangtan Universe does not reflect the members' actual lives, but some ARMY followed the experience by theorizing the fictional narrative arc. Some fans also created YouTube videos that analyzed and mapped out theories for understanding the fictional stories. This content not only builds fan connections as they work together to understand and unpack the story but also offers another route for fans to enter and experience the range of content.

ARMY performs many of the fan practices mentioned in this chapter: organizing for streaming and charting, circulating news and content created by fans, and connecting with BTS over social media. But this fandom is also recognized for its social and humanitarian projects, inspired by BTS's messages. These range from reflections on the love, fear, and angst around growing up and adulthood to critiques of social injustice and encouraging people to find their passion. These messages have universal power because they appeal to many shared experiences regardless of age, gender, or ethnicity. While some start from a South Korean context or perspective, these issues are not limited by borders and languages.[46] BTS invites ARMY and other listeners to consider issues rather than setting out to advocate for one particular outcome or follow one particular directive. No outcome or response is privileged over another. The fan base's strength is its desire to reflect the joy and connection they have experienced due to BTS's music.

Although organizing around social issues is not unique to ARMY, what distinguishes ARMY's philanthropic work from the rest is the scale, effort, and diversity in the range of causes. Perhaps one of the most recognized BTS messages has come from their aforementioned *Love Yourself* album series and their work with the United Nations Children's Fund (UNICEF). In November 2017, BTS and Big Hit partnered with the Korean Committee for UNICEF to join the #ENDviolence campaign. The focus was on preventing violence against young people. The group's participation and support of this campaign, described as an extension of BTS's lyrics and music videos, attested to the importance of self-love. It was part of the overarching concept for the *Love Yourself* albums – to echo the importance of loving oneself as a first step toward fostering self-respect and awareness of one's place in the world.[47] One of the ARMY responses to this message created One in an ARMY (OIAA), a fan-driven organization that helps raise funds and awareness about various human rights and social issues, composed of ARMY volunteers worldwide. For each BTS member's birthday, they will run a campaign in their name and honor. These volunteers receive input from other ARMY members regarding which nonprofit organizations they will support, and they use Twitter to organize calls for microdonations. They have done campaigns for various nonprofits, from those that support literacy for incarcerated teens to support for the elderly to COVID-19 relief. Their reach and impact for the birthday projects are extensive, raising just over a total of $49,000 in 2019 in honor of each of the seven BTS members' birthdays alone.[48] This amount didn't include additional projects, such as flash fundraisers and ongoing projects that celebrate acts of kindness that may not be attached to monetary donations. A September 2020 Weverse magazine article, "BTS & ARMY, We Walk Together," highlights the philanthropy of ARMY and notes that its donation history totaled $2,018,020,000 won, roughly US$1,713,802.[49]

ARMY's response to these efforts is impressive because of the money raised and the opportunities it provides for people to learn about issues they otherwise might be unaware of. OIAA stresses the importance of projects that reflect the messages found in BTS: "The vision behind OIAA is driven by our belief that the comfort we get from BTS can be given back to the world in abundance. It also aligns with our objective, as individuals, to work in making this world a better place."[50] This desire to reflect the gratitude for BTS through efforts to help communities who may not even be aware of the group or its fandom has been quite effective for the fundraising efforts. However, more crucial than the amount raised is that these activities provide opportunities to educate about social issues. For example, an October 2020 birthday campaign in honor of a BTS member, Jimin, raised money for Free the Girls, an organization that helps girls rescued from sex trafficking. Using Twitter threads to spur conversation throughout the month of the campaign, OIAA posted links for donations and a series of questions about the issue to encourage discussion and share knowledge about the subject. The questions encouraged readers to move between local and global contexts and see connections between issues often related to more significant structural inequalities: "FTG, through their programs have emerged as great entrepreneurs who are adapting to the needs of the time by trying to expand to an online model, like an online marketplace. How do you think online channels and the global reach of the internet help them in their endeavors?"[51] They also ask ARMY to think about how sex trafficking connects to other issues about the kinds of social support and infrastructure needed to help victims: "How do you think our structures and institutions contribute to creating the divide and what in your opinion can one do on their end to bridge the gap?"[52] These are opportunities for critical conversation and learning, which are just as crucial for social change as donations.

Similarly, an examination of how some ARMY members responded to the #BLM movement in 2020 sheds light on the fandom's ability to mobilize with impressive donations and educate from within around issues of race, racism, and violence. In the wake of George Floyd's killing and ensuing protests of racial violence against Black people, there were con-certed efforts within the fandom to raise money and awareness for BLM. These efforts, many of which started before BTS announced in support of BLM and made public that they had donated $1 million to support the movement, were driven by fans. The magnitude of ARMY's response to BLM resulted in the #MatchAMillion campaign. Although fans started this outside OIAA, the organization helped track logistics for the campaign to match funds. Before the announcement that BTS had donated $1 million, OIAA found that ARMY had raised approximately $50,000. Again, the ability to organize and the amount raised are undoubtedly crucial, but the attempts to educate the public deserve attention. Before BTS's announce-ment, fans tweeted resources that helped explain the history of anti-Black racism in both American and global contexts. In particular, there were efforts to help Korean fans understand the importance of this movement and moment. The #BLM hashtag was circulating within the ARMY community before BTS tweeted their message of support on June 4, 2020; on June 1, 2020, another hashtag appeared in the ARMY community: #WeLoveBlackARMY. This was created by Dr. Jiyoung Lee, a Korean-ARMY academic who used the hashtag in conjunction with #BlackLivesMatter to show support and draw attention to the issue. Dr. Lee's tweet directed toward K-ARMY, first written in Korean and later translated into English, reads:

> I'd like to ask you, K-ARMYs.
>
> The current situation in the U.S. is so severe that I'm apprehensive about the pain felt by the Black ARMY. Wouldn't it provide a little bit of strength to them if you showed you're with them? Why don't you write a message of encouragement with the hashtags?
>
> I'm worried about people who might be hurt beyond our expectations. Especially our overseas fans. We know so well about the protest site filled with fear and anger. I hope our support and backing can help them to turn their despair into hope.[53]

Under the hashtag, a range of conversations ensued from people asking to learn more about the incident to links to blog posts that articulated Korean-ARMY's own attempts to understand race and racism in this context. The hashtag functioned to call attention to the issue, offer support, and provide a space to exchange resources and educate one another about the problems. This moment also represented a potential opportunity for learning and activism that transcended BTS.

ARMY takes finding ways to support one another just as seriously as supporting BTS. In addition to organizing to help with philanthropic efforts, fans have developed several subgroups that provide communal support, such as Korean-language-learning opportunities, tutoring services for a variety of subjects, book clubs, mental health support, cooking lessons, and sharing of employment resources. The Bangtan Academy is an ARMY-sponsored free language-learning program operated through a Discord server that supports students who are learning Korean using several different curricula. Self-paced classes utilize YouTube Korean language channels supplemented with homework assignments designed by Bangtan Academy teachers; all this is augmented by support and encouragement from teachers and other students through chats. There are also language courses taught by volunteers who design their own curricula and provide materials for students. In addition, there are opportunities for learning and discussion around Korean history and culture.[54] ARMY Academics provide free tutoring across a host of subjects taught by

ARMY volunteers. Those seeking help complete a form and partner with a tutor. ARMY Academics also sponsors free programs to help students navigate the process of applying to college, choosing majors, and transitioning from high school to college (ARMY Academy).

Another example of this intracommunity support is the BTS ARMY Job Board, coordinated by ARMY volunteers who circulate job advertisements worldwide. They describe the impetus for their establishment as wanting to provide help for ARMY as inspiration from "the examples of kindness and compassion shown by BTS through their words and their actions" (ARMY Job Board "History"). On Twitter, they share a range of potential job opportunities. This group also supports other fans around issues of career-related concerns.

These fan-driven efforts are not directly related to BTS's success but rather exemplify fans' willingness and desire to support the community formed around this group. ARMY's desire to support BTS has manifested into a desire to help one another in ways inspired by but not limited to music.

Conclusion

Korean popular music fandoms are vibrant communities comprising unique individuals. While the records these fandoms help their artists to reach are impressive, equally impressive is how fandom communities are helping their local and global communities find meaningful ways to impact the world. Broadly, fandoms support artists through purchasing music and content, creating original content inspired by the artists, and taking up volunteer efforts promoting social good. The mechanics of this work change over time given social and material conditions, the artists, and the fans who make up these communities. Attention is often given to fandom for its ability to support its artists. Perhaps we can also learn how the joy and comfort expressed in the music inspire ripples of action throughout communities, some of whom may have never even listened to Korean popular music. The ARMY fandom, similar to BTS, demonstrates possibilities in uncharted territory.

References

Anderson, Crystal. "K-Pop Fandom 101." *Kpopkollective*, December 8, 2013, https://kpopkollective.com/2013/12/08/k-pop-fandom-101/2013.

Arun, Thanmay. "K-Pop Singer IU Celebrates 12th Anniversary by Donating $86,000, Thanks Fans for Their Support." *International Business Times*, September 20, 2020, www.ibtimes.com/k-pop-singer-iu-celebrates-12th-anniversary-donating-86000-thanks-fans-their-support-3049758.

Bhandari, Aditi. "The Mobilising Power of the BTS Army." Reuters, July 14, 2020, https://graphics.reuters.com/GLOBAL-RACE/BTS-FANS/nmopajgmxva/.

Bruner, Raisa. "How K-Pop Fandom Operates as a Force for Political Activism." *Time*, July 25, 2020, https://time.com/5866955/k-pop-political/.

Chin, Bertha, and Lori H. Morimoto. "Towards a Theory of Transcultural Fandom." *Participations: International Journal of Audience and Receptions Studies* 10/1 (2013): 92–108.

Cho, Michelle. "3 Ways That BTS and Its Fans Are Redefining Liveness." Flow. journal, May 29, 2019, www.flowjournal.org/2018/05/bts-and-its-fans/.

Cohen, Jonathan. "Mediated Relationships and Media Effects: Parasocial Interaction and Identification." In Robin L. Nabi and Mary Beth Oliver (eds.), *The SAGE Handbook of Media Processes and Effects* (Los Angeles, CA: Sage, 2009).

Dodson, P. Claire. "BTS's Growing Fanbase Isn't Just Teens, It's Their Moms." Instyle.com, July 2, 2020, www.instyle.com/celebrity/bts-fans-over-35-map-of-soul (accessed November 1, 2020).

Dooley, Ben, and Su-Hyun Lee. "BTS's Loyal Army of Fans Is the Secret Weapon behind a $4 Billion Valuation." *New York Times*, October 14, 2020. www.nytimes.com/2020/10/14/business/bts-ipo.html.

Duffett, Mark. *Understanding Fandom: An Introduction to the Study of Media and Fan Culture*. New York: Bloomsbury, 2013.

Frater, Patrick. "BTS' 'Bang Bang Con: The Live' Claims Record Viewership for Online Concert." *Variety*, June 14, 2020, https://variety.com/2020/digital/asia/bts-big-bang-con-the-live-record-online-concert-1234635003/.

Gibson, Jenna. "How K-Pop Broke the West: An Analysis of Western Media Coverage from 2009–2019." *International Journal of Korean Studies* 22/2 (2019): 24–46.

Han, Benjamin. "K-Pop in Latin America: Transcultural Fandom and Digital Mediation." *International Journal of Communication* 11 (2017): 2250–2269. https://ijoc.org/index.php/ijoc/article/view/6304/2048.

Hemmeke, Katelyn. "Planting Rainforests and Donating Rice: The Fascinating World of K-Pop Fandom." *Korea Exposé*, February 20, 2021. www.koreaexpose.com/fascinating-world-k-pop-fandom-culture/.

Hinck, Ashley. *Politics for the Love of Fandom: Fan-Based Citizenship in a Digital World*. Baton Rouge: Louisiana State University Press, 2019.

Horton, Donald, and R. Richard Wohl. "Mass Communication and Para-Social Interaction: Observations on Intimacy at a Distance." *Psychiatry: Interpersonal and Biological Processes* 19/3 (1956): 215–229.

Jenkins, Henry. *Textual Poacher: Television Fans and Participatory Culture*. Updated twentieth anniversary edition. New York: Routledge, 2013.

Jung, Sun. "Fan Activism, Cybervigilantism, and Othering Mechanisms in K-Pop Fandom." *Transformative Works and Cultures* 10 (2012), https://doi.org/10.3983/twc.2012.0300.

Jung, Sun, and Dooboo Shim. "Social Distribution: K-Pop Fan Practices in Indonesia and the 'Gangnam Style' Phenomenon." *International Journal of Cultural Studies* 17/5 (2014): 485–501. https://doi.org/10.1177/1367877913505173.

Kang, Haeryun. "K-Pop's Digital 'Army' Musters to Meet the Moment, Baggage in Tow." NPR, June 24, 2020, www.npr.org/2020/06/24/882867577/k-pops-digital-army-musters-to-meet-the-moment-baggage-in-tow.

Kelley, Caitlin. "Meet the BTS Fan Translators (Partially!) Responsible for the Globalization of K-Pop." *Billboard*, February 8, 2018. www.billboard.com/articles/columns/k-town/8078464/bts-fan-translators-k-pop-interview.

Kim, Rieun, Hyunkyung Lim, Minji Oh, and Yejin Lee. "BTS & ARMY, We Walk Together: BTS & ARMY's Story during the Pandemic." *Weverse Magazine*, September 21, 2020, https://magazine.weverse.io/article/view?lang=en&colca=3&num=1.

Kim, Suk-Young. *K-Pop Live: Fans, Idols, and Multimedia Performance*. Stanford, CA: Stanford University Press, 2018.

Kim, Youngdae. *BTS the Review: A Comprehensive Look at the Music of BTS*. Trans. H. Chung. Seoul: RH Korea, 2019.

King-O'Riain, Rebecca Chiyoko. "'They were having so much fun, so genuinely . . .': K-Pop Fan Online Affect and Corroborated Authenticity." *New Media & Society* 23/9 (2020): 2820–2838.

Lee, Eunbyul. "When Korean Wave Flows into the Islamic World." In Tae-Jin Yoon and Dal Young Jin (eds.), *The Korean Wave*, 163–181. Lanham, MD: Lexington, 2017.

Lee, Jeeheng. *BTS and Army Culture*. Trans. O. Han. Seoul: Communication Books, 2019.

Lee, Jiyoung. *BTS, Art Revolution: BTS Meets Deleuze*. Trans. C. Yi and S. Kim. Seoul: Parrhesia, 2019.

[@JeeLee06767883]. "#WeLoveYouBlackARMY." Twitter, June 1, 2020, https://twitter.com/JeeLee06767883/status/1267519009303326720.

Lee, Minji. "New Korean Learning Kit Aims to Help More Fans Study Korean with BTS." Yonhap News Agency, April 28, 2021, https://en.yna.co.kr/view/AEN20210428003500315.

McLaren, Courtney., and Dal Young Jin. "'You can't help but love them': BTS, Transcultural Fandom, and Affective Identities." *Korea Journal* 60/1 (2020): 100–127. https://kj.accesson.kr/assets/pdf/8511/journal-60-1-100.pdf.

Min, Wonjung, Dal Young Jin, and Benjamin Han. "Transcultural Fandom of the Korean Wave in Latin America: Through the Lens of Cultural Intimacy and Affinity Space." *Media, Culture & Society* 41/5 (2019): 604–619.

Moon, Kat. "Inside the BTS ARMY, the Fandom with Unrivaled Organization." *Time*, November 18, 2020. https://time.com/5912998/bts-army/.

Morris, Seren. "Kpop Fans Are Spamming the Grand Rapids Police after Crashing the Dallas Police App." *Newsweek*, June 3, 2020, www.newsweek.com/kpop-spamming-fancams-grand-rapids-police-department-protest-evidence-1508043.

One in an ARMY. "Black Lives Matter." 2020. www.oneinanarmy.org/black-lives-matter.

"OIAA Rewind 2019" (video). YouTube, January 31, 2020, www.youtube.com/watch?v=GMmbz7Dzolc.

"On the Impetus behind ARMY Charitable Giving." Medium, July 2030, 2020, https://oneinanarmy.medium.com/on-the-impetus-behind-army-charitable-giving-.

One in an ARMY Charity Project [@OneInAnARMY]. "Hey ARMY! Are you up for a lil conversation about the cause and the org (@freethegirls) we are supporting for #KeepGoingWith Jimin?" Twitter, October 9, 2020.,https://twitter.com/OneInAnARMY/status/1314558725601071110.

Otmazgin, Nissim, and Irina Lyan. "Hallyu across the Desert: K-Pop Fandom in Israel and Palestine." *Cross-Currents: East Asian History and Culture Review* 9/1 (2013): 68–89.

Rohr, Nicolette. "Where the Fans Are: Listening to Music and Fandom." *The American Historian*, February 2019, www.oah.org/tah/issues/2019/february/where-the-fans-are-listening-to-music-and-fandom/ (accessed September 1, 2021).

Sherman, Maria. *Larger Than Life: A History of Boy Bands from NKOTB to BTS.* New York: Black Dog and Leventhal, 2020.

Siriyuvasak, Ubonrat, and Shin, Hyunjoon. "Asianizing K-Pop: Production, Consumption and Identification Patterns among Thai Youth." *Inter-asia Cultural Studies* 8 (2007): 109–136.

Stanfill, Mel. "Straighten Up and Fly White: Whiteness, Heteronormativity, and the Representation of Happy Endlings for Fans." In Lucy Bennett and Paul Booth (eds.), *Seeing Fans: Representations of Fandom in Media and Popular Culture*, 187–196. New York: Bloomsbury, 2018.

Song, Sooho. "The Evolution of the Korean Wave: How Is the Third Generation Different from Previous Ones?" *Korea Observer* 51/1 (2020): 125–150.

Yoon, Haein. "Hangeul Holds the ARMY World Together." *Weverse Magazine*, October 9, 2021, https://magazine.weverse.io/article/view?lang=en&colca=6&num=250.

Yoon, Kyong. "Korean Wave | Cultural Translation of K-Pop among Asian Canadian Fans." *International Journal of Communication* 11/17 (2017): 2350–2366. https://ijoc.org/index.php/ijoc/article/view/6303/2053

"Transnational Fandom in the Making: K-Pop Fans in Vancouver." *International Communication Gazette* 81/2 (2018): 176–192.

Notes

1 Nicolette Rohr, "Where the Fans Are: Listening to Music and Fandom," *The American Historian*, February 2019, www.oah.org/tah/issues/2019/february/where-the-fans-are-listening-to-music-and-fandom/ (accessed September 1, 2021).

2 Mel Stanfill, "Straighten Up and Fly White: Whiteness, Heteronormativity, and the Representation of Happy Endings for Fans," in L. Bennett and P. Booth (eds.), *Seeing Fans: Representations of Fandom in Media and Popular Culture* (New York: Bloomsbury), 187–196.

3 Ben Dooley and Su-Hyun Lee, "BTS's Loyal Army of Fans Is the Secret Weapon behind a $4 Billion Valuation," *New York Times*, October 14, 2020, www.nytimes.com/2020/10/14/business/bts-ipo.html.

4 Mark Duffett, *Understanding Fandom: An Introduction to the Study of Media and Fan Culture* (New York: Bloomsbury, 2013), 5.

5 Ashley Hinck, *Politics for the Love of Fandom: Fan-Based Citizenship in a Digital World* (Baton Rouge: Louisiana State University Press, 2019).

6 Hinck, *Politics for the Love of Fandom*, 9–10.

7 Duffett, *Understanding Fandom*, 5.

8 Henry Jenkins, *Textual Poacher: Television Fans and Participatory Culture* (New York: Routledge, 2013), 12.

9 Maria Sherman, *Larger Than Life: A History of Boy Bands from NKOTB to BTS* (New York: Black Dog and Leventhal, 2020).

10 Stephanie Choi, "Why Are BTS Fans Always Dismissed as 'Hysterical Teenage Girls'?," *Hello Asia*, June 21, 2019, www.helloasia.com.au/news/whare-bts-fans-always-dismissed-as-hysterical-teenage-girls/.

11 Kyong Yoon, "Korean Wave | Cultural Translation of K-Pop among Asian Canadian Fans," *International Journal of Communication* 11/17 (2017): 2350–2366.

12 Bertha Chin and Lori H. Morimoto, "Towards a Theory of Transcultural Fandom," *Participations: International Journal of Audience and Reception Studies* 10/1 (2013): 92–108.

13 Sooho. Song, "The Evolution of the Korean Wave: How Is the Third Generation Different from Previous Ones?," *Korea Observer* 51/1 (2020): 125–150.

14 Suk-Young Kim, *K-Pop Live: Fans, Idols, and Multimedia Performance* (Stanford, CA: Stanford University Press, 2018).

15 Song, "The Evolution of the Korean Wave."

16 Ju Oak Kim, "BTS as Method: A Counter-Hegemonic Culture in the Network Society," *Media, Culture & Society* 43/6 (2021): 1061–1077.

17 Youngdae Kim, *BTS the Review: A Comprehensive Look at the Music of BTS*, trans. H. Chung (Seoul: RH Korea, 2019).

18 Rebecca Chiyoko King-O'Riain, "'They were having so much fun, so genuinely . . .': K-Pop Fan Online Affect and Corroborated Authenticity," *New Media & Society* 23/9 (2020): 2820–2838.

19 Crystal Anderson, "K-Pop Fandom 101," *Kpopkollective*, December 8, 2013, https://kpopkollective.com/2013/12/08/k-pop-fandom-101/2013.

20 Benjamin Han, "K-Pop in Latin America: Transcultural Fandom and Digital Mediation," *International Journal of Communication* 11 (2017): 2250–2269; K. Yoon, "Korean Wave | Cultural Translation of K-Pop among Asian Canadian Fans."

21 Jin Ha Lee and Anh Thu Nguyen, "How Music Fans Shape Commercial Music Services: A Case Study of BTS and ARMY," Proceedings of the International Society for Music Information Retrieval Conference (2020).

22 Michelle Cho, "3 Ways That BTS and Its Fans Are Redefining Liveness," Flow.journal, May 29, 2019, www.flowjournal.org/2018/05/bts-and-its-fans/.

23 Cho, "3 Ways That BTS and Its Fans Are Redefining Liveness."

24 xCeleste, "BTS Hardships: Antis, Plagiarism, Sajaegi, Petitions," YouTube, June 9, 2018, www.youtube.com/watch?v=NidD1d73tXI.

25 Jenna Gibson, "How K-Pop Broke the West: An Analysis of Western Media Coverage from 2009–2019," *International Journal of Korean Studies* 22/2 (2019): 24–46.

26 Jeeheng Lee, *BTS and ARMY Culture*, trans. O. Han (Seoul: Communication Books, 2019).

27 Caitlin Kelley, "Meet the BTS Fan Translators (Partially!) Responsible for the Globalization of K-Pop," *Billboard*, February 8, 2018, www.billboard.com/articles/columns/k-town/8078464/bts-fan-translators-k-pop-interview.

28 P. Claire Dodson, "BTS's Growing Fanbase Isn't Just Teens, It's Their Moms," www.instyle.com/celebrity/bts-fans-over-35-map-of-soul (accessed November 1, 2020).

29 Y. Kim, *BTS the Review*.

30 Minji Lee, "New Korean Learning Kit Aims to Help More Fans Study Korean with BTS," Yonhap News Agency, April 28, 2021, https://en.yna.co.kr/view/AEN20210428003500315.

31 Sun Jung, "Fan Activism, Cybervigilantism, and Othering Mechanisms in K-Pop Fandom," *Transformative Works and Cultures* 10 (2012), https://doi.org/10.3983/twc.2012.0300.

32 S.-Y. Kim, *K-Pop Live*.

33 S. Jung, "Fan Activism, Cybervigilantism, and Othering Mechanisms in K-Pop Fandom."

34 "Journey of Love Myself," Love Myself, https://love-myself.org/eng/journey-of-love-myself.

35 Thanmay Arun, "K-Pop Singer IU Celebrates 12th Anniversary by Donating $86,000, Thanks Fans for Their Support," *International Business Times*, September 20, 2020, www.ibtimes.com/k-pop-singer-iu-celebrates-12th-anniversary-donating-86000-thanks-fans-their-support-3049758.

36 Haeryun Kang, "K-Pop's Digital 'Army' Musters to Meet the Moment, Baggage in Tow," NPR, June 24, 2020, www.npr.org/2020/06/24/882867577/k-pops-digital-army-musters-to-meet-the-moment-baggage-in-tow.

37 Katelyn Hemmeke, "Planting Rainforests and Donating Rice: The Fascinating World of K-Pop Fandom," *Korea Exposé*, February 20, 2017, www.koreaexpose.com/fascinating-world-k-pop-fandom-culture/.

38 Aditi Bhandari, "The Mobilising Power of the BTS Army," Reuters, July 14, 2020, https://graphics.reuters.com/GLOBAL-RACE/BTS-FANS/nmopajgmxva/; Seren Morris, "Kpop Fans Are Spamming the Grand Rapids Police after Crashing the Dallas Police App," *Newsweek*, June 3, 2020, www.newsweek.com/kpop-spamming-fancams-grand-rapids-police-department-protest-evidence-1508043.

39 Qtd. in H. Kang, "K-Pop's Digital 'Army' Musters to Meet the Moment, Baggage in Tow"; Raisa Bruner, "How K-Pop Fandom Operates as a Force for Political Activism," *Time*, July 25, 2020, https://time.com/5866955/k-pop-political/.

40 Patrick Frater, "BTS' 'Bang Bang Con: The Live' Claims Record Viewership for Online Concert," *Variety*, June 14, 2020, https://variety.com/2020/digital/asia/bts-big-bang-con-the-live-record-online-concert-1234635003/.

41 Y. Kim, *BTS the Review*; Courtney McClaren and Dal Young Jin, "'You can't help but love them': BTS, Transcultural Fandom, and Affective Identities," *Korea Journal* 60/1 (2020): 100–127; J. O. Kim, "BTS as Method," 36.

42 J. Lee, *BTS and ARMY Culture*, 36.

43 Y. Kim, *BTS the Review*, 20.

44 Donald Horton and R. Richard Wohl, "Mass Communication and Para-Social Interaction: Observations on Intimacy at a Distance," *Psychiatry: Interpersonal and Biological Processes* 19/3 (1956): 215–229; Jonathan. Cohen, "Mediated Relationships and Media Effects: Parasocial Interaction and Identification," in R. Nabi and M. B. Oliver (eds.), *The SAGE Handbook of Media Processes and Effects* (Los Angeles, CA: Sage, 2009).

45 "BTS Leader RM's Special Love of Korean Painting," *The Korea Herald*, October 15, 2019, www.koreaherald.com/view.php?ud=20191015000829.

46 Jiyoung Lee, *BTS, Art Revolution: BTS Meets Deleuze*, trans. C. Yi and S. Kim (Seoul: Parrhesia, 2019).

47 Y. Kim, *BTS the Review*.

48 One in an ARMY, "OIAA Rewind 2019" (video), YouTube, January 31, 2020, www.youtube.com/watch?v=GMmbz7Dzolc.

49 Rieun Kim, Hyunkyung Lim, Minji Oh, and Yejin Lee, "BTS & ARMY, We Walk Together: BTS & ARMY's Story during the Pandemic," *Weverse Magazine*, September 21, 2020, https://magazine.weverse.io/article/view?lang=en&colca=3&num=1.

50 One in an ARMY, "On the Impetus behind ARMY Charitable Giving," Medium, July 30, 2020, https://oneinanarmy.medium.com/on-the-impetus-behind-army-charitable-giving-.

51 One in an ARMY Charity Project [@OneInAnARMY], "Hey ARMY! Are you up for a lil conversation about the cause and the org (@freethegirls) we are supporting for #KeepGoingWith Jimin?," Twitter, October 9, 2020,
   https://twitter.com/OneInAnARMY/status/1314559887607824384.

52 One in an ARMY Charity Project [@OneInAnARMY], "Hey ARMY!"

53 J. Lee [@JeeLee06767883], "#WeLoveYouBlackARMY," Twitter, June 1, 2020, https://twitter.com/JeeLee06767883/status/1267519009303326720.

54 Haein Yoon, "Hangeul Holds the ARMY World Together," *Weverse Magazine*, October 9, 2021, https://magazine.weverse.io/article/view?lang=en&colca=6&num=250.

PART VI

Circuits of K-Pop Flow

12 K-Pop and the Participatory Condition

Vicarity, Serial Affect, and "Real-Life Contents"

MICHELLE CHO

IHEARTRADIO: Why do you think K-pop is growing in America?

RM: I think, first, we're doing K-pop, right? And K-pop is a great mix of music, music videos and performance, choreographies, and social media and *real life contents*. So, I think, when you get into our music, for example, you search YouTube and you can search, you can look for our chemistry and the, like, contents, and they and you could look for the, like, social medias. And so, it's like really easy for them to, like, get to us, so, I think, that's why K-pop is popular. And, for us, I think we're talking about, uh, we write and produce our music ourselves, and we're talking about the young people, young people's lives, like, every day, like, us, like you. So, uh, I think there is a specific contemporary characteristic for the young, between all the young people in the world. And, thanks to our fans, they translate our lyrics and our interviews into their languages, and that's how they could resonate and *feel the same feelings with us*. And that's why they pay attention to us. And the performances, of course.

—"BTS Favorite American Music + Fan Questions | Exclusive Interview," iHeart Radio YouTube Channel, posted December 12, 2017[1] (emphasis added)

In a December 2017 web interview with iHeartRadio.com, the leader of the K-pop idol group BTS, Kim Namjoon (RM, also known then as Rap Monster), defined K-pop as "a great mix of music, music videos and performance, choreographies, and social media and *real-life contents*." I emphasize the phrase "real-life contents" because it highlights the equivocation between "real life" and "contents" that I argue is at the heart of K-pop's appeal and the media practices of fan comportment that are the focus of this chapter. Further in his comment, RM encapsulates the impacts of K-pop's transmedia modalities (music, video, performance, social media) and fans' participatory responses (content translation and sharing): They allow fans to *"feel the same feelings with us."*

This chapter analyzes fan and idol participation in the video ecosystem of K-pop fandom in order to argue that the ideal of co-feeling, "feel[ing] the same feelings" with K-pop idols and with other fans, produces unique and emergent media forms characterized by vicarity, seriality, and surplus

[231]

enjoyment. These vicarious media – or media intent on producing vicarious experiences – rely on structures of visual identification as well as the ability of twenty-first-century media platforms to transform acts of consumption into spectacles in their own right. Fan acts of identifying with and consuming K-pop idol celebrity and youth culture take multiple forms, ranging from K-pop dance covers to *meokbang* (broadcast-eating videos) to reaction videos (fan-recorded reactions to K-pop content), all of which illustrate RM's claim that the relay of vicarious experience binds K-pop idols to their fans and fans to each other, in the process producing ever more "real-life contents." I argue that vicarity relies on the ubiquitous reflexivity that defines social media platforms as sites of subject formation via media production and consumption. While the term "metamedia" has historically referred to computing mechanisms by which digital media remediate older media forms, I argue that the habitual use of digital media necessarily produces metaconscious awareness of metamediation; social media participation constitutes an immersive, everyday form of metamedia as a prompt for reflexivity, by which vicarious substitution through video induces intense affective experiences of identification.

Moreover, vicarious media seem to suggest a proxy for politics as an expression of collective sentiment – the ways media platforms bridge the private and the public through the antinomies of the social. Traditional modes of political organizing, which until recently seemed foreign to a fan habitus, are newly central to the activities of fan collectives since the youth-led uprisings in Chile (2019) and the United States (2020). My goal is therefore to articulate how K-pop fandom exemplifies contradictory impulses for intense individuation – for example, social media platforms' structures of monetizable recognition – and the corresponding longing for utopian community and collective agency that we see across multiple nodes of media consumption.

The Participatory Condition

In the 2016 edited collection *The Participatory Condition in the Digital Age*, volume editors Darin Barney, Gabriella Coleman, Christine Ross, Jonathan Sterne, and Tamar Tembeck argue that digital media in Western liberal democratic societies have generalized participation from mere "relational possibility" to a requirement of contemporary cultural life and practices of selfhood.[2] In their words, "The participatory condition names the situation in which participation – being involved in doing something and taking part in something with others – has become both environmental (a state of affairs) and normative (a binding principle of right action)" (i). According to Barney et al., participation goes beyond specific practices of engagement. Instead, it is the very core of democratic society itself: "fundamentally, [participation] is the promise and expectation that one can be actively involved with others in decision-making processes that affect the evolution of social bonds, communities, systems of knowledge, and organizations, as well as politics and culture" (viii). Here, the authors seem to suggest that the *idea* of participation is crucial to the *act* of participation. In other words, the ideology of participation as social contract inheres in every participatory utterance or gesture.

However, the ways digital technologies generalize participation – from the interpellating call of social media platforms to the infrastructures of data collection in which we participate through the mere act of searching for information or streaming music on a smartphone or internet-connected PC – require us to revise this traditional concept, as participation now clearly exceeds the domain of rational discourse in the Habermasian public sphere. Moreover, the authors of the volume use the qualifiers "the West" and "Western" to situate their analyses of the participatory condition, when a "West and rest" binary no longer offers descriptive value in today's media ecologies. In their view, the impasse of the participatory condition – the fact that media participation is a means of both empowerment and subjection – calls for resistance to the "depoliticization" of digitally mediated participation, again hewing to a narrow understanding of normative participation as the sort in which rational citizen-subjects engage in order to articulate political claims. In what follows, I argue that we must overcome this dualism between properly and normatively political participation and illiberal, excessively passionate and insufficiently reasoned participation. Digitally mediated participatory cultures do not simply sort into the polarized categories of what Jodi Dean calls "communicative capitalism," on one hand, and politically progressive, anticapitalist, rhizomatic media networks, on the other.[3] K-pop media cultures range across these categories and often combine them. Thus, we must think beyond this binary to theorize the full implications of the participatory condition in global media and fan cultures such as those that constitute the transmedia worlds of K-pop. K-pop refuses the abstract generality of "the West" and demands specific historical and geopolitical consideration, as a media phenomenon that operates both in the center (of East Asian culture industries and on corporate-owned platform giants of US provenance) and at the margins (eliciting participation from audiences across the global south).[4]

Henry Jenkins introduced the framework of participatory cultures of popular media consumption in the influential fan studies work *Textual Poachers: Television Fans and Participatory Cultures*, published in 1992 (notably, a time before widespread internet use). He proposed a division between media consumers and "poachers," arguing that the latter appropriate and repurpose commercial media in fandom, for the sake of community building through the formation of fan counterpublics.[5] This division, in Jenkins's account, maps onto a common division prevalent in media and communications theory and critiques of mass culture between the passive consumer – trained by mass media formats and technologies to be ever more receptive to the dictates of capitalist cultural industries and their manufacture of desire – and the active audience that uses commercialized culture as textual material to be refashioned for progressive or resistant ends. This triumphalist approach to fan engagement and secondary creation as "participatory" has since been criticized for its one-sided celebration of fan activity and identity, while nevertheless remaining a keystone in the field of Anglophone fan studies.

Jenkins himself issued such a critique of participatory culture and participatory media, or media texts that aim to elicit fan participation, as media texts and franchises began to expand across a rapidly transforming media ecology with the advent of digital distribution. Since the mid-2000s, he and other scholars have continually returned to the problematic of participatory culture, especially as the internet and networked communications shape the collective consciousness of youth. Participatory culture requires a focused media literacy curriculum, in Jenkins's view, yet subsequent work in fan studies often gets stuck in the now deeply etched groove that connects the poles of celebration and condemnation of the participatory condition of technologically mediated, networked fandom.

Jenkins's foundational analyses of convergence culture in Euro-American contexts also anticipated the further co-option of fan activity as commodified attention in the platform ecosystem of twenty-first-century media consumption. More recent analyses of social media continue to confront the dilemmas of a thoroughly mediated social arena that seems to confound the distinction between private and public that has been so important to modern political theory. Media scholar and theorist Laikwan Pang has written about the political potential of privatized social media platforms in Hong Kong's umbrella movement, returning to political philosopher Hannah Arendt's discussion of the social as the liminal space between the private and public.[6] For Arendt, the individual's desires and needs as an embodied self – the domain of the private economy of the household – must be rigorously excised from the public domain, in contrast to the social, which is constituted by the intermingling of the private and public. The problem, for Arendt, is the steady replacement of the public with the confounding fuzziness of the social, where the projection of the individual's private concerns clouds extra-individual claims in the properly public realm of the political.[7] Studies of the democratic uses of social media and platforms often take as a signal case the counterhegemonic use of Twitter in the Arab Spring to celebrate expressly political activity that appropriated global north technologies for left-populist ends, such as online organizing through hashtag campaigns.[8] This scholarship does not often attend to the political potential of platform engagement in fannish modalities – for entertainment, parasocial fantasy and world building, or lateral connectivity among fans.

Gender and sexuality studies scholarship, as well as feminist and queer political discourses, emphatically reject the divisions between public, private, and social, as the second-wave feminist slogan "the personal is political" has become a crucial epistemological orientation for developing knowledge about the ways social categories and identities condition citizenship and subjectivity in numerous contexts. In foundational texts in cultural studies, especially as formulated by the Birmingham School (now often referred to as British Cultural Studies), popular culture is undeniably political in its hegemonic force, as regimes of representation convey social divisions and power relations within society. The primary tenet of cultural studies scholarship throughout the late twentieth and twenty-first centuries is that culture is a system of signs that produces meaning in a contingent manner with nonetheless material effects. Thus, culture is not fixed, essential, or inherent to the materiality of forms, objects, or practices, nor does it conform to categorical distinctions between private/individual and public/collective modes of human experience. Crucial to this understanding of the ways seemingly private experience cannot be thought outside the realm of publicity is the question of race and other forms of visible difference, and the political claims and impositions that such forms produce. Thus, critical race theory extends the insight that all of culture operates as an apparatus of meaning production to the problematic of embodiment, and the ways visible difference undergirds contemporary power relations built on a foundation of colonial semiotics of racial signifiers.

I situate my analysis within the above cultural studies frameworks to extend my conclusions on the specific phenomenon of K-pop beyond the narrow signifying function of ethnicity or national consciousness. The cultural history of K-pop has been discussed elsewhere in this volume; I seek to contribute an analysis of how K-pop's digital mediation produces a corresponding cultural mediation that is shifting norms through emergent cultural forms in the mediated community of K-pop fandom as microcosm. The signifying function of these new media forms, however, is relational. K-pop's participatory fan culture has no central locus in any nationally defined signifying system, not even that of contemporary South

Korean culture and the role of popular media within it, since K-pop fandom is dispersed, transcultural, and translational. New norms of mediated participation, however, are emerging in the ways that fans attempt to overcome such dispersal by foregrounding the singularity *and* commonality of their embodied fan experience. The next section specifies these forms of mediation and analyzes the mechanisms by which fan reactivity – a specific type of participation – establishes vicarious experience as a core collective pursuit in K-pop fandom.

Metamedia and Fan Mediation

What I am defining as a "reactive" tendency in K-pop fandom relies on individual fans' metaconsciousness of the ways platforms and social media networks operate. To discuss the mechanisms of such a reactive impulse and its technological supports, or the medium-specificity of K-pop's participatory fan culture, I begin by revisiting new media theorist Lev Manovich's early 2000s discussion of metamedia.[9] He writes that "a meta-media object contains both language and metalanguage – both the original media structure (a film, an architectural space, a sound track) and the software tools that allow the user to generate descriptions of, and to change, this structure." In the context of computing, when analog media are digitized (or when digital media seek to mimic the function or aesthetic of analog media – e.g., digital photographs), they are transformed into metamedia or metadata by their processing by software that enables images, text, or video to be mapped, searched, selected, zoomed into, zoomed out of, filtered, and so on. The transformation of media into metamedia also allows for accessing old media in forms that are now embedded in our quotidian use of digital technology.

Beyond particular software interfaces, metamedia also express a logic that manifests aesthetically. According to Manovich, "the logic of metamedia fits well with other key aesthetic paradigms of today – the remixing of previous cultural forms of a given media (most visible in music, architecture, design, and fashion), and a second type of remixing – that of national cultural traditions now submerged into the medium of globalization."[10] In Manovich's terms, metamedia echo the logics of remix dispersed across temporal and spatial axes, that is, historical and geographical extension, as a third type: "the remixing of interfaces of various cultural forms and of new software techniques – in short, the remix of culture and computers."[11] To restate Manovich's argument, then, the cultural logic of pastiche or remix necessarily inflects the aesthetic and operational design of metamedia. A key practical example of the overarching cultural principle of metamedia as remix is hypertext, or the embedding of links to other digital media into online text. Hypertext – the nesting of other media within textual media – is a common technique of intertextuality that is all too familiar in the interactive sphere of social media engagement. It is almost impossible to participate on social media platforms without also referencing, citing, or juxtaposing other mediated communicative utterances or gestures. Social network interfaces are designed to maximize sharing through hyperlinking, through the repost, reblog, and retweet, as well as the like and the filtering capacity of the hashtag. One of the primary aims of fan organization in K-pop fan culture as well as other media fandoms is the skillful use of metamedia to amplify the visibility of one's favorite artist or celebrity within algorithmic ecosystems.

Political theorist and communications scholar Jodi Dean argues that the thorough integration of visual signs – such as emojis, gifs, and photos – within the structures and practices of participatory media results in a new language of communication irreducible to any of the individuated forms whose combination has quickly become the conventional idiom of the internet: speech, writing, and image. Dean calls this visual-linguistic remix "secondary visuality."[12] Drawing on the concept of secondary orality – "the transmission of spoken language in a print culture" – from cultural and religious historian and literary scholar Walter J. Ong, Dean develops the framework of secondary visuality to theorize the transforming function of visual images into (meta)textual objects in social media and platform communications.[13] This capsule communicative genealogy goes from "face-to-face interaction, to print (the written letter, perhaps with photographs included), to voice (telephone), to immediate text (e-mail, SMS), to photo-sharing (Flickr) to social media incorporating writing and photos, to personal communication conducted through combinations of words, photographs, images and short videos (GIFs)."[14] In the context of secondary visuality, images lose their singularity in order to become common ideas that mobilize their force as generic concepts through rapid and easy shareability. The common use and expression of generic images – the most "spreadable" – constitute a digital commons.[15] "Out of repetition," Dean asserts, "emerge trends, bubbles and aggregates, common images through which collectivity momentarily shines."[16]

For Dean, a forceful example of secondary visuality is the photographic form of the selfie – a radical overturning of the individuated aura of the portrait into a generic face, a "commonface" (playing on the notion of commonplace): "A selfie is a photo of the selfie form, the repetition of a repeated practice."[17] In order to elaborate the above "common-ing," or making-generic of faces, Dean offers examples from daily life – her use of

Facebook, her daughter's daily SnapChat conversations with friends, and, most pertinent for the discussion of "real-life contents" in K-pop, Dean's experience of following the British boy band One Direction on Twitter and absorbing the metamediatic reactions (tweets and retweets) of the group's passionate fandom. Dean explains, "When tweeting their reactions to various One Direction–related happenings … fans would use photos of the band members … to express their feelings. For many fans, words alone could not convey the intensity of their emotions."[18] This describes the curious capacity of the celebrity persona to signify both generality and singularity at the same time. The uptake of images of One Direction members as both substitute emojis and fan avatars illustrates this duality: "One Direction photos communicated the feelings of One Direction fans to each other, to the world, or at least to Twitter.… Funny or clever tweets accumulated thousands of retweets and likes. Sometimes there would only be three or four. The overall effect was of *immense flows of feeling streaming off the screen*" (emphasis added).[19] These three examples "point towards the constant generation and regeneration of a visual commons of circulating images."[20]

Surprisingly, Dean, who condemns circulating communicative texts in her theory of communicative capitalism, sees the same mechanisms as a visual commons, most convincingly supported by the case of fandom. Integrating the conceptual tools offered by Manovich and Dean allows us, then, to foreground the everyday experience of metamedia as metatextual awareness *and* interface design and the potential "common-ing" use of metamediated social connection to expand the sphere of collective activity. Incorporating embodied activities of K-pop fandom, social media's remix culture builds a visual commons through fandom's gift economy. RM's use of the term "real-life contents" straightforwardly and unsentimentally remarks on the way that social media transforms experience into data or metamedia – "real life" rendered by digital media representation and social media interfaces into "contents" or bits of textuality.

"Real-Life Contents"

In the iHeartRadio interview, RM does not elaborate whether "real-life contents" are distinct from or a subcategory of "social medias"; however, it is fair to connect the term to two categories of content production that distinguished BTS from their K-pop peers in their early years: "Bangtan Bombs," backstage antics captured in short video clips produced and curated by their management company, and "Bangtan Vlogs," video content of BTS members directly addressing fans in the simulated intimacy of a video chat. Although prior K-pop groups also produced backstage and "making-of" footage, this content was usually distributed as extra features on official concert DVDs. The other customary venue that purports to highlight pop idols' "real-life" personalities are guest segments on variety shows broadcast on South Korean cable or network television. In contrast, Bangtan Bombs and Bangtan Vlogs have been produced and distributed on the Bangtan TV YouTube channel alongside official music videos, music video teasers and album previews, dance practice/choreography videos, and longer "making-of" or "behind (the scenes)" videos that are labeled "Episodes." Big Hit Entertainment (now HYBE), the group's management company, established Bangtan TV in December 2012, before the group's official debut, suggesting that the company planned to foreground the group's "real-life contents" as its core marketing strategy from the beginning.

As of February 2021, Bangtan TV had 44.1 million subscribers, 1,403 uploaded videos, and 8,340,701,825 aggregated views. Other platforms that house the ever-expanding archive of BTS-related video content are VLive, the celebrity live-streaming, vlogging app developed by Korean portal giant Naver; Twitter; TikTok; the HYBE-owned fan engagement platform WeVerse; Weibo; Tudou; and Niconico, not to mention nonsanctioned, fan-uploaded content on the aforementioned video-sharing apps as well as Vimeo and Dailymotion.[21] Big Hit/HYBE formats BTS's "real-life contents" to maximize fan participation as secondary creation and media production, from fanfic to fanvids/video edits to reaction videos, dance cover videos, concert vlogs, theory posts/videos, and merch unboxing videos, to offer a nonexhaustive list, to which I will turn in the next section. "Real-life contents" are also structured to maximize parasocial engagement through direct address to fans, which the K-pop industry (as well as other East Asian pop industries including J-pop and C-pop) codifies as "fanservice."

Parasociality has been theorized from a variety of perspectives in fields as diverse as media/communications, marketing and consumer research, psychology, and human development. First introduced by anthropologist Donald Horton and sociologist R. Richard Wahl in 1956, when television was rapidly popularizing as a mass medium in the United States, parasociality has also been key to conceptualizing celebrity culture.[22] What may be unique to Asian pop idol industries' cultivation of parasocial bonds is the foregrounding of the fan-idol relationship; the K-pop industry specifically invests resources in producing parasocial relationships through the emphasis on "real-life contents." The category thus reconsiders the agency of the parasocial; rather than such engagement being an effect of media reception, media producers elicit it by design, and providing "real-life contents" is their primary tactic.

As the K-pop industry focuses all the more on cultivating empathetic connection as a basis of community, to what extent is "feeling the same feelings" becoming the only form of connection? And how does *feeling* recode participation? These questions are crucial for thinking about the effects of digitally mediated community beyond fandoms, since "community" names a bond of common interests based on shared positionality vis-à-vis institutions and modes of subjection. This is the realm of the political, requiring the ability to organize regardless of whether one can imagine the self as the other. The dangers of overemphasizing empathic identification are very clearly taken up in studies of populism as a derangement of social bonds by their substitution with empathetic/sympathetic identification, which is also a form of narcissism – imagining that the other feels exactly the way that you do. But, as RM emphasizes in his interview, the point is to give fans the idea that they can "feel the same feelings as us. And that's why we're popular."

Key to establishing empathic connection and parasocial intimacy as the primary form of participation in mediated fandom community is the capture of ever more diverse forms of liveness. As Jane Feuer argued in her seminal essay, "The Concept of Live TV: Ontology or Ideology," liveness is not simply a description of the ontology of television as the broadcast of one source to many viewers in temporal synchrony. It is instead an ideology that suffuses the broadcast medium itself, regardless of content.[23] Important work by Suk-Young Kim delineates the ways K-pop's performance culture maintains liveness as its core ideology of fan engagement, despite relying ever more explicitly on media technologies, even in the space of live concert performances. Kim also connects the ideology of K-pop's liveness to the medium of television by explaining the crucial intermediation of K-pop's choreographic and emotional labor by South Korean broadcast networks.[24]

If ideology, as Gramsci alerts us, tries to conceal itself by masquerading as fact, then the ideology of liveness has become the naturalized core of "real-life contents." In the case of live performance, liveness has undergone a process of conceptual revision as mediated forms supplement or supplant the traditional notion of liveness as designating the spatial convergence of audience and performer in theater and other genres of stage performance.[25] Dean's proposal of the "commonface" offers a useful summary of the paradox of liveness in a "mediated habitus" by capturing the coexistence of the singularity of the individual as connoted by the face as a metonym of the individual's interior experience and the generality of the common.[26] The deindividuating operation of secondary visuality in digital (meta)media nevertheless relies on the specificity of individually felt and transmitted feelings, in a generalized relay of serialized affects and vicarious experience, which I elaborate on in the following section.

Serial Affect and Vicarious Media

I turn now to seriality and vicariousness – the ways forms of collectivity and co-feeling have multiplied as platforms generate liveness beyond temporal synchrony. The form of serial affect that I identify in K-pop fandom is best illustrated by reaction videos, in which individuals record their act of consuming other media, converting their spectatorship itself into spectacle as a genre of "contents." The reaction video is native to YouTube, and I have written elsewhere on how the genre codifies authenticity by popularizing the capture of, and thus theatricalizing, "spontaneous" affect in media reception – usually the viewing of another video.[27] Seriality, in the context of reaction videos' performance of empathic connection, amplifies the pleasure of spectatorial identification: the more layers of reaction can be captured and transmitted in a video relay, the more the image of others' pleasure supplements one's own emotional and affective response. Thus, serial affect refers to both sequential affect in a video series – videos produced in response to other videos – and seriality without linear duration but featuring intertextual simultaneity, in the multiplying levels of co-feeling and re-mediation enclosed by the frame of a single reaction video. To illustrate these two interconnected types of serial affect, I share the following examples.

The first is from a subgenre of reaction video: the reaction video compilation (Figure 12.1). Here, I refer to the video "BTS (방탄소년단) 'DNA' Official MV reaction mashup," posted on September 27, 2017, but this is simply one among many examples.[28] Reaction video compilations are videos in which fans edit individual fan reactions to the same work

Figure 12.1 A screenshot from "BTS 'DNA' Official MV Reaction Mashup" edits together individual reaction videos into a single frame, to produce the semblance of a crowd response.

(usually a music video or live performance) into a single video, to produce a new spectacle of aggregate reactivity. "BTS 'DNA' Official MV reaction mashup" compiles separately filmed and uploaded reactions to BTS's music video for their single "DNA" and arranges them as tiles in a single frame, so that the multiple reactors take on the semblance of a mass audience. The compilation preserves each reactor's recorded sound, so the cacophony of their exclamations amplifies each individual reaction into a crowd response, simulating a concert experience. BTS's "DNA" music video had been viewed 22.3 million times within twenty-four hours of being uploaded to YouTube on September 18, 2017, so the reaction video mashup also draws significance from the metric culture created by the platform's built-in quantification tool, to extrapolate the image of mass reaction to this imagined community of millions of viewers. Moreover, the reaction video mashup itself has garnered 1.2 million views as of February 2021; through the view count, YouTube viewers, even those who eschew recording their reactions as secondary content, become participants in the ever-growing "crowd" response, reactivating liveness, no matter how temporally removed they are from the filmed fans' reactions.

Foreshortening the duration of the individually filmed reaction series, the compilation video amplifies the affective force of the series of video reactions, compressed to the length of the original music video/musical track. By condensing the series into a composite image, the fan author of this compilation creates a new spectacle that visualizes the additive structure of surplus enjoyment. The fan's enjoyment of the spectacle of the original music video is filtered through the enjoyment expressed and captured in each reaction video, which adds to the original enjoyment; I call this "surplus enjoyment" because the spectacle of the composite reaction, while new, is never complete without the image of the original stimulus – the BTS music video. Therefore, all of the reactions index and extend the music video, rather than supplanting it. Surplus enjoyment is also transformed into surplus value, as the platform extracts the fandom's collective labor of looking to produce surplus value or profit.[29]

The second illustration of serial affect in fan video production is somewhat more complex, but its relational dynamics are similar to that of the reaction video mashup. This series refers to the co-feeling of embodied experience of consuming and producing kinesthetic intimacy through K-pop dance cover videos. Here, I present a series of group dance covers solicited by the K-pop management giant SM Entertainment in 2017, when they sponsored a cover dance contest to market their group NCT 127's music video and single "Cherry Bomb."[30] Such contests are a way of producing the type of serial reaction and surplus enjoyment of serial fan affect employed by several K-pop companies, underscoring the importance of dance to K-pop's parasocial relations and participatory fan culture. Indeed, capturing on video the kinesthetic intimacies of popular dance is now a staple of pop cultural participation beyond K-pop. For example, this is the impetus behind the many viral dance challenges on TikTok, a microblogging, video-sharing platform that uses the format of very short videos and features a suite of editing tools that allow users to score their own soundtrack. To briefly sketch the video series I present here, the first video features members of the group NCT 127 reacting to selected videos that were submitted for the dance cover contest. This video culminates in the group's reaction to the contest-winning video by East2West. In the second video, the East2West dancers react to NCT 127's reaction to their cover, in a relay that aptly demonstrates the seriality of affect that I want to highlight. The streams of co-feeling between idol and fan are grounded in what Karen Wood calls "kinesthetic empathy" – her term for a viewer's bodily experience or sensation while watching screen dance – which emerges as the primary criterion for judging the excellence of East2West's performance. The idol stars' admiration for the cover dance group's ability to kinesthetically empathize with the idols by accurately reflecting the idol group's physical comportment in their dance cover becomes a mirror of the fans' delightful recognition of co-feeling by "playing" the idol in the cover performance. The compression of the idols' reaction video in East2West's reaction-to-the-reaction video also exemplifies the production of surplus enjoyment characteristic of K-pop reaction videos.[31]

East2West was established in 2010 in Montreal, Canada, and has maintained a YouTube channel – East2WestOfficial – since that year, where the group uploads dance cover videos as one of its main activities. East2West also hosts regular K-pop choreography workshops and produces an annual live performance showcase. The group's members are all nonprofessional dancers. In 2017, a subunit of nine East2West dancers tied for first place in the NCT 127 "Cherry Bomb" Dance Contest hosted by SM Entertainment and 1TheK – a Korean entertainment video content production company whose YouTube channel boasts over 20 million subscribers. As a prize for winning the contest, which was advertised as being judged by the members of the group themselves, 1TheK filmed NCT 127 reacting to the top entries in a video posted to its YouTube channel. In response, the "Cherry Bomb" cover dancers in East2West filmed their own reaction to NCT 127's reaction, in a video titled "[EAST2WEST] NCT 127 REACTED TO OUR COVER???" I describe both reaction videos and the serial relay of affective response displayed in the videos' mise-en-abyme visual structure (Figure 12.2).

The NCT 127 reaction video places all members of the group in front of a monitor, presumably playing the videos to which they are reacting. In the

Figure 12.2 Screenshot from East2West's "[EAST2WEST] NCT 127 REACTED TO OUR COVER???"

video's mise-en-scene, the video being reacted to is shown in a small window at the bottom of the screen, as is customary for the reaction video genre.[32] While the general format follows the conventions of fan-made reaction videos, the video producers also introduce cuts, close-ups of particular members' reaction shots, and onscreen text of the sort commonly found in Korean variety content (*yeneung*). As East2West's cover video begins, the leader of NCT 127 states the name of the group, and the video within the video clearly identifies the cover performance by nationality. As East2West's performance begins, several members react verbally – "Woah," "Oh my god!" – as onscreen intertitles in pink lettering echo their expressions. Throughout, NCT 127's reactions take the form of both nonverbal exclamations and spoken commentary.

Notably, East2West's winning dance cover is the sole entry featured in the reaction video that swaps the dancers' gender: The East2West cover is performed by nine women playing the roles of NCT 127, a male idol group. At first, the members of NCT 127 seem focused on this point, commenting on the way that the East2West dancers infuse a feminine energy into the choreography. As their reaction continues, however, the group leader, Taeyong, incredulously remarks that the dancer who is covering his part is dancing very similarly to him – putting the same energy into the dance: "if she dances like that, I know it must be painful. The next day your neck is … [miming a stiff neck]." Later, at the end of the song's last chorus, where the dancer playing Taeyong does a standing backbend into a seated position, another group member tells Taeyong that he's given the cover dancer a huge burden in having to master that movement, as members express their amazement: "She's doing the best because she's so flexible!" These comments center on vicarious bodily sensation and embodied identification between dancer and idol as the idols take in the novel spectacle of the fans cosplaying them in their dance routine. This contrasts slightly with NCT 127's comments about the contest submission they react to just prior to East2West's video. This entry (tied for first place) is by K-boy, a male dance group from Thailand, and what impresses the idols most about their dance cover is how K-boy has painstakingly re-created their music video's mise-en-scene, with the same videographic elements and extremely accurate costumes – the emphasis is on the care taken to reproduce the "Cherry Bomb" video text. For East2West, on the other hand, the group members focus on the vicarious experience induced by the dance cover video, expressing kinesthetic intimacy with the dancers.

East2West's filmed reaction to NCT 127's reaction to their winning video submission assembles the group of dancers in an entirely different guise than they appear in the dance cover. Instead of channeling the charismatic energy of NCT 127 members, the East2West dancers are young, excited fans reacting to their celebrity idols. As the 1TheK video did not have English subtitles at the time of the women's reaction, they are limited to responding solely to the nonverbal affective cues in NCT's reaction – the oohs, ahhs, and jaws dropping, which the women then echo in their spectatorial excitement. Interestingly, however, East2West emit the loudest reactions in response to *themselves*, when the 1TheK video presents full-screen images of the dance cover to emphasize particularly striking parts of the performance. In these moments, the cover dancers express vicarious identification with the idols as *spectators* who are consuming the content of their dance cover video. These moments of vicarious substitution are intense, though fleeting. The video's capture and containment of these mobile identifications in the video within the video within the video bring into simultaneous view the amplifying delight of the fan dancers' co-feeling in their cover performance, refracted through the idols' experience of kinesthetic empathy, and then compounded again in East2West's double identification as idol and fan. As Dean writes, "enthusiasm arises out of experience of collective imitation because the collectivity comes into being as collectivity by feeling itself amplified, strengthened … Pleasure accrues through repetition … we see others as they see with us."[33] The reaction to the reaction's vicarious structure allows the accumulation of experiences of substitution; the fan feels a collective fan delight over the spectacle of the idols while also accessing the idol's affect, which the reaction video makes available. Hence the fan is doubly delighted by the idol's recognition of the fan's delight.

Conclusion

My goal in this chapter has been to articulate how K-pop fandom exemplifies the contradictory impulses for intense individuation – for example, social media platforms' structures of monetizable recognition – and the corresponding longing for utopian community and collective agency that we see across multiple nodes of media consumption. Serial affect and vicarious media are key frameworks for understanding how these impulses are negotiated in the networked, metamediatic spaces of fan-idol parasocial engagement. In the video examples, which feature the visual common-ing of fan reactions, the genre conventions of the reaction video blur the boundary between self and other in a serial affective relay. This relay or series has no formal conclusion, but can be imagined repeating and amplifying forever in the streams of feeling that reverberate through K-pop fandom's digital platform ecosystem. Vicarious experience is a way of resisting the alienating impacts of surveillance capitalism and platforms' attention economies, whose capacities have always been latent in digital media's metamediatic operations. K-pop's ancillary fan videosphere produces forms of microcelebrity like that of East2West – they are widely known among K-pop fans through their YouTube channel (with over 1.5 million subscribers). But at the same time their gestures are not only their own but also a form of kinesthetic mediation. Their bodies become platforms that express the choreographed movements, pleasure, and excitement that fans share as collective embodied intimacy.

To return to the question of the participatory condition, we might now ask, What sort of participation is this? Fan mediation has geopolitical dimensions – the dance cover contestants identifying by nationality, for instance – and reflects the unevenness of K-pop's reliance on media infrastructures. Without access to media equipment, studio space, time/leisure to learn the choreography, and social media savvy, fans cannot elevate their fandom to the level of platform visibility. But there is also an investment in a *dis*possessive individualism in these fan responses, a delight in the other's delight that characterizes fandom's participatory condition. Identities are mobile and ever-changing in fandom's gift economy. As a global phenomenon, K-pop and its uniquely mediated practices, as well as its symbolic significance as a non-Western popular culture produced by a "middle power" (in international relations parlance) punching well above its weight in the cultural sphere, call for serious consideration, beyond the framework of national culture as a subfield of area studies knowledge production. K-pop's media matrix offers many new directions for research about media, transnational fandom (or imaginations of transnationalism), and imagined communities beyond national and linguistic borders.

K-pop fandom models reactivity as the operative form of participation as social behavior – the act of responding to a prompt to create a relay of reactions that constitute collective identity. In terms of civic participation, there are also usually prompts for the subject's participatory reaction. This goes far beyond interpellation as the subject's reaction to the hailing call of the law, but could give us a new way of thinking about participation as primarily spurred by lateral relations. Rather than defining participation as "taking part" in or "being part" of the social body as determined by hierarchical social organization, K-pop's participatory condition allows us to think about the way that normative horizons emerge in relation to collective identities based on shared delight. However, this is not to assert that fan-inflected participation – the forms and conventions of new media forms that aim at vicarious experience as the basis for community bonds – constitutes a utopian space of collectivity. Although these media forms often aspire to a kind of universalism to transcend the political limitations of cultural and linguistic particularity and subordinate identity positions and focus on ostensibly acultural elements of bodily sensation and sensory motor impulses or reflexes, the videos cannot but emphasize fandom as a practice of self-making – identity formation through embodiment and mediated self-representation. The significance of these practices depends entirely on context, for example, in the phenomenon of Kazakh fandom of K-pop promoting nonnormative gender representation in post-Soviet Eastern Europe, or of Chilean K-pop fans coming together as youth who are often dismissed by the political establishment. In the case of East2West, K-pop cover dance allows a group of young people, who are mostly members of visible minority groups, to take up space in public in a context in which the dance and theater communities are predominantly white and display documented bias against minority interests. These are just some of the many areas of much-needed future research in fan, media, platform, and performance studies, spurred by K-pop's vicarious media.

Notes

1 www.youtube.com/watch?v=NMSAOKtgxtg. See Ben Sisario and Michael J. de la Merced, "The Radio Giant iHeartMedia Prepares for Possible I.P.O.," *New York Times*, April 3, 2019.

2 Darin Barney, Gabriella Coleman, Christine Ross, Jonathan Sterne, and Tamar Tembeck (eds.), *The Participatory Condition in the Digital Age* (Minneapolis: University of Minnesota Press, 2016).

3 Jodi Dean, "Communicative Capitalism: Circulation and the Foreclosure of Politics," *Cultural Politics* 1/1 (2005): 51–74 , and *Democracy and Other Neoliberal Fantasies: Communicative Capitalism and Left Politics* (Durham, NC: Duke University Press, 2009). See also Jodi Dean, "Faces as Commons: The Secondary Visuality of Communicative Capitalism," Open! Platform for Art, Culture, and the Public Domain, December 31, 2016, 1–10; at www.onlineopen.org/faces-as-commons.

4 See Minjung Won, "Korean Wave Reception and Participatory Fan Culture in Latin America: What Lies beyond the Media Reports," in Tae-Jin Yoon and Dal Yong Jin (eds.), *The Korean*

Wave: Evolution, Fandom, and Transnationality (New York: Lexington Books, 2017), 145–162; Eunbyul Lee, "When the Korean Wave Flows into the Islamic World: *Hallyu* in Tunisia," in the same volume, 163–182.

5 Henry Jenkins, *Textual Poachers: Television Fans and Participatory Cultures* (New York: Routledge, 1992). See Michael Warner, *Publics and Counterpublics* (New York: Zone Books, 2002), and Benedict Anderson, *Imagined Communities: Reflections on the Origin and Spread of Nationalism* (New York: Verso, 1983).

6 Laikwan Pang, "Retheorizing the Social: The Use of Social Media in Hong Kong's Umbrella Movement," *Social Text* 35/3/132 (2017): 71–94.

7 Pang synthesizes Arendt's argument in *The Human Condition* (Chicago: University of Chicago Press, 1958), 58.

8 See Zeynep Tufekci, *Twitter and Tear Gas: The Power and Fragility of Networked Protest* (New Haven, CT: Yale University Press, 2017), and Sarah J. Jackson, Moya Bailey, and Brooke Foucault Welles, *#Hashtag Activism: Networks of Race and Gender Justice* (Cambridge, MA: MIT Press, 2020).

9 Lev Manovich, "Understanding Meta-media," *CTheory* 2005, https://journals.uvic.ca/index.php/ctheory/article/view/14459.

10 Manovich, "Understanding Meta-media."

11 Manovich, "Understanding Meta-media."

12 Dean, "Faces as Commons," 2.

13 Dean, "Faces as Commons," 2.

14 Dean, "Faces as Commons," 3.

15 Henry Jenkins, Sam Ford, and Joshua Greene, *Spreadable Media: Creating Value and Meaning in a Networked Culture* (New York: New York University Press, 2013).

16 Dean, "Faces as Commons," 4.

17 Dean, "Faces as Commons," 6.

18 Dean, "Faces as Commons," 2.

19 Dean, "Faces as Commons," 2.

20 Dean, "Faces as Commons," 2–3.

21 See Marc Steinberg, *The Platform Economy: How Japan Transformed the Consumer Internet* (Minneapolis: University of Minnesota Press, 2019).

22 Donald Horton and R. Wohl, "Mass Communication and Parasocial Interaction: Observations on Intimacy at a Distance," *Psychiatry* 19 (1956): 215–229; Alice Marwick and Danah Boyd, "To See and Be Seen: Celebrity Practice on Twitter," *Convergence: The International Journal of Research into New Media Technologies* 17 (2011): 139–158.

23 Jane Feuer, "The Concept of Live TV: Ontology or Ideology," in E. Ann Kaplan (ed.), *Regarding Television: Critical Approaches – An Anthology* (Los Angeles, CA: AFI, 1983).

24 Suk-Young Kim, *K-Pop Live: Fans, Idols, and Multimedia Performance* (Stanford, CA: Stanford University Press, 2018).

25 For a review of this literature in the performance studies context, see Suk-Young Kim, *K-Pop Live*, especially pp. 10–16. In particular, Kim builds on Philip Auslander, *Liveness: Performance in a Mediatized Culture* (New York: Routledge, 2008).

26 Dean, "Faces as Commons."

27 See Michelle Cho, "Pop Cosmopolitics and K-Pop Video Culture," in Joshua Neves and Bhaskar Sarkar (eds.), *Asian Video Cultures: In the Penumbra of the Global* (Durham, NC: Duke University Press, 2017), 240–265.

28 This particular video was posted on a South Korea–based YouTube channel called SoJam Radio (Sojaem sa-yeon radio), whose most popular content consists of K-pop reaction video compilations. www.youtube.com/watch?v=k-zWBsgvhO8&t=1s.

29 I adapt the concept of "looking as labor" from Jonathan Beller, *The Cinematic Mode of Production: Attention Economy and the Society of the Spectacle* (Hanover, NH: Dartmouth College Press, 2016).

30 www.facebook.com/1theK/videos/1377526255627899.

31 Karen Wood, "Kinesthetic Empathy, Conditions for Viewing," in Douglas Rosenberg (ed.), *The Oxford Handbook of Screendance Studies* (Oxford: Oxford University Press, 2016).

32 The reaction video remains on 1TheK's YouTube channel: "Let's Dance: NCT 127_'Cherry Bomb' Dance Cover Contest Reaction Video," www.youtube.com/watch?v=5Vp-FqpzjlI.

33 Dean, "Faces as Commons," 5.

13 Idol Shipping Culture

Exploring Queer Sexuality among Fans of K-Pop

THOMAS BAUDINETTE

Within a webcomic published in early 2018 (Figure 13.1), a passionate fan of Korean boy band BTS who identifies online as Myra (@MyraKM9597) charts the process by which she came to identify as a member of ARMY, the BTS fandom group. Beginning with her enraptured discovery of BTS, continuing with her learning to be part of ARMY through engaging with the band's social media, and ending with a rebuffed attempt to convert her friend into a supporter of the global superstars, Myra's webcomic depicts a narrative that would be easily recognizable to most K-pop fans.[1] From exploring the struggles of international fans who lack Korean-language proficiency to strong feelings of wonderment and attraction to the handsome and talented members of BTS, Myra's webcomic also dramatizes the pleasures and pains central to the fandom culture that has emerged around K-pop idols both within and without South Korea. But one section is particularly interesting. In the fifth portion, entitled "Shipwars," Myra explores an aspect of K-pop fandom called "shipping" that may seem somewhat confusing to outside observers but is integral to the celebration and consumption of K-pop idol culture. In this artistic retelling of her journey, Myra explores how her strong attraction toward how two of the boy band's members interact produced an immense affective response that led her to begin "a blog for her ship." Via the narrative she creates within this comic, Myra argues that the phenomenon termed "shipping" is integral not only to becoming part of ARMY but also to becoming a K-pop fan.

Known variously as "coupling" in South Korea (*keoppeuling*) and Japan (*kappuringu*) and "slash," "real person shipping," or simply "shipping" in Anglophone contexts, the practice to which Myra alludes is the fannish celebration of the relationship – the word from which the term "shipping" derives – between two members of a K-pop idol group. More than just referring to the celebration of idols' real-world friendships, however, the terms "coupling" and "shipping" are more commonly utilized by K-pop fans to refer to the practice of imagining the members of their favorite bands in romantic or sexual relationships.[2] As idol shippers, fans like Myra create visual art such as comics or illustrations and write fan fiction in

[249]

Figure 13.1 Myra's webcomic (read left to right, top to bottom). Courtesy of Kuro Mai.

which they explore the erotic potentials of imaginary same-sex idol relationships.[3] Indeed, shipping practices that reimagine the members of popular K-pop boy groups such as H.O.T., TVXQ, and BTS within romantic or homoerotic relationships are especially common among both heterosexual female fans and fans from queer communities.[4] As Myra's webcomic suggests, shipping is a common practice within K-pop fandom culture. Ultimately, it is a social practice whereby fans deploy homoerotic imaginaries, or what theorist Jungmin Kwon terms "gay FANtasy,"[5] not only to explore their sexual desires for the attractive idols but also to express the intensely affective experience of fandom itself.

In this chapter, I explore the homoerotic practice of shipping idols as a lens into the broader study of gender and sexuality in relation to K-pop, demonstrating the importance of fans' sexual desires to fandom culture. I draw on ethnographic research into K-pop fandom in Australia, Japan, and the Philippines that I conducted between 2015 and 2020 to theorize the role queer sexuality plays within fandom culture. These three countries represent under-researched contexts for the reception of transnational K-pop, and my hypothesis was that the significant cultural differences among them would strongly influence shipping, allowing for interesting contrastive analysis. I pay especially careful attention to how societal norms influence both fans' shipping practices and their understandings of shipping itself. In focusing on queer sexuality, I go beyond a simple exploration of sexual orientation and deploy queer as a radical hermeneutic focused on "whatever is at odds with the normal, the legitimate, the dominant" to account for sexual desires and practices that foundationally challenge the societal status quo.[6] Although the desires and beliefs of fans from queer communities form an important part of the analysis, my main focus in this chapter is to explicate how the sexual desires evoked through shipping challenge and subvert both patriarchy and heteronormativity within the myriad cultural contexts in which K-pop fans are embedded around the globe.

I begin by charting the emergence of shipping practices within South Korean fandom, exploring how K-pop production companies strategically encourage young women to consume K-pop through shipping, thus producing spaces within the patriarchal society where women's sexual desires can be safely explored. The chapter then turns to an analysis of international shipping practices, presenting a comparative case study of BTS shipping within Japanese and Anglophone (Australian and the Philippines) fandom spaces. While BTS shipping in Japan tends to draw on rigid logics that conceptualize homoerotic relationships between men via sexual practices and behaviors divorced from identity, Anglophone shipping tends to instead overtly deploy LGBTQ identity politics to make sense of fantasy relationships between band members. Nevertheless, I argue that both practices possess queer potentials that allow fans to affectively explore their sexuality, affirming their sexual desires for K-pop idols. This process, I suggest, is particularly important for fans from queer communities seeking visibility within the global K-pop fan community.

The Emergence of Idol Shipping in South Korea: A Queer Feminist Practice

The practice of imagining idols within homoerotic pairings developed together with the broader emergence of K-pop and idol culture in the early 1990s as South Korea's entertainment industries underwent reforms tied to the democratization of society and the concomitant liberalization of the Korean popular culture landscape.[7] That is to say, from the very genesis of K-pop, shipping was central to the development of fandom culture. Kwon identifies the emergence of idol shipping in the 1990s as part of a broader social phenomenon where young heterosexual female consumers became increasingly interested in "gay FANtasy," a term Kwon coined to denote "female fans' interest in and desire for gay male erotic relationships" and "the subjectivity and cultural power of these enthusiastic media consumers."[8] Other examples of this influential culture include South Korean young women's investment in Japanese Boys Love manga comics – a genre I discuss further in the following section which is also sometimes called *yaoi* – and gay-themed American sitcoms such as *Will and Grace*.[9] As these further examples make clear, South Korean young women's interest in male homoeroticism emerged in the 1990s partly as a result of the gradual removal of the nationalist protectionism that had typified the postwar South Korean media landscape until the late 1980s.

The historical emergence of idol shipping thus owes much to the ideology of globalization known as *segyehwa* and resultant policies aimed at structurally reforming the Korean economy implemented by the administration of President Kim Young-sam (Gim Yeongsam). As Suk-Young Kim highlights, despite the economic failure of these structural reforms, *segyehwa* was ideologically instrumental in the historical development of K-pop, particularly through policies lifting the ban on the importation of Japanese cultural products.[10] This opening up to Japan played a crucial role in introducing South Korean women to the pleasures inherent to shipping. Almost at the same time as entertainment companies began producing idol boy bands in the 1990s, a fandom for the homoerotic Boys Love manga of Japan exploded among young women in South Korea.[11] Thus, as these young women were enthusiastically supporting and discussing the handsome idols from the so-called first generation of K-pop bands such as H.O.T., Sechs Kies, and Shinhwa on online forums, they were also enthusiastically consuming the fan-translated Boys Love manga from Japan that were available on these sites.[12] Unsurprisingly, these two fandoms merged as young women began to ship handsome male idols from their favorite bands together, imagining them in romantic or sexual relationships similar to those depicted on the pages of translated homoerotic manga as a way to express both their fannish devotion and their sexual desires.[13]

The literacies from these Boys Love manga, which I introduce more fully below, strongly affected the ways that young female consumers learned to "read" interactions between the handsome idols central to K-pop's emerging performance norms in the 1990s and thus educated K-pop fans about the affective and erotic potentials of male-male intimacy.[14] Within the heteronormative social context of South Korea, where expressions of same-sex desire are socially censured, the importation of Japanese popular culture queered young women's viewing habits, introducing a queer gaze that celebrated radical sexual expression and continues to challenge the conservative gender ideologies of the society. But shipping also represents a queer transformative practice in other important ways. South Korea's patriarchal society has traditionally denied women the ability to express their sexual desires actively, instead positioning them as objects upon which the desires of heterosexual men are enacted.[15] For Kwon, shipping represents a radical feminist act since its explicit facilitation of women's exploration of their attraction to handsome male idols provides young female fans the sexual agency to express their desires within a social context where such expression is often routinely silenced.[16] Thus shipping centers women's sexual desires at the heart of K-pop fandom culture.

As businesses chiefly targeting young female consumers, K-pop production companies strategically manage the star personae of their idols. Historically, this has meant implementing dating bans and controlling media reporting through their considerable economic clout to ensure that idols remain unattached and thus potentially available as objects of romantic investment to their fans. As the K-pop industry matured, Kwon argues, shipping was co-opted into the developmental logics of South Korea's idol culture as a safe way for female fans to consume media about their idols without compromising this theoretical availability.[17] K-pop production companies now explicitly support shipping practices, such as when SM Entertainment invited fans of their megagroup TVXQ to participate in an officially sanctioned fanfic contest focused on imagining members of the band in romantic relationships (sexually explicit fictions were, however, strictly banned).[18] In strategically deploying shipping in their marketing and production practices, Korea's popular culture industries have expanded and diversified their markets by absorbing what was once an underground subculture into the mainstream.[19] It has become routine for K-pop idols to perform "fan service," often involving "skinship" and other acts of "performed intimacy" that passionate fans subsequently draw on in the production of fan fiction and fan art.[20] In so doing, K-pop production companies are borrowing already well-established fan service practices from the Japanese idol industry (most notably from Johnny's and Associates, the largest producer of boy bands in Japan).[21] Further, as a result of the cultural influence of K-pop idol shipping, in recent years companies have created "bromance films" wherein handsome idol actors perform "intimate but not sexual" relationships designed to attract young female fans of gay FANtasy while not alienating more conservative audiences.[22]

The above historical narrative reveals that shipping is primarily practiced by female fans of male idols, the chief market in South Korea for K-pop. But emerging research by anthropologist Layoung Shin reveals that shipping also initially informed the practices of same-sex-desiring female fans active within the "fancos" (fan costuming) community. Many lesbian-identified K-pop fans would enjoy cross-dressing as their favorite male idols in the 1990s not only to celebrate their fandom but also to express their own sexual attraction to members of the same sex through the strategic embodied performance of shipping through costume play.[23] Kwon's interviews with gay Korean men show that many view gay FANtasy culture such as idol shipping positively, recognizing its potential to shift public attitudes toward homosexuality in positive directions, although none of Kwon's gay interlocutors actively participated in such practices.[24] There is a dearth in research into queer fans of K-pop within South Korea itself, but, as my research in Australia and the Philippines reveals, idol shipping has become increasingly popular among queer communities around the globe. It is thus likely that shipping is practiced by queer fans in contemporary South Korea.

Shipping BTS in Japan: The Influence of Boys Love Manga

In the early 2000s, a passionate Japanese fandom for Korean popular culture developed; anthropologist Millie Creighton identified the ratings success of *Winter Sonata* (*Gyeoul Yeonga*) in 2004 and the subsequent domination of Japan's pop music charts by South Korean superstars BoA and TVXQ as catalysts for the Korean Wave in Japan.[25] By the mid-2010s, Japanese fandom for Korean popular culture had become embedded within preexisting women's consumer cultures, with female teenagers and women in their twenties emerging as the primary fans of K-pop idol groups.[26] Discussions I had with young women fans during a trip to Tokyo in 2020 revealed that they did not see K-pop fandom as separate from their broader consumption of Japanese women's media.[27] In fact, many indicated that it was "obvious" (*atarimae*) that Japanese women would be attracted to Korean popular culture since it represents just one facet of what one interlocutor termed "girls' culture" (*shōjo bunka*).[28] My observations and conversations with fans between 2015 and 2020 revealed that K-pop fandom had entered into dialogue not only with Japan's own established idol culture but also with the *shōjo* manga (girls' comics) at the heart of Japanese girls' culture.[29]

One genre of *shōjo* manga played an especially prominent role in influencing how young women consumed and enjoyed media about K-pop idols in Japan: the aforementioned Boys Love manga. It is via Japanese fans' engagement with this popular culture form that they learn about and begin to practice shipping. The connection is unsurprising since K-pop developed in part due to production companies' earlier adaptation of these very practices to the South Korean context. Indeed, in a book focused on the lasting appeal of TVXQ in Japan, cultural critic Ono Toshirō points to "K-pop idol *yaoi*" among female fans of the boy band as one reason for the group's continued success in the Japanese market.[30] Highlighting that Japan's long tradition of Boys Love manga provided women the "necessary knowledge" to produce homoerotic fantasies, Ono notes that "playing with *yaoi*" (*yaoi de asobu*) represents an important "method of experiencing pleasure" through K-pop idol consumption.[31] Interestingly, the Japanese character that Ono uses in his writing to refer to pleasure (愉) typically connotes sexual forms of pleasure, especially orgasm. Just as idol shipping allows women in South Korea to explore their sexual desires, Ono argues, shipping idols through the logics of Boys Love provides young Japanese women a form of sexual release often denied them within Japan's patriarchal society.[32]

Emerging out of *shōjo* manga in the mid-1970s, Boys Love focuses on intimate relationships between beautiful male youths and possesses narrative logics born out of Japanese conceptualizations of gender and sexuality.[33] One particularly important narrative trope is the so-called *seme-uke* rule, which stipulates that one member of a male-male couple is characterized as an *uke* (receiver) who is passively initiated into male-male romance by an aggressive *seme* (attacker) who subsequently "leads" their relationship.[34] Cultural critic Nishimura Mari argues that this *seme-uke* relationship is typified by a power imbalance usually signaled to readers via set representational strategies known in Japanese as the "noble path" (*ōdō*).[35] First, the *seme* is typically depicted as taller, older, and considerably stronger than the *uke*.[36] Second, the *seme* is regularly characterized as reserved and stoic, but with a strong and uncontrollable sexual desire that is awakened by the virginal innocence of the *uke*.[37] Third, the *uke* represents the partner who is penetrated during sex and is typically presented as "soft" and "effeminate" compared to the penetrating *seme*, usually depicted as comparatively "harder" and more "masculine."[38] This *seme-uke* rule was transplanted to South Korea, where K-pop idol shippers similarly position couples as containing a *gong* (*seme*) and a *su* (*uke*) member.

When examining how the members of BTS are typically shipped in Japan, it becomes apparent that this *seme-uke* rule also strongly influences how Japanese fans of K-pop both practice and understand idol shipping. According to a representative chapter on shipping in *The BTS Fanatic's Manual*, one of fifteen BTS "mooks" (magazine books) I have gathered during trips to Japan between 2018 and 2020, all of which contain a section addressing shipping, the so-called love-love relationships between the members naturally fall into *seme-uke* couples.[39] The "mook" lists eleven particularly popular ships, providing a brief introductory text as well as ratings for each potential couple's "love level" and "likelihood of appearance." The following ships are presented to the reader in order of apparent popularity among Japanese fans: Jimin x Jungkook, RM x J-Hope, Jin x V, Suga x Jungkook, Jimin x V, Suga x V, V x Jungkook, J-Hope x Jungkook, Jin x J-Hope, J-Hope x Jimin, and RM x Suga. The use of the "member x member" method of framing the ships is significant and ultimately derives from Boys Love fan practices where "*seme* x *uke*" has become the standard way of naming a male-male couple.[40] Speaking about the role of the *seme-uke* rule with three Japanese idol shippers I met at a K-pop merchandise store in Ikebukuro in 2020, I learned that it was rare for the authors of Japanese shipping fan fiction or comics to position members as switching their sexual roles. Further, these women reinforced the idea that an *uke* is somehow "feminine" (*onnarashii*), with one fan suggesting that the youngest member of BTS, Jungkook, was like a "young princess (*ohime-sama kyara*) protected by six knights."[41]

Except for two prominent examples both involving RM, the leader of BTS, an older member of BTS is always presented as the *seme* and a younger member is presented as the *uke* within each of the BTS ships listed above. The texts in the "mook" stress the brotherly nature of each pairing, such as in the following description of the Jimin x Jungkook couple: "whenever he has free time, somehow Jimin *nii-san* (older brother) comes over to Jungkook. Usually Jungkook treats Jimin as if he is some kind of nuisance, but it is clear that Jungkook enjoys being spoiled by this loving older brother."[42] Following the narrative and characterization conventions of the *seme-uke* rule, the status of one member as an "older brother" provides him with power and thus positions him as a logical *seme* for Japanese fans. Further, the focus on "watching over" (*mimamoru*) and "spoiling" (*amaeru*) in the descriptions in this "mook" of each couple's *uke* replicates common-sense understandings of romantic relationships in Japan, where a man (or "masculine" *seme*) is expected to take charge of a relationship with an innocent woman (or "feminine" *uke*). The two cases where this age-based shipping is not practiced in the eleven potential couples from *The BTS Fanatic's Manual* are where the group's leader RM is positioned as the *seme*. Within the texts of these two ships, rather than RM's age, it is his status as leader of BTS that positions him as a powerful *seme*, particularly in the description of the RM x Suga couple, where the two members are described as the group's "father and mother" (*fūfu kappuru*) figures, respectively.[43]

This brief example shows that Japanese idol shippers follow logics that appear somewhat rigid, slotting K-pop band members into a predetermined gendered formula based on traits such as age or position in the band. What appears most important within the Japanese context is the broader positioning of boy band members as either *seme* or *uke*, which in turn influences how consumers present the gendered identities of the characters within their derivative fan works. It is for this reason that the fans I met in Ikebukuro fantasized about Jungkook being a "princess" protected by six older "knights." The categories of *seme* and *uke* are not understood by fans as identities, however; many young women I interviewed strongly disavowed the idea that the characters appearing within fan works were gay men defined by their sexual desires. Rather, our conversations revealed that the descriptors *seme* and *uke* were used to make sense of idol behaviors, either in reality or within fan works, with debates over who represents a *seme* or an *uke* producing an affective response known in Japanese as *moe*. Indeed, these K-pop shipping practices mimic how Japanese Boys Love manga fans also derive explicit pleasure from their supposed "*moe* talk" (*moebanashi*).[44] Fans thus creatively manipulate the character tropes of the *seme* and *uke* to produce homoerotic relationships between male idols that are charged with romantic or erotic potential, providing meaningful ways for them to celebrate the K-pop idols they adore.

While the logics of Boys Love manga have rightly been criticized as replicating heteronormative relationship structures by implicitly positioning the *seme* and *uke* as figurative men and women,[45] I do not want to dismiss the queer potentials of such fandom practices. Through fantasies of homoeroticism created through the manipulation of the *seme-uke* rule, Japanese female fans mobilize queer sexuality as an important method to express their own attraction to K-pop idols and thus produce pleasures that theorists such as Ono acknowledge as explicitly sexual.[46] The *seme-uke* rule therefore provides a framework and vocabulary with which to vocalize and celebrate the inherently erotic affects induced by K-pop fandom. Ultimately, Japanese fans draw on a preexisting tradition with a long history in Japanese girls' culture as one of many methods to make sense of their attraction to the members of popular K-pop groups. K-pop idol shipping thus represents a significant emerging practice in Japan's girls' culture that deploys queer sexual expression to conceptualize young Japanese female fans' sexual and gendered identities.

Shipping BTS in Anglophone Fandom: Queer Sexuality and the Politics of Identity

One Saturday in January 2020, I joined over a hundred passionate fans of BTS at an inner-city gallery in Sydney to attend a photography exhibition dedicated to members Jimin and Jungkook that had been collaboratively organized by Australian and South Korean social media fan sites. As I wandered and interacted with fans throughout the day, I learned that many of those who had gathered in the gallery had come to celebrate what an organizer termed the "close relationship" between Jungkook and Jimin,[47] as well as to purchase fan-produced merchandise featuring this popular pair. Although the event was advertised as targeting all ARMY, a significant portion of the attendees with whom I interacted identified as shippers of Jimin and Jungkook, a pairing known in Anglophone fandom as "Jikook." Unlike in Japan, however, many of the shippers I met at this Sydney gallery were gay men who viewed their K-pop fandom as intrinsically tied to their queer sexual identities (throughout the day I met eight such fans). This did not surprise me, as previous research I had conducted among LGBTQ consumers of Japanese and Korean popular culture in the Philippines, where K-pop fandom is particularly prevalent in the LGBTQ community,[48] showed that queer Philippine fans also practice K-pop idol shipping. My experiences with English-speaking BTS fans in Australia and the Philippines confirmed that K-pop idol shipping was common in Anglophone fandom spaces.

Unlike in Japanese and South Korean fandom, where the logics of the *seme-uke* rule and influence from Boys Love manga fandom have strongly shaped shipping practices, idol shipping within Anglophone contexts appears more closely aligned to an identity-based conceptualization of queer sexuality born out of LGBTQ identity politics. By LGBTQ identity politics, I refer to the common tactic within Western queer liberation activism where concrete identity categories such as gay, lesbian, bisexual, and transgender are deployed as a form of strategic collective action.[49] My conversations with fans in Australia and the Philippines who actively participate in idol shipping culture online – typically reading and writing fan fiction or engaging in shipping debates on social media such as Twitter – found that Anglophone fans tend to conceptualize shipping as an explicit reimagining of idols as identifying as members of the LGBT community. Marcus,[50] a gay Australian fan of both K-pop and Japanese manga, explained to me during a conversation in 2019, "When I ship BTS, it's kind of like a fantasy where I imagine my bias [favorite member] is gay and likes boys."[51] Likewise, a bisexual fan of BTS in the Philippines named Maria noted that she liked "taking the members of BTS and making them gay," explaining that shipping was a process of "turning the boys queer."[52] Interestingly, Maria viewed idol shipping as a political act that helped to "raise the visibility" of "queer identity" in the context of the "heteronormative culture of the Philippines."[53]

Another queer Filipino fan named Leon likened K-pop idol shipping to "gay porn," noting that both queer and straight fans "imagine our favorite members fucking" as a way to enjoy explicit sexual fantasies of "hot boys who turn us on."[54] I also encountered this positioning of K-pop idol shipping as a form of pornography during a conversation with a gay male fan and his heterosexual female friend at the gallery event in Sydney, with both suggesting that the "power" of "shipping Jikook" came from repurposing the two members' close "brotherly" relationship as a "hot gay fantasy."[55] Even many heterosexual female fans I met in Australia made similar comments. For instance, a Chinese Australian K-pop fan named Lisa explained to me in 2018 that while she did not practice shipping herself, she understood it as a form of "gay porn" among some Australian fans.[56] As these narratives suggest, K-pop idol shipping is one method through which fans celebrate and express sexual attraction to idols through erotic fantasy play. In so doing, they consciously utilize the language of LGBTQ identity politics to label the members as explicitly same-sex attracted, making this the central focus of the fantasy.

In English-language fan fiction for BTS on Archive of Our Own, one of the world's largest online fan fiction repositories,[57] most of the uploaded shipping fics position at least one of the members as directly identifying with their same-sex attraction (e.g., identifying as gay, bisexual, queer, or poly[amorous]). A search for the word "gay" reveals that 60.3 percent (61,497/101,964) of male-male BTS fan fiction hosted on the site deliberately deploy the term to either identify a character or describe the sex acts that occur between members. A minority of BTS fan fiction takes this even further, strongly tying the shipping of idols within erotic, romantic, or pornographic contexts to explicit LGBTQ activism. One example is a fan fiction entitled *The Paradiso Lounge*, which explicitly situates a highly pornographic romance between BTS members Suga and Jimin within the context of New York City's 1990s BDSM community. Tagged as specifically concerned with "social justice," the fic reimagines Yoongi (Suga's real name) as a queer activist photographer who eventually falls in love with Jimin, a sex worker at an underground leather bar. The following excerpt provides an example of how *The Paradiso Lounge* ties K-pop idol shipping to broader LGBT activism:

> "Oh, you document the community?" Jimin asked in an interested tone, retrieving an ashtray from the edge of the table to place it down in the middle for them to share. "Does that mean you travel around the city a lot? Snapping photographs of gay establishments and safe spaces? Going to the HIV and AIDS protests, and all the other marches and protests? Is that what you document?"
>
> "I've been 'round," Yoongi said with a lazy nod, finding it far easier to study the glowing cherry of his cigarette than to hold the other man's gaze. "I've been right to the heart of the community, y'know, the protests, the condom and needle drives, the fundraisers – the social aspect that keeps us going in this toxic society. But I've been to the fringes too like, uh, the radicals, the militants. The radical feminist lesbians, the pinko faggots; the kinda gays that exist in our community that the gatekeepers don't talk 'bout 'cos they're a threat to the heteronormative society far too many think we should accept a part in, rather than refuse to conform to."[58]

Throughout my conversations with Anglophone fans, I learned that most who practiced idol shipping were keenly aware that it was based in fantasy, and none believed that the members of BTS who they shipped together were actually attracted to the same sex. Rather, as Marcus explained to me, idol shipping was a kind of "play" designed to enjoy their fandom for BTS in "exciting and sexy ways."[59] In this sense, despite the logics that influenced their conceptualization of shipping being radically different, both Japanese and Anglophone BTS shippers are involved in a highly creative and affective practice tied to their desires as fans. For Sandy, a bisexual female fan in Australia, shipping BTS (and she noted that she also shipped members of the K-pop girl group 2NE1) represented just one of many methods to "express my love for the members of the band."[60] She explained it was a "release valve" for the sexual tension that fans of BTS often express, suggesting rather humorously that "you have to do something to scratch that itch when you see the boys grinding against each other on stage!"[61] Ultimately, K-pop idol shipping possesses queer potentials through its celebration of male-male erotica, which allow fans to vocalize and explore their sexual attraction, acknowledging that sexual desire plays an important role in broader K-pop fandom.

Not all fans of BTS in Anglophone contexts view K-pop idol shipping positively. Within Western fandom spaces there have been long-running historical debates concerning the ethics of "real person shipping."[62] In an article polemically titled "Your OTP Is Not Real: Why Idol 'Shipping' Has No Place in K-Pop," a contributor to the K-pop blog Seoulbeats argues that shipping is "a potentially harmful activity to both the fans and idols in question" because it supposedly promotes skewed understandings of same-sex relationships among fans.[63] The author concludes by arguing that shipping is a "self-indulgent activity when real people with real feelings are the ones being manipulated for the sake of entertainment and fantasy," suggesting that instances where K-pop production companies produce content aligned with shipping represent "a step too far."[64] This is a pervasive discourse within Anglophone spaces that seems to be absent within both South Korean and Japanese K-pop fandom, and some BTS shippers I interviewed in the Philippines had strong criticisms for those who held such views. A bisexual fan named Zoe argued that such critiques neglected the fact that fans understand that they are involved in fantasy play, strongly disassociating shipping from reality.[65] As Maria strongly believed shipping was a queer political act, she likewise viewed such attempts to censure shipping as a form of heteronormative backlash designed to silence fans engaged in subversive practices.[66] While there are important ethical debates to be held over shipping real people, especially within highly pornographic fan fiction, this does not negate the fact that the fantasy shipping produces is a legitimate way to explore the sexual desires central to K-pop fandom.

Concluding Remarks

As Myra suggests in the webcomic that opens this chapter, idol shipping is a fundamental element of global K-pop fandom that deploys queer sexuality to produce affective responses among fans. Initially emerging as a bottom-up fan practice that allowed young women in South Korea to express and play with their sexual desires safely in the context of societal patriarchy, idol shipping was soon co-opted into the production processes of K-pop by entertainment companies keen to exploit young women's significant economic clout. Through a case study of shipping practices among fans of BTS in Japan, Australia, and the Philippines, this chapter has demonstrated that while the cultural context in which a fan is situated shapes shipping practices, fans around the globe practice idol shipping as a method to explore the sexual desires for the handsome idols that sit at the heart of the K-pop industry. Whether understanding the imagined homoerotic relationships as tied to the *seme-uke* rule central to Boys Love manga in Japan or drawing on the logics of LGBTQ identity politics in Anglophone contexts, fans are united in their commitment to idol shipping as a form of fantasy play. This fantasy play, I argue, both queers dominant social understandings of sex and gender and allows for the expression of fans' own gendered and sexual identities as desiring subjects.

To conclude this chapter, I wish to briefly reflect on the importance of K-pop idol shipping to the LGBTQ community. My conversations with queer fans of K-pop in Australia and the Philippines routinely raised the issue that while K-pop fandom is often considered to be a safe space for same-sex desiring and gender-nonconforming individuals, the contents of mainstream K-pop production often lack explicit queer visibility. Sandy, for instance, recognized that while her K-pop fandom had helped her to understand her sexuality as a bisexual woman, South Korea remains a homophobic society and there are very few openly queer idols (Sandy spoke positively of Holland, however, who is an indie idol famous for explicitly centering his identity as a gay man within his performance).[67] For such fans, idol shipping injects a necessary corrective into K-pop fandom. Sandy drew on the logics of the LGBTQ identity politics that influence Anglophone fans' conceptualizations of shipping to suggest that the practice helps ameliorate the lack of queer representation within the K-pop industry and would eventually lead to changes to social attitudes in South Korea.[68] In this way she echoed the opinions of my Philippine interlocutor Maria, who viewed idol shipping as a necessary queer political act.

Within her work on gay FANtasy, Kwon celebrates the potential of K-pop idol shipping to transform the heteronormative nature of the South

Korean media landscape through increasing positive visibility of queer communities.[69] She finds through her interviews with gay men in South Korea that many view practices such as idol shipping as positively shifting the conversation on queer sexuality among K-pop fans.[70] I have encountered similar beliefs among gay Japanese men who are fans of K-pop. As Aki, a twenty-two-year-old man, explained to me in 2015, K-pop idol shipping "bridged the considerable gap" between heterosexual female and gay male fans in Japan.[71] Although he did not practice shipping himself, Aki firmly believed that such fan practices among the "typical female fans of K-pop" would "open their minds to the presence of gay fans" and thus produce a more inclusive fandom culture.[72] More investigation of the entanglements of K-pop idol shipping and LGBTQ fans will be necessary to fully understand the transformative potentials of shipping in increasing queer visibility within this global fandom. Nevertheless, K-pop idol shipping plays a transformative queer role in a variety of cultural contexts, demonstrating how queer sexuality is fundamental to K-pop fandom culture.

Recommended Reading
Kwon, Jungmin. *Straight Korean Female Fans and Their Gay Fantasies*. Iowa City: University of Iowa Press, 2019.

Notes

1 Sarah Keith, "'Becoming-a-fan' Stories: *Hallyu* in Australia," in Gil-Sung Park, Nissim Otzmagin, and Keith Howard (eds.), *Transcultural Fandom and the Globalization of Hallyu* (Seoul: Global Research Institute, Korea University, 2019), 129.
2 Jungmin Kwon, "Queering Stars: Fan Play and Capital Appropriation in the Age of Digital Media," *The Journal of Fandom Studies* 3/1 (2015): 102–103.
3 Kwon, "Queering Stars," 103.
4 Kwon, "Queering Stars"; Ono Toshirō, *Sore demo Tōhōshinki wa yuru ga nai: Itande iku kanryū joshi to kenkan no nami* (TVXQ remain unaffected: Korean wave fan girls and the anti-Korean wave) (Tokyo: CYZO, 2015), 63–70.
5 Jungmin Kwon, *Straight Korean Female Fans and Their Gay Fantasies* (Iowa City: University of Iowa Press, 2019), 4.
6 David M. Halperin, *Saint Foucault: Towards a Gay Hagiography* (Oxford: Oxford University Press, 1997), 62.
7 Suk-Young Kim, *K-Pop Live: Fans, Idols, and Multimedia Performance* (Stanford, CA: Stanford University Press, 2018), 27–30.
8 Kwon, *Straight Korean Female Fans*, 11.
9 Kwon, *Straight Korean Female Fans*, 162–164.
10 Kim, *K-Pop Live*, 28–29.
11 Kwon, *Straight Korean Female Fans*, 43.
12 Kwon, *Straight Korean Female Fans*, 44.
13 Kwon, *Straight Korean Female Fans*, 48–49.
14 Kim Hyojin, "*Hanguk dongin munhwa-wa yaoi: 1990 nyeondae-reul jungshim-euro*" (The culture of Korean derivative works and *yaoi*: Focusing on the 1990s), *Manhwa Aenimaesheon Yeongu* 30 (2013): 263–291.
15 Kwon, *Straight Korean Female Fans*, 92–93.

16 Kwon, *Straight Korean Female Fans*, 94.

17 Kwon, "Queering Stars."

18 Kwon, "Queering Stars," 104.

19 Kwon, *Straight Korean Female Fans*, 18–19.

20 Kwon, "Queering Stars," 102–103.

21 Lucy Glasspool, "From Boys Next Door to Boys' Love: Gender Performance in Japanese Male Idol Media," in Patrick W. Galbraith and Jason G. Karlin (eds.), *Idols and Celebrity in Japanese Media Culture* (Houndmills: Palgrave Macmillan, 2012), 120–123.

22 Kwon, *Straight Korean Female Fans*, 170.

23 Layoung Shin, "Queer Eye for K-Pop Fandom: Popular Culture, Cross-Gender Performance, and Queer Desire in South Korean Cosplay of K-Pop Stars," *Korea Journal* 58/4 (2018): 87–113.

24 Kwon, *Straight Korean Female Fans*, 153–158.

25 Milli Creighton, "Through the Korean Wave Looking Glass: Gender, Consumerism, Transnationalism, Tourism Reflecting Japan-Korea Relations in Global East Asia," *The Asia-Pacific Journal: Japan Focus* 14/7 (2016), unpaginated, http://apjjf.org/2016/07/Creighton.html.

26 Kim Sung-Min, *K-Pop: Shin-kankaku no media* (K-pop: A new style of media), (Tokyo: Iwanami Shinsho, 2018), iii.

27 I have translated all excerpts from interviews with fans in Japan from their original Japanese to English.

28 See Thomas Baudinette, "Reflecting on Japan-Korea Relations through the Korean Wave: Fan Desires, Nationalist Fears, and Transcultural Fandom," *Transformative Works and Cultures* 36 (2021), unpaginated, https://journal.transformativeworks.org/index.php/twc/article/view/2045.

29 Baudinette, "Reflecting on Japan-Korea Relations."

30 Ono, *Sore demo Tōhōshinki*, 69.

31 Ono, *Sore demo Tōhōshinki*, 63.

32 Ono, *Sore demo Tōhōshinki*, 69–70.

33 Mark McLelland and James Welker, "An Introduction to 'Boys Love' in Japan," in Mark McLelland, Kazumi Nagaike, Katsuhiko Suganuma, and James Welker (eds.), *Boys Love Manga and Beyond: History, Culture, and Community in Japan* (Jackson: University Press of Mississippi, 2015), 3.

34 Nishimura Mari, *BL karuchā-ron: Bōizu rabu ga wakaru hon* (A cultural theory of BL: A book for understanding Boys Love) (Tokyo: Seikyūsha, 2015), 127.

35 Nishimura, *BL karuchā-ron*, 70.

36 Nishimura, *BL karuchā-ron*, 71.

37 Nishimura, *BL karuchā-ron*, 71.

38 McLelland and Welker, "An Introduction," 10.

39 *Bōdan Shōnendan Nekkyō Manyuaru* (The BTS fanatic's manual) (Tokyo: M.B MOOK, 2019), 75.

40 See Kaneda Junko and Shion Miura, "'Seme X uke' no mekuru meku sekai: Dansei shintai no miryoku o motomete" (The world surrounding 'seme X uke': Searching for the attractiveness of male bodies), in *Yurīka. Fujoshi Manga Taikei* (Tokyo: Seidōsha, 2007).

41 Interview with anonymous Japanese fans, January 17, 2020, Tokyo, Japan.

42 *Bōdan Shōnendan*, 76.

43 *Bōdan Shōnendan*, 83.

44 Patrick W. Galbraith, "*Moe* Talk: Affective Communication among Female Fans of *yaoi* in Japan," in McLelland et al. (eds.), *Boys Love Manga and Beyond*, 153–168.

45 Hitoshi Ishida, "Representational Appropriation and the Autonomy of Desire in *Yaoi*/BL," trans. Katsuhiko Suganuma, in McLelland et al. (eds.), *Boys Love Manga and Beyond*, 210–232.

46 Ono, *Sore demo Tōhōshinki*, 69.

47 Interview with anonymous organizer of K-pop fan event, January 11, 2020, Sydney, Australia.

48 See Alona U. Guevarra, "Creating a Safe Space for Queer Teens? Some Initial Findings on Queer Teens in K-Pop Cover Groups and Fan Community," *AIKS Korean Studies Conference Proceedings* 1 (2014): 102–119.

49 Mary Bernstein, "Celebration and Suppression: The Strategic Uses of Identity by the Lesbian and Gay Movement," *American Journal of Sociology* 103/3 (1997): 531–565.

50 The names of fans presented in the following sections are pseudonyms.

51 Marcus, interview by author, Sydney, Australia, February 23, 2019.

52 Maria, interview by author, Quezon City, Philippines, July 11, 2019.

53 Maria, interview by author, Quezon City, Philippines, July 11, 2019.

54 Leon, interview by author, Makati, Philippines, July 17, 2019,

55 Interview with anonymous fan at K-pop fan event, Sydney, Australia, January 11, 2020.

56 Lisa, interview by author, September 8, 2018, Sydney, Australia.

57 Judith Fathallah, "Digital Fanfic in Negotiation: LiveJournal, Archive of Our Own, and the Affordances of Read–Write Platforms," *Convergence* (Online First), 3–8, https://doi.org/10.1177/1354856518806674.

58 Per the request of the original author, a hyperlink to the fiction has not been provided for privacy reasons.

59 Marcus, interview by author, Sydney, Australia, February 23, 2019.

60 Sandy, interview by author, Sydney, Australia, August 30, 2018.

61 Sandy, interview by author, Sydney, Australia, August 30, 2018.

62 Jennifer McGee, "In the End It's All Made Up: The Ethics of Fan Fiction and Real Person Fiction," in Phyllis M. Japp, Mark Meister, and Debra K. Japp (eds.), *Communication Ethics, Media and Popular Culture* (New York: Peter Lang, 2005), 161–180.

63 "Your OTP Is Not Real: Why Idol 'Shipping' Has No Place in K-Pop," *Seoulbeats*, December 23, 2011, https://seoulbeats.com/2011/12/the-dangers-of-shipping/.

64 "Your OTP Is Not Real."

65 Zoe, interview by author, Quezon City, Philippines, September 21, 2019.

66 Maria, interview by author, Quezon City, Philippines, July 11, 2019.

67 Sandy, interview by author, Sydney, Australia, August 30, 2018.

68 Sandy, interview by author, Sydney, Australia, August 30, 2018.

69 Kwon, *Straight Korean Female Fans*, 160.

70 Kwon, *Straight Korean Female Fans*, 158.

71 Aki, personal communication, December 27, 2015.

72 Aki, personal communication, December 27, 2015.

14 Following the Footsteps of BTS

The Global Rise of K-Pop Tourism

YOUJEONG OH

The globalization of K-pop is not only about outward expansion with more export market penetration. The outward circulation of Korean entertainment has spawned inbound global flows by drawing in its audience as tourists and shoppers. As Korean popular culture functions as a window through which audiences come to know South Korea (hereafter Korea), specific places within the country have emerged as physical sites through which K-culture experiences can be extended.[1] This chapter explores K-pop tourism, which is reshaping the tourist landscape in the country. Despite the temporary decrease after the THAAD conflict with China in 2017, Korea's popularity as a tourist destination continually surged until 2019, before the outbreak of the COVID-19 pandemic.[2] The global craze for K-pop and its associated lifestyles, such as K-beauty and K-food, are the primary contributors.[3] According to the statistics released by the Korea Tourism Organization (KTO), the proportion of tourists in their twenties has continually increased since 2015 and was the highest demographic of international tourists in Korea in 2019.[4] The same survey asked foreign tourists' reasons for selecting Korea as a travel destination; "K-pop/Korean Wave" accounted for 12.7 percent.[5] Other major purposes, such as shopping, food, and elegant culture/fashion trends, are not entirely separate from the lifestyles that Korean popular culture exhibits. Given the obvious link between the global fever of K-pop and increasing inbound tourism, this chapter focuses on specific practices of K-pop tourism: what motivates fans to visit Korea, what specific destinations draw fans' desire, how they experience K-pop–related places, and what implications K-pop tourism has for both the K-pop and tourism industries. In order to illustrate the actual behaviors and lived experiences of K-pop tourism, discussions will revolve around its most thriving route: the "Bangtan Tour."

Bangtan Tour: Sentimental Pilgrimage

There is little dispute that BTS (Bangtan, or Bulletproof, Boys) is the most successful K-pop idol group, garnering worldwide recognition and popularity. BTS has a huge and devoted worldwide fan base, known as ARMY (an acronym for Adorable Representative M.C. for Youth). The international fandom includes talented translators and savvy promotors of BTS music through streaming and systemic purchase. ARMY generates extraordinary volumes of social media postings on Twitter, Tumblr, Instagram, Facebook, and YouTube, easily driving world trends. With its mighty numbers, ARMY immediately bought out all the tickets for the BTS World Tour in 2018 and 2019.[6] The concert venues are always ringing with fan chants. Inspired by BTS and their music, international members of ARMY desire to learn the Korean language, know more about Korea, and, most importantly, visit Korea, where they can follow in the footsteps of BTS.

Global fans come to Seoul, the world's capital city of K-pop, not only to attend concerts and music shows but also to trace the paths of K-pop idols they admire. The stomping grounds of BTS have turned into destinations. The basic idea of the "Bangtan Tour" is visiting any BTS-related places, such as where the group filmed music videos and had album jacket photo shoots, or simply places BTS members frequented, and taking "proof photos" to verify that fans have been there as well. How is the Bangtan Tour lived, experienced, and told? What "images, feelings, desires, thoughts, and meanings" constitute this tour?[7] To answer these questions, in July 2019 I embarked on the "Bangtan Tour" to several places associated with BTS. At first sight, all the places I visited turned out not to have any touristic qualities of sightseeing, heritage, leisure, or Instagrammable images. Then the question is, why and how do those places attract fan-tourists? What are the perceived values of these places to fans, and how do they appreciate the places? The following sections aim to answer in terms of authenticity, storytelling, and everydayness. In all three categories, the role of fan-tourists constitutes, rather than consumes, place values.

Authenticity

In *Pop City*, I discussed three types of pleasures in K-pop tourism: expectation, connection, and knowledge accumulation.[8] The very anticipation of having a chance to meet their beloved idols in person provides fans with excitement. By attending live music events (concerts, music shows, fan meetings, etc.), fans enjoy being connected not only with stars but also with fellow fans they encounter. Over the course of K-pop tourism, fans collect information about stars and star-associated places, and such knowledge accumulation itself brings them joy. The pleasure derived from K-pop tourism culminates in the desire for connection. Celebrity tourism is similar to pilgrimage in that it evokes "pilgrims' personal experiences of connection with their faith."[9] What draws members of ARMY across the globe to Seoul is their aspiration to be more deeply connected with BTS and develop affective intimacy with them.

The old office of Big Hit Entertainment (the agency of BTS, now HYBE), located on a back street of Gangnam in Seoul, is the primary pilgrimage destination to anchor desires for emotional attachment. Although Big Hit has moved to other locations, the old agency building is the birthplace of BTS, a "sacred site" where BTS came into being. The landlord keeps the old Big Hit sign at the entrance, authenticating the place's stature on the BTS tourist trail. In tourism studies, authenticity "is used to characterize a criterion of evaluation used by the modern tourist as observer."[10] In celebrity tourism, however, the concept of authenticity transcends the modern/premodern, Western/non-Western, and self/other binaries. Revolving around the celebrity's existence, authenticity is what "legitimizes" fans' personal relationship with idols.

What renders the old agency building even more authentic is BTS's own coming-of-age narrative. Before achieving their current status as a global icon, BTS struggled in the early years. Given the monopolistic landscape of the K-pop industry dominated by three major agencies, a band produced by a small agency like Big Hit did not enjoy privileged treatment by broadcasters; sometimes their performances were cut from broadcasts, and the band was often forced to perform shorter versions of their songs, resulting in limited exposure to the public. BTS was also harshly criticized by underground rappers who did not see the group as legitimate hip-hop artists due to their idol status. Some members received insulting comments from "netizens" (anonymous internet users) for their appearances that did not fit the stereotypical mold of perfect-looking idols. When BTS initially won first place on a music chart show, netizens accused Big Hit Entertainment of *sajaegi* – a scheme to buy their own artists' albums to achieve a top rank on the music charts, thus boosting further sales – because no one believed BTS could sell more than 100,000 album copies in 2015. BTS was also attacked for plagiarism of other groups' concepts[11] and constantly scrutinized for any minute faults. Multiple BTS songs are reactions to such struggles and oppression, expressing pain and anger, as well as gratitude for fan support that became the source of comfort and resilience. What built and consolidated the strong fan base (ARMY) was BTS's honest and sincere sharing of their transformative journey with their fans. The peculiar aura of the old agency building emanates from its authenticity as a place of humble beginnings.

The building's façade presents an astonishing view. All walls, stairs, window frames, and even handrails are entirely covered with millions of scribbles by fans. Fans' graffiti can be categorized into largely three types: thanks, love, and anticipation. "Thank you for your music." "Thank you for changing my life." "You're my Most Beautiful Moment of Life." ARMY fans thank the group for how they were touched by BTS and their songs, and how they were comforted by them. Expressions of infinite love and support for members are obvious: "Jasmine♥JK," "Jin♥SylIA," "I Love BTS." Fans also leave their names, their home countries, and inviting notes – "Singapore ARMY," "Italy ARMY," and "Come 2 Hawaii" – in anticipation of BTS someday revisiting the site and seeing the messages. Fans' graffitiing is a performative act to reinscribe the meaning of this place, sustaining and reproducing its authenticity. ARMY fans are informed about this building via diverse media and feel motivated to visit. One of the sources is BTS's own Twitter account (@bts_twt). On May 31, 2015, RM posted a selfie standing at the outdoor stairway of the agency building. But fans are not merely doing the ritual of "quotations" by repeating preframed and fixed photographic practices. By staging their stories, messages, and aspirations, ARMY fans rework the sacredness of this place. Visiting the old agency building is beyond merely consuming it. Rather, inscribing aspirations via imprinted messages into a physical space is an act of reconstructing the pilgrimage site.

The authentic status of the old agency building can be compared to the new HYBE locations where there are no visual marks left by fans. This could be due to the fact that the current landlord and HYBE do not allow graffiti. A more persuasive explanation, however, is that fans care more about BTS's "humble beginnings" than their current world-star status. Since ARMY has been built and expanded upon BTS's history of struggles, its members have strongly empathized with the narrative that casts the group as underdogs. The "blood, sweat, and tears" (a title of their song) BTS shed at a small building where Big Hit could afford to rent only two floors make the old agency building a "true" BTS place.

Just a few steps from the old Big Hit location is Yoojung Sikdang, under which BTS's old practice room was located. This Korean BBQ restaurant was frequented by BTS after hours of hard practice during their trainee period and in the early days after their debut. In BTS's reality show *Rookie King* (2013), the restaurant was featured with the members' complimentary comments on dishes and how the place is closely associated with their pre-debut era. RM said, "[Even] during vacation, we would eat two of our meals here." Suga added, "[The owner's] food was like my mom's homemade meals." In an interview on the show, the owner remarked, "I love them like they're my own children. They're all so polite, kind, and bright. I truly believe that they'll be successful."[12]

Humble Korean BBQ restaurants like Yoojung Sikdang usually serve workers from nearby offices and neighborhood regulars; they are places where middle-aged folks wine and dine for entertainment. By no standards does Yoojung Sikdang fit the taste of younger generations; it is neither fancy nor Instagrammable. However, the majority of current customers are ARMY fans from across the globe; inside the restaurant the four walls and even the ceiling are completely covered with BTS photos, banners, stickers, and posters. During my visit, the restaurant owner, who garnered fame and admiration from ARMY thanks to the interview, kindly welcomed each guest, asked about a favorite member, and handed out a photo card of the member. She seemed very accustomed to treating international guests and advised them on their menu selections by hinting about each member's favorite dishes. Like the old agency building, Yoojung Sikdang is an "authentic" place BTS inhabited, where they lived their everyday life and endeavored to achieve their dreams. The reward for fans visiting is having the same food that once brought comfort and satisfaction to BTS, allowing the tourists to imagine the group's modest early days. The possibility of sharing in BTS's memories by dining there is a spice to lure more fans to this place.

Storytelling

What distinguishes BTS from other K-pop idol groups is that they produce their own music and participate in the writing/composition of their songs. The conventional production of K-pop idols centers around cultivating desirable images, and idols perform music designed to highlight the images given to them by their agency.[13] From their beginning, however, BTS was encouraged to write lyrics and melodies through which to reveal their true personalities and share their voices with the audience. Rather than grooming immaculate appearances, the journey of BTS involved finding their worldviews and communicating them to audiences. Their debut trilogy albums, *2 COOL 4 SKOOL* (2013), *O! RUL8, 2?* (2013), and *SKOOL LUV AFFAIR* (2014), dealt with teenage anxiety, dreams, happiness, and love. Although industry insiders comment that the school theme was banal and already overexploited, it was natural for the BTS members, aged fifteen to twenty at that time, to talk about school. The debut title song, "No More Dream," urges teenagers to "follow their own dreams rather than fall prey to society's expectations."[14] The self-reflective lyrics, not scripted by industry experts but emanating from the band members' own voices, are blunt and crude, but resonate closely with fellow youngsters.

BTS's "confessional lyrics" proved real and developed further in the trilogy HwaYangYeonHwa (meaning "The Most Beautiful Moment in Life," hereafter HYYH), under which three albums were released: *HYYH: Pt.1* (2015), *HYYH: Pt.2* (2015), and *Young Forever* (2016). The HYYH trilogy is a coming-of-age story narrating "the struggles the boys face[d] while transitioning from childhood to adulthood, from being caterpillars to becoming butterflies."[15] All the songs, music videos, concept films, and photos are organized around the theme of youth and the feelings that come with it: angst, grief, confusion, volatility, pain, laughter, and dreams. After releasing *HYYH: Pt.1*, Big Hit released *HYYH On Stage: Prologue*, a twelve-minute video, which is an overarching bridge connecting several videos for songs on the trilogy albums. The prologue is a story after the music video for "I NEED U" (the title song of Pt.1) was released in May 2015, and a preview of *HYYH: Pt.2* and *HYYH: Young Forever*. The film starts with a scene of V with bloodied hands and suffering from guilt.[16] Then he is lying on a mattress at an abandoned outdoor pool with no water. In a few seconds, the other boys arrive at the pool and join V. Later, they realize that Jin is video-recording these scenes. Greeting Jin, the boys continue to have "the most beautiful time" together. Soon a quote appears onscreen: "You can smile as long as we are together."

The HYYH trilogy, including the *On Stage: Prologue* film, has attracted numerous interpretive communities in which fans actively decipher the hidden meanings of BTS storytelling narrated and represented in music videos and lyrics. According to some of these fan interpretations, the abandoned swimming pool implies Neverland, where boys (childhood friends) remain innocent, playful, and oblivious to the cruelty of the real world.[17] These nostalgic scenes were filmed at an abandoned pool at Seoul National University. Tucked inside the forest far from the main campus, the pool and surrounding buildings appear dilapidated. The four walls of the pool are filled with multiple layers of graffiti, originally created for filming and now augmented by fans. The bottom of the pool is covered with coarse moss, littered with bizarre-looking props. This secluded, deserted, and creepy space, were it not for its association with BTS, does not possess any quality to attract visitors. However, it is one of the must-visit BTS places, thanks to the power of storytelling.

BTS fans visit this place not to consume it but to appreciate the stories visualized through it. The abandoned swimming pool is meaningful and worth visiting only to those who empathized with the HYYH narrative. Here ARMY fans reflect on their youth – the most beautiful moment in life. Here their pain and angst are consoled, and their joys and dreams uplifted. ARMY fans' manner of telling their tourism story verifies the point; post-tour blog postings show scenes from the film and photos fans took at the same spots in an alternating manner, relating the HYYH stories to their own feelings at the site. Since the group has effectively constructed an "authentic narrative" based on their own lived experiences, the place is suffused with "true and sincere" stories to draw fans.[18] Touring the abandoned swimming pool reaffirms fans' affective affinities with BTS and their music. Fan-tourists, however, are not limited by sentimentalism alone. One fan noted after their visit, "Once my friend played 'Butterfly,' which was mainly the background song for their *On Stage: Prologue*, it still felt nostalgic."[19] Affective interpretation processes spill into the pool and redefine the material space.[20] The embedded storytelling is enriched through fans' diverse sensorial activities and bodily performances.

Sensing emotional connections through the place leads to the materialization of emotions. ARMY fans have left personal messages of love and support for BTS as graffiti on the walls. Drawings of BT21 cartoon characters (based on the actual group members) make up parts of the graffiti. The affective place created through narrative construction is constantly reconfigured by fans' performative activities added to the original site. By looking at the fan-generated graffiti, ARMY fans not only become connected to BTS but also feel camaraderie with fellow fans. A blog post comments about a message written on the wall, "Thanks for Teaching me How to Love Myself," by reacting "The feeling is mutual" (*naduyo*).[21]

BTS's socially conscious and interactive lyrics fully blossomed in their album *You Never Walk Alone* (2017). The title song, "Spring Day" (*Bomnal*), exudes feelings of longing for missing friends or loved ones who may not be with us anymore. Although there has been no confirmation from BTS themselves, many fans relate the story in "Spring Day" to the Sewol ferry tragedy (for an account on this incident, see Chapter 10). Starting with the phrase "I miss you, When I say this I miss you more," the lyrics portray loss and grief. "It's only winter here. Even in August, winter is here" denotes that their loneness and despair persist during all seasons. Toward the end, the lyrics move to imply the willingness for reunion: "The morning will come again, Because no darkness, no season can last forever. When cherry blossoms are blooming, the winter is ending … If you wait a little more, if you stay up a few more nights, I will come see you, I will come pick you up." Despite the nuanced symbolism, this song conveys condolences for victims and their families, as well as consolation for the "Sewol generation" – young South Koreans traumatized by witnessing the death of so many young people.

Jumunjin Beach (or Hyangho Beach) in Gangneung city (located on the east coast of the Korean Peninsula) is where BTS took the cover photo for their sensational album *You Never Walk Alone*. The photo displays an empty seaside bus stop, which was constructed for the shoot; inside the album, "concept photos" depict BTS members sitting at the bus stop individually and together. "BTS 'YOU NEVER WALK ALONE' cover shooting sketch" on their YouTube channel shows behind-the-scenes episodes of the concept photo shoot.[22] Other than the beach, the location features nothing spectacular. Yet this place is now flooded with tourists. KTO held a popularity poll to ask ARMY (more than 22,000 members in 137 countries) which place they most wished to visit of all BTS filming locations. Receiving more than 21 percent of the votes, this Jumunjin Beach bus stop ranked number one.[23] The Gangneung city government installed a replica of BTS's bus stop at Jumunjin Beach, complete with the set's signpost, stating, "This place is the shooting location of BTS's YOU NEVER WALK ALONE album cover." Inside the bus stop is a little bus station schedule map, on which all the stations are named after BTS songs. Why do so many (international) fans take extra time and energy to visit a small regional city outside the Seoul metropolitan region, only to see this "replica" bus stop? They are not consuming the location per se, but the stories associated with the place. Sitting at the same spot where BTS once sat, they contemplate the comforting and encouraging message the album delivers: "You never walk alone." It is also a great place for fans to take memorable photos that confirm "ARMY is where BTS was," thereby reaffirming their loyalty and commitment.

Everydayness

Worshipping idols is not limited to consuming music and celebrating the iconic aura of stars on stage. Fans want to "know" about each idol not only as a star but also as a person. Celebrity consumption, therefore, involves accumulating knowledge about them – birthday, favorite food, movie choices, how they behave in certain circumstances, personal fashion style, and so on. Even the most trivial information is precious to fans. As discussed elsewhere, reality-variety shows conventionally function as a channel through which K-pop idols reveal their offstage personalities.[24] Partly because they did not have opportunities to appear on reality shows given that the collaborative partnership between major agencies and leading broadcasters dominated television shows, BTS has proactively utilized social media platforms – YouTube, Twitter, Instagram, Facebook, Weibo, Weverse, and TikTok – to promote themselves. The members of BTS were some of the first K-pop idols on Twitter. The majority of their YouTube channel (BANGTANTV) content consists of Bangtan Bomb, short videos focusing on the members having fun behind the curtains of TV music shows, award ceremonies, promotional events, and live stages; there is a "Log" section to share individual members' daily lives and thoughts. The savvy reliance on social media played a role in effectively forming a global fan base.

BTS has tapped social media platforms for promotion of their music, but also for interaction and building intimacy with fans. Most other K-pop groups' official social media accounts are managed by agencies solely for promotional purposes – release of a new album, new music video, or concert schedule – and individual members run their own accounts for more personal posts. BTS has one collective Twitter account that the seven members share to post about their daily lives: everyday selfies, funny photos of birthday celebrations, post-performance "thank you" videos for fans, or travel photos and other information about their whereabouts.[25] The shared BTS Twitter account made fans not only invest in it with concentrated energy and loyalty but also find immense pleasure in discovering BTS members as fellow human beings. Fans "study" such casual postings: what kinds of fashion items they don, how they spend free time, what they want to say to ARMY. Getting to know the group members' everyday personae helps build affective intimacy for the audience. Fans are primarily captivated by idols' stardom built upon their impeccable physical qualities, their stellar performances, and the ubiquity of their images. The highly iconic status, however, also creates a star-fan distance that should be bridged in order to make the latter truly attached to the former. Developing familiarity by revealing everyday personalities of idols is a critical step to transform an interested audience into devoted fans. Once strong affective intimacy is formed, it can in turn generate profits from selling products and places. Affective intimacy turns fans into motivated pilgrims, inspiring them to embark on the "Bangtan Tour."

Places BTS members have visited during their free time have emerged as "pilgrimage" sites among fans. Daeo Bookstore (*Daeo seojeom*), the oldest bookstore in Seoul, is located in Seochon, a district known for preserving old ways of life in the city. After visiting there twice in 2016 and 2019, RM, the leader of BTS, posted selfies taken at this place on Twitter. The bookstore proudly exhibits one of the photos from 2016 at the same spot where RM took it. Adorned with tons of used books and antiques, exuding an exotic aura of the "recent past" of the city, the bookstore is an Instagrammable place soon to become a destination for BTS pilgrims. The very spot where RM took his selfie is popular, an affective place where fans can feel the "personal side" of their beloved idol. Now even the KTO posts information about this bookstore featuring BTS. The MIN's café is a place BTS frequented during their early days. Owned by Lee Changmin from the K-pop idol group 2AM and Homme, it is run by Changmin's parents, who provide little BTS anecdotes to fans. Inside the café, visitors can find a wide array of BTS memorabilia, including pictures, autographs, albums, and handwritten letters from the members. BTS posted photos relaxing at their regular table at this café several times on Twitter. When I visited, I witnessed minor but fierce competition among customers, holding a favorite beverage of their *choeae* (bias, or favorite idol), to take BTS's regular table. By sharing the same place (albeit with time lags) and imitating stars' behaviors, ARMY's affective relationship to BTS is extended bodily, materially, and spatially.

The members of BTS have run their own online variety shows, *RUN BTS!* and *Bon Voyage*, exclusively released on Naver Corporation's V Live channel, a live video-streaming service. *RUN BTS!* usually includes games and "extraordinary experiences" in various settings such as cooking, camping, visiting a water park, and pottery making. In episode 45, BTS met a professional barista who taught them how to make a shot of espresso, taste and appreciate one, and make latte art.[26] After a brief tutorial, each member was asked to make signature drinks that would be evaluated by the barista. The episode was filmed at "&gather café," a humble location in a quiet Seoul neighborhood far from bustling commercial centers and typical tourist destinations. It is now attracting ARMY fans who must seriously study a map to get there. There is nothing special about the café's interior design except the popular purple neon sign displaying "Time, stay a while, you're so beautiful (*sungana meomchueora neo jeongmal areumdapguna*)," underneath which BTS members took a photo. However, ARMY fans do not visit here only to take a photo under the sign. The café is imbued with BTS's real-life personalities. Variety shows like *Run BTS!* inevitably display offstage aspects of the group: laughter, challenges, trials and errors, and chemistry among group members. What captivates fans is revelations about how the world-class celebrities are "imperfect" beyond their comfort zones. Being "flawed" is considered charming to fans, who feel BTS is relatable. &gather café is a place where fans can grasp the textures and ambiance of such intimacy. The café owner stated that the place was particularly crowded around BTS's fifth and sixth anniversaries and each member's birthday. A mundane space became a sacred place in which fans can sip beverages "created" by BTS.

Celebrity Merchandise Shops as Destinations

BT21 is a brand consisting of eight cartoon characters (Koya, RJ, Shooky, Mang, Chimmy, Tata, and Cooky, each representing one of the group members, and VAN, representing BTS's fandom ARMY) produced through a collaborative project between BTS and Line Friends. BTS members participated in the entire process of creating the characters, from drawing sketches to design and elaboration. The eight characters are now copiously reproduced on all kinds of commodities – such as cushions, pens, T-shirts, cups, and bags – that are sold at Line Friends stores.

Elsewhere, I defined K-pop idols as a metacommodity "to sell other products, including music, celebrity merchandise, and K-pop places as pseudo-avatars of K-pop idols. Once images are cultivated, they can be endlessly reproduced in products, virtual shows, and experimental tours."[27] Idol merchandise is a secondary product with symbolic value cultivated through the affective intimacy forged between idols and fans. Once affective relations are formed, fans try to deepen such connections by consuming tangible avatars. Yet BT21 is slightly different from conventional celebrity goods produced by professional designers, which conventionally feature images of idols. Cup featuring Mang (a character J-Hope produced), for example, is fundamentally different from a cup on which J-Hope's face is simply wrapped, since the character was created by J-Hope, whose personality, characteristics, and inspirations were embedded in it. BTS also created stories in order to generate character traits that somewhat resemble the members' own personalities. For instance, RJ (representing Jin) loves cooking and eating and has a compassionate soul that makes everyone feel right at home. Miniprankster Shooky (correlating to Suga) loves pulling pranks, especially on friends; one thing he hates is milk. Moreover, BT21 characters frequently appear on *RUN BTS!* episodes, partly because both Line Friends and the V Live channel are owned by the Naver Corporation. In episode 43, Suga appears on the show wearing the costume of RJ, as punishment for losing a quiz game in a previous episode.[28] Jin is wearing Cooky's costume in episode 45.[29] Such intertextual appearances of BT21 characters make them more familiar to fans by adding more story lines. Through a repeated personification process, BT21 characters become affective avatars of BTS.

Among many stores in Seoul, the Itaewon Line Friends Flagship Store holds a more sacred aura because it was where BTS members held meetings to build concepts for their respective characters.[30] The store is equipped with multiple screens that repeatedly show scenes from BT21 Universe episodes featuring the character-building process.[31] The second floor of the store is exclusively reserved as a BT21 Zone in which huge BT21 characters are placed and all kinds of BT21 merchandise are displayed. BT21 Zone also exhibits the artifacts of the character-building process, such as original sketches, concept pieces, dolls, and posters signed by BTS. The third floor is a café that offers a BT21-themed menu, such as "Chimmy drink" – a mango slush. During fieldwork I witnessed a crowd filling the entire store, particularly in the BT21 zone. Fans were milling around the store window-shopping various products, busy taking selfies in the BT21 Zone with characters, or relaxing at the café. Here, I was able to have conversations with some overseas ARMY fans. They commented, "It *is* a tourist destination full of photo spots. It is so much fun to take pictures with life-size BT21 characters." I wondered why they buy BT21 characters and what kinds of pleasure such merchandise generates. The question was answered with a very self-convinced statement, "Chimmy is Jimin. When I touch Chimmy, I can smell Jimin's odor, I can listen to Jimin's breathing."[32] The affective avatars are great souvenirs for fan-tourists who can feel BTS's personal presence through the characters.

BTS and City Promotion

K-pop tourism is highly demand-driven; the fan-driven influx of tourists "often surprises the receiving destinations."[33] Some municipalities belatedly recognize the explosive power of K-pop-induced mobilities and start to employ K-pop artists in tourism promotion. Given their exponentially increasing international impact, the members of BTS are among the most sought-after celebrities by Korean cities and provinces. The winner of the intermunicipal competition to court BTS was Seoul Metropolitan City, which employed BTS as an Honorary Tourism Ambassador for three consecutive years starting in 2017. Every year, the city government produced Seoul advertisement videos released on social media (Facebook, YouTube, and Instagram) and broadcast through television channels: "KBS World aired in 58 million households in 117 countries and on the tvN Asia Channel that is available to 9 million households in nine Southeast Asian countries."[34] The 2017 video titled "BTS Life in Seoul" introduced major landmarks of Seoul, including Hangang Park and the newly constructed Seoullo 7017 overpass. In 2018, besides the advertisement music video "With Seoul," an additional seven special playlists featuring thematic explorations of Seoul were promoted: Delicious Seoul, Relax Seoul, Extreme Seoul, Historic Seoul, K-Wave Seoul, Fashionable Seoul, and Exclusive Seoul. A transition in points of view occurred in the 2019 video from the previous introduction of the city by Seoulites to the viewpoints of foreign tourists, who are encouraged to create and share special experiences. Both individual versions created by each BTS member and integrated versions featuring all BTS members aim to elicit tourists' desires to live and spend time in Seoul like BTS.[35]

Both the tourism market and the city government have found that BTS's endorsement power has been much greater than initially estimated.

According to the Hyundai Research Institute, out of the 10.41 million tourists, 7.6 percent of the visits in 2017 were influenced by the Korean pop group.[36] The same report also stated that one in every thirteen foreign tourists in 2017 visited South Korea solely due to BTS. "It is rare for any country to have a boost in the tourism industry contributed by a specific group of people rather than sights or events."[37] The Seoul Metropolitan Government credited BTS for revitalizing the city's tourism, which had stagnated since the THAAD ban.[38] The city government also thanked BTS for their fidelity and private promotion – such as uploading multiple Seoul-related postings on their social media accounts – in addition to the official promotion activities. City officials are confident about potential risks arising from the volatile nature of celebrity-centered promotion, stating, "Their attitudes are humble and full of gratitude, there are no signs of arrogance or boasting. Since all members are aware about it, I am confident that there will be no scandals."[39] Based on trust and reliability, the city hopes to renew its contract with BTS.

BTS's Fifth Muster (annual fan meeting), "Magic Shop," in celebration of their sixth anniversary, took place in Busan Metropolitan City. The city government and the Busan Tourism Organization (BTO) took full advantage of the event, and their strategies merit a close analysis. The city adorned major Busan landmarks – Gwangan Bridge, Busan-Hang Daegyo Bridge, and the Busan Cinema Center – with purple lights, BTS's signature color, to welcome both BTS and ARMY fans. The BTO came up with special tours that followed the traces of two BTS members (Jimin and Jungkook) born and raised in Busan. Each consisted of locations – such as popular coffee shops, restaurants, and heritage sites – where Jimin and Jungkook lived or spent time during their childhood. The manner in which BTO introduced the Jimin Tour and Jungkook Tour is also intriguing. Holding a hand fan in which Jimin's face is printed, a BTO staff introduces locations in Geumjeong-dong as if Jimin is walking through the neighborhood. Similarly, watching the photos of Manduck-dong presented by BTO, the audience would feel that Jungkook is walking through his hometown.[40] Inspired by these promotions, fans amble along Jimin's and Jungkook's memory lanes. ARMY fans could also spot multiple banners hung by neighborhood residents: "BTS Jimin, son of Geumjeong, congratulation on your sixth anniversary concert. Jimin-ah, we love you!!" Humble residential neighborhoods are suddenly recast as "K-pop places" replete with BTS stories. ARMY fans' practices of relaying their experience – how they feel about areas, how they come to know more about BTS and thus become more attached to them – constitute the affective qualities of place.

Ahead of a BTS fan meeting in Busan, V posted photos of himself walking in Busan Citizens Park, commenting, "Busan is nice" in the dialect of Gyeongsang (the province where Busan is located). Only a few days later, the Busan Infrastructure Corporation (BISCO), which manages the park, set up a "footprints" signpost at the same spot where V stood. They also posted a map introducing "V's photo spot" on their Facebook page with the comment: "ARMY! This is the trail. Please refer to the map. You can now walk the path V once walked."[41] Busan Citizens Park also contains layers of painful history: During Japanese colonial rule (1910–1945), it was used as a horse racing track and later as a storage yard for military supplies serving the Imperial Japanese Army headquarters in Busan. After liberation in 1945, the US military occupied the site and operated Camp Hialeah until it was closed in 2006; only in 2010 was the site transferred to the city of Busan, and the park was opened in 2011. Despite the risk of obscuring this contentious history and being known only as a place associated with BTS, the park has become a popular destination among the ARMY, who love to take "been there" photos at the same spot.

Conclusion

K-pop tourism is illustrative of how the tourism landscape is changing. Any places, even though they do not possess traditional touristic qualities, associated with K-pop or with specific K-pop idols can emerge as the hottest tourism destinations. Places of K-pop idols' birth, dreams, and career path have become "authentic places," a pilgrimage route for K-pop fans. K-pop tourism entails a significant amount of multifaceted storytelling: Anecdotes of stars, messages of K-pop music, and narratives presented in music videos and photos construct the meanings of place. Reflecting upon such stories, fan-tourists make strong connections to both stars and places. K-pop tourism that follows the footsteps of stars collapses the barrier between celebrity and fans, helping to develop strong affective bonds between them. By traveling to star-related places, fans can share the idols' offstage everyday life. The desire to do this enables ordinary spaces to be stripped of quotidian, mundane features and endows those spaces with affective qualities. In K-pop tourism, perceived values of expectation, enjoyment, and experiences matter more than physical, social, and cultural qualities of place. The role of fandom in K-pop tourism, however, is not limited to place consumption. Through various performances – photographic practices, graffiti, and post-visit social media circulation – fans reconfigure, enrich, and fortify the socially constructed meanings of those places. If stars are human magnets to draw fan-tourists to certain places, fans are agents to amplify and further publicize the value of their tourist trail.

Further Reading

Beeton, Sue. *Film-Induced Tourism*. Clevedon: Channel View Publications, 2005.

Choe, Youngmin. *Tourist Distractions: Traveling and Feeling in Transnational Hallyu Cinema*. Durham, NC: Duke University Press, 2016.

Edensor, Tim. "Staging Tourism: Tourists as Performers." *Annals of Tourism Research* 27/2 (2000): 322–344.

Kim, Kyung Hyun, and Youngmin Choe (eds.). *The Korean Popular Culture Reader*. Durham, NC: Duke University Press, 2014.

Kim, Suk-Young. *K-Pop Live: Fans, Idols, and Multimedia Performance*. Stanford, CA: Stanford University Press, 2018.

Kim, Youna (ed.) *The Korean Wave: Korean Media Go Global*. New York: Routledge, 2013.

Oh, Youjeong. *Pop City: Korean Popular Culture and the Selling of Place*. Ithaca, NY: Cornell University Press, 2018.

Notes

1 For a more detailed account, see Youjeong Oh, *Pop City: Korean Popular Culture and the Selling of Place* (Ithaca, NY: Cornell University Press, 2018).

2 Korea Tourism Organization, "Korea Tourism Statistics" (2020), www.index.go.kr/potal/stts/idxMain/selectPoSttsIdxMainPrint.do?idx_cd=1653&board_cd=INDX_001. In March 2017, the US government established the Terminal High Altitude Area Defense (THAAD) missile system in South Korea. While both the US and the South Korean government insisted that it was a measure to prevent North Korea's provocation, it irritated China. In response, the Chinese government and citizens boycotted South Korean products and companies and banned group tourism to South Korea. Only in October 2017 did Seoul and Beijing agreed to normalize relations again.

3 Korea Tourism Organization, "Increase in Foreigners' Recognition of and Preference for South Korea as a Tourist Destination" (press release, 2019), https://kto.visitkorea.or.kr/kor/notice/news/press/board/view.kto?id=441344&isNotice=false&instanceId=42&rnum=1 .

4 Ministry of Culture, Sports and Tourism (MCST), *2019 International Visitor Survey*.

5 Ministry of Culture, Sports and Tourism (MCST), *2019 International Visitor Survey*, 27.

6 Although the exact number is not available, as of August 2020, BTS's Twitter account (@bts_twt) had 28.4 million followers and their YouTube channel (BANGTANTV) had 35.5 million subscribers.

7 Edward Bruner, *Culture on Tour: Ethnographies of Travel* (Chicago: University of Chicago Press. 2005), 19.

8 Oh, *Pop City*, 151–155.

9 Yaniv Belhassen, Kellee Caton, and William Stewart, "The Search for Authenticity in the Pilgrim Experience," *Annals of Tourism Research* 35/3 (2008): 668–689.

10 Erik Cohen, "Authenticity and Commoditization in Tourism," *Annals of Tourism Research* 15 (1988): 374.

11 For the meanings and practices of "concept" crafting in the K-pop industry, see Oh, *Pop City*, 111–112.

12 From *Rookie King: Bangtan Channel*, episode 1, aired on SBS MTV (2013).

13 Oh, *Pop City*, 111–112.

14 Tamar Herman, "BTS' Most Political Lyrics: A Guide to Their Social Commentary on South Korean Society," Billboard.com, February 13, 2018, www.billboard.com/articles/columns/k-town/8098832/bts-lyrics-social-commentary-political/.

15 The Bangtan Theory, "BTS INU, PROLOGUE & RUN: RETAKES ON INNOCENCE LOST & THE HARDSHIPS OF GROWING UP" (2016), https://thebangtantheory.wordpress.com/.

16 In the original version of the "I Need U" music video, the ending scenes suggest that V symbolically kills his abusive father in order to protect his sister. Because of the age-restricted content, this part is omitted in the official version.

17 The Bangtan Theory, "BTS 'PROLOGUE' TRAILER EXPLAINED // THE BUTTERFLY THEME" (2016), https://thebangtantheory.wordpress.com/2016/07/26/bts-prologue-mv-explained/.

18 Courtney McLaren and DalYong Jin, "'You can't help but love them': BTS, Transcultural Fandom, and Affective Identities," *Korea Journal* 60/1 (2020): 100–127.

19 "Butterfly" is included in the album *The Most Beautiful Moment: Pt. 2.* "Reign," "BTS Tour" (2018), http://outsidethebottle.net/2018/09/30/bts-tour-abandoned-pool-at-snu/.

20 For more about affective interpretation, see Matt Hills, *Fan Cultures* (London: Routledge, 2002).

21 https://blog.naver.com/jieun__328/221573945800 (accessed March 14, 2021).

22 "BTS 'YOU NEVER WALK ALONE' Jacket Shooting Sketch," YouTube, www.youtube.com/watch?v=46qWWmnK4F0 (accessed March 14, 2021).

23 Korea Tourism Organization, "The Best 'Bangtan Tour' Destination Selected by Foreigners," https://kto.visitkorea.or.kr/kor/notice/news/press/board/view.kto?id=431482&rnum=9 (accessed March 14, 2021).

24 Oh, *Pop City*, 114–116.

25 BTS also holds an official account managed by BigHit Entertainment (@bts_bighit).

26 V Live, "Run BTS! 2018 – Ep. 45," www.vlive.tv/video/63564 (accessed March 14, 2021).

27 Oh, *Pop City*, 123.

28 The episode was aired on March 6, 2018. V Live, "Run BTS! 2018 – Ep. 43," www.vlive.tv/video/61788 (accessed March 14, 2021).

29 V Live, "Run BTS! 2018 – Ep. 45," www.vlive.tv/video/63564 (accessed March 14, 2021).

30 I found, as of April 2020, this store is permanently closed. But there are eight Line Friends stores in Seoul, two in Gyunggi Province, and two more in Busan.

31 BT21 Universe webpage, https://bt21.com (accessed March 14, 2021).

32 Interview by author, July 2019.

33 Cristine Lundberg and Maria Lexhagen, "Bitten by the Twilight Saga: From Pop Culture Consumer to Pop Culture Tourist," in Richard Sharpely and Phillip Stone (eds.), *Contemporary Tourist Experience: Concepts and Consequences* (London: Routledge, 2012).

34 Hyun-bin Kim, "BTS to Promote Seoul Tourism," *Korea Times*, October 10, 2018, www.koreatimes.co.kr/www/nation/2018/10/281_257357.html.

35 All promotion videos can be accessed at https://english.visitseoul.net/index (accessed March 14, 2021).

36 Min Jung, Jun-bum Oh, Yooran Shin, and Seunghee Ryu, *The Economic Effects of BTS* (Seoul: Hyundai Research Institute, 2018).

37 Wandering Shadow, "The 'BTS Effect' on South Korea's Economy, Industry and Culture," May 30, 2019, https://shadow-twts.medium.com/the-bts-effect-on-south-koreas-economy-industry-and-culture-975e8933da56#:~:text=It%20is%20rare%20for%20any,rather%20than%20sights%20or%20events.

38 See note 2.

39 Dae-ro Park, "Seoul Metropolitan City Enjoys Hiring BTS Whose Global Influencer Status Heightened," *NEWSIS*, May 5, 2019, https://newsis.com/view/?id=NISX20190503_0000640904.

40 Busan Tourism Organization, "ARMY's Suggestions of BTS Places in Busan," https://blog.naver.com/busanto1115/221559609443 (accessed March 18, 2021).

41 BISCO, https://ko-kr.facebook.com/bisco.pr (accessed March 18, 2021).

Index

numbers in **bold**= table, *italics*=figure

Printed in the USA
CPSIA information can be obtained
at www.ICGtesting.com
CBHW080246201124
17695CB00008B/304